UNIX® Shell Objects

UNIX® Shell Objects

Christopher A. Jones

Foster City, CA ♦ Chicago, IL ♦ Indianapolis, IN ♦ New York, NY

UNIX® Shell Objects

Published by
M&T Books, an imprint of IDG Books Worldwide, Inc.
An International Data Group Company
919 E. Hillsdale Blvd., Suite 400
Foster City, CA 94404
www.idgbooks.com (IDG Books Worldwide Web site)

Copyright © 1998 IDG Books Worldwide, Inc. All rights reserved. No part of this book, including interior design, cover design, and icons, may be reproduced or transmitted in any form, by any means (electronic, photocopying, recording, or otherwise) without the prior written permission of the publisher.

Library of Congress Catalog Card No.: 98-071857

ISBN: 0-7645-7004-8

Printed in the United States of America

10 9 8 7 6 5 4 3 2 1

1B/SU/QX/ZY/FC

Distributed in the United States by IDG Books Worldwide, Inc.

Distributed by Macmillan Canada for Canada; by Transworld Publishers Limited in the United Kingdom; by IDG Norge Books for Norway; by IDG Sweden Books for Sweden; by Woodslane Pty. Ltd. for Australia; by Woodslane (NZ) Ltd. for New Zealand; by Addison Wesley Longman Singapore Pte Ltd. for Singapore, Malaysia, Thailand, Indonesia, and Korea; by Norma Comunicaciones S.A. for Colombia; by Intersoft for South Africa; by International Thomson Publishing for Germany, Austria, and Switzerland; by Toppan Company Ltd. for Japan; by Distribuidora Cuspide for Argentina; by Livraria Cultura for Brazil; by Ediciencia S.A. for Ecuador; by Ediciones ZETA S.C.R. Ltda. for Peru; by WS Computer Publishing Corporation, Inc., for the Philippines; by Unalis Corporation for Taiwan; by Contemporanea de Ediciones for Venezuela; by Computer Book & Magazine Store for Puerto Rico; by Express Computer Distributors for the Caribbean and West Indies. Authorized Sales Agent: Anthony Rudkin Associates for the Middle East and North Africa.

For general information on IDG Books Worldwide's books in the U.S., please call our Consumer Customer Service department at 800-762-2974. For reseller information, including discounts and premium sales, please call our Reseller Customer Service department at 800-434-3422.

For information on where to purchase IDG Books Worldwide's books outside the U.S., please contact our International Sales department at 650-655-3200 or fax 650-655-3297.

For information on foreign language translations, please contact our Foreign & Subsidiary Rights department at 650-655-3021 or fax 650-655-3281.

For sales inquiries and special prices for bulk quantities, please contact our Sales department at 650-655-3200 or write to the address above.

For information on using IDG Books Worldwide's books in the classroom or for ordering examination copies, please contact our Educational Sales department at 800-434-2086 or fax 317-596-5499.

For press review copies, author interviews, or other publicity information, please contact our Public Relations department at 650-655-3000 or fax 650-655-3299.

For authorization to photocopy items for corporate, personal, or educational use, please contact Copyright Clearance Center, 222 Rosewood Drive, Danvers, MA 01923, or fax 978-750-4470.

LIMIT OF LIABILITY/DISCLAIMER OF WARRANTY: AUTHOR AND PUBLISHER HAVE USED THEIR BEST EFFORTS IN PREPARING THIS BOOK. IDG BOOKS WORLDWIDE, INC., AND AUTHOR MAKE NO REPRESENTATIONS OR WARRANTIES WITH RESPECT TO THE ACCURACY OR COMPLETENESS OF THE CONTENTS OF THIS BOOK AND SPECIFICALLY DISCLAIM ANY IMPLIED WARRANTIES OF MERCHANTABILITY OR FITNESS FOR A PARTICULAR PURPOSE. THERE ARE NO WARRANTIES WHICH EXTEND BEYOND THE DESCRIPTIONS CONTAINED IN THIS PARAGRAPH. NO WARRANTY MAY BE CREATED OR EXTENDED BY SALES REPRESENTATIVES OR WRITTEN SALES MATERIALS. THE ACCURACY AND COMPLETENESS OF THE INFORMATION PROVIDED HEREIN AND THE OPINIONS STATED HEREIN ARE NOT GUARANTEED OR WARRANTED TO PRODUCE ANY PARTICULAR RESULTS, AND THE ADVICE AND STRATEGIES CONTAINED HEREIN MAY NOT BE SUITABLE FOR EVERY INDIVIDUAL. NEITHER IDG BOOKS WORLDWIDE, INC., NOR AUTHOR SHALL BE LIABLE FOR ANY LOSS OF PROFIT OR ANY OTHER COMMERCIAL DAMAGES, INCLUDING BUT NOT LIMITED TO SPECIAL, INCIDENTAL, CONSEQUENTIAL, OR OTHER DAMAGES·

Trademarks: All brand names and product names used in this book are trade names, service marks, trademarks, or registered trademarks of their respective owners. IDG Books Worldwide is not associated with any product or vendor mentioned in this book. UNIX is a registered trademark licensed exclusively through X/Open Company, Ltd. Linux is a registered trademark of Linus Torvalds in the United States and other countries.

 is a trademark under exclusive license to IDG Books Worldwide, Inc., from International Data Group, Inc.

 is a trademark of IDG Books Worldwide, Inc.

ABOUT IDG BOOKS WORLDWIDE

Welcome to the world of IDG Books Worldwide.

IDG Books Worldwide, Inc., is a subsidiary of International Data Group, the world's largest publisher of computer-related information and the leading global provider of information services on information technology. IDG was founded more than 25 years ago and now employs more than 8,500 people worldwide. IDG publishes more than 275 computer publications in over 75 countries (see listing below). More than 90 million people read one or more IDG publications each month.

Launched in 1990, IDG Books Worldwide is today the #1 publisher of best-selling computer books in the United States. We are proud to have received eight awards from the Computer Press Association in recognition of editorial excellence and three from *Computer Currents'* First Annual Readers' Choice Awards. Our best-selling *...For Dummies*® series has more than 50 million copies in print with translations in 38 languages. IDG Books Worldwide, through a joint venture with IDG's Hi-Tech Beijing, became the first U.S. publisher to publish a computer book in the People's Republic of China. In record time, IDG Books Worldwide has become the first choice for millions of readers around the world who want to learn how to better manage their businesses.

Our mission is simple: Every one of our books is designed to bring extra value and skill-building instructions to the reader. Our books are written by experts who understand and care about our readers. The knowledge base of our editorial staff comes from years of experience in publishing, education, and journalism — experience we use to produce books for the '90s. In short, we care about books, so we attract the best people. We devote special attention to details such as audience, interior design, use of icons, and illustrations. And because we use an efficient process of authoring, editing, and desktop publishing our books electronically, we can spend more time ensuring superior content and spend less time on the technicalities of making books.

You can count on our commitment to deliver high-quality books at competitive prices on topics you want to read about. At IDG Books Worldwide, we continue in the IDG tradition of delivering quality for more than 25 years. You'll find no better book on a subject than one from IDG Books Worldwide.

John Kilcullen
CEO
IDG Books Worldwide, Inc.

Steven Berkowitz
President and Publisher
IDG Books Worldwide, Inc.

Eighth Annual
Computer Press
Awards ≥1992

Ninth Annual
Computer Press
Awards ≥1993

Tenth Annual
Computer Press
Awards ≥1994

Eleventh Annual
Computer Press
Awards ≥1995

IDG Books Worldwide, Inc., is a subsidiary of International Data Group, the world's largest publisher of computer-related information and the leading global provider of information services on information technology. International Data Group publishes over 275 computer publications in over 75 countries. More than 90 million people read one or more International Data Group publications each month. International Data Group's publications include: **ARGENTINA:** Buyer's Guide, Computerworld Argentina, PC World Argentina; **AUSTRALIA:** Australian Macworld, Australian PC World, Australian Reseller News, Computerworld, IT Casebook, Network World, Publish, Webmaster; **AUSTRIA:** Computerwelt Österreich, Networks Austria, PC Tip Austria; **BANGLADESH:** PC World Bangladesh; **BELARUS:** PC World Belarus; **BELGIUM:** Data News; **BRAZIL:** Annuário de Informática, Computerworld, Connections, Macworld, PC Player, PC World, Publish, Reseller News, Supergamepower; **BULGARIA:** Computerworld Bulgaria, Network World Bulgaria, PC & MacWorld Bulgaria; **CANADA:** CIO Canada, Client/Server World, ComputerWorld Canada, InfoWorld Canada, NetworkWorld Canada, WebWorld; **CHILE:** Computerworld Chile, PC World Chile; **COLOMBIA:** Computerworld Colombia, PC World Colombia; **COSTA RICA:** PC World Centro America; **THE CZECH AND SLOVAK REPUBLICS:** Computerworld Czechoslovakia, Macworld Czech Republic, PC World Czechoslovakia; **DENMARK:** Communications World Danmark, Computerworld Danmark, Macworld Danmark, PC World Danmark, Techworld Danmark; **DOMINICAN REPUBLIC:** PC World Republica Dominicana; **ECUADOR:** PC World Ecuador; **EGYPT:** Computerworld Middle East, PC World Middle East; **EL SALVADOR:** PC World Centro America; **FINLAND:** MikroPC, Tietoverkko, Tietoviikko; **FRANCE:** Distributique, Hebdo, Info PC, Le Monde Informatique, Macworld, Reseaux & Telecoms, WebMaster France; **GERMANY:** Computer Partner, Computerwoche, Computerwoche Extra, Computerwoche FOCUS, Global Online, Macwelt, PC Welt; **GREECE:** Amiga Computing, GamePro Greece, Multimedia World; **GUATEMALA:** PC World Centro America; **HONDURAS:** PC World Centro America; **HONG KONG:** Computerworld Hong Kong, PC World Hong Kong, Publish in Asia; **HUNGARY:** ABCD CD-ROM, Computerworld Szamitastechnika, Internetto online Magazine, PC World Hungary, PC-X Magazin Hungary; **ICELAND:** Tolvuheimur PC World Island; **INDIA:** Information Communications World, Information Systems Computerworld, PC World India, Publish in Asia; **INDONESIA:** InfoKomputer PC World, Komputek Computerworld, Publish in Asia; **IRELAND:** ComputerScope, PC Live!; **ISRAEL:** Macworld Israel, People & Computers/Computerworld; **ITALY:** Computerworld Italia, Macworld Italia, Networking Italia, PC World Italia; **JAPAN:** DTP World, Macworld Japan, Nikkei Personal Computing, OS/2 World Japan, SunWorld Japan, Windows NT World, Windows World Japan; **KENYA:** PC World East African; **KOREA:** Hi-Tech Information, Macworld Korea, PC World Korea; **MACEDONIA:** PC World Macedonia; **MALAYSIA:** Computerworld Malaysia, PC World Malaysia, Publish in Asia; **MALTA:** PC World Malta; **MEXICO:** Computerworld Mexico, PC World Mexico; **MYANMAR:** PC World Myanmar; **NETHERLANDS:** Computer! Totaal, LAN Internetworking Magazine, LAN World Buyers Guide, Macworld Netherlands, Net, WebWereld; **NEW ZEALAND:** Absolute Beginners Guide and Plain & Simple Series, Computer Buyer, Computer Industry Directory, Computerworld New Zealand, MTB, Network World, PC World New Zealand; **NICARAGUA:** PC World Centro America; **NORWAY:** Computerworld Norge, CW Rapport, Datamagasinet, Financial Rapport, Kursguide Norge, Macworld Norge, Multimediaworld Norge, PC World Ekspress Norge, PC World Nettverk, PC World Norge, PC World Norge, PC World ProduktGuide Norge; **PAKISTAN:** Computerworld Pakistan; **PANAMA:** PC World Panama; **PEOPLE'S REPUBLIC OF CHINA:** China Computer Users, China Computerworld, China InfoWorld, China Telecom World Weekly, Computer & Communication, Electronic Design China, Electronics Today, Electronics Weekly, Game Software, PC World China, Popular Computer Week, Software Weekly, Software World, Telecom World; **PERU:** Computerworld Peru, PC World Profesional Peru, PC World SoHo Peru; **PHILIPPINES:** Click!, Computerworld Philippines, PC World Philippines, Publish in Asia; **POLAND:** Computerworld Poland, Computerworld Special Report Poland, Cyber, Macworld Poland, Networld Poland, PC World Komputer; **PORTUGAL:** Cerebro/PC World, Computerworld/Correio Informático, Dealer World Portugal, Mac*In/PC*In Portugal, Multimedia World; **PUERTO RICO:** PC World Puerto Rico; **ROMANIA:** Computerworld Romania, PC World Romania, Telecom Romania; **RUSSIA:** Computerworld Russia, Mir PK, Publish, Seti; **SINGAPORE:** Computerworld Singapore, PC World Singapore, Publish in Asia; **SLOVENIA:** Monitor; **SOUTH AFRICA:** Computing SA, Network World SA, Software World SA; **SPAIN:** Communicaciones World España, Computerworld España, Dealer World España, Macworld España, PC World España; **SRI LANKA:** Infolink PC World; **SWEDEN:** CAP&Design, Computer Sweden, Corporate Computing Sweden, Internetworld Sweden, it.branschen, Macworld Sweden, MaxiData Sweden, MikroDatorn, Natverk & Kommunikation, PC World Sweden, PCaktiv, Windows World Sweden; **SWITZERLAND:** Computerworld Schweiz, Macworld Schweiz, PCtip; **TAIWAN:** Computerworld Taiwan, Macworld Taiwan, NEW ViSiON/Publish, PC World Taiwan, Windows World Taiwan; **THAILAND:** Publish in Asia, Thai Computerworld; **TURKEY:** Computerworld Turkiye, Macworld Turkiye, Network World Turkiye, PC World Turkiye; **UKRAINE:** Computerworld Kiev, Multimedia World Ukraine, PC World Ukraine; **UNITED KINGDOM:** Acorn User UK, Amiga Action UK, Amiga Computing UK, Apple Talk UK, Computing, Macworld, Parents and Computers UK, PC Advisor, PC Home, PSX Pro, The WEB; **UNITED STATES:** Cable in the Classroom, CIO Magazine, Computerworld, DOS World, Federal Computer Week, GamePro Magazine, InfoWorld, I-Way, Macworld, Network World, PC Games, PC World, Publish, Video Event, THE WEB Magazine, and WebMaster; online webzines: JavaWorld, NetscapeWorld, and SunWorld Online; **URUGUAY:** InfoWorld Uruguay; **VENEZUELA:** Computerworld Venezuela, PC World Venezuela; and **VIETNAM:** PC World Vietnam.

Credits

ACQUISITIONS EDITOR
Laura Lewin

DEVELOPMENT EDITOR
Laura E. Brown

TECHNICAL EDITOR
Samuel Ockman

COPY EDITOR
Eric Hahn

PROJECT COORDINATOR
Ritchie Durdin

BOOK DESIGNERS
Jim Donohue
Kurt Krames

GRAPHICS AND PRODUCTION SPECIALIST
Stephanie Hollier

QUALITY CONTROL SPECIALISTS
Mick Arellano
Mark Schumann

GRAPHICS TECHNICIANS
Linda J. Marousek
Hector Mendosa

PROOFREADER
Arielle Carole Mennelle

INDEXER
Liz Cunningham

COVER DESIGN
© mike parsons design

About the Author

Christopher A. Jones works as a consultant on Internet applications development, specializing in distributed, object-oriented, Web-based applications. He has a UNIX systems administration background, and has developed software in C++, Java, Perl, and the shell for both Windows and UNIX machines. Chris lives in Seattle with his wife Barb and son Miles. He's an avid music fan and musician.

For my wife Barb, the best dang woman in all of King County.

Preface

Although the UNIX shell is often considered a simple scripting language, it can provide the power of compiled languages, such as C++ and Java. *UNIX Shell Objects* demonstrates advanced programming techniques that enable this pleasant and convenient language to accommodate complex and ambitious tasks.

Who Should Read This Book

Whether you're a UNIX programmer, Webmaster, network engineer, or system administrator, this book changes your view of shell programming. Unlike texts that demonstrate simple shell syntax, *UNIX Shell Objects* shows how the capabilities of the shell can be expanded tenfold by bringing object-orientation and distributed programming to the Korn shell.

As a former UNIX systems administrator and current Internet applications developer, I use the shell as part of my everyday work. Whether I'm packaging an application, integrating runtime components, or trying to personalize my UNIX account, I usually write shell scripts. In *UNIX Shell Objects*, I show you exactly how to integrate the shell into your own work.

The Topic at Hand

UNIX Shell Objects shows you how to bring object-oriented programming (OOP) to the shell. OOP is conceptual, and not limited to any one language. OOP reduces the amount of time needed to develop and improve the functionality of your software. Software development is moving from the simple client-server paradigm into the distributed objects paradigm. The next generation of systems development bridges multiple tiers across the network, thus connecting new and existing systems into large distributed applications. As the long-standing standard workhorse of UNIX systems, the shell will remain important far into the future.

UNIX Shell Objects also presents a good measure of CGI programming and shows you how to tap network API power from the shell through the use of Java. As this book shows, customizing APIs for use in shell scripts brings unimaginable power to your scripting – enabling you to create commands for Internet sockets, messaging, and other advanced programming techniques.

What's in the Book

Chapters 1 and 2 discuss object-orientation in general, and quickly review common shell programming constructs. These topics bring you up to speed on both the nature of OOP as well as many of the shell syntax and programming techniques used throughout the book.

Chapters 3, 4, and 5 demonstrate how to create objects in the shell, and cover such topics as inheritance, encapsulation, polymorphism, messages, and component architecture. All of the code written in the shell is portable and powerful.

Chapters 6 and 7 show how Java can enhance shell programming by tapping into Java's powerful networking support. You use Java to create Internet sockets, thus allowing for interprocess communication between shell scripts. You tie the Java processes to the shell via the coprocess technique, and your shell scripts start to use named-pipes (First In First Out) that cross the network.

Chapter 8 examines completely new ground in shell programming by developing an object request broker (ORB). The ORB enables you to incorporate an object into your code that can exist across the network. Using an object through the ORB appears in a similar manner as using a local one, but the ORB approach offers extremely valuable flexibility to the programmer. Services once isolated across the network can now be tightly integrated into your code.

Chapters 9 and 10 build a system management utility (SMU) from distributed objects. This application brings together many objects to accomplish high-level operations. A series of operation objects are developed that encapsulate complex, multi-object tasks behind a simple, repetitive interface. This process allows for the easy hookup of a graphical user interface through the Web, Java, or native client code.

Chapter 11 extends the ORB architecture with the addition of callback capabilities. This concept allows for a distributed object loaded by client code to turn around and invoke methods on the client, thus switching the roles of client and server.

Chapters 12 and 13 feature an in-depth look at CGI programming from the shell by developing "request" and "response" objects to encapsulate scripts from the details of HTTP requests. These objects allow quick and easy parsing and decoding of complex URL encoded data, and make CGI programming rapid and simple. In culminating the SMU application, Chapter 13 develops a Web site that acts as a distributed front end to the complex array of distributed objects created previously to manage system activities.

To review, Chapters 3–5 encompass the shell objects themselves, which are treated as a fairly standalone entity. You may regard the objects as the most interesting and powerful issue presented in this book. The ORB and supporting components are developed in Chapters 7–9 and remain fairly autonomous. The SMU application is developed on top of the ORB in Chapter 10 and is bound to the rest of the code presented in the first half of the book. The CGI objects presented in Chapters 12 and 13 can readily be applied in any Internet application, and have no dependency on the ORB or some of the other techniques presented in the book.

This Book's Approach

Before you dash off to code a shell ORB and its objects, consider the following issues. The ORB is a complex application that uses IPC to bridge code running on any number of machines. This ORB is written entirely in the shell. The complexities of network programming are intense, and you may occasionally sit on one end of the network chain and wonder why your object isn't responding. Keep in mind that as many as eight processes could be running between you and your final object, and a small glitch could be located in any of the processes.

As a rule, approach the material in this book on a piece-by-piece basis. Instead of trying to launch the ORB right off the CD-ROM and code from the back of the book to the front, try to build and gain an understanding of each small piece. As you start to combine these processes, you'll become more familiar about their operations and potential problems. Eventually, you also will be able to debug the more complex acrobatics attempted in this book.

Small icons occur throughout the text to indicate items of interest, tips, cautions, and CD-ROM information that may warrant closer inspection.

The Note icon indicates interesting information related to the text.

The Tip icon uncovers additional, helpful information that can save time.

The Caution icon denotes an issue that warrants careful consideration. These items may be system-specific behaviors or warnings when typing in a delicate command.

 The CD-ROM icon points out where you can find the software discussed in the book on the CD-ROM.

About the Software

The code in this book was developed on both Linux (Slackware with a 2.0.29 Kernel) and Solaris (2.5, 2.6). While the shell objects are very portable, I experienced different behavior regarding synchronous pipe I/O between Solaris and Linux. Overall, I recommend that if you intend to run the ORB, first get it working on Linux, and then port and adapt it to your target platform.

The public domain Korn shell is enclosed on the CD-ROM. You can write shell objects in any shell flavor, but the `shcc` converter presented in Chapter 3 only works with the Korn shell. I have successfully compiled pdKsh5.2.12 on both Linux and Solaris.

The CD-ROM also contains the Apache Web server. As an exercise, a system management application is created using the distributed techniques in this book. The Web server creates a browser-based interface that attaches to the distributed objects to provide a means of remote administration for UNIX servers. Apache is bundled with most Linux distributions, and your Apache server configuration should work properly.

The Java components in this book are developed with JDK 1.1 for Linux. If you have a fairly recent distribution of Linux, you may already have it installed. If not, the most recent release is available from `http://www.blackdown.org`.

Contacting the Author

I find shell programming very exciting and welcome any comments. You can reach me via e-mail at `chris@perpendicularuniverse.com` or visit my Web site at `www.perpendicularuniverse.com`.

Acknowledgments

Without the comments and feedback of both Laura Brown and Sam Ockman, this book would be much harder to understand. Of course, this book wouldn't have been possible without Laura Lewin.

I might not have finished without the perseverance and support of my wife Barb and our beautiful baby boy Miles, who watched me shrivel away in front of my computer while skipping episode after episode of *The X-Files*. Needless to say, I wouldn't have gained my technical skills without the support of my mom, whose help has been well-appreciated over the years.

Finally, without the comments, satire, and smell of Drew, the world would be a much duller place — although there would be a lot more cheese.

Contents at a Glance

	Preface viii
	Acknowledgments xii
Chapter 1	The Nature of Object-Oriented Programming 1
Chapter 2	The Shell as a User and Programming Environment 19
Chapter 3	The Syntax of Writing Classes 47
Chapter 4	Using Shell Objects. 79
Chapter 5	Object Communication 111
Chapter 6	Using Java from the Shell 139
Chapter 7	Encapsulating the Network with Components 161
Chapter 8	Distributed Objects. 191
Chapter 9	Designing an Object-Oriented System. 231
Chapter 10	Creating a Shell-Based Distributed Application. . . 253
Chapter 11	Rethinking an Object-Oriented System 287
Chapter 12	Using Shell Objects with CGI 323
Chapter 13	Connecting from the Web. 357
Appendix A	GNU General Public License 389
Appendix B	About the CD-ROM 397
	Index 401
	End-User License Agreement 430
	CD-ROM Installation Instructions 436

Contents

Preface viii

Acknowledgments xii

Chapter 1   The Nature of Object-Oriented Programming 1
            Mastering Class Basics 2
            Exploring Encapsulation........................... 4
                Access Rights 4
                Interface Design 5
            Examining Inheritance 6
            Understanding Polymorphism....................... 8
                System Backup................................ 9
                Dynamic Binding.............................. 9
            Building a Universe with OOP..................... 10
                Creating a Continuum Class 11
                Originating an Atomic Class 12
                Making a Planetary Class..................... 13
                Giving Birth to a Galaxy Class............... 14
                Establishing a Universe 15
            Applying OOP in the UNIX Shell 16
            Summary 17

Chapter 2   The Shell as a User and Programming
            Environment 19
            Shell Concepts 20
                File Descriptors 20
                Redirection.................................. 21
                Pipes 24
                Built-In Variables and Identifiers 25
                Parameter Substitution....................... 27
            Shell Programming................................ 29
                if-then Evaluation 29
                while Loops 31
                for Loops 32
                case Statements 33
                Functions.................................... 34
            Programming Examples 35
            Programming Concepts............................. 41
            Considering the Environment...................... 43
            Summary 45

Chapter 3	**The Syntax of Writing Classes** 47	
	Shell Object Syntax 47	
	Object Interfaces.................................. 49	
	Inheritance...................................... 50	
	Polymorphism 50	
	Other Object Relationships 51	
	Object Design.................................... 52	
	Getting Started with a Real Script 52	
	Class Architecture................................. 53	
	Constructors.................................... 55	
	Access Functions 57	
	Data Members and Properties..................... 58	
	Methods.. 60	
	Destructors..................................... 62	
	Class Programming Considerations.................... 63	
	Variable Scope and Data Clashing 63	
	Debugging 65	
	How Shell Objects Work............................ 68	
	Using the eval Keyword 68	
	Taking Apart shcc................................ 70	
	Summary 77	
Chapter 4	**Using Shell Objects.** 79	
	Strategies 79	
	Functional Considerations 79	
	Inheritance, References, and Aggregation 80	
	Functional Classes 81	
	Object References................................ 88	
	Object Lists..................................... 94	
	Inheritance 96	
	unixServer Class................................... 99	
	Remote Machine Operation Commands 99	
	Composition................................... 100	
	Class Factories 104	
	Summary 109	
Chapter 5	**Object Communication** 111	
	Messages.. 112	
	Object to Object Communication..................... 113	
	Events... 114	
	Updating the objlist Class........................ 115	
	Creating the msgHandler Class.................... 117	
	Demonstrating Messaging with Classes 119	
	Critical and Operational Events Example 122	

		Event Handling Example 123
		Improving the disk Class 124
		Improving the unixServer Class 126
		Process Boundaries 131
		Named Pipes 131
		Coprocesses 132
		API Level Solutions 133
		Named Pipes for IPC 134
		Summary 136
	Chapter 6	**Using Java from the Shell** **139**
		Choosing Java 140
		Applets and Applications 140
		Portability 140
		Other Java Features 141
		Examining Java's Syntax and Object-Orientation 142
		Getting Started 144
		Class Interaction Example 146
		References 148
		Exploring Input and Output 150
		Understanding Java Language Features 152
		Interfaces 152
		Inheritance 155
		Threads 157
		Other Features 159
		Summary 160
	Chapter 7	**Encapsulating the Network with Components** **161**
		Understanding Networking 162
		TCP/IP 163
		The Sockets API 164
		Pipes Revisited 165
		The Shell Architecture 166
		Using Sockets 166
		Exploring the Socket Command 173
		The Client 173
		The Server 178
		Investigating Shell Examples 182
		Creating a Socket Class for the Shell 186
		Summary 190
	Chapter 8	**Distributed Objects** **191**
		Exploring Distributed Services 191
		The Advantages of Distribution 192
		Distributed Interfaces 193

	Distributed Servers.............................. 194
	Distributed Clients 195
	Distributed Proxies.............................. 196
	Examining Distributed Architecture 196
	A Word about Pipes............................. 197
	Connections and Objects 197
	The Big Picture................................ 201
	Understanding Korn Shell Object Protocol............ 202
	Requesting an Interface 203
	Defining the Interface 203
	Invoking a Method.............................. 203
	Releasing an Object 204
	Coding the Client Proxy 204
	Launching the Request.......................... 205
	Building the Object............................. 206
	Creating the Release Method 208
	Dissecting the Connection Manager 210
	Creating Persistent Connections 210
	Creating Multiple Connections 211
	Creating the Object Request Broker.................. 213
	Examining the ORB Process 213
	Creating the Instance Script 222
	Registering Interfaces with the Server................. 225
	Creating ORB Examples 226
	Starting the Server.............................. 227
	Starting a Client................................ 227
	Running the Examples........................... 228
	Summary 230
Chapter 9	**Designing an Object-Oriented System 231**
	Grasping the Goals of an Object-Oriented System 231
	Building Components........................... 232
	Breaking Apart the Application 234
	Examining Runtime Components................... 235
	Saving the Day with Object-Orientation.............. 236
	Exploring Application Objects 237
	Understanding Distributed Runtime Components....... 238
	Using Interfaces to Facilitate Scalability 239
	Identifying Application Goals....................... 239
	Providing Features.............................. 240
	Exploring User Management 240
	Tracking Disk Space............................ 241
	Rebooting Servers 242
	Tracking Applications 243

Understanding Required Services..................243
Creating a Comprehensive Design....................244
    Grasping Server Details.........................244
    Creating a UNIX Server Facade 245
    Examining the Object Request Broker 245
    Dissecting the Network..........................247
    Hooking Up Commands 248
    Understanding the Web Server
      and CGI Application 250
    Exploring the Interface.........................250
Understanding the Big Picture 250
Summary 252

Chapter 10 Creating a Shell-Based Distributed Application... 253
Creating the Core Base Classes 253
    Discovering the Operation Base Class..............254
    Creating the New uServer.cls Class.................255
    Deriving a sunUserver Class......................262
Creating the Operation Classes 263
    Add Account Operation 264
    Delete Account Operation........................266
    Operation for Rebooting Servers 269
    Operation to View Disk Space 270
    View Disk Statistics Operation....................272
    Load Average Operation.........................272
    View Process Table Operation 274
Deploying Operation Objects in the Repository.........277
    Taking Care of Dependencies 277
    Creating Object Definition Files 277
Creating a Distributed Client Application 278
    Creating a Nondistributed Client 278
    Creating a Distributed Client 283
Summary 286

Chapter 11 Rethinking an Object-Oriented System 287
Modifying an Object-Oriented System 287
    The Magic of Interfaces 288
    Suggestions for Your System 289
Implementing Object Callbacks......................294
    Callback Overview 294
    Server Object Responsibilities.....................295
    Client Object Responsibilities.....................295
Modifying the KSOP Protocol........................296
    Formatting the Server String 297

	Formatting the Client String................................ 297
	Modifying proxy.sh... 297
	Recoding the Virtual Function 297
	Completing a Callback 299
	Modifying the ORB Server 303
	Modifying the Instance Process 307
	Modifying the Connection Manager 310
	Creating an Example Callback Application..................... 312
	Creating object1 312
	Creating object2 313
	Creating the Server Component 314
	Creating the clientCb Stub Code and Base Class.......... 317
	Creating the Object Repository .def Files 319
	Running the Demo Script..................................... 320
	Summary 322

Chapter 12	**Using Shell Objects with CGI 323**
	Discovering Practical Applications for Shell Objects...... 323
	Application Menus... 323
	Application Glue 324
	Examining CGI... 324
	Uncovering CGI 325
	Configuring the Web Server.................................. 325
	Revealing the Mysteries of HTTP 327
	Creating an HTTP Request 328
	Receiving the HTTP Response................................ 328
	Handling Forms 328
	Understanding the CGI Environment 329
	The CGI User 329
	CGI Variables 330
	Creating CGI Objects... 332
	Creating a Request Object................................... 333
	Creating a Response Object 342
	Developing CGI Examples...................................... 346
	Completing a Simple CGI Program.......................... 346
	Examining a Questionnaire 348
	Creating a Gateway Application.............................. 350
	Summary 356

Chapter 13	**Connecting from the Web 357**
	Connecting the Components.................................... 357
	Getting the Environment Ready 358
	Testing the Environment 358
	Creating the Interface....................................... 359

	Creating index.html 359
	Creating Template Files 361
	Creating CGI Error Scripts. 363
	Creating the Application. 365
	Server Configuration 365
	The Main Form. 369
	Object Interface 376
	Security 386
	Summary 387
Appendix A	GNU General Public License 389
Appendix B	About the CD-ROM 397
	Index 401
	End-User License Agreement 430
	CD-ROM Installation Instructions 436

Chapter 1

The Nature of Object-Oriented Programming

IN THIS CHAPTER

- Polymorphism
- Encapsulation
- Inheritance
- The structure of objects
- How objects appear in code

OBJECT-ORIENTED PROGRAMMING (OOP) has a certain magic. Object-oriented techniques can provide unprecedented power and functionality to the software developer. These techniques can minimize the hassles and rework brought about by the demands of new software, new platforms, changing requirements, redesigns, redirection, and every other sort of software-breaking problem that plagues modern development. While there are certain tradeoffs depending on how many levels of encapsulation your environment needs and the abstraction of your interfaces, many agree the time saved in constant rewriting and development far outweighs slight processor overhead. Processors and hardware are only getting faster, while software development is only growing more complex.

Object-oriented techniques benefit any language. While this book focuses on the UNIX shell, the techniques presented can be applied to any language, such as C++, BASIC, Perl, and so forth. Object-oriented programming is a concept, not a language; it's a method of decomposing software systems into functional components for greater flexibility and reuse.

Object-oriented concepts can be hard to visualize, and often, your imagination only makes it more difficult. The abstract notion of objects mysteriously floating about cyberspace interfacing with each other confuses many programmers. What's more, translating these concepts into code can seem daunting. In the simplest sense, an object can simply contain a variable's definition, together with a function declaration capable of changing the variable. Although object-oriented techniques become much more complex, the basic idea stays the same. For now, you can think of *objects* as collections of data and the functions that operate upon them.

Mastering Class Basics

The most basic element in object-oriented programming is the *class*, which acts as the blueprint for an object and, in many systems, is the only static element. Complex systems often use "Factory" techniques and automate the object construction process, but you won't be using that approach in the UNIX shell at first. In these systems, by avoiding the hard-coded construction of a particular object, you can concentrate on putting together the right kinds of interfaces and provide greater flexibility in your system (Chapter 4 discusses this topic in depth).

A class is usually a simple text file that details the design of your object. If you're familiar with scripting or programming, you're probably already familiar with the idea of a function. You declare a function, and then use its code by simply calling out the function's name somewhere in your program, as follows:

```
say_hello() {
    print "Hello!"
}
```

Many lines later, you invoke this function simply with the following:

```
say_hello
```

This code outputs the appropriate message. Classes provide the same sort of capability, but in a slightly different way. In fact, you can achieve many of the same benefits of object-oriented programming through the use of function libraries and modular programming. As you'll see, however, object-orientation is the natural progression of these techniques and provides more advantages.

As mentioned previously, you can safely think of objects as collections of data members (variables) and the functions that operate upon them. You create a class to hold these variables and functions. You can later *instantiate*, or create an instance in code of an object of your class that holds these variables and functions and keeps them specific to the instance. Your class could define a variable called `hello_message` and a function called `print_message` to display `hello_message`. The functions and data are internal to the class — when you create an object of this class, the object contains `hello_message`, and `print_message` as in the following:

```
#!/bin/ksh
   ## class message
   id=$1  ## assign the object a name
   ## data member
   eval "${id}_helloMessage=\"Hello! I'm a message.\""
   ## operation
eval "${id}_printMessage() {
   print \$$${id}_helloMessage
   }"
```

Chapter 1: The Nature of Object-Oriented Programming

This simple class lets you create objects that contain a message, along with a function to display that message. You create an object and use its functionality as in the following:

```
## create object
. message MyFirstMessage
## use it
MyFirstMessage_printMessage
```

The previous code shows how you create an object in the Korn shell. As the standard scripting language, the Korn shell is ubiquitous to UNIX systems. It is used primarily in administrative tasks, application integration, and system-level programming. The Korn shell excels over languages like C/C++ in its capability to parse files easily, handle strings, and allow easy access to configuration files and handle multiple tasks concurrently through the use of coprocesses. As a language, the Korn shell's primary data type is the string. The $ operator indicates strings, and even integer types are referenced this way. The shell supports arrays and arithmetic expression, though it doesn't have the user-defined types and data structures found in C.

Due to the shell's simple data typing, you can use its string handling combined with its function constructs to support object-orientation. The Korn shell wasn't originally designed to be object-oriented, so you need to pull a few strings (no pun intended) to get the shell working properly. If you're familiar with shell scripting and think the preceding code is obfuscated with brackets (}) and slashes (\), don't worry. Fortunately, the brackets and slashes are always the same, and a script can be written to add the evaluation statements and brackets. An example script is presented in Chapter 3 as shcc. This script enables you to leave out the obfuscating characters:

```
# operations
_message() {
   # constructor function
   _helloMessage="Hello! I'm a message"
}
_printMessage() {
   print $_helloMessage
}
```

As you can see, this version of the class is pure, ordinary shell code. You can run this version, but you can't assign object identifiers to the functions and data members. Also, this version of the class uses a constructor function, which is a normal feature of classes. The constructor function is called first to initialize the object — more on this later. The shcc script resolves the cumbersome syntax of adding eval "{ObjectId}" to your code, creates destructor functions, and plumbs in debugging code.

An object refers to all of its data members and operations with its own name. An object called `MyObject` calls its operations in C++ in a syntax like `MyObject.function()`. To provide this same sort of functionality within the Korn shell, prefix a class's data members and functions with the name of the object that wants to own them: `MyObject_function`.

Toward the end of this chapter, an interesting pseudoapplication is created that illustrates some of the benefits of object-oriented design and programming. Before examining this pseudoapplication, let's study some of the key concepts of OOP in greater detail.

Classes do more than just hold functions and operations for your object. They allow for *encapsulation* of object data from the clients that use it. That is, you can hide all the implementation-specific details behind the "public" operations you provide for any script or program that wants to use your object. Classes can also be inherited by other classes to reuse the code. Classes provide functions identical to the functions implemented by other classes, thus allowing both types of objects to be used by any client object that expects the common interface. Objects provide for greater flexibility than afforded by function libraries and modular programming.

Exploring Encapsulation

Encapsulation enables you to hide your code and its operations behind an object's public methods. As a result, you can change the implementation of the class without "breaking" the code that depends on it. For instance, you have a function `InsertUser` that inserts a new user's name into a password file on a computer system. You write other classes and code that use the `InsertUser` interface to accomplish work. At a future point, you decide to have the password database centered on a network machine using NIS. You can go back and recode the `InsertUser` method to add a user to the remote password file — instead of the local one. Any code that depends on this interface won't be affected by this change. The change is invisible because it is encapsulated behind the object. The interface is the point of control for all client code. What goes on behind the interface is invisible to the client.

Object-oriented programming often uses these *black-box* methods — methods where the functionality and implementation are hidden as often as possible to allow for greater flexibility. As long as you develop the right interface, and reuse it in other classes or derived classes, the code that depends on these interfaces doesn't have to be changed when the object's implementation changes.

Access Rights

Specifying whether an object's data members and methods are public or private is another means of furthering encapsulation in some languages, including C++. These monikers are assigned at creation and determine who can access the method or data member. The reasoning behind this approach is also to encapsulate the implementation-specific data. If client code knows what kind of data types and variables the object uses, the wily programmer, believing himself a quick-fixer, may be tempted to code directly with the object when the right situation arises. For example, a programmer knows that a drawing class you've written accepts integers and assigns them to internal data members before plotting them onto the screen. Caught in a sticky situation, the programmer has just been given all of your code with which to work and decides that when he needs to draw a line, he will simply assign his own values to your object's internal data members and call the object's draw function. The problem in this situation arises when you rewrite your class to increase performance or provide additional functionality. Suddenly, all of the client code that the programmer has developed is broken because you've redesigned your object's internal line drawing functions. Now bugs appear in the system, and code on both sides will have to be rewritten. This scenario can be avoided by using encapsulation, and specifying private and public members and operations.

If your object's implementation-specific operations are declared private, only an object instance of your class can access its own internal functions. This forces any client code to work with the public interfaces you've provided. In the preceding example, you could have redefined the internal drawing functions, but as long as you did not change the public interface, none of the client code has to be changed. You use this approach by creating access functions.

When you develop classes in the UNIX shell, you will not be using private and public specifiers, but you will implement access functions. Examples in this book, however, demonstrate how access rights can be specified and internal data "locked" down if needed. In these examples, internal code is not included in the "header" area at the top of the class file, and the intended interface operations should be clear to any programmer who wishes to use your class. The shell classes consist of several lines of comments at the top of each file declaring what operations are intended to be used by client code, and what data members are accessible to them. Specifying access avoids the poor programming practice of allowing someone to delve into the code and try to tweak the internal operations. If you are developing a class where this functionality is critical, then this book's methods for specifying private and public access should be well worth implementing.

Interface Design

Apart from private and public specification, the real power of encapsulation is in using interfaces. By publishing the public "handles" with which to use your object, you ensure that the class remains flexible — you can always change the internal implementation to adapt to changes in requirements or the environment. One key to making encapsulation work is proper interface design. If your interface is too specific, you run the risk of coupling the interface too tightly to any situation.

For example, if you have a function that can open a socket connection to another machine, you should try to make the function as simple as possible. The method could require two values: one representing the message to be sent and one representing the listening remote machine or service. A poor design requires more information from the client, such as the specific port number, the specific length of the message, and perhaps even instructions for what the recipient is supposed to do with the message. This kind of interface design is useless because it's practically impossible to change the implementation behind the object without changing the interface. You should keep the interfaces as simple and flexible as possible and put the dirty details of the operations within the object. The key to object-oriented programming is the use and reuse of interfaces. A good interface can be implemented by more than one class, thereby maximizing the encapsulation available to a system. As this book demonstrates, effective use of object-oriented techniques takes careful planning.

Examining Inheritance

In the simplest sense, inheritance represents direct code reuse in object-oriented programming. If you create a class that performs certain functionality, you can derive another class directly from it through inheritance and retain all of the exact same code, plus add any additional features needed. For example, you have a class that represents UNIX machines living on a network. You put all of the operations and data members relevant to all UNIX machines in your class. Some machines have more operations capability than others, however. This matter needs to be addressed with a new type of object. Through inheritance, you derive another class and keep all of the original functionality and code, and just add the needed functions. This direct form of inheritance promotes code reuse by allowing different types of objects that share similar attributes to reuse the same common code. When developing OO systems, you often strive to decompose different aspects of the system into areas that can reuse common functionality, with the goal of factoring out this functionality into base classes.

Developing base classes for every single shared interface in the system and deriving objects accordingly is a poor use of inheritance. Excessive inheritance and base-classing can result in a broad, useless array of feature-shallow objects. Inheritance is used when an object closely resembles another object, and can be considered a type of the first object. For example, an apple is a type of fruit. An orange is a type of fruit. You could create classes that represent the "functionality" or properties of apples and oranges and share their base code to a class of fruit:

```
# Class Fruit
## data members
   _isRound
   _hasSeeds
## operations
   _fallFromTree()
   _rot()
```

Chapter 1: The Nature of Object-Oriented Programming

The preceding class, Fruit, has defined data members that represent its "roundness" and the fact that it has "seeds." Also, Fruit has operations that allow it to "fall from a tree" or "rot." This is a good base class, and this code can be reused by subclasses like apple and orange:

```
# Class Orange Inherits Fruit
## data
   _isOrange
## operations
   _squirtJuice()
```

The class Orange directly inherits all of the features of Fruit. An orange certainly _isRound and hasSeeds, but an orange is a special kind of fruit and its color isOrange. Additionally, not all fruit can squirtJuice() quite like an orange. This sort of inheritance is a direct reuse of code.

Another feature of inheritance is the capability for a derived class to redefine or override the operations declared by its parent. A preceding section discussed a class that could represent a UNIX system on a network. The vendor-specific implementation details involved in configuring a specific type of UNIX system is an annoying problem facing system administrators. The configuration files are often kept in slightly different places and while all of the common commands are present, often there are subtle variations on the syntax that implements them. Inheritance is an excellent way to remedy this problem. A UNIX class can define functions such as LaunchXwindow and RebootSystem. While these functions may be the same for many UNIX machines, some machines are slightly different. By creating a base class that provides an interface Reboot, you can have subclasses inherit and redefine this function to represent the command necessary to reboot their particular system.

```
# Class UNIXSystem
## operations
   _Reboot()
   {
     /etc/shutdown -ry now
   }
```

This partial class listing implements a function called Shutdown that successfully shuts down a particular UNIX machine. This shutdown command does not work on all machines; therefore, the following subclass is created that inherits and redefines this function.

```
# Class AnotherUNIXSystem
## operations
   _Shutdown()
   {
     /etc/shutdown -r 0
   }
```

This class redefines `Shutdown` to function correctly on a different type of UNIX system. The power of this class is the capability to keep the functionality transparent to client code. Any script that needs to shut down a collection of network machines doesn't need to know which version of `Shutdown` is implemented on the remote machines — only that they have objects that present the correct usable interface. This technique enables you to create a long list of network machines and create a five-line script that successfully reboots them, regardless of their UNIX type. The implementation-specific details are encapsulated behind the object and the interface is shared through inheritance.

```
#!/bin/ksh
# use UNIX object interface to reboot network
for each in $(< machines)
do
  # create class object
  . UNIXSystem ThisMachine $each
  # call operation
  ThisMachine_Shutdown
done
```

Provided a shell class called `UNIXSystem` exists, the preceding script creates an object for each machine contained in the file list `machines` and then calls the `Shutdown` function for each object. This type of script occurs throughout the book.

Understanding Polymorphism

Polymorphism is the magical method by which one object can masquerade as another. It is the mechanism used to write code that depends on interfaces, not implementation. By writing your code to use interfaces, you maximize the encapsulation and flexibility of an object-oriented system. The interface can be inherited and redefined, or it can be implemented by a new and unforeseen class to accomplish new functionality. Polymorphism is not necessarily the result of inheritance — instead, it is the intentional reuse of an interface. In the preceding example, many different types of objects could implement the `Shutdown()` interface. The client script that uses the code never needs to know what kind of object is on the implementation side.

If you are writing an application that needs to use database services, you should stay flexible regarding database management systems and database objects. This is an excellent place for polymorphic techniques. You can create a database object that deals with the dirty task of opening a connection to a database, opening a flat text file, or storing information into another device such as a tape drive. You could then create different types of data objects; one each for people, systems, and other items. These objects could track any desired type of data. You can implement two common interfaces for these data objects. One streams the data into the database, while the other reads the stream back out. Keep this interface the same for all of your data objects. Your database object, the one taking care of the device-dependent dirty work, should only expect to deal with either receiving a data stream from an object or returning the stream to the object. The database object simply "feeds" this stream to the appropriate device. In fact, if you have a wide array of different data storage devices, you can invoke other objects as well to deal with their specifics.

This process enables you to create data objects with varying types and lengths of fields. You only need to create the streaming functions. The database object use these functions to transfer data to and from the hardware or network storage medium. The database object has no idea which object's methods it invokes — it only knows that the object provided the proper interface.

System Backup

Likewise, if you are creating classes in the shell to deal with backing up a system, you can create a storage object and a backup object. The backup object simply builds lists of files that need to be backed up. It can deal with incremental backups or an entire system copy, and store this information internally and forward it onto the storage object. The storage object does not need to know anything about the object with which it deals except that the object provides a method with which to retrieve a list of filenames. The storage object can then implement whatever means desired to store the information: a tar file, a Solaris installable package (to be used with `pkgadd`), or a binary stream fed to a raw disk device or copied onto an NFS mount or remote server across the network. The flexibility is provided through the storage object's interface. Just sending a message changes the method of backup. Any written script can use the backup object without worrying about a change in the interface or the sort of activity carried out on the other side. Also, different types of backup-like objects can be created to do different tasks. You can implement a derived object to package up a Web site, or build lists of individual user files. All of these objects can use a storage object as long as they provide the proper interface for the storage object to use.

Polymorphism adds to system flexibility regarding the type of objects you're tossing about at runtime. While this isn't apparent in the shell, because the shell is an interpreted language, it does show up in compiled code.

Dynamic Binding

Dynamic binding occurs when objects meet each other for the first time while an application is in execution. When an object expects the interface of another object, it only knows of the interface, not the implementation. You can swap one object out and replace it with another while a system is running. In the shell, this process is as easy as replacing a file. In compiled code, however, there is overhead. Optimization and mapping can't be done at compilation time because the object code to be implemented may not have been written yet. The overhead associated with broad encapsulation and heavy use of polymorphism won't be apparent in the shell, because you can mix and match your objects at runtime just as easily as at design time. This capability derives from the shell's quality as an interpreted language. Every line of code is interpreted by the Korn shell, which usually lives at /bin/ksh on UNIX systems, and the scripts are written in plain text files. Swapping out an object's functionality in one of your shell systems simply replaces a file at the opportune moment.

When developing an application in C or C++, you compile your text file into a binary executable that the processor can run. The file you've written in C++ is turned into a bunch of numbers that represent understandable instructions to processor. You're free to program in this language, but the amount of instructions you must provide to print a word on the screen is much longer than print "hello, world!". The processor has a smaller set of simple instructions than available to a (slightly) higher level language like C++.

When a program is compiled, the compiler makes note of where certain functions are called from your code and performs its mapping at that time. This process results in a quickly executing program. These conditions change when you introduce polymorphism, however. If you write a class capable of receiving any object's common interface, the compiler can't map the function call to the code because the code may be different every time the function is invoked. This approach provides flexibility for object-oriented developers, but causes overhead in compiled code.

This book's examples make ample use of the capability to change the functionality of objects dynamically. Because the language is already being interpreted by the processor, there is no gain in overhead and you essentially just add new lines to a text file.

Building a Universe with OOP

Let's dive right in with an ambitious example that models the entire universe (well, with four or five objects). While not exact, this example presents an entertaining example of a functional object-oriented system. The model you create in this example consists mostly of Korn shell function pseudo-code, leaving out the "hooks" that turn the classes into objects. The shcc program, presented in a following section of this book, converts these undecorated functions into object-generating class scripts with a minimal amount of effort.

The models in this example illustrate an object-oriented approach to a complex design, and many of the common benefits of OOP techniques are presented. The overall system represents an architectural representation of the entire cosmos in extremely simple structural terms. You start (and end) with the most basic structure, called *continuum*, and trace it up through increasingly complex structures spanning atomic and celestial levels. The objects at each level only need to know of their relative position, their relative size, and the child objects that compose them. A common interface throughout lets the objects indicate their appearance and girth, and

Chapter 1: The Nature of Object-Oriented Programming

makes sure the objects that compose them also reveal this information. On the viewing end of this system is the Display object, which is capable of rendering a representation of the dynamic structure. The flexibility built into this system becomes apparent when different levels of resolution are required, or when the display device changes from a computer monitor to something more sci-fi, like a holodeck. The display object acts as an adapter, creating a bridge from the structural objects' draw methods to the operating systems' display device interface.

Now, imagine your boss has come to you with a special problem. She needs you to reproduce the physical universe within her palmtop computer for mysterious reasons (everyone suspects she wants to create a virtual universe to hide in). First, you want to define what is fundamental to every object in the universe. You will use the most basic structure you can find, and use it as your abstract base class. This enables you to derive all other objects from this granddaddy, and try to represent the physical universe.

Creating a Continuum Class

Because you want to be thorough, you start this exercise with a base class called Continuum. The Continuum class represents the most common object relationship in the universe. Every object has one thing in common: it is and it has that which composes it. The Continuum class represents the functionality necessary to realize each object. With a willing suspension of disbelief and a slant toward the humorous and Zen, you derive your class hierarchy and launch your dynamic system to model the universe. To that end, your first class in pseudo-code follows:

```
# Class Continuum
## member variables
  _size[x]       ## Relative size to display's "_scale" factor
  _co-ords[x]    ## Three-dimensional spatial co-ordinates
  _components[x] ## List of composing objects
 _strDisplay    ## Name of display object adapter

  ## functions
  _Draw()
  {
   ## first, draw our children
   if [[ -n $_components ]]; then
     for each in ${_components[*]}
     do
       ${each}_Draw()
       ((x+=1))
     done
   fi

   ## then draw our self!
   ## send info to display obj
   ${_strDisplay}_Draw $_size $_co-ords
  }
```

```
_Move()
{
##no implementation defined
}
```

Your class has two functions: `Draw()`, which defines the default behavior for all derived Continuum objects; and `Move()`, which _Draw will call draw on all of its components and then take care of drawing itself. You could create a class `quark`, and it could define its version of `draw()` to represent quarks successfully. For brevity and to avoid absolute ridiculousness, however, skip the quantum level and go straight for the atomic.

Originating an Atomic Class

Now you have to start making decisions. Do you really know what atoms look like structurally? Do you really know how their structure affects their behavior? Can you represent atoms in a structural way similar to architecture? These are all relevant, complex questions, and as far as this book is concerned, the answer is an emphatic yes!

You move straight to Atom. While you could create classes for what composes an atom, there is no behavioral differentiation at that level (at least, not right now) and no reason to implement these classes with a subtype. As this example will demonstrate, however, it is entirely possible to implement any level of representation without much code rewriting. The structure you develop takes care of representation recursively, so implementing a new object is a breeze — it is realized automatically by its parent.

You won't create a separate class for an Atom; instead, you create a Continuum object, called Atom, with an atomic size specification. This simply defines its structural representation with a numeric size value; you coincide this number with an elements value on the periodic chart. The value represents the spherical diameter of your representative atom. Accordingly, a hydrogen atom has a size value of 1, while a monster uranium atom constitutes a 238 (or something similar). This numeric value is held by the object's size value. The value is multiplied by the universal constant you define named `scale` (a member of the Display class). This allows for multiple levels of resolution. Because this is the smallest member of the hierarchy (for now), an Atom's size should equal the universal constant `scale`. If scale is equal to 1, than hydrogen (a very small atom) is equal to 1, also. If you demand a higher level of resolution and define scale to be 10, a hydrogen atom's size is also 10, thus allowing for 10 units of resolution within an atom. Respectively, a uranium's size is defined as `238 * scale`. Because an atom in this universe is spherical, its size member can be a single integer that represents its diameter.

As for the larger objects you compose, their `co-ords` value are a series of integers that represent them spatially in three dimensions. Of course, when you need to represent an object from its size array, the scale factor is used to determine resolu-

Chapter 1: The Nature of Object-Oriented Programming

tion; meaning, on a screen 640 pixels wide, a hydrogen atom represents 10 pixels if the scale is 10. Conversely, the display mechanism can also contain a ratio factor to redefine the scale to a more realistic representation. For now, don't become too involved with representation — just continue creating your objects.

You also leave molecules as static objects, which are capable of changing their size and position, but you define no movement for them. They are created as objects directly from the Continuum class. In fact, because you are achieving such a broad scale of perspective in this hypothetical model, you won't be using any new subtypes until the planetary level.

Making a Planetary Class

The class used to define planet objects actually works for anything that follows an orbital path. Because both stars and planets usually move in a circular motion, you create them from the same class: OrbObject. You inherit directly from Continuum and implement the virtual Move() function to accomplish your planetary traveling. The code for the OrbObject class follows:

```
## Class OrbObject Inherits Continuum
 . Continuum $args ## function will "source"
## continuum code (see shcc)
## implement the move function and keep everything else
 _Move()
 {
  _co-ords[x] = $(IncrementCircularMotion $co-ords[x])
 }
```

As you can see, you keep all of the original functionality and data members of the Continuum class and simply implement the code you need, which is the Move function. You conveniently pass your current co-ordinates to the hypothetical IncrementCircularMotion function, which adjusts them accordingly.

This example omits some critical parts of your object classes. In most languages and the UNIX shell, all classes usually have constructor and destructor functions that pass necessary parameters and configuration settings when the object is first constructed. The constructor is the first called function of an object and destructor, obviously, is the last. Typically, a destructor is implemented automatically in some languages and is used to free up any of the memory being used by the object.

In the hypothetical scenario, constructors pass initial size and spatial co-ordinate parameters to your objects, not to mention an indication of the types and quantity of the objects of which they are composed. This scenario leaves out a few other elements, but you need to start thinking in object-oriented terms before tackling any real code. A constructor for a planet object, for example, might take parameters to indicate its size and co-ordinates. It also might indicate the fact that it is composed of a gazillion water molecules, nitrogen atoms, oxygen atoms, and so forth. These, in turn, have their constructors called, and initialize their co-ordinates based on the co-ordinates of their parent.

The OrbObject represents planets and stars. You give the same type of movement to both of these celestial bodies. When a star takes the creation of its composite planet objects into account, it indicates their position to be outside of the star, as opposed to your other atomic and molecular objects that contain the objects they create.

Giving Birth to a Galaxy Class

Your next celestial object creation is a galaxy. You derive a Galaxy class from Continuum that implements the Move function accordingly. A Galaxy class contains the same functionality as the Continuum class — it has a size, a position (determined by the co-ords), and is composed of other objects (namely planets and stars) that in turn are composed of atomic and molecular objects. The Galaxy class implements its Move function to increment its position and check its proximity to other galaxies. You make another convenient call to a function ComputeGravitationalPull, which alters your co-ords accordingly based on the gravitational influence of other distant Galaxy objects. The pseudo-code used in a Galaxy class follows:

```
# Class Galaxy Inherits Continuum
  . Continuum $args   ## function to "source" continuum code
## keep most of the functionality of continuum
  _Move()
  {
    ## adjust co-ords based on the gravitational influence
    ## of other galaxies
    co-ords[x] = $(ComputeGravitationalPull $co-ords[x])
  }
```

Because the Continuum object calls the draw function for all of its components, you can collectively group objects together in one large galaxy object. Essentially, you use this approach when you declare a molecule object to be a collection of atom objects. They are both objects of class Continuum except they have different sizes, and of course, the atoms are contained within the molecule. Using these object-oriented techniques, you can just as easily create an atom object containing molecules made up of planets, which are in turn composed of galaxies. You focus on the structure — not the functionality and behavior. Imagine a geometric structure, which contains smaller geometric structures. The function that displays these structures is called *recursively* (that is, one object calls the function for itself and all of the objects within it). This sort of technique enables you to treat groups of objects through the same interface you would treat individual objects. If you move your planet, you also move the thousands of objects you placed within it.

Establishing a Universe

The last object is the Universe. The Universe object is directly implemented from the Continuum class. If you use the classes you've constructed here, you need to indicate how many stars the universe contains when you construct your Universe class in code. In turn, you need to indicate their number of orbiting planets and the number of molecules and atoms of which those planets consist. You have many options for configuring your universe, including default numbers for and the composition of planets and stars. You can also create constructor functions that use some sort of algorithm or other means of determining how to compose the objects. One strong point in this scheme is the draw function. You only need to call `Draw()` on the universe object, and the rest falls into place. Also, because of the object-oriented nature, it's easy for you to go in and redefine the behavior of planets, stars, and atomic components to create your universe in any manner.

For a more realistic representation of the universe, you probably would have wanted to model reality a little more closely. You could have focused on the atomic level, implemented a variety of chemical behavior at that level, and let it dictate the behavior of larger compositions. You also could have coupled the objects to the smallest elements, as opposed to linking to the largest element, the universe. By connecting the atomic objects to a class Energy or some other "ether-like" substance, you could use that class as the message medium to communicate to the objects. The chain of events and workings of the universe on a larger scale would be directly based on the atomic and chemical fluctuations that the small objects would represent. Remember that an average rock or sponge is made up of billions of atoms, though. Any processor would be very busy if given the task of creating all of the atoms contained in a galaxy.

To conclude the model, you start the universe with two commands:

```
Continuum Universe
Universe_draw
```

This example assumes that you created default constructors to call the stars and planets with the necessary instruction to pass along to their components. Following this scheme, all construction is just passed along to the components until it finally ends up in the hand of the atomic objects. Everything is eventually made up of those objects, and they would really be the only items instantiated. Everything else is merely designated as a certain collection of atom objects. Think of it as a long list of container boundaries, each pointing to smaller boundaries as what it contains, until finally, you substantiate the only material in our system, which is the continuum structure itself.

You can subsequently pass the highest level object (instantiation) onto the smallest implemented class (atom). You can actually build this sort of functionality into the Continuum class. As a result, you instantiate a universe with `Continuum Universe` and (ultimately at the bottom of every recursive chain) call `Continuum`

`Universe` again at the atomic level. Thus, you ensure infinite recursion and an infinite number of universes!

You don't want to crash your computer, however. As you can see, object-oriented techniques provide for much greater flexibility than mere function libraries. While this sort of design may seem appropriate for large applications, you may be asking, "Why would I want to do this from the Korn or Bash shell?"

Applying OOP in the UNIX Shell

As you use this book to leverage object-oriented techniques within the Korn shell, you tap into powerful UNIX APIs with Java. You can either install and compile these APIs off the CD-ROM, or type them in yourself if you want the experience. The CD-ROM contains a directory that corresponds to each chapter in the book. These tools encapsulate much of the UNIX API functionality usually only available to languages like C/C++ and Java. You can create shell scripts capable of opening socket connections, writing to network pipes, and doing all other sorts of useful activities. Coupled with object-oriented techniques, this allows for the development of fairly sophisticated applications, including an Object Request Broker for the shell in Chapter 8. This lightweight ORB allows client objects on one machine to code directly with remote objects as if they were local.

If you're involved in UNIX software development, system administration, CGI and Web application design, or just want to customize your shell account, you can benefit from OOP techniques. From a system administrator's point of view, many of the objects within this book should become very useful.

As a system administrator, you probably write scripts to automate all sorts of management tasks. These tasks may include backing up the system to killing rogue processes, creating new user accounts, and tracking security mechanisms. OOP techniques can make this automation easier. Often a system administrator writes a lengthy script to edit and modify system files across a network. Undoubtedly, this involves many exceptions for different systems where the file to be edited is in a different location or the proper arguments for a command are slightly different. These scripts often become long, plodding routines that slowly go out across the network and do their menial tasks. With OOP techniques, you can encapsulate system-specific behaviors behind an object that holds a common interface. You program to this interface from your shell scripts, thereby making your life much simpler and improving the efficiency of your program. You abandon using the network commands `remsh` and `rsh` in place of a dedicated socket connection that attaches your code to a remote machine. You can create system monitoring objects and access them from a Web browser running on a PC at your desk. The possibilities for object-oriented system programming are unlimited and surpass traditional techniques in most cases. As demonstrated in the following chapters of this book, you can build and customize your own system management application by constructing a system from reusable components.

Summary

This chapter discussed some OOP basics and what can be applied within the shell. If you've only used the shell to configure your account or create a customized backup or tar file, you will find a new approach to shell programming within this book. The shell programs created here are fully functional component-based applications.

The next chapter delves deeper into shell programming and discusses the basic constructs that the shell offers as a language.

Chapter 2

The Shell as a User and Programming Environment

IN THIS CHAPTER

- Customizing the shell environment
- Examining functions
- Looking at parameter substitution
- Understanding shell syntax

THIS CHAPTER ACQUAINTS you with shell commands and effective programming techniques. Although this chapter assumed you've logged on to a UNIX machine and are familiar with commands such as `ls`, `cp`, and `mv`, you do not need to be familiar with other shell concepts such as pipes and redirection. You need not be familiar with advanced shell programming concepts, either. If you are already an experienced shell programmer and just want to learn object-oriented techniques, you can safely skip this chapter. Otherwise, this chapter functions as a quick-paced tutorial.

The Korn shell is a commercially available product that ships with most commercial versions of UNIX. The Korn shell has many features that set it apart from other shell implementations such as the Bash and Bourne shells. These features are only available on the KSH 93 version. Therefore, to maintain compatibility and portability, the examples and techniques presented here and in the rest of this book are designed to operate primarily with the pdKsh-5.2.12 (the public-domain Korn shell) and Bash with little or no modification. Of course, all examples also work in commercial implementations of the Korn shell.

Shell Concepts

If you're not familiar with a shell account, you may be a little intimidated at first. When you're using the shell, you can't drag and drop files, you can't undo deletions from the recycle bin, and you can't plop a file on top of a printer icon and expect it to come streaming out of your InkJet. You can, however, take advantage of many powerful techniques for manipulating files, changing the behavior of the operating system, and actually developing scripts to automate tasks. The shell is also a powerful programming language, which is the focus of this chapter.

File Descriptors

File descriptors can be considered numbers, or identifiers, that represent files. The most important file descriptors are commonly referred to as STDIN (standard input) and STDOUT (standard output). If you've ever typed in a command from the command line, you've used these file descriptors. STDIN and STDOUT are ubiquitous to computing and are even used in MS-DOS based programs. Basically, any output that a program returns is sent to STDOUT. By default, this STDOUT is usually the screen, unless it's been redirected to a file or another program. STDIN, by default, is the keyboard, but it can also be the output of another command if you've set up a pipe or redirection. Most UNIX utilities take their input from STDIN and write their output to STDOUT. These file descriptors are represented with a number in the UNIX shell. The number 0 represents STDIN, the number 1 represents STDOUT, and the number 2 represents STDERR. Many programs choose to write error messages to STDERR (standard error). By default, STDERR is usually redirected to STDOUT so that you view it. Logging and application debugging can easily be set up by redirecting STDERR to a file.

If you want to redirect STDERR to a file in UNIX, type the following:

```
exec 2> errors.txt
```

The preceding command writes all output intended for STDERR (file descriptor 2) to the file `errors.txt`. Be careful: if you try this command, your command prompt may disappear. The command prompt is often written to STDERR. You can also type a syntax error and the results (the shell's complaint) are forwarded to `errors.txt`:

```
pS -EAF # not a command, syntax error...
```

The shell does not complain (at least visibly), but if you check the contents of `errors.txt`, you see something like the following:

```
ksh: pS: not found
```

Chapter 2: The Shell as a User and Programming Environment

To retrieve your error messages and once again see your mistakes, redirect STDERR to be a duplicate of STDOUT like the following:

```
exec 2>&1
```

You can create your own file descriptors in the UNIX shell. File descriptors can be any number between 0 and 9, and can be used in redirection, pipes, and as STDIN.

To create a file descriptor number 4 and open it for writing to the file `text.txt`, type the following:

```
exec 4> text.txt
```

You can then write to the file, or have other commands write to the file, by referencing file descriptor 4.

Redirection

Redirection enables you to take the contents of a file and use it as STDIN, or take the output of any command and send it to a file or a file descriptor. To send the output of a `ps` command to the file `processes.txt`, type the following:

```
ps -eaf > processes.txt
```

The preceding command creates the file `processes.txt` if it does not exist, or overwrites it if does exist. If you want to append to the file `processes.txt`, you can use the >> operator instead:

```
ps -eaf >> processes.txt
```

This command leaves the original contents in place and appends the new output to the end. You can also redirect the contents of a file to be used as STDIN by a command:

```
read these are my good vars < words.txt
```

This command sets the values of `these`, `are`, `my`, `good`, and `vars` to the first five space-separated words in the file `words.txt`. For example, if `words.txt` only contains `hello my name is UNIX`, the values set by the preceding command are the following:

```
echo $these $are $my $vars
hello my name is UNIX
```

The command `read` takes the five variable names as parameters and reads their values from the file `words.txt`.

As you can see, redirection works both ways. For example, you can use the "here document" concept to send several lines of text to STDOUT within a shell script. For example, examine the following script `menu.sh`:

```
#!/bin/ksh
# menu.sh
##########
cat << END_OF_MENU

Welcome to the Menu System!
  1. Eat Lunch
  2. Eat Dinner
  3. Make a cup of coffee
  4. Reboot!
Enter Selection:
END_OF_MENU
read selection
echo "You chose $selection"
```

If executed, the preceding script writes everything after the `cat` statement to STDOUT until it encounters the word `END_OF_MENU`; command execution then resumes. This process is useful when you need to output large quantities of text without having to type an individual print statement for each line. You can also redirect the "here document" to a file like the following:

```
cat << END_OF_TEXT >> myfile.txt
These are the words I'm sending
to your file, enjoy!
END_OF_TEXT
```

The preceding creates or appends to the file `myfile.txt` all of the words following the `cat` command prior to the word `END_OF_TEXT`.

Also, you can send several commands to the shell, any other shell interpreting program such as the Perl executable, or even a SQL interpreter, as follows:

```
/bin/ksh << END_OF_SCRIPT
echo "hello, my name is UNIX"
uptime
END_OF_SCRIPT
```

The preceding sends the commands to the shell and outputs `"hello, my name is UNIX"` and then the system's `uptime`. You can also write to the Perl interpreter as follows:

```
/usr/bin/perl << END_OF_SCRIPT
print "Sorry, this book is not about Perl\n";
END_OF_SCRIPT
```

Chapter 2: The Shell as a User and Programming Environment

The preceding, of course, writes everything before END_OF_SCRIPT to the Perl interpreter. As a rule, any command that can take input from STDIN can be given the contents of a file or any list with the < operator. In the Korn shell, you can execute a for each loop with the contents of a file in the following way:

```
for each in $(< words.txt)
do
  banner $each
done
```

The preceding expands words.txt into a list for use in the loop. A less efficient and commonly abused method of this process follows:

```
for each in $(cat words.txt)
do
  banner $each
done
```

You do not need to invoke the cat command to present the contents of words.txt. The shell can more easily and efficiently take care of presentation through redirection. In the Bash shell, similar results can be achieved through the following:

```
while read var
do
  banner $var
done < words.txt
```

TIP Many UNIX utilities take filenames as parameters such as grep, awk, and cat. You usually do not need to set up a pipeline to send the contents of a file to one of these utilities.

The preceding achieves the same results as the less efficient example, although it's important to note that the for each loop reads each space-separated string within the file. By contrast, the while read loop reads each line up to the new line character into the value of $var. This difference can be useful when trying to parse a file up into pieces; you can either break it into each line or into any character. By default, any white space, tab character, or new line character separates lists in a UNIX file.

 The Internal Field Separator variable (IFS) defines what character is used as the default delimiter. You can easily set this variable to be a semicolon or a comma when delineating text files with the following: `IFS=;`. Make sure to reset the IFS variable back to its default if your program will be doing other statements that use the IFS character.

Pipes

Pipes are another means of redirection that differ in several powerful ways. A pipe, represented with the character `|`, can send the output of one command to the standard input of another. While redirection is most commonly used on files, pipes are used on processes. A pipeline can be constructed with one process leading into the next. For example, the following pipeline lists all of the process IDs owned by the user `chrisj` on a System V-ish system like Solaris:

```
ps -eaf | grep chrisj | cut -c10-15
```

Also, if you have the proper access rights, you can kill all of `chrisj`'s processes with the following pipeline:

```
ps -eaf | grep chrisj | cut -c10-15 | xargs kill
```

Pipes can also be used inefficiently, especially when coupled with the `cat` command, as follows:

```
cat file.txt | grep string
```

The preceding can be written much more efficiently as follows:

```
grep string file.txt
```

If the command does not take filenames as parameters you can use redirection as follows:

```
tr X \# < file.txt
```

The preceding translates all instances of `X` to `#` within the file `file.txt` and writes it to STDOUT. As a rule, you almost never need to use the command `cat` when you are trying to send the contents of a file to a command. The shell takes care of this process much more efficiently.

Pipes can be used with many UNIX commands. For example, you can pipe the processes running on a system to your friend via the `mail` command:

Chapter 2: The Shell as a User and Programming Environment

```
ps -eaf | mail dbatch@voicenet.com
```

You can also forward the entire contents of your mail box through redirection (provided the environment variable `MAIL` is set to your mailbox):

```
mail dbatch@voicenet.com < $MAIL
```

Pipes are used to "tie" together the ends of processes. Most UNIX commands are designed to read from STDIN and write to STDOUT; this attribute makes them very flexible and allows the usage of pipes. Using pipes to customize UNIX utilities together is very easy.

Built-In Variables and Identifiers

The shell uses many built-in identifiers and operators that you need to know about to be successful at shell programming. Apart from the slew of provided environment variables, the shell also provides special character variables that can indicate the return status of executed commands, the number of arguments passed to a function or file, and even each individual parameter passed to a function or file. These special variables are the same in most cases for the Bash and Korn shells.

Start with a few important ones. Variables in the shell are prefixed with the character `$`, which is a reserved character and shouldn't be used within variable names. You cannot type variables in the shell and `$X` can be either a text string, a whole number, or a floating-point figure. All variables are treated as character strings in the shell, but arithmetic evaluation can be performed in both the Bash and Korn shells by surrounding the expression with double parentheses `(( ))`. For example, the following expression literally prints "4 + 4":

```
x=4
print $x + $x # prints " 4 + 4 " literally
```

The following statement prints the total, 8, however:

```
x=4
print $(( x + x ))
```

Generally speaking, all variables in the shell can be considered character strings. You should know the following basic built-in identifiers:

```
#!/bin/ksh
# dumpvars.sh
##############
# the number of positional parameters (arguments)
print "Params: $#"
# the current process' pid
print "My PID: $$"
# All parameters
```

```
print "All the arguments: $@"
# the return status of the last command
print "Return status of last command: $?"
# the command line arguments (Positional Parameters)
print "Arg0, the command itself: $0"
print "Arg1: $1"
print "Arg2: $2"
print "Arg3: $3"
print "Arg4: $4"
print "Arg5: $5"
print "And the rest, if any!: $6, $7, $8, $9"
```

These one character variables contain items relevant to a shell program. If you type this script and execute it with a varying number of nonsensical arguments, you see different results. Command line arguments are interpreted by your shell program as positional parameters represented by the numbers 0-9, with 0 being the called command or function. The command shift shifts the positional parameters to the left by one. For example:

```
#!/bin/ksh
# ex3.sh
while [[ -n $1 ]]   # while $1 is not null
  do
    print "arg: "$1
    shift
  done
```

If you execute the preceding command, you see all of the command line arguments printed as follows:

```
$ ex3.sh these are my command line arguments hey!
arg: these
arg: are
arg: my
arg: command
arg: line
arg: arguments
arg: hey!
```

You can also create this effect by using the built-in variable $@ as follows:

```
#!/bin/ksh
# ex4.sh
for each in $@   # for each arg
do
   print "arg: "$each
done
```

Chapter 2: The Shell as a User and Programming Environment

The shell environment also contains variables that may be of use to your shell program. You break apart the .profile file in a following section, where you analyze all the steps taken in a typical .profile. One of the more interesting ones is $RANDOM, which generates a random integer between 0 and 32767:

```
for each in 1 2 3 4 5 6 7 8 9 0
do
  print $RANDOM
done
```

The preceding prints 10 randomly generated integers. The shell also provides many environment variables; some are dynamic, while others are static. To see all of the variables in your current environment, issue the set command:

```
set
```

By using set, your environment scrolls out.

Depending on how your environment is configured, the set command may not be available. In this case, you can try the env command.

Parameter Substitution

Another feature of the Bash and Korn shells is the capability to substitute parameters. You may have a program that needs to test whether a variable is null. If the variable is null, you need to set the value accordingly, or leave it alone if something has already been done with it. Without substitution, you have to code that operation as follows:

```
if [[ ! -n $myvar ]]; then    # is lengthy
    myvar="Hello!"
fi
```

You may also test your variable to be null as follows, which can generate a syntax error if the variable has not yet been defined:

```
if [ $myvar = "" ]; then    # may generate syntax error
    myvar="Hello!"
fi
```

If the variable `myvar` has not been set yet, the preceding may generate a syntax error from the test command ([ ). Because the expression is interpreted as if [= " "], the test command complains that it expects an argument. By quoting the variable $myvar, you can test it without the syntax error, but the best solution would be to code it using substitution as follows:

```
myvar=${myvar:-Hello!}   # good
```

With this substitution, you can't go wrong. If the variable is unset, it is set to Hello!; if `myvar` already has a value (for example, it is set to "Goodbye!"), it is left alone. The shell has a number of substitution expressions that are applicable in many situations.

Another feature of shell string evaluation is the capability to modify parts of a parameter. For example, the following script has two functions. The first function renames all the files in a directory with a .bak extension, which signifies them as backup copies. If the originals are destroyed, you can move them back with the second function, `restore`.

```
#!/bin/ksh
# backup.sh
backup() {
  for each in *
  do
if [ ! -d $each ]; then   # if not a directory
      cp $each $each.bak
    fi
  done
}
restore() {
for each in *bak   # only backed up files
  do
mv $each ${each%%.bak}   # rename without bak extension
  done
}
```

The substitution is the key to the preceding script. The shell allows variables to be substituted by patterns, as demonstrated by the following:

```
string="files.txt.backup.files.txt"   # what an ugly string!
# version 1
print ${string##*files}       # generates .txt
# version 2
print ${string#*files}        # generates .txt.backup.files.txt
# version 3
print ${string%files*}        # generates files.txt.backup.
# version 4
print ${string%%files*}       # generates nothing
```

As you can see, the command deletes the pattern from `string`, depending on which operator you supply. One #, or one % sign, deletes the smallest portion of the pattern, either starting at the beginning (#) or at the end (%). Using %% or ## deletes the largest version of the pattern that occurs. The following program examples put this technique to use — if it seems confusing now, don't worry. Learning by example is often the easiest way.

Shell Programming

This section describes many programming techniques involved in shell scripting. Evaluation, testing, loops, and functions are all covered with realistic examples. Shell programs are usually written to solve small problems. These small problems often generate huge headaches, so scripting can be very powerful. This section presents typical, efficient solutions to both simple and complex programming problems. Many of these examples can be used in almost any type of script.

if-then Evaluation

The `if-then` type of evaluation is often used for evaluating certain conditions. Whether you're trying to get the status of the last executed command, validate a collection of filenames, or retrieve input from the user, you almost always test the results brought back to you. `if-then` evaluations usually take the following form in the shell:

```
if <list>; then
   <list> was true, do code
 else
   <list> was false, do more code!
 fi
```

In this situation, `list` can be anything from a series of commands to testing a string, file, or arithmetic expression. To test if a string exists within a file, you could use the following:

```
if grep error log.txt; then
   echo "I found errors in log.txt!"
 else
   echo "Errors are not found within log.txt"
 fi
```

Likewise, if you want a negation test, you could use the following:

```
if ! grep success log.txt; then
   echo "Success not found in log file!!!"
 fi
```

The ! is the negation or "not" operator. You can also evaluate strings, arithmetic expressions, and other items through an if-then evaluation:

```
#!/bin/ksh
read string   # get input from user
if [ "$string" = "hello" ]; then
  echo "Well, hello yourself!"
else
  echo "That's no greeting..."
fi
```

The preceding tests the contents of string to be equal to "hello". You can also do an arithmetic evaluation, as follows:

```
#!/bin/ksh
read number
if (( number > 4 )); then
  echo "Its bigger than 4!"
else
  echo "Its not bigger than 4."
fi
```

The test command [is not a direct part of the if statement, but is often used in conjunction with if to create a testing list. You can test for a variety of conditions by using the built-in capabilities of the test command. The following lists some examples:

```
#!/bin/ksh
read string   # our string to test
#
# test for null
  if [[ ! -n $string ]]; then
    echo "NULL!"
  fi
#
# test if string is a file
  if [[ -f $string ]]; then
    echo "$string IS FILE"
  fi
#
# test if string is a readable file
  if [[ -r $string ]]; then
    echo "$string IS READABLE"
  fi
#
# start program again?
  echo "Run program again [y/n]: "
  read answer
  if [[ $answer = "y" || $answer = "Y" ]]; then
exec $0   # run program again using pos param 0
  fi
```

The test command has an extensive amount of testing options. Many of these options can get the desired results far quicker than trying to test for something the "long way." Testing a string to see if it is a file with the -f option is less complicated than trying to execute a list or a read on the file. Reducing the number of outside process calls to other commands makes your shell scripts far more efficient.

while Loops

The while loop is a cousin to the if-then evaluation. The while expression takes the same form as if-then, as follows:

```
while <list>
do
  # commands
done
```

As long as list is true, the commands between do and done execute. To do something ten times and then quit, you could do the following:

```
#!/bin/ksh
((x=0))  # set number x to zero
  while (( x < 10 ))
  do
     echo "Counting, X = $x"
     ((x=x+1))
  done
```

The loop executes until x has incremented to ten – then the loop exits. Similarly, you can also test a string's value, as follows:

```
#!/bin/ksh
while [ "$string" != "please" ]
do
   echo "What's the magic word?"
   read string
done
```

Here, string is tested to be equal to "please". If string is not equal to "please", you are prompted again. The loop exits when the user types in the magic word, "please".

The while command tests for <list> to be true; therefore, you can make something always true by doing the following:

```
while true
  do
     echo "I will be true forever!"
     echo "Keep going?"
     read answer
```

```
       if [[ $answer = "n" || $answer = "q" ]]; then
         exit
       fi
done
```

The preceding expression while true is always true, with the loop continuing until the user replies with an "n" or "q". The "||" is the or operator, enabling you to test two conditions. In this case, it's an "either or evaluation" – you could also use "&&" to do a "if-this-and-that" kind of test.

for Loops

The for loop is another shell expression.

```
for <var> in <list>
do
  # commands
done
```

The variable <var> holds the value of each member in <list> each time the loop is executed until <list> is completed. The <list> can be any tab- or space-separated list like those used in other UNIX utilities or what is defined by the internal IFS variable within the shell's environment.

To perform operations on a series of files in your current directory, you can use the following example:

```
#!/bin/ksh
for myfiles in *    # * will be every file in the current dir
  do
    print "Doing cp on $myfiles"
    cp $myfiles $myfiles.bak
  done
```

The list supplied to a for loop can be anything, including the contents of the executing script. If you save the following script, you can give it a try:

```
#!/bin/ksh
for each in $(< $0)   # $0 is this script (see above)
do
  echo "These are the contents of $0: $each"
done
```

You can also explicitly show the contents of your list in a for loop:

```
#!/bin/ksh
((total = 0))  # initalize total to zero as number
for nums in 56 23 45 1 78 84 23 45
do
```

```
    total=$((total + nums))
 done
 print $total
```

The preceding totals all of the numbers listed after the `for` statement. You can also build a list on the fly and perform actions upon the members. For example, you can use the `who` command to list the individuals logged onto a UNIX machine, and then execute the `finger` command upon each one to see more information about them:

```
#!/bin/ksh
# lets finger everybody!
for person in $(who | cut -c0-10| sort -u)  # clip their name from
 the
             # output of the who command
do
  finger $person
done
```

When you know the specific location of the desired information, use a more efficient command like `cut`, as opposed to `awk`. Awk can handle more complex operations, but in this case it isn't necessary. You notice a significant slowdown if you execute the same script via `awk`, as follows:

```
#!/bin/ksh
# lets finger everybody with awk!
for person in $(who | awk '{print $1}')  # clip the first field from
             # output of the who command
do
  finger $person
done
```

This script executes slower because `awk` involves more overhead than `cut`. Note, however, that `awk` is designed for more sophisticated applications and can often make quick work of varying content or complexly arranged files. Often, though, `awk` simply cuts out one field or series of characters where `cut` could do a more efficient job. A following section focuses on reducing calls to outside commands as a means of increasing the execution time of scripts.

case Statements

The capability to do `case` statements is another handy feature for shell scripting. Instead of a long series of `if-then` evaluations, you can test for different possibilities in one place. The following example shows a menu program that launches other commands based on what the user selects:

```
#!/bin/ksh
# case example
```

```
cat << end_of_menu   # here document

Menu Selections:
  1. List the contents of this directory
  2. Telnet to a remote machine
  3. Execute a shell command
Please enter your choice:
end_of_menu
# get user input
read choice
case $choice in
  1)
     ls
;;  # list the directory
  2)
     echo "remote host:"
     read host
     telnet $host
;;  # telnet to another machine
  3)
     echo "command:"
     read command
     /bin/ksh $command
;;  # execute command
  *)
     echo "please enter a valid choice:"
     $0
;;  # restart script
esac
```

The `case` statement takes the following form:

```
case <var> in
  <selection> )
      # commands
      ;;
  <selection> )
      # commands
      ;;
esac
```

In the preceding form, `<var>` can be any variable and `<selection>` can be all of the possibilities. A `case` statement is ended like `if` with the reverse, an `esac`.

Functions

The shell also supports functions. Functions can take arguments and are interpreted in the same way as the positional parameters. The following example function takes a string as an argument and checks its value against `/etc/passwd`:

```
chkUser()
{
USER=$1    # take first arg as username
  if ! grep ^$USER /etc/passwd; then
return 1   # user does not exist
  fi
  return 0
}
```

This function assigns the value of the first passed parameter $1 to USER. It then attempts to grep the user out of the password file. If the user does not exist, the function returns non-zero, which indicates failure. If the user does exist, the function returns 0, or true. The following function can be used in a script in the following way:

```
if ! ChkUser chrisj; then
  echo "User not found on this system"
fi
```

In the preceding example, you check the return value of the function chkUser to validate a user ID. The function chkUser can also do more sophisticated checking, such as querying NIS or checking other system files to find the user.

Programming Examples

You can put all of the programming concepts presented so far in Listing 2-1's example program. This program performs global search and replace operations on any number of files. It's menu-driven and allows patterns to be entered by the user for both files and search and replace criteria. This script is compatible with both commercial versions of the Korn shell as well as the public domain pdKsh, which is available for Linux.

Listing 2-1: serep.ksh

```
#!/bin/ksh
##################################################################
#
# serep.sh
# - perform global search and replace on multiple files
#
##################################################################

# function declarations

# WaitForInput()
#
```

```
# waits for user to press return, then exits
#
WaitForInput()
{
  echo "press return..."
  read input
  return 0
}

# doValidateFiles()
#
# Checks to see that files, and search and
# replacement criteria have been set
#
doValidateFiles()
{
  if [[ "$SELFILES" = "" || \
        "$SEARCHCRITERIA" = "" ||\
        "$REPLACEMENT" = "" ]]; then
     clear || cls # if not clear, try cls
     echo "In order to perform a search and replace you define"
     echo "the files to be operated upon, and both the search"
     echo "and replacement criteria."
     echo;echo
     WaitForInput
     return 1
  fi
  return 0
}

# selFiles()
#
# Defines list of files to be used during search & replace
#
selFiles()
{
  clear || cls
  echo "DEFINE FILE SELECTION"
  echo
cat << END_OF_TEXT
This section allows you to define which file you would
like to perform the search and replace operation on.
You may enter a file pattern with regular expressions,
or an exact filename, or an entire directory.  For example,
to select all C source files in a particular directory
you might enter:

       /var/home/chrisj/*.c

Which would indicate all the files that have
a .c extension.

Please enter your file pattern:
```

```
END_OF_TEXT
  read pattern
  echo; echo
  echo "Based on the pattern you entered these files will be"
  echo "selected:"
  #
  # show selected files and define list
  #
  SELFILES=""
  for each in $pattern
  do
     if [[ -w $each && -f $each ]]; then
        echo $each
        SELFILES=$SELFILES" "$each
     fi
  done
  WaitForInput
  return 0
}

# defSearch()
#
# Defines the pattern
#
defSearch()
{
  clear || cls
  echo "DEFINE SEARCH CRITERIA"
cat << END_OF_TEXT

The pattern to be searched for needs to be entered
using "Regular Expression" syntax.
Some examples follow:

  Reg Expr &  Meaning

Regex:  ^#*
All occurrences of a "#" as the first character of a
line, followed by one or more characters. This,
basically, would match comments in a shell program.

Regex:  ?*[c|C]
Matches anystring at least one character, followed by
zero or more characters, with a lowercase or capital C
as the last character.

Please enter search criteria in regular expression syntax:
END_OF_TEXT
  read SEARCHCRITERIA
  echo;echo "You've typed: $SEARCHCRITERIA"
  WaitForInput
  return 0
}
```

```
#
# defReplace()
#
# Defines replacement for $SEARCHCRITERIA
defReplace()
{
  clear || cls
  echo "DEFINE REPLACEMENT TEXT"
  #
  # here document
  cat << END_OF_TEXT

Please enter the text you would like to act as
the replacement for the pattern you've
selected: $SEARCHCRITERIA

Note that this pattern cannot be a regular
expression, but must be hard text.
Enter replacement text:
END_OF_TEXT

  # read replacement text
  read REPLACEMENT
  echo; echo "You've typed: $REPLACEMENT"
  WaitForInput
  return 0
}

#
# doPreview()
#
# Allows you to see the changes before they're made
doPreview()
{
  if ! doValidateFiles; then
     return
  fi
  clear || cls
  echo;echo
  echo PREVIEW
  echo "You've indicated the following files to be changed:"
  for eachfile in $SELFILES
  do
     echo $eachfile
  done
  sleep 2
  echo "Within those files, you indicated that all occurrences"
  echo "of: $SEARCHCRITERIA"
  echo "be replaced with: $REPLACEMENT"
  echo "Hit return to preview these changes on all the files"
  read input
  for eachfile in $SELFILES
```

Chapter 2: The Shell as a User and Programming Environment

```
   do
      eval sed "s/$SEARCHCRITERIA/$REPLACEMENT/g" $eachfile
      echo "=================================================="
      echo "FILE SEPARATOR"
      echo "=================================================="
   done | more
   WaitForInput
   return 0
}

# doSearchReplace()
#
# change selected files
#
doSearchReplace()
{
   if ! doValidateFiles; then
      return
   fi
   clear || cls
   echo "SEARCH AND REPLACE"
   echo
   echo "The following files will be altered:"
   for each in $SELFILES
   do
      echo $each
   done
   echo
   echo "Would you like to make backup copies of the"
   echo "originals? [y/n]"
   read answer
   echo "DEBUG: answer = $answer"
   if [ $answer = "y" ]; then
      for each in $SELFILES
      do
         echo "Creating backup of $each"
         cp $each $each.bak
      done
   fi
   echo;echo "Beginning Search and Replace"
   echo;
   for thisfile in $SELFILES
   do
      echo "Examining file: $thisfile"
      eval sed "s/$SEARCHCRITERIA/$REPLACEMENT/g" $thisfile \
         > $thisfile.new
      echo "Finished edit, updating file..."
      mv $thisfile.new $thisfile
      echo "=================================================="
   done
   echo "Completed...."
   WaitForInput
   return
```

```
}
#
# main loop - display menu
#
while true; do # infinite loop
  clear || cls
  echo "SEARCH AND REPLACE"
  cat << END_OF_MENU

  1) Select Files
  2) Enter Search Criteria
  3) Enter Replace Criteria
  4) Perform Search and Replace
  5) Preview

  Select ==>
END_OF_MENU
  #
  # get input from user
  #
  read choice garbage
  #
  # case statement for menu
  #
  case $choice in
     1)
        # call selfiles function
        selFiles
        ;;
     2)
        # call define search criteria function
        defSearch
        ;;
     3)
        # call define replace criteria function
        defReplace
        ;;
     4)
        # do search and replace
        doSearchReplace
        ;;
     5)
        # preview changes
        doPreview
        ;;
     q|Q|exit)
        # exit
        exit
        ;;
     *)
        # display error message
        echo "Please enter a valid option."
```

```
        sleep 2
        ;;
  esac
done
```

Programming Concepts

One key item in creating efficient shell scripts to minimize calls to outside shell commands. This technique has been illustrated in some of the preceding examples with the misuse of awk and cat. This section exposes some common mistakes that slow shell programs, and also uses the time command to test how fast things really execute. The following short program takes a user's name and searches for that name in the system records. If the user has an account, the program reports the last time the user logged in. The following first version is lengthy and full of code that can be easily condensed:

```
#!/bin/ksh
# chkuser.sh - long version
#
user=$1
if [ "$user" = "" ]; then
  echo "Usage: $0 <userid>"
  exit
fi

# check for user in passwd file
RESULT=$(cat /etc/passwd | grep $user )
validuser=${RESULT%%:*}
if [ "$validuser" = "$user" ]; then
  echo "$user is verified in /etc/passwd...."
  echo "determining last login time..."
else
  echo "$user does not exist in /etc/passwd"
  exit
fi
RESULT=$(last | grep $user | head -1)
print $RESULT
```

Upon execution, this program functions properly but runs slightly slow. Use the time command to check its execution speed, as follows:

```
time chkuser.sh chrisj
....output ignored...
real: 0m1.09s
user: 0m0.25s
sys: 0m0.35s
```

Now optimize this script and check its execution time, as follows:

```
#!/bin/ksh
# chkuser.sh - faster, shorter version
#
user=${1:?"Usage: $0 <username>"}
if grep ^$user /etc/passwd > /dev/null; then
    echo "$user is verified in /etc/passwd..."
    echo "determining last login time..."
    last | grep $user | head -1
else
    echo "User is not found in /etc/passwd"
fi
```

This script executes slightly faster and is much shorter. First, you eliminate checking the value of $1 by exiting with an error message if $1 is not set. You also consolidate testing and variable assignment instead of drawing it out across several lines.

TIP   Many factors can affect a UNIX system's performance, including applications, users, and network activity. Make sure to consider the state of the system before evaluating an application's performance. A good tool for measure is the `uptime` command.

If successful execution — not the output — of a command is important, you should just test the return result. If the data you need to parse from a string is always in the same place (in this case, the beginning of the string), then use `cut` or a regular expression, as opposed to `awk`. Now when you time this command, you see the following results:

```
time ./fast.sh chrisj
... output ignored ...
real: 0m0.88s
user: 0m0.19s
sys:  0m0.27s
```

The `time` command prints the values according to the `real` time elapsed during the command, the time spent in execution of the command `user`, and the time spent in the system `sys`. Of course, the results of these tests can vary accordingly to what other processes consume CPU.

Optimization usually comes down to a few simple rules. First, if speed is important or the code is going to be heavily reused (such as in a function), then eliminating outside commands is paramount. Second, if you are performing some sort of complex operation or evaluation, check if an existing utility can complete the task for you. While outside calls should be minimized, they certainly don't have to be eliminated. You don't want to spend your time reinventing the wheel. You can use the sort command if you don't want to write your function to do ASCII collating. Then again, if the code is going to be reused heavily, investing in optimization time wouldn't be wasted. Using redirection and pipes properly is another consideration for optimizing your shell scripts. With the Korn shell, there is an infinite number of ways to do things. Any one piece of code in this book could be rewritten to execute faster, because nearly all of them could be optimized in one way or another. Optimization is a good goal that is not always achieved.

Considering the Environment

This section discusses some of the shell environment factors that can affect your scripts and applications. You start by examining the .profile (or .bash_profile in the bash shell), which usually exist in your home directory. Many environment variables are initialized in the profile. If you execute the command set, you get back all of your current environment variables.

When you first start your shell session, your .profile is executed if you have a profile. If you don't have one, the system-wide default /etc/profile may be sourced. The following example profile could exist for a user named jdoe on a Solaris system:

```
stty istrip
PATH=/usr/bin:/usr/ucb:/etc:/usr/openwin/bin
PATH=$PATH:/var/home/jdoe/bin:/usr/sbin:/usr/dt/bin
  PATH=$PATH:/var/home/jdoe/objects:.
GODZILLA_HOME=/var/home/jdoe/NETSCRAPE
LD_LIBRARY_PATH=$GODZILLA_HOME
DISPLAY=miles:0.0
MANPATH=usr/share/man:/usr/openwin/man:/opt/local/man:/opt/SNWvxva/m
  an
MANPATH=$MANPATH:/opt/SUNWconn/man:/opt/local/man:/usr/share/man
MANPATH=$MANPATH:/usr/openwin/share/man:/usr/openwin/man:/opt/SUNWvx
  vm/man
export PATH GODZILLA_HOME DISPLAY MANPATH LD_LIBRARY_PATH
#
# If possible, start the windows system
#
if [ 'tty' = "/dev/console" ] ; then
  if [ "$TERM" = "sun" -o "$TERM" = "AT386" ] ; then
    if [ ${OPENWINHOME:-""} = "" ] ; then
      OPENWINHOME=/usr/openwin
      export OPENWINHOME
    fi
    echo "" echo "Starting Windows (type Control-C to interrupt)"
    sleep 5
    echo ""
```

```
            $OPENWINHOME/bin/openwin

     clear    # get rid of annoying cursor rectangle
     exit     # logout after leaving windows system
  fi
fi
if [ -f .kshrc ]; then
  . .kshrc
fi
```

This .profile is fairly simple. The words in all capital letters are environment variables. As you can see, the PATH and MANPATH are set in the beginning. PATH is the environment variable searched when you enter a command at the command prompt. If your path is not set, commands as simple as ls do not work, as the shell cannot locate the executable /bin/ls. Your path must be set for any commands to be found. Also, note that the dot (.), or current working directory, should only be placed at the end of your path. As a security risk, a dot at the beginning of your path forces the shell to look for commands starting in your current directory. While this may not seem harmful, a user can easily place a script deviously called ls within a public directory. Those who have a . as the first element in their path execute this devious script when they enter the public directory, as opposed to the real /bin/ls. If the user makes a script such as the following, names it ls, and places it in a publicly traveled directory, he could effectively copy a shell of each user who attempts to type ls within that directory. This shell has the effective user ID of the user to which it belongs but could be executable by anyone – this rogue user could steal the identity of each person who happens to fall into his trap:

```
# rogue ls
# if you have a dot as the first element in your path
# this script will execute instead of the real /bin/ls

# copy the shell to A secret place
cp /bin/ksh /rogue/user/shell

# chmod it Set-uid on execution
chmod 4755 /rogue/user/shell

# execute the real ls with original options
/bin/ls $@
```

The preceding script, if named ls, effectively steals the identities of those who execute it. As a result, the rogue user (or anyone) could simply execute /rogue/user/shell and have your euid; meaning, he would have all your authority. This situation is particularly bad if you are the root user. Therefore, make sure you do not have a dot as the first element in your path. If your path includes all the important binary paths, you can place a dot at the end of your path.

Chapter 2: The Shell as a User and Programming Environment

In addition to the `PATH` variable, the `MANPATH` variable is set. This points to the directories that contain man pages.

In the preceding example profile, other variables are also set. Sometimes, applications store information regarding components in environment variables, as is apparent in the `GODZILLA_HOME` variable in the preceding example.

The profile also sets up terminal options and launches the X-Window system. At the end of the profile, there is a test for a file called .kshrc; if this file exists, it is executed. Often, personalizations such as aliases are kept in this file. If this file doesn't exist, it is skipped. If the file does exist, its contents are sourced into the current shell.

The .kshrc that this profile sources could look like the following:

```
stty erase ^H
set -o vi
alias px='ps -eaf | grep $1'
alias ll='ls -l'
export PS1="[$(hostname)]"
```

This .kshrc file sets two aliases: one shortcut for hunting down processes via a `ps` command and another shortcut to the `ls -l` command. Also, the erase key is set to what amounts to a backspace (the ^H appears on the command line if you type a backspace before setting this) and the command line is set to use Vi-style editing. If you've learned the Vi editor, you can carry this knowledge into command line editing. The last command in this file sets the prompt (PS1) to be equal to the hostname within brackets — if the hostname was boris, you receive [boris] for a prompt.

Summary

The best way to learn shell programming is by example. In the remainder of the book, when trying to figure out how to test for a certain situation or evaluate an expression, feel free to refer back to this chapter. Also, don't worry if you're still a bit foggy on shell programming after reading this chapter; you'll keep picking it up as you move along. Because most of the concepts in this chapter are used throughout the book's code, you have many more opportunities to see them work.

The next chapter embarks on a new area of shell programming: object-orientation.

Chapter 3

The Syntax of Writing Classes

IN THIS CHAPTER

- The mechanics behind shell script object-orientation
- Shell object syntax
- Escaping variables
- Writing classes
- Compiling classes with the `shcc` converter script

A CLASS IS similar to a blueprint. In the architecture of object-oriented programming, classes are created before any objects are instantiated, before any logic is executed, and before anything *happens*. A class defines the functionality of an object. In your class file, you indicate what operational methods your object contains, the requirements and sequence of its construction, what data members it owns, how it is to live and die, and what sort of public functionality it presents. A class gives your object its character. Classes also define the inheritance to occur and the relationships between superclasses and subclasses. You apply polymorphic techniques and can reuse existing class code in classes.

Shell Object Syntax

In the simplest of objects, a class can simply be a function declaration, as follows:

```
# class person.cls
_person() {
_strName=$1
}
```

The preceding `person` class has one operation and one variable defining the person's name. In this example, the function `_person` assigns the value of the first parameter to the variable `_strName`.

When a class is first called, it usually takes a series of parameters as construction arguments. These parameters define the initial state of the object. The parameters passed to an account object can indicate the owner, the starting balance, and other information. The object then stores these values internally and can provide operations for altering them. Once again, you can think of objects as collections of data and the functions that operate upon them. The class also defines all of the object's operations and the means of carrying out its destruction when necessary. Once all of this information has been read, an object is instantiated and begins its life.

The operations that a class presents as publicly accessible functions may alter the internal state of the object's data. The account object, for example, has functions to increment and decrement the balance, and indicate the status of the account if it is past due or in good standing. An account object may also have methods for tracking when payments have been made, and have the capability of signaling an alert when a billing cycle is closing and it's time to send a bill to the customer. All of these methods are centered around the object's data. The methods are a means of accessing and controlling that data. In this area, object-orientation is different from procedural and traditional languages. While scripts and code have the notion of scope, object-oriented languages have the notion of object ownership and of public and private data members. In the shell, for example, a function has the capability to access any data member in the current process. That is, one function can alter the value of X, and another function can turn around and alter the value of X, without actually passing the value of X between functions. The scope of X's value exists throughout the whole process address space – in other words, the entire program. The following object-oriented scripts practice how to pass objects and their data back and forth when another object needs to manipulate another's data. When a piece of code needs the value of an object's data member, it uses that object's published interface for accessing the value. The idea of object-centric data is important to OOP.

One of the reasons for internalizing and protecting class data is because the data reflects the object's state and is a substantiation of that state. An account object has internal data reflecting the balance, the status of the account, a list of recent payments, and perhaps directions to a database or location where archived information may be contained. The data is owned by the object, and only the owner should have the ability to induce change. Figure 3-1 shows the properties of a class and its methods.

Public and private specifiers won't be used in the chapter's shell objects, but those capabilities are easily implemented and examples are provided. Instead, this chapter focuses on creating a well-carved public interface as the logical way to interact with the object. By providing well-documented access functions and considering how you document and comment your classes, you can provide an apparent means of using the object. Any person who wants to manipulate your object's internal data directly has to spend time digging through your code to uncover the guts to implement such poor programming practice.

unixServer
Attributes: _strDevices[x] _nLoad _nUsers
Operations: _getDiskUsage _getLoad _getUsers _getWindow

Figure 3-1: A class diagram with data members and methods

When an object reaches the end of its viability and relevance, its destructor method is usually called to destroy its instance. In many cases, objects may not be destroyed directly. Instead, the process that owns the object exits, taking all of its data with it. Some languages also implement garbage collection in which unused memory is reclaimed by the operating system. This book's example scripts can call an object's _delete method to unset all of its data members and functions in the shell, but in many cases, the process that owns the object simply exits.

 When a shell process exits, all of the memory it was using is released back to the operating system.

Object Interfaces

Objects are a collection of functions that surrounding and protecting data – the core of the object and the representation of its state. The data is internal, and the internal workings of the object are private. The published interfaces, however, are intended to be the only way of interacting with the object, and thus constitute the object's visible appearance.

When you start to view objects this way, you can see how concepts such as polymorphism and inheritance are accomplished. Two objects may have the same published interface, but they may implement the details in completely different ways. This approach pays off in an environment whose details consist of subtle differences. A network of UNIX servers is often littered with small platform-specific differences. By creating similar objects with the same published interfaces, you can create code that can interoperate with all the machines on the network – while dealing with the same interface and never knowing the specifics of the black box on the other side. This is a primary goal of object-orientation. By programming toward interfaces, and not towards their implementation, you create reusable and extensible code. Keeping the interface as the focus, you are free to mix and match what is on either side without disturbing dependencies. Furthermore, by decomposing large systems into smaller interoperable components, you can leverage flexibility and reduce configuration problems simultaneously. As the network topology becomes more complex and involves more disparate, distributed systems, the granularity and atomization of the objects can be increased and the flexibility and simplicity maintained through interfaces that provide common, well-known services. Figure 3-2 shows the inheritance and reuse of a common interface in a UNIX server object.

Inheritance

Inheritance is best used when an object closely resembles another object and should be a type of the other object. Chapter 1 shows how oranges and apples are a type of fruit and thus shared some common features. Inheritance is used to share code directly. All types of fruit share some common ground, and this common ground can and should be shared explicitly. In these cases, the common functionality is factored out into a base class, and subtypes of this class, oranges and apples, inherit this base code. A class can redefine the functions it inherits and add new operations that may not be appropriate for the base class.

Polymorphism

Inheritance is quite different from polymorphism, which is the reuse of an interface definition and not so much the reuse of code. The collection of distributed servers shown in Figure 3-2 is an example of polymorphism. Each of the classes subscribes to this published public interface, known as unixServer, to make themselves accessible to clients. With this approach, clients only need to know of the unixServer interface to use the services of these objects. In actuality, each of these classes implement the unixServer interface in completely different ways and no code is shared. Every class that implements the unixServer interface inherits from the base class unixServer, but as you will see, the base class itself contains no code or the code is completely overridden in the subclasses. So, while inheritance is a mechanism of polymorphism, the two concepts are certainly different.

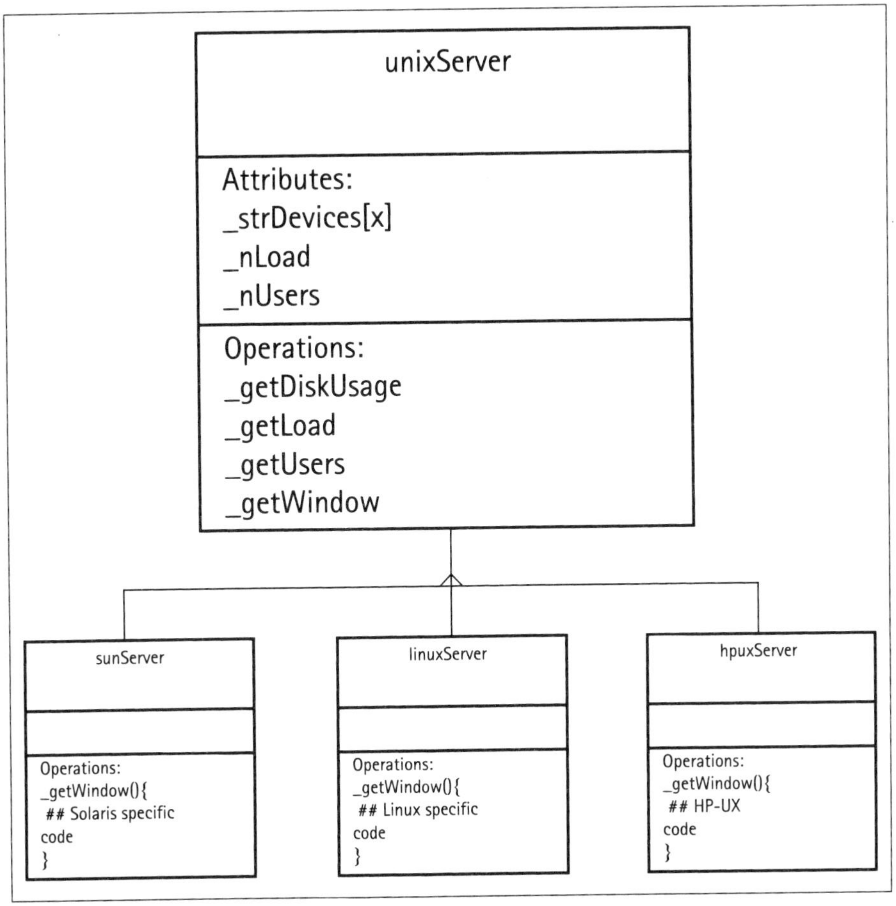

Chapter 3: The Syntax of Writing Classes

Figure 3-2: Inheritance relationships between unixServer and its subclasses

You need to be able to distinguish between the advantages of polymorphism and inheritance. While similar in functionality, the results are very different. Inheritance enables you to reuse an interface and code, while polymorphism is really just the reuse of the interface.

Other Object Relationships

Other relationships can also exist between objects. In addition to reusing an interface, you can give one object to another and form a *has-a* relationship, as opposed to the *is-a* relationship achieved through inheritance. For example, you create an object to represent UNIX machines. At first, you code the object to track disk usage on the machine via a method _getDiskUsage. During the development of your system, you decide that all disk-related information should be kept within a disk object. You create a disk class and give all of your UNIX system objects a disk object for each disk on the system. This can be indicated in the class and obtained at instantiation as the server takes stock of its environment. Giving an account object or a system object knowledge of file interactions only make these objects cumbersome and rigid. By allowing these objects to obtain and call upon file objects when needed, you are free to change the implementation of either object as long as you maintain the interface. You can change your file class to use a default umask or increase the efficiency on inserting and appending text, as well as adding methods for search and replace editing. Trying to implement these features within an object of an unrelated type only complicates the design process. When you want to change something regarding file usage, you must change every class that uses files, rather than change *the* class that represents files.

Object Design

Good design is another aspect of creating objects. When you design a class, you must consider the system in which your object will operate and the changes that will occur to that system over time. In most cases, you should keep your objects simple. For example, an account object shouldn't be responsible for opening and closing files that hold account data. A file object shouldn't be concerned with text editing. A text editing object shouldn't be concerned with display hardware. As you create classes that you intend to reuse, you will see the patterns of development emerge. You will find yourself discovering new objects as the functionality is repeated in objects of different types and you decide to consolidate that functionality into its own object. Through developing the applications in this book and creating your own applications, you will increase your knowledge of object-oriented design.

Getting Started with a Real Script

If you've not yet installed the software off the CD-ROM, you may want to do so now. In particular, this section uses utilities in the /Tools directory. The script shcc takes a simple-looking collection of shell functions created in a class file and performs quoting and keyword additions that allow them to become object-oriented. The name shcc is short for "shell CC" derived from CC, the standard C++ compiler on UNIX systems. An explanation of how shcc uses the eval word to quote your functions occurs in a following section, but this section uses the script to create executable versions of our object classes. shcc involves two simple rules for effective use: the required use of a constructor function in your class and the prefixing of all class-specific data members and methods with an underscore character (_).

Chapter 3: The Syntax of Writing Classes

To install the tools, run the `install` script located in the `/Tools` directory. This creates a couple of `class` and `bin` directories that should be added to your path. The default location for the installation is `/usr/local/shellobj`, but you can install them in your own directory if you don't have root access. Regardless of the location, these directories need to be added to your PATH environment variable, which is usually defined in a file called .profile or .kshrc within your home directory. If you've accepted the default installation location, you can add the following lines to your profile. If you've installed elsewhere, substitute the following path accordingly:

```
PATH=$PATH:/usr/local/uso/classes
PATH=$PATH:/usr/local/uso/bin
```

 The CD-ROM has a README file that details the installation process and some considerations you may need if you run into any problems running the installation script.

Class Architecture

Now, let's attempt to break apart the structure of a class as represented in shell code. After you've decided what your class is to represent, and you have some idea of the data it will contain and the methods that will operate upon that data, you can begin coding your class.

The following simple class emulates the basic architecture:

```
#
# person.cls
#
# a basic class
#
## constructor function, called when object is created
_person() {
_strName=$1
_nAge=$2
}
#
## access functions for the _strName property
_getName() {
echo $_strName
}
```

```
_setName() {
_strName=$1
}
#
## access functions for the _nAge property
_getAge() {
echo $_nAge
}
_setAge() {
_nAge=$1
}
```

The preceding class implements a constructor, which takes parameters indicating the object's internal data properties name and age. The constructor is called first, when you first instantiate an object from your class. Use the program shcc and give the class a spin. If you've saved the preceding as person.cls, you can run shcc from your command prompt as follows:

```
$> shcc person.cls
```

You can then use the object from the command line:

```
$> . ./person myperson Bob 43
```

Now, call the get methods:

```
$> myperson_getName
Bob
$> myperson_getAge
43
```

Now use the set methods and check the results:

```
$> myperson_setName Bozo

$> myperson_getName
Bozo
$> myperson_setAge 100

$> myperson_getAge
100
```

This object implements basic access functions to alter the object's internal data. If you look at the code created by shcc, you see that it calls your constructor function with the values you pass in when you instantiate your object. When you use inheritance, you actually call the parent class's constructor within your constructor, passing it the necessary values.

One note about the scheme used in variable names: you may have noticed most variables either prefixed with _n or _str. This prefix is for readability. The underscore implies object ownership and is also required by the shcc script. The n and str represent integers and strings, respectively. The shell is a language with no typing. That is, a number, a collection of letters, and even an array are all handled the same way. To improve readability, the general type of variables are indicated through a short prefix. For example, in the shell you can add two variables together:

```
X=$(( X + X ))
```

This example works, but the shell won't complain if you set *X* to be equal to "Hello". The shell just gives you an error such as X: Bad number when you attempt addition. You cannot discern a variable's type by looking at a shell script. In contrast, languages such as Java and C++ have strong typing in which variables have to be forwardly declared, as in int X or char* name. These languages don't necessarily need a prefixing scheme. Also, for those familiar with Hungarian notation in Win32/MFC code, this is not an attempt at or justification of that scheme!

Constructors

You should write constructors first. Normally, you initialize an object's internal data within the constructor. For example, if you are creating a rectangle object, you might pass in the height and width parameters, along with color or fill pattern information, as follows:

```
_rectangle() {
_nWidth=$1
_nHeight=$2
_strFill=${3:-solid}
}
```

In this case, the width and height of the rectangle are taken from the first two parameters passed to the constructor, but the third parameter for the fill pattern is optional. If the third positional parameter ($3) is not set, its value is substituted with solid. You can test for the parameters supplied by using the substitution techniques presented in Chapter 2. If the caller does not give you all the necessary parameters, fill in the missing ones with default values. By initializing all of the internal data in the constructor, you make sure that the data will be available for other methods as they are invoked. For example, if you had set and get methods for a person's name in a person object, you wouldn't want a caller to be able to call getName before the name has been initialized. Getting everything organized in the constructor is always a good practice.

 The constructor function should provide your object with all the necessary data to sustain itself. Your object should be able to function just after construction.

In some OO languages, you can create overloaded constructors that can take a variable number of arguments. This approach allows for objects to be created under different circumstances. You can readily do this in the shell through a number of methods. You can test for the number of parameters that are actually given, or you can check the values or types of passed-in parameters and differentiate among them in that way. The goal is to figure what you've been handed and invoke the correct version of the constructor to accomplish the job. The preceding example fills in defaults for a parameter if it wasn't set. You could have also invoked different versions of the constructor based on the number. By testing the reserved variable $#, you could have chosen the correct version. This approach is good when you have a wide variety of client code that may need to instantiate objects in different situations, and all of the information cannot be provided at construction.

In most cases, however, you don't need to use overloaded constructors. Your constructor can also tell whether or not it's been called correctly. The following version of the person.cls constructor returns an error message if its constructor is not used appropriately:

```
#
# person.cls
#
# a basic class
#
## constructor function, called when object is created
_person() {
if (( $# != 2 )); then
print -u2 "_person: constructor does not take\
$# parameters"
return 1
fi
_strName=$1
_nAge=$2
}
```

In the preceding example, the constructor indicates (with an annoying message that some of you may recognize from your favorite C++ compiler) if at least two values are not passed to a constructor. Your objects will not function correctly if they are not constructed correctly, so you should check what is passed into your constructor function.

Access Functions

Many beneficial features of object-oriented programming are accomplished with access functions. As previously stated, access functions form the heart of interface definitions and allow for techniques like polymorphism. Usually, access functions provide simple methods for accessing a data member without revealing the variable's name. As in the preceding `person.cls` example, `set` and `get` methods are used to change an object's properties, thus enabling you to encapsulate the inner workings of the class. You can also rewrite versions of the class and change internal variable names without worrying about breaking any client code that depends on the objects.

Access functions are a key part of interface design. In your `person.cls` example, you created a simple function, `_getName`, which returned the person's name to STDOUT. By keeping this interface and publishing it, you could integrate code where an account object is handed a person object and retrieves the person's name via the access function:

```
.
.
. (deep within an account class)
.
_getAccountOwner() {
# takes person object as parameter
pRef=$1
#
# call _getName on person object
#
_accOwner=$( ${pRef}_getName )
print $_accOwner
}
```

By using this interface instead of trying to go after the person class variable `_strName` directly, you can change the way you implement a person object. You could change the person class to do a SQL (Structured Query Language) lookup on a database to get the correct username. As long as you eventually write the response to STDOUT, the account class doesn't need to know what's occurring, and is blind to the changes. This approach maximizes your ability to change classes without breaking dependencies. When you write systems that are distributed across a network, the capability to make changes without having to modify all of the software across the network will be a blessing.

 **TIP** Access functions are a key ingredient in creating reusable interfaces.

In addition to retrieving a data member's value, an access function is also responsible for defining the value of variables. As in the preceding example, you can code a _setName function that sets a user's name in a database, as opposed to updating the information in a flat file or editing the password file. All dependent code is able to alter the value of a person object's name property by using the set method:

```
_setName()  {
_strName=$1
}
```

You can also customize this simple version to do other things, such as leave the value of _strName as is, if the method was invoked without a parameter:

```
_setName()  {
_strName=${_strName:-1}
}
```

Here, _strName is either left alone or set to the value of the parameter $1, provided $1 is set and not null.

Chapter 8 develops a request-broker for shell objects that enables you to distribute your objects across different machines. One key aspect to this design is using access functions. By keeping most object interaction down to functions, you can create (in a relatively simple manner) proxy objects that forward requests back and forth between the local client and the remote machine where the object is actually implemented. In this scenario, local proxy objects appear to the client as the remote object; in actuality, they forward requests off to the broker, and listen for the return results that come back. This process remains transparent for the client, who can act as though it is coding with the real thing.

Data Members and Properties

An object's data members and properties are its prize possessions. They represent the object's current state and comprise the core of what the object represents. The concept of state may be foreign to you if you're used to programming in procedural terms. Because an object encapsulates all of its properties, interacts with other objects and the rest of the system through its public methods, and exists for a given period of time, it's easy to apply the concept of state to an object. The object's state is represented by its data members at any given time. For something as simple as an account object, its state may not vary much except with respect to its balance. You create a _dumpState function for any of your objects and write out the object's current state to a log file or the screen, for example. For an object representing a process on a UNIX system, you can check its state in the following way:

```
_dumpState() {
   echo $_nPID
   echo $_strProcessOwner
   echo $_strProcessName
   echo $_strCPUTime
   echo $_nParentPID
}
```

You can periodically call this method on the object and check its data members, and eventually build a graph tracking the object's state through time. While the concept of state may not seem critical to the system applications you develop, object-oriented programming in general lends itself well to modeling any sort of real world environment, where the concept of state can be very critical in determining the patterns of a system or toward which state it tends to evolve. For example, if you create objects to represent processes running on a PC, you can track their state through time. All of the objects eventually come to an end: either through user initiated exit, or generating a "General Protection Fault" (GPF) error or something similar. You could then use this data to determine toward what state the system seems to evolve. Your conclusion might be: PCs tend to go toward a state of GPF, and lock up!

More realistically, your object represents data members and properties. C++ has the notion of private, public, and protected data members. In the shell, you can create private data members – that is, variables that can only be modified by the object that owns them (in a variety of ways). Although this book doesn't commonly use access specifiers, let's discuss one such scheme for enforcing access rights.

In the shell, when your object is initially created, you can make a copy of the built-in variable $RANDOM and prefix all of your object's data members in this way. Your object remembers and applies this number when it needs to access private members. Other code running in the system has no means of accessing the names used in your object. Your class file lists the variables as follows (provided you set rndmID=$RANDOM):

_strName${rndmID}

In this case, all instantiations of this class hold a different value for _strName${rndmID}. Although someone actually using your object from the command line could just type $> print $rndmID to unlock the mystery, the example generally works for script use.

The whole notion of private and public access specifiers is not designed for security, but rather to enforce encapsulation in software design. Generally, this book designs classes with appropriate access functions without bothering to document the internal workings of the class, thus making it logical to work with the class in its intended manner.

Methods

Your object may have many functions besides access specifiers. You can include functions to perform complex operations, retrieve system statistics, create user accounts, and execute a number of other tasks. Most of the functions in the shell provide return results in just a few ways. The return may be the success or failure of the operation indicated with a 1 or 0, the function may set internal data to reflect the retrieved information, or the method may write information to STDOUT. The following example returns a success or failure code from a method that retrieves user information from /etc/passwd:

```
_getUserFields() {
  _user=$1
  if ! grep $_user /etc/passwd | read _fields; then
    print -u2 "$_user not found in /etc/passwd"
    return 1
  else
    return 0
  fi
}
```

The expression echo word | read var does not always set var to the value of word. The implementation is shell-dependent and may not work on all versions of the KSH. In the worst case, you can always use an expression like fields=$(grep $_user /etc/passwd), though the subprocess may have side effects.

The preceding function attempts to set an internal variable _fields with user information from the system file /etc/passwd. If the command fails (returns non-zero), the function prints an error message and returns non-zero itself. This allows for a client to use this function in the following way:

```
if _getUserFields; then
  echo "User information: $_fields"
else
  exit
fi
```

Chapter 3: The Syntax of Writing Classes

In a similar way to the function it calls, the process exits if the result is not a success. The function _getUserFields prints an error message, so you don't have to print another error message in the second example – it's safe just to exit.

Returning one or zero is an ideal way to execute shell functions. Programming in this manner enables you to use the if command to test the success of your operations. Also, shell commands themselves function in this way. Applying this technique throughout your programming enables you to incorporate it in everything you do, because it is so widely used by other system utilities.

Another means of executing shell object functions sets a variable with the information that the method returns. You can also return one or zero to indicate whether this retrieval and assignment is successful. If you have a function _getDiskUsage that retrieves disk statistics and then sets internal variable _diskStats to represent the data, you could use the function in the following way:

```
if _getDiskUsage; then
  for each in _diskStats;
    do
      print "Disk Usage: $_diskStats"
done
else
  print "No disk information available"
fi
```

The preceding is essentially the same mechanism as the first example. Instead of setting an object-owned data member, however, you can set the return of a method to a publicly known variable, which can comprise a large amount of information.

Another way to treat the information retrieved by a method writes it to STDOUT. You've done this process already with the person class, which writes the results of its get methods to STDOUT. This approach allows for your client code to choose how it wants to handle the information. It can forward it to the screen, write it to a log file, or store it in a variable. If you create a user object that represents user accounts on a UNIX system, you would probably write a _getFields method that retrieves the user's information. Initially, this object (actually created in Chapter 4) pulls the information out of the /etc/passwd file, and sets internal data members accordingly. This object also has a method that simply returns all of the user's information to STDOUT. Client code could handle the object in the following way:

```
#
# insert user into /etc/passwd
#
# uRef is instantiated user object with altered information
echo $( uRef_getFields ) > /etc/passwd
```

The preceding three ways comprise the primary ways you should handle how functions operate. These methods, also used with access functions, allow the most interoperability between objects. The next chapter uses objects together and actually passes them off to each other, letting the receiver invoke methods on the object it receives. At that point, you'll see that using an access function to get at an object's data is much easier than trying to grab one of its internal members. Generally, when you hand an object to another object, you can invoke a method in the following way:

```
#
_createAccount() {
  # user object is first parameter
  uRef=$1
  #
# invoke get fields method to create account
  echo $( ${uRef}_getFields ) > /etc/passwd
}
```

This example is similar to the preceding example, but in this case, you don't know the explicit name of the object you were passed when you first wrote the function. Therefore, you have to invoke methods based on a variable set to the name of the object that was passed in. In this case, uRef was not an actual object instance, but a variable representing an object instance — hence the necessary enclosure in brackets.

Destructors

Destructor methods are called when an object is no longer needed and its space in memory should be reclaimed for other uses. In languages like C++, the delete keyword automatically calls an object's destructor and takes care of freeing the allocated memory. In the shell objects, you can reclaim an object's occupied memory space in a number of ways. The script shcc (included on the CD-ROM and presented in a following section) creates a simple _delete method for you. This _delete method actually parses through the environment of the current shell process and executes the built-in unset command on every variable and function using your object's ID. While this approach is reclaiming most of the memory, a tiny residual remains, due to the nature of the shell. Different implementations of the Korn and Bash shells behave differently, but in some versions of the Korn shell, the unset command has no effect on functions. As a result, while you can easily delete all data internal to your object, the actual function definitions persist until the shell exits. The overhead varies depending on the size of your object, but is usually just a few bytes. If you leave a process running that continually creates and deletes objects in the hundreds, the process space steadily grows at a rate of approximately

30 bytes per object instance. You would have to create and delete approximately 10,000 objects to build up a residual process space of 300K. This residual process space is relatively small when you consider many large binary programs claim a few megabytes of RAM while executing. Regardless, you must consider this situation in your applications.

One obvious solution occasionally `exits` or re-`exec`s a new shell process, replacing the memory used by the previous instance; that is, you have a system monitoring application that continually monitors your system. While it may take days for a residual amount of memory to build up, you can have your system's main process periodically restart itself, rotate or flush log files, and then restart with a fresh system process. This approach is usually the norm for daemons and processes intended to be left running. Regardless of the environment, long-running processes often do strange things and eventually wind up consuming lots of system resources. This sequence is true of many commercial applications running on a variety of hardware.

The application developed in following chapters of this book effectively manages its memory. It invokes objects into separate processes and uses them until they cease to exist, thus avoiding many problems. Also, the system is distributed across several servers and most of its functionality is broken across smaller, short-lasting processes.

In general, destructor methods are called to destroy an object. The `shcc _delete` method works well for most situations, but due to the shell's nature, you should restart your processes on a periodic basis.

Class Programming Considerations

When instantiating objects in your shell scripts, you should be aware of a few considerations. Historically, shell scripts have been small and didn't contain much data. By default, shell scripts have a global scope for all data in the process; that is, you can reference the same variable in any function and always deal with the one and only instance of that variable. Global scope in a shell process is unavoidable and other mechanisms must be in place to protect data.

Variable Scope and Data Clashing

Your objects have better data management because all data in your object belongs to the object instance of which it is a part. You have to reference your variables in this way. For example, if you create an instance of a person object named `MyPerson`, its data members have to be referenced as the following:

```
$> print $MyPerson_Name
Bob
$> print $MyPerson_Age
25
```

The variables _Name and _Age don't exist except in the context of an object that owns them. This approach prevents the mix-up of data between objects.

Be aware though, that you have to specify when you want data to be owned. If you prefix your variable with an underscore, shcc makes the association for you. If you do not, you run the risk of confusing object instances. Compare the snippet of class code from a list class, as follows:

```
_AddItem() {
  _itemList[x]=$1
  ((x=x+1))
}
```

This function _AddItem takes a parameter and inserts it into the _itemList array at the current position of *x*. It then increments *x* by one, so that the next insertion won't clobber the last. This appears to work fine, right? It does work, except when there are two or more instances of list objects. The problem: at any given time, when _AddItem is called by any instantiated object, the value of *x* is shared between them. For example, you create one list object (list1) and insert four items into the list. You create a second list object (list2), and insert one item into the list. Then you go back and insert another item into list1. If you dump your list arrays, you would see the following:

```
list1[0]=item
list1[1]=item
list1[2]=item
list1[3]=item
list2[4]=item
list1[5]=item
```

The problem here is that list1 has five elements but is blank at location 4, while list2 has 1 item but resides in location 4. This problem occurs because the variable of *x* is shared between both object instances.

 All variables within a shell script are global, which can be an important consideration when you're using lots of objects within the same program. Make sure that all variables have unique names within the same shell script.

This sort of variable clashing can cause serious bugs. Always internalize your variables by prefixing them with an underscore and letting shcc create an object ownership relationship.

Debugging

Debugging is always a part of any complex programming effort. The shell does not have a visual run-time debugger where you can select watch variables and place break points. Despite this omission, you have a variety of ways to debug your code. The shell command `set -vx` provides a fairly adequate glimpse into your shell scripts execution. Every shell statement and transaction is printed to the screen and you can easily see how the shell is interpreting your code. If you type `set -vx` from the command line, all of your subsequent commands are put through this debugger. You can issue `set +vx` to stop the output. For example:

```
$> set -vx

$> print hello
+ print hello
hello

$> string="goodbye"
+ string=goodbye!

$> print $string
+ print goodbye!
goodbye!
```

This approach can be powerful because it enables you to see how the shell is interpreting code. If you prefer the output to go to a file, you can redirect STDERR. This approach works well in a shell script to create a log file of all things that went right or wrong. You need a command similar to the following in your code:

```
exec 2> errorlog.txt
set -vx
```

When placed at the top of your script, this command allows for everything to be logged as it executes. Note that `set -vx` has scope only in the current shell process, and actually doesn't branch out into function calls. Therefore, it's necessary to place this debugging command within the body of function definitions you want to debug.

`shcc` can take `debug` as the first parameter to turn on debugging in your shell objects. This approach tracks down unexpected behavior in your classes. To recompile the `person.cls` class with debugging, try the following:

```
$> shcc debug person.cls
```

The resulting version of the class produce copious debugging output when you instantiate objects. Listing 3-1 shows an example of running a person object from the command line with debugging on:

Listing 3-1: Debugging output

```
[probing]. person MyPerson Bob 25
. person MyPerson Bob 25
+ . person MyPerson Bob 25
#!/bin/ksh
set -vx
+ set -vx
###############################################################
## ClassFile: person.cls
##    Created: Sun Jan 25 11:37:44 PST 1998
###############################################################
ObjectId=$1
+ ObjectId=MyPerson
args=$@
+ args=MyPerson Bob 25
#
# person.cls
#
eval "${ObjectId}_person() { set -vx
${ObjectId}_strName=\$1
${ObjectId}_nAge=\$2
}"
+ eval MyPerson_person() { set -vx
MyPerson_strName=$1
MyPerson_nAge=$2
}
MyPerson_person() { set -vx
MyPerson_strName=$1
MyPerson_nAge=$2
}
eval "${ObjectId}_setName() { set -vx
${ObjectId}_strName=\$1
}"
+ eval MyPerson_setName() { set -vx
MyPerson_strName=$1
}
MyPerson_setName() { set -vx
MyPerson_strName=$1
}
eval "${ObjectId}_getName() { set -vx
echo \$${ObjectId}_strName
}"
+ eval MyPerson_getName() { set -vx
echo $MyPerson_strName
}
MyPerson_getName() { set -vx
echo $MyPerson_strName
}
eval "${ObjectId}_setAge() { set -vx
${ObjectId}_nAge=\$1
}"
```

Chapter 3: The Syntax of Writing Classes

```
+ eval MyPerson_setAge() { set -vx
MyPerson_nAge=$1
}
MyPerson_setAge() { set -vx
MyPerson_nAge=$1
}
eval "${ObjectId}_getAge() { set -vx
echo \$${ObjectId}_nAge
}"
+ eval MyPerson_getAge() { set -vx
echo $MyPerson_nAge
}
MyPerson_getAge() { set -vx
echo $MyPerson_nAge
}

eval "${ObjectId}_Delete()  { set -vx
set | grep ^$ObjectId | while read var
        do
                unset \${var%=*}
        done

}"
+ eval MyPerson_Delete()  { set -vx
set | grep ^MyPerson | while read var
        do
                unset ${var%=*}
        done

}
MyPerson_Delete()  { set -vx
set | grep ^MyPerson | while read var
        do
                unset ${var%=*}
        done

}
#
# Construction
# -called when class first executes.
#
call_args=${args#*\ }     # remove objname from arglist
+ call_args=Bob 25
${ObjectId}_person $call_args  # Call constructor with arglist
+ MyPerson_person Bob 25
+ MyPerson_strName=Bob
+ MyPerson_nAge=25
[probing]
```

The `set -vx` switch dumps functions as they are defined, and then shows the expansion of all of the internal variables as it evaluates the quoted functions. At the end of the output, you see the actual work of the constructor being carried out:

```
+ MyPerson_person Bob 25
+ MyPerson_strName=Bob
+ MyPerson_nAge=25
```

If you rerun `shcc` without the debugging switch, your class functions normally again.

How Shell Objects Work

At this point, you may be wondering exactly how shell objects work. If you've coded in the shell before, you know that though the preceding functions and classes work, they certainly aren't object-oriented.

Using the eval Keyword

Well, no complicated trick or magic coding is involved. In the simplest terms, objects are created by using the `eval` keyword on a quoted function. Your goal is to take all of the variables within your function and add an object ID tag to them; that is, if you have a variable named `_myvar` within your function, you want to expand it to be called `${objectID}_myvar`. If `objectID` is set to `MyObject`, the actual variable name in the shell can be referenced as `$MyObject_myvar`. This sequence requires use of the `eval` keyword.

Here's an actual example. You define a variable called `foo` to be equal to `This is`. You create a second variable, `bar`, to be equal to `Crazy!`. Finally, you create a variable called `mywords` that is equal to `foobar`. Using the `eval` keyword, you can print these values in a variety of different ways:

```
$> foo="This is"

$> bar="Crazy!"

$> mywords="foobar"
```

You can now print the sentence in the following way:

```
$>print ${foo}${bar}
This is Crazy!
```

You can also define a variable called `foobar`:

```
$> eval foobar='${foo}${bar}'
```

Chapter 3: The Syntax of Writing Classes

In the preceding, `eval` expands the values of `foo` and `bar`, and presents the assignment `foobar="This is Crazy!"` to the shell. You can also use `eval` to print the sentence by evaluating `mywords`:

```
$> eval print \$$mywords
```

Before this command line is presented to the shell interpreter, `eval` expands it to look as follows:

```
$> print $foobar
```

Of course, based on the preceding assignment of setting `foobar` equal to the contents of `$foo` and `$bar` respectively, the following output is expected:

```
This is Crazy!
```

This simple example creates object-orientation in the shell.

`shcc` (and what you would do by hand if you code your objects) quotes a function definition, and expands all instances of `ObjectID` before presenting the function definition to the shell. The value of `ObjectID` is passed in from the command line. An example of a simple function quoted and ready for object expansion follows:

```
#!/bin/ksh
# dynamically named function!
ObjectID=$1
eval "{ObjectID}_printit() {
print Hello!
}"
```

The preceding script defines a function called `_printit` prefixed with whatever the first argument was set to. Save the preceding snippet as `function.sh`, and try the following:

```
$> . function.sh hello
$> hello_printit
Hello!
```

Before the function `printit` is defined by the shell, `eval` searches and replaces all instances of `ObjectID` with the first command line argument, which is `hello` in this case.

Taking Apart shcc

Now let's examine in greater detail exactly what shcc does to your scripts. Use the example person.cls with which you've been working throughout this chapter. For reference, Listing 3-2 lists person.cls again, prior to alteration by shcc:

Listing 3-2: person.cls

```
# person.cls
#
_person()  {
  _strName=$1
  _nAge=$2
}
_setName()  {
  _strName=$1
}
_getName()  {
  echo $_strName
}
_setAge()  {
  _nAge=$1
}
_getAge()  {
  echo $_nAge
}
```

Now try running shcc on person.cls, and note the output created as it parses your class in Listing 3-3:

Listing 3-3: The output of the shcc command

```
$> shcc debug person.cls
Escaping $args for inheritance...
Escaping quotations...
Escaping Dollar Signs...
Escaping escape Characters...
Replacing $args for inheritance...
Escaping \}_ (referenced object method calls) from parser...
Removing temporary file: person.cls.temp
Removing temporary file: person.cls.temp1
Removing temporary file: person.cls.preparse
Removing temporary file: person.cls.preparse1
Generating header...
Parsing file:
shcc: --> # <--
shcc: --> # person.cls <--
shcc: --> # <--
shcc: --> _person()\tab \{ <--
shcc: --> _strName=\\$1 <--
shcc: --> _nAge=\\$2 <--
shcc: --> \} <--
```

```
shcc: --> _setName()\tab \{ <--
shcc: --> _strName=\\$1 <--
shcc: --> \} <--
shcc: --> _getName()\tab \{ <--
shcc: --> echo \\$_strName <--
shcc: --> \} <--
shcc: --> _setAge()\tab \{ <--
shcc: --> _nAge=\\$1 <--
shcc: --> \} <--
shcc: --> _getAge()\tab \{ <--
shcc: --> echo \\$_nAge <--
shcc: --> \} <--
Replacing \}_'s (referenced object method calls)...
```

Shcc indicates what it is parsing from your file. This is good information if you ever receive unexpected results and you're trying to trace exactly what happened. The file that shcc generates for you, in this case person, looks like Listing 3-4:

Listing 3-4: The converted version of person.cls

```
$> cat person
#!/bin/ksh
set -vx
########################################################################
## ClassFile: person.cls
##   Created: Sun Jan 25 11:37:44 PST 1998
########################################################################
ObjectId=$1
args=$@
#
# person.cls
#
eval "${ObjectId}_person() { set -vx
${ObjectId}_strName=\$1
${ObjectId}_nAge=\$2
}"
eval "${ObjectId}_setName() { set -vx
${ObjectId}_strName=\$1
}"
eval "${ObjectId}_getName() { set -vx
echo \$${ObjectId}_strName
}"
eval "${ObjectId}_setAge() { set -vx
${ObjectId}_nAge=\$1
}"
eval "${ObjectId}_getAge() { set -vx
echo \$${ObjectId}_nAge
}"
```

```
eval "${ObjectId}_Delete() { set -vx
set | grep ^$ObjectId | while read var
    do
            unset \${var%=*}
    done
}"
#
# Construction
# -called when class first executes.
#
call_args=${args#*\ }        # remove objname from arglist
${ObjectId}_person $call_args  # Call constructor with arglist
```

You can see how all of the functions have been expanded to include the dynamic naming convention that was demonstrated in preceding sections. shcc also creates a _Delete function as well as mechanisms for using inheritance. All of these tasks are easy enough to do by hand, but if you're going to use a script to quote your functions, why not do some other automation? shcc is not perfect, and you have to follow a simple guideline when creating your classes to have them parsed correctly. This guideline is very basic and is probably how you would want to create shell objects anyway. The basic structure is illustrated quite well in person.cls, but Listing 3-5 shows a simplified, annotated version you can use as a reference.

Listing 3-5: template.cls

```
#
# template.cls  - a template for creating classes for use with shcc
#
# comments are ok, and can appear anywhere.
#
# Note that there is no shell escape, as in #!/bin/ksh, shcc will
# add this for you.
#
# Construct function - required. Initalize member variables and
# whatever else you like
_template() {
  echo "Constructor doing nothing!"
_dataMember=100
}
#
# Functions and data must begin with an underscore _, and functions
# should end with a close-bracket on a line by itself.
_tempMethod() {
  echo $_dataMember
}
#
# You can also accept objects parameters, and invoke their functions
_tempMethod2() {
  objRef=$1
  #
```

Chapter 3: The Syntax of Writing Classes

```ksh
    # invoke method on objRef
    ${objRef}_getProperty
    #
    # Assign output of method invoaction to variable
    _result=$( ${objRef}_getProperty )
    print $_result
}
# no destructor or delete method is needed
```

You should tinker with and customize shcc. While it has several complex parsing algorithms, you can add your own to suit your coding style. Listing 3-6 shows the code for shcc:

Listing 3-6: The shcc **converter program**

```ksh
#!/bin/ksh
#######################################################
#
# shcc    -    Shell Object Converter
#
# Version: 1.0
#
# Usage: shcc [debug] <infile> [<outfile>] [<shell>]
#
# Examples:
#   shcc debug myclass.cls
#     -creates outfile: myclass with debugging
#
#   shcc myobject
#     -creates outfile: myobject.out
#
#   shcc aobject bobject
#     -creates outfile: bobject
#
#   shcc debug barney.class barney /bin/zsh
#     -create outfile: barney with debugging using the Zshell!?!
#
# Documentation:
#   See full documentation for usage. shcc converts ordinary
#   function bodies into object-oriented function bodies.
#
#######################################################
# determine if debugging has been set
#
if [[ "$1" = "debug" ]]; then
   DEBUG="set -vx"
   shift
fi

# set output filename
#
FileName=$1
```

```
if [[ $FileName = @(*.cls) ]]; then
  Outfile=${FileName%%.cls}
else
  if [[ $2 = "" ]]; then
    Outfile=$FileName.out
  else
    Outfile=$2
  fi
fi

# set shell environment for header
#
SHELL=${3:-/bin/ksh}

# Escape all quotes and dollarsigns
#
print "Escaping \$args for inheritance..."
  sed "s/\$args/STRING_ARGS/g" $FileName > $FileName.temp
print "Escaping quotations..."
  sed "s/\"/\\\\\"/g" $FileName.temp > $FileName.temp1
print "Escaping Dollar Signs..."
  sed "s/\\$/\\\\$/g" $FileName.temp1 > $FileName.preparse
print "Escaping escape Characters..."
  sed "s/\\\/\\\\\\\/g" $FileName.preparse > $FileName.preparse1
print "Replacing \$@ for inheritance..."
  sed "s/STRING_ARGS/\$args/g" $FileName.preparse1 \
> $FileName.preparse2
print "Escaping }_ (referenced object calls) from parser..."
  sed "s/}_/ROM/g" $FileName.preparse2 > $FileName.esc

# cleanup temporary files
#
for each in $FileName.temp \
      $FileName.temp1 \
      $FileName.preparse \
      $FileName.preparse1
do
  print "Removing temporary file: $each"
  rm $each
done

# print header to Outfile
#
print "Generating header..."
cat << End_Header > $Outfile
#!${SHELL}
${DEBUG:-#}
######################################################################
## ClassFile: $FileName
##   Created: $(date)
######################################################################
ObjectId=\$1
args=\$@
```

```
End_Header

# begin parsing loop
#
print "Parsing file:"
while read each
do
echo "shcc: --> $each <--"

  case $each in
    #
    # Parsing patterns
    #

    @(#*)   )
      ## skip comments!
      ;;
    +(* _*|*[a-z]_[a-z]*)  )
      each=$(echo $each | sed "s/^_/\${ObjectId}_/g")
      each=$(echo $each | sed "s/\ _/\ \${ObjectId}_/g")
      each=$(echo $each | sed "s/\$_/\$\${ObjectId}_/g")
      ;;
    @(_*\(\)*)  )
      each="eval \"\${ObjectId}"${each}
      if [[ "$DEBUG" != "" ]]; then
        each=${each}" $DEBUG"
      fi
      ## each=$(echo $each | sed "s/_/\${ObjectId}_/g")
      ;;
    ?(* _*|*{_*)  )
      each=$(echo $each | sed "s/_/\${ObjectId}_/g")
      ;;
    @(*\$_*)  )
      each=$(echo $each | sed "s/_/\${ObjectId}_/g")
      ;;
    @(*}_*)  )
      ## do nothing
      ;;
    @(_*)   )
      each=$(echo $each | sed "s/_/\${ObjectId}_/g")
      ;;
    @(}*)   )
      each=${each}\"
      ;;
  esac

  print $each > $Outfile

done < $FileName.esc

# create a Delete function and Constructor call
#
cat << end_of_fn >> $Outfile
```

UNIX Shell Objects

```
eval "\${ObjectId}_Delete() { $DEBUG
  set | grep ^\$ObjectId | while read var
     do
              unset \\\${var%=*}
     done
}"
#
# Construction
# -called when class first executes.
#
call_args=\${args#*\ }        # remove objname from arglist
\${ObjectId}_$Outfile \$call_args  # construct with arglist
end_of_fn

# cleanup temporary files
#
print "Replacing }_'s (referenced object method calls)..."
  sed "s/ROM/}_/g" $Outfile > $Outfile.new
  mv $Outfile.new $Outfile
rm $FileName.esc
rm $FileName.preparse2
chmod a+x $Outfile
```

The preceding script is certainly not object-oriented, and does its job in a makeshift fashion. At first, shcc escapes characters that should avoid evaluation; that is, some variables should stay variable. You only want to expand the object identifier handed to your script at creation. After this escaping is done with the sed command, the whole file is then parsed through a loop, which translates variables, functions, and referenced objects into their prefixed versions. For example, the following regular expression grabs functions:

```
@(_*\(\)*)
```

The @(......) is used in the shell for pattern matching; that is, you can write an if or case statement and try to match a word with the regular expression enclosed between @(...). The regular expression is actually on the inside: _*\(\)*, which translates into _<anyword>()<anyword> or function declarations:

```
_MyFunction()
_yourFunction() { #comments
_theirFunction(){
```

The other expression patterns in `shcc`'s main `case` loop perform similar duties. Some patterns try to determine when you are invoking a method on a referenced object, and what is just a plain variable. `shcc` works works well for every example in this book, but don't be surprised if some of your superhuman shell gymnastics throw it off a bit. You should be able to customize `shcc` to your liking.

Summary

By now, you should have a good understanding of class functionality in object-oriented programming. Also, you should have solved any mysteries regarding how this is actually accomplished in the shell. OOP can be implemented in any language — you just need to provide all of the correct mechanisms to implement the object-oriented features. Your scripts need the capability to inherit from each other, to overload and redefine inherited functions, and to be able to invoke methods on objects that are passed as parameters.

In the next chapter, you begin using objects together and start uncovering the relationships that make object-oriented programming beneficial.

Chapter 4

Using Shell Objects

IN THIS CHAPTER

- ◆ Creation of useful objects
- ◆ Use of objects together
- ◆ Aggregation versus acquaintance
- ◆ Lists of objects
- ◆ Strategies for using objects

NOW THAT YOU have a solid understanding of classes, you can begin to construct useful objects. Many of the classes you create here are reused in the development of a distributed systems management application. In this chapter, you strive to create simple, function-oriented objects that are not complicated with unnecessary and unrelated tasks. You also develop relationships between objects that have yet to be explained, including composition, inheritance, aggregation, and factory classes.

Strategies

Certain strategies can be used when developing objects. A poorly designed class holds little benefit. If you couple your classes too tightly to each other or add unnecessary functionality to your classes, you wind up with a class that isn't extensible and has to be rewritten for every situation in which it's applied. Creating classes with appropriate and extensible functionality usually means keeping your classes simple. Objects should be modeled after the real-world entities they represent. This approach means reducing object functionality to what is essential, composing objects with other objects, and requesting the services of other objects when needed.

Functional Considerations

One way to start the design process creates a list of the concepts, entities, and operations that will exist in your system and decide what can be collected into an object. In your system management application, you will attempt to manage a network of servers. You obviously want to create objects to represent the distributed servers themselves. You could add operations for checking system devices and application states. But at what level do you stop decomposing larger entities into the objects of which they're composed? A server is really a collection of disks, interface cards, printers, modems, and any number of other devices. Processes, applications, file systems, and configuration schemes also make up the system. At what point does the granularity cease? Should you create objects to represent network protocols? What about individual processes? Threads? Shell commands? What concepts do you abstract into objects?

As mentioned earlier, you don't want to provide a system class with file knowledge – likewise, you don't want to provide a file object with text editing capabilities. Recognizing these characteristics in your objects is not always easy, and often depends on the environment in which you are working and toward what angle your solution is geared.

The resolution or granularity of your system depends on two questions: How much detail does your application need to function correctly? How much extensibility and flexibility will your system eventually require? In this chapter, you whip up a quick version of a unixServer class that provides a lot of functionality right out of the box. While this object is expanded and redesigned throughout the book, in this chapter it illustrates some useful object concepts. The unixServer class actually contains two other classes, namely a list object that holds an array of references to the server's disk objects. You also create an account and user object that demonstrate object interoperation.

Inheritance, References, and Aggregation

In addition to the functional design considerations you need to make, you can also use strategies for using objects together. These relationships are often the true power of object-oriented systems. For example, in giving the unixServer object the capability to own a disk object (a concept known as *aggregation*), you decouple disk-specific operations from the unixServer class, which provides you with disk-related methods. A disk object is capable of keeping track of its size, percentage of used space, the disk's mount point, and device specifics. A unixServer object can use a disk object to retrieve this information. By keeping the unixServer blind to the implementation details of disks, you allow for both objects to grow over time, coupling them via a simple interface. If you had given the unixServer class the necessary code to gather disk statistics, you would be tying the implementation of disk operations to the unixServer class where they don't belong. By encapsulating disk properties in a separate disk object, you are free to change your disk class and even subtype the disk class out to other devices that can still provide a disk-like interface.

In this chapter, your objects use other objects in three key ways. A few classes actually inherit code from other classes, implementing a few subtle changes where necessary. These subclasses closely resemble the object from which they inherit and can be considered a type of the first object.

The second relationship you discover is the capability for an object to use the services of another via a reference or acquaintance to the other object. In this case, one object knows of another object instance by name, and has the capability to invoke methods on this object. The object's lifetimes can be unrelated, however, and while one is not talking to the other, they can be independent.

The third relationship you create is aggregation, when an object actually contains another object that is privately bound to the owner for its lifetime. The owner always creates the contained object, and their lifetimes are intertwined. Other objects may have no knowledge of the contained object and its existence may be invisible.

Functional Classes

A file is one of the first items you represent with an object. The file class you create is basic and just holds the properties of a standard UNIX file. When you do an `ls -l` command from the shell, you receive key information regarding a file. In particular, its permissions, the number of hard links to the file, the owner, the group, the name, the size, and the last modified time are shown. This information is easily abstracted into an object. Your file class will have no operations for files other than changing the owner, group, or name. It will have access functions for the remaining read-only properties such as size and last-modification time. The file class will have no editing operations upon a file, but the file class is eventually inherited by a class edit file and another class Web file, which are methods for displaying the file's contents after printing the appropriate HTTP header.

Your class is named `sfile`, since the word `file` is an actual UNIX command. The class listing `sfile.cls` is shown in Listing 4-1.

Listing 4-1: `sfile.cls`

```
#
# sfile.cls
#
# Methods
#
#   _setOwner
#   _setGroup
#   _setName
#
# Data Members
#
#   _strPerms
#   _nLinks
#   _strOwner
#   _nGroup
#   _nBytes
```

```
#    _strMonth
#    _strDay
#    _strTime
#    _strName
#
# Construction
#
#    . sfile <ref> <[filepath]filename>
#
########################################################################

_sfile() {
  if [[ -r $1 ]];then
    _privsetStats $(ls -l $1)
  else
    print -u2 "Construction failed: Unable to read file $1..."
    return 1
  fi
}

_privsetStats() {
  #
  # This function parses output of an ls -l, and should
  # only be called after an update or change to the file.
  #
  _strPerms=$1
  _nLinks=$2
  _strOwner=$3
  _nGroup=$4
  _nBytes=$5
  _strMonth=$6
  _strDay=$7
  _strTime=$8
  _strName=$9
}

#
# Access functions for user-modifiable parameters
#
_setOwner() {
  if ! chown $1 $_strName
  then
    print "Cannot change owner to $1"
    return 1
  fi
  _privsetStats $(ls -l $_strName)
}

_getOwner() {
  echo $_strOwner
}

_setGroup() {
```

```
  if ! chgrp $1 $_strName
  then
    print "Cannot change group to $1"
    return 1
  exit
  fi
  _privsetStats $(ls -l $_strName)
}

_getGroup() {
  echo $_nGroup
}

_setName() {
  _newName=$1
  if ! mv $_strName $_newName
  then
    print "Cannot change $_strName to $1"
    return 1
  fi
  _privsetStats $(ls -l $_newName)
}

_getName() {
  echo $_strName
}

_setPerms() {
  if ! chmod $1 $_strName; then
    print "Unable to change permissions on $_strName"
    return 1
  fi
  _privsetStats $(ls -l $_strName)
}

_getPerms() {
  echo $_strPerms
}
```

sfile.cls contains some simple access functions and a few related properties. Interestingly, you've created a private function _privsetStats that actually gleans the file's real-time properties from the ls -l command. The other functions in the class call this operation whenever there is a change in the file's properties. If another process or user modifies the file while you're using the same file, this operation enables your object to reflect the new changes the next time it is queried. This process surpasses the method of simply querying the file's properties once and writing the changes when the object is destroyed. By always referencing the physical file your object represents, you safeguard yourself against unexpected changes, and you also create an object that more closely resembles its real-world counterpart.

Files can change at any time, and your object should reflect that possibility. You can use `sfile` from the command line:

```
$> . sfile afile /etc/passwd
$> afile_getOwner
root
$> print $afile_nBytes
873
```

 Many of you will need to use a syntax like `../sfile afile /etc/passwd` when instantiating objects. You can leave out the `./` for clarity and convenience. This approach requires a dot (.) in your path. A dot is okay to have in your path if you've included all relevant binary directories and the dot is placed at the end. For those of you diametrically opposed to placing the dot in your path, you have to "path-out" your objects when instantiating them. See the end of Chapter 2 for details on the security issues concerning the dot in your path.

Another object, `disk.cls`, also resembles `sfile.cls` in design. Your disk class can hold a standard disk's device properties as viewed by the file system; that is, this object contains the same information you get via a `df -k` or `bdf` statement. The disk class represents mounted file systems – not expressly the actual devices connected to the hardware. A UNIX file system, or disk, can have one mount point and a certain capacity, but be physically striped across several different physical volumes or hardware devices. Your disk object represents disks – an available number of file system megabytes mounted at a certain location in the server's file system – as they appear to the operating system and the user. The object reflects the name of the mounted disk, the size in kilobytes, the number of kilobytes used and available, the percentage of disk space used, and the mount point of the disk within the file system.

The `disk.cls` class implements some typical access functions and holds data members to reflect the disk's properties. This type of object can be used by application logging that needs to determine the best place to start putting large files. This object can also be used to monitor file system capacity and send alerts when a dangerous situation arises. Every system administrator knows too well the havoc wreaked by overflowing file systems.

Listing 4-2 demonstrates `disk.cls`.

Listing 4-2: `disk.cls`

```
_disk() {
  if (( $# < 4 )); then
    print "Unable to construct disk object."
    return 1
  fi
  _strName=$1
  _nKbSize=$2
  _nKbUsed=$3
  _nKbAvail=$4
  _nCapacity=$5
  _strMount=$6
}
_getName() {
  echo $_strName
}
_getPercentUsed() {
  echo $_nCapacity
}
_getKbSize() {
  echo $_nKbSize
}
_getKbUsed() {
  echo $_nKbUsed
}
_getKbAvail() {
  echo $_nKbAvail
}
_getMount() {
  echo $_strMount
}
_getFullList() {
  print -n "Device: $_strName Mounted At: $_strMount"
  print " Percent Used: "$_nCapacity
}
```

Another abstraction you will choose to make in your system is for the user's benefit – you'll create an object to represent users on the server. As you probably suspect, this object will have access functions to change and view the user's properties. Your user object will contain information similar to what is contained in the UNIX accounting file /etc/passwd. Besides a user's password, which /etc/passwd rarely contains these days, additional important information is also kept in the file. A user's login name is kept in /etc/passwd. Their user ID (UID), group ID (GID), home directory, real name, and login shell are also indicated in this file.

Some aspects usually associated with users are not included in the operations implemented by this object. The creation and deletion of server accounts are not controlled by a user object. While the information in /etc/passwd is world-readable, the capability to create and delete accounts is only allowed by the system administration account. All applications that can use user objects should not be able to modify or create user accounts.

You construct a user object by passing a login name as the first parameter when instantiating the class. The user object implements a method _getFields that returns all of the user's information in a colon-delimited string as it appears in /etc/passwd. The operation _getFields can optionally take a number from 1 to 7, specifying which field in particular to return. For example, to get the user's real name or gecos information, you could do the following:

```
$> . user myuser melvin

$> myuser_getFields 5
Melvin Boris, x4532
```

You can also reuse a user object by calling the constructor again with a new parameter:

```
$> myuser_myuser root

$> myuser_getFields 1
root of all evil,,,,,
```

Root of all evil,,,,,, if you're wondering, is included in the gecos field for root in the default installation of Slackware3.2 for Linux/x86. The gecos field, as it's sometimes called, contains information either reflective of the user's real name or other descriptive information regarding the account. In a more secure environment, the gecos field is often left blank or minimally decorated.

The code listing for user.cls is shown in Listing 4-3.

Listing 4-3: user.cls

```
#
# user.cls
#
# Methods
#
#   _user <userID>
#   _setFields <field:field:field:field:field:field:field>
#   _getFields [<field number>]
#
# Data Members
#
#   _strName
#   _strPasswd
#   _nUID
#   _nGID
#   _strGecos
#   _strHomeDir
#   _strShell
```

```
#
# Construction
#
#   . user <ref> <userid>
#
#####################################################################


_user() {
  # You must keep use of IFS local, as this function
  # will be used amongst many others in the same
  # shell process

  if [ "$1" = "" ]; then
    print -u2 "$0: please supply username to constructor"
    return 1
  fi
  user=$1
  oldIFS=$IFS
  IFS=:
  _strFields=$(grep ^$user /etc/passwd)
  _setFields $_strFields
  IFS=$oldIFS
}

_setFields() {
  if (( $# > 3 )); then
    _strName=$1
    _strPasswd=$2
    _nUID=$3
    _nGID=$4
    _strGecos=$5
    _strHomeDir=$6
    _strShell=$7
_strFields="$_strName:$_strPasswd:$_nUID:$_nGID"
_strFields="$_strFields:$_strGecos:$_strHomeDir:$_strShell"
  else
    if [[ "$2" = "" ]]; then
      print -u2 "_setFields: argument is null..."
      return 1
    fi
    _newValue=$2
    case $1 in
      1) _strName=$_newValue      ;;
      2) _strPasswd=$_newValue    ;;
      3) _nUID=$_newValue         ;;
      4) _nGID=$_newValue         ;;
      5) _strGecos=$_newValue     ;;
      6) _strHomeDir=$_newValue   ;;
      7) _strShell=$_newValue     ;;
      *) print -u2 \
         "_setFields: Invalid field number: $1..."
         ;;
```

```
      esac
_strFields="$_strName:$_strPasswd:$_nUID:$_nGID"
_strFields="$_strFields:$_strGecos:$_strHomeDir:$_strShell"
  fi
}

_getFields() {
  if [[ "$1" = "" ]]; then
    echo $_strFields
  else
    case $1 in
      1) echo $_strName         ;;
      2) echo $_strPasswd       ;;
      3) echo $_nUID            ;;
      4) echo $_nGID            ;;
      5) echo $_strGecos        ;;
      6) echo $_strHomeDir      ;;
      7) echo $_strShell        ;;
      *) return 1               ;;
    esac
  fi
}
```

Object References

Your next functional object is responsible for user accounts on the system. In a departure from previous classes, this class actually requires a reference to an existing user object. All account actions involve users, and as a result, a reference to an object is required. The reference in this case is simply a name of an instantiated class. If you create a user object with the ID myuser, as in the preceding example, you can pass this name to an account object at construction. Also, the account class contains operations to change the account owner or user reference, and retrieve the name of the owner. Figure 4-1 shows an account object holding a reference to a user object.

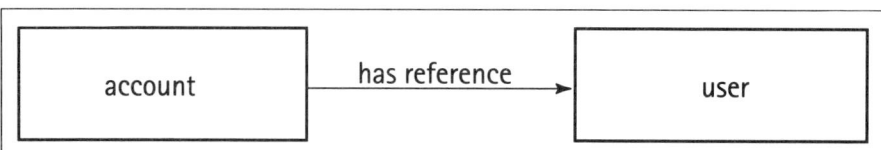

Figure 4-1: An account object holding a reference to a user object

When a class receives an object reference, it can invoke methods on the object. Your account class invokes the _getFields method of your instantiated user object to retrieve information for account maintenance. This allows the user object to change independently of the operations that an account object performs. An account object always queries a user object for the most recent information before performing any actions. This relationship is sometimes referred to as an acquaintance or a casual relationship, because the object's lifetimes and operations aren't bound together. The user object can come from anywhere, and it may change or go away at anytime. Their implementations are also independent and an account object can be passed any object that implements user-like behaviors. Specifically, any class that provided a _getFields method can be used with an account object. The account class is blind to the operations performed by the user object. It only knows of the existence of the correct interface.

This concept can be extended to other situations as well. If you want to store information in flat text files to be used as a database by applications, you create a database object capable of performing insertions and deletions on the various data files. This database object tries to invoke one of two methods on any object reference it is handed: _toStream and _fromStream. These methods simply provide a long stream of data to the database object that either writes it to, or extracts it from the various data files. The database object can use these simple operations to create a whole variety of different data files. The objects passed to the database are responsible for providing the _toStream and _fromStream methods. A person class can write a varying number of fields indicating name, age, address, and so forth on a _toStream operation, and expect the same format string upon invocation of a _fromStream method. Every class can implement these functions in any way, with any data string or format size. The only dependency, or coupling, between a data class and a database class is the _toStream and _fromStream methods. This sort of encapsulation is an excellent example of decoupling reusable functionality from the objects that wish to perform it. This enables you to change the way your database class stores data from flat text files to a relational database management system using SQL without breaking class dependencies. None of the data objects have to change to use the new format.

Your account class uses a similar method when querying a user class. Instead of giving account objects knowledge of /etc/passwd and the capability to glean information straight from that file, you enforce encapsulation by requiring accounts to query user objects for user-related information. Using this method in a distributed environment, you may pass an account object a reference to a user object that doesn't currently have information in /etc/passwd on that particular machine. This method also gives us the needed encapsulation to prevent tight coupling between user and account classes.

TIP The term *reference* is used to indicate when an object knows of another object, but does not contain it. This usage differs from the meaning of "reference" to a C/C++ programmer.

In your shell classes, you can invoke a method on a referenced object by putting the variable representing the reference in brackets. For example, if a class provides a _getReference method that returns the name of a current object reference it holds (as in an account object returning a reference to its user object), you can invoke methods as follows:

```
# set newRef to object instance name
#
newRef=$( object_getReference )
#
# invoke a method using value of newRef
${newRef}_Operation
```

The actual name used by an object instance can constantly change. Therefore, your class must use a variable representing an instantiated object to invoke its methods. In the preceding example, newRef is simply a variable holding the value of a currently instantiated object. The brackets are used to separate the variable newRef from _Operation for the shell.

The account.cls class contains a data member _uRef, which is set to an instance of the user class. This instance, reference, or ObjectID name – whatever you choose to call it – is passed to the account class at construction, but can be changed using the _setOwner method. Also, if your class is handed an account object, you can get a reference to its current user object by calling _getOwner. If this method seems a little confusing now, the example script should help clarify matters. First, Listing 4-4 shows the class account.cls.

Listing 4-4: account.cls

```
#
# account.cls
#
# Methods
#
# _account <user object>
# _createAccount
# _deleteAccount
# _getOwner
# _setOwner
# _writeError <msg>
#
# Data Members
#
# _strOwner
#
# Construction
#
# . account <ref> <user>
#
###########################################################
```

```
_account()         {
  _uRef=$1
  if [[ $? != 0 ]]; then
    _writeError "_account construction failed..."
    return 1
  fi
}

_validUser()           {
  #
  # validate uRef data
  #
  UID=$( ${_uRef}_getFields 3 )
  GID=$( ${_uRef}_getFields 4 )
  if grep ":$UID:" /etc/passwd > /dev/null; then
    _writeError "_createAccount: user ID already in use..."
    return 1
  fi
  if ! grep ":$GID:" /etc/group > /dev/null; then
    _writeError "_createAccount: Group does not exist..."
    return 1
  fi
  #
  # valid user
  #
  return 0
}

_createAccount()          {
  if _validUser; then
    print -u2; "_createAccount: creating account..."
    print $( ${_uRef}_getFields ) > /etc/passwd
    if [ -f /etc/shadow ]; then
      print $( ${_uRef}_getFields 1 )"::" > /etc/shadow
    fi
  fi
  if [ ! -d $( ${_uRef}_getFields 6 ) ]; then
    mkdir $( ${_uRef}_getFields 6 )
    chown $( ${_uRef}_getFields 3 ) $( ${_uRef}_getFields 6 )
    chgrp $( ${_uRef}_getFields 4 ) $( ${_uRef}_getFields 6 )
  fi
}

_deleteAccount()          {
  if ! grep $( ${_uRef}_getFields 1 ) /etc/passwd; then
    _writeError "User not found in /etc/passwd..."
    return 1
  fi
  print -u2; "_deleteAccount: deleting account..."
  print -u2; "_deleteAccount: modifying /etc/passwd..."
  if ! grep -v ^$( ${_uRef}_getFields 1 ) /etc/passwd \
```

```
      >> etc/passwd.new
    then
      _writeError "create new passwd file..."
      return 1
    fi
    if ! mv /etc/passwd.new /etc/passwd; then
      _writeError "mv new passwd file..."
      return 1
    fi
    if [ -f /etc/shadow ]; then
      print -u2; "_deleteAcccount: modifying /etc/shadow..."
      if ! grep -v ^$( ${_uRef}_getFields 1 ) /etc/shadow \
      >> /etc/shadow.new
       then
         _writeError "create new shadow file..."
         return 1
      fi
      if ! mv /etc/shadow.new /etc/shadow; then
        _writeError "mv new shadow file..."
        return 1
      fi
    fi
}

_getOwner()    {
  #
  # This function returns a reference to the user object
  #
  echo $_uRef
}

_setOwner()    {
  _uRef=$1
}

_writeError()    {
  _msg=$1
  print -u2; "$ObjectId failed on: $_msg"
  return
}
```

Many methods in the user class write their output to STDOUT. To contain the results in a variable, the account class executes these method calls in a subprocess contained in parentheses. For example, if you want to set a variable `filestuff` to the output of an `ls -l` command, use the following:

```
$> filestuff=$(ls -l)
```

The variable now contains the output of the command. Likewise, if you need to set a data member to the output of another object's method, you use the same technique:

```
_myVar=$( object_Method )
```

If that object is a reference and not a known instance, use the following:

```
_myVar=$( ${ref}_Method )
```

The script example1.sh, shown in Listing 4-5, depicts the use of references in user and account classes. The script first creates two user instances followed by an account instance. The script then queries the account for the current owner, invokes methods on the returned reference, sets the account owner to a new object, and uses the same process to obtain once again a reference to the account's owner and invoke methods.

Listing 4-5: example1.sh

```
#!/bin/ksh
#
# simple example, account and user interaction
# note: substitute chrisj with valid account on your system!

. user ua chrisj
. user ub root
. account aa ua

print "Calling get owner on account object:"
 #
 # Set temporary variable 'owner' to $aa_strOwner
 # via access function
 #
 owner=$(aa_getOwner)

print "Owner object reference is: $owner"
print "Calling _getFields method on object reference..."
 #
 # Invoke method on referenced object
 #
 ${owner}_getFields

print "Changing account owner..."
 #
 # Give a new user object reference to the account
 # object
 #
 aa_setOwner ub

print -n "New owner on account object is: "
 #
 # Again, set 'owner' to $aa_strOwner via
 # access function
 #
 owner=$(aa_getOwner)
```

```
print $owner
print "Calling _getFields method on object reference..."
#
# Invoke method on referenced object
#
${owner}_getFields
```

The following shows the output of `example1.sh`:

```
Calling get owner on account object:
Owner object reference is: ua
Calling _getFields method on object reference...
chrisj:x:501:500:Chris Jones:/home/chrisj:/bin/ksh
Changing account owner...
New owner on account object is: ub
Calling _getFields method on object reference...
root:x:0:0:root of all evil,,,,:/root:/bin/bash
```

Object Lists

You often need to maintain several references to objects. You may create a collection of server objects of various subtypes and want to contain them in some sort of list. Because all of these objects implement the same interface to accomplish different tasks, you can invoke the same operation on them in a loop. If you have five server objects of different flavors (named after cartoon characters, of course), and want to invoke the `_checkDisks` or similar method, you can do the following:

```
for each in bugs daffy tweety sylvester itchy
do
${each}_checkDisks
done
```

In this approach, each object instance can be of completely different types, as long as they implement the `checkDisks` interface. If these objects represented flavors of UNIX, a different command could be necessary for creating disk statistics for each object. The method `_checkDisks` encapsulates the specifics behind its common published method name. This powerful example of polymorphism enables you to create simple scripts that invoke complex operations on disparate servers. This one aspect of object-orientation is powerful enough to justify applying the paradigm to Korn shell scripting. Shell scripts are most often used for these type of operations.

In many cases, you won't want to line up all of your objects in this fashion. In some instances, you may want to create lists dynamically. Therefore, you can create a list object to maintain lists of object references. While this object can be used for any sort of lists, it provides an operation for invoking a method on every object within the list, so it is particularly geared for managing lists of object references. The `objlist.cls` class provides the methods `_addItem`, `_removeLastItem`, `_getLastItem`, and `_execute`. `Objlist.cls` is a simple stack that does not contain operations for inserting items into the middle of a list. (You will perform this fairly easy task in a later chapter.) For now, the most valuable method in `objlist.cls` is the `_execute` method. To accomplish the results shown in the preceding example, you can create an instance of an object list and add items to it. When the collection is complete, you can call the `_execute` method to perform operations on the list.

```
$> . objlist mylist
$> mylist_addItem bugs
$> mylist_addItem daffy
$> mylist_addItem tweety
$> mylist_addItem sylvester
$> mylist_addItem itchy
$> mylist_execute checkDisks
```

This example has the same effect as the preceding example, but here the list has persistence and can be maintained and updated.

Listing 4-6 shows the code to `objlist.cls`.

Listing 4-6: `objlist.cls`

```
#
# objlist.cls
#
# Methods
#
#   _addItem
#   _getItem
#   _getAllItems
#   _removelastItem
#   _execute <objref> <method> <arguments>
#
# Data Members
#
#   _list[_lastItemUsed]
#
# Construction
#
#   . objlist <ref>
#
##################################################
(( _lastItemUsed=0 ))

_objlist() {
  echo
  # construct, do nothing
}
```

```
_addItem() { ITEM=$1
  _list[_lastItemUsed]=$ITEM
  (( _lastItemUsed = _lastItemUsed+1 ))
}

_getItem() { pos=$1
  echo ${_list[pos]}
}

_getAllItems()      {
  echo ${_list[*]}
}

_removelastItem() {
  _list[_lastItemUsed-1]=" "
  (( _lastItemUsed = _lastItemUsed-1 ))
}

_execute() { method=$1 ARGS=$2
  for object in $( _getAllItems ); do
    ${object}_${method} $ARGS
  done
}
```

Inheritance

As discussed in Chapter 3, inheritance is the direct reuse of code in object-orientated programming. When a class inherits from another class, the parent's code is directly included in the child, allowing for all parent operations to be performed in the name of the child. The logical application of this technique creates a common parent or base-class that contains functionality needed by many classes. You then derive these classes from the parent, reusing the parent's code and also inadvertently maintaining version control and encapsulation. Because the code is inherited at construction, any changes that occur in the parent's implementation are propagated throughout the children.

Implementing inheritance in the Korn shell is rather easy. In your class, simply source the parent class into the current shell process with a dot in the same way you create an object – for inheritance, however, you pass the same arguments passed to your class.

For example, you have a class customer that you want to inherit from class person. You write your class as follows:

```
#
# customer.cls, inherits from person.cls
#
. person $args
#
_customer() {
```

```
  _person $1 $2   # pass name and age
                  # off to person's constructor
_nAcctNumber=$3
}
_getAcctNumber() {
  echo $_nAcctNumber
}
_setAcctNumber() {
  _nAcctNumber=$1
}
```

Always remember to source your super-class object into your class before any function definitions.

The preceding code has two interesting characteristics. First, you invoke a person object into your class with the mysterious parameter $args. This parameter substitutes for $@, which is the shell reserved variable that lists all arguments passed to a script or function. You want to preserve all parameters that are passed to your class customer, and in turn, you want to pass them along to the class person. So, why aren't you using the following code?

```
. person $@
```

The answer derives from the way your classes execute. When shcc takes your .cls file and turns it into an object generating script, it also performs other tasks. First, it inserts a line at the end of the script that calls your constructor function after all the functions have been declared. This insertion allows all of your class's functions to be defined before calling your object's constructor. This enables you to make calls to other methods in your class from your constructor. This insertion also allows for the concept of constructor functions altogether. The only other method initializes all data at the top of the class script, and then defines all of your functions accordingly. Traditionally, a constructor function is used to initialize an object in OO languages. This approach has many advantages and this book seeks to preserves the use of constructor functions in shell objects.

Constructor functions alone do not explain why you can't get inheritance by using the $@ variable, however. The answer: $@ has no persistence. The shell is constantly redefining $@ to be equal to the current string of parameters supplied to either a command or function. When your inherited class is instantiated, it takes $@, calls its constructor, and executes shift to move about the positional parameters constituting $@. Therefore, to maintain persistence in the arguments that are initially passed to your class, copy them to $args. shcc completes this work for you —

just make sure you use this reserved word, $args, when inheriting classes in your shell objects. Also, when you source a super-class into your script, your arguments are automatically passed to the super-class constructor. This subsequent call to the constructor in the subclass custom-tailors what you want handed to the super-class constructor. Because the technique is used in other OO languages like C++, controlling the inheritance in the subclass's constructor function also makes more logical sense.

Be careful using reserved characters within your objects. Most characters are transient and their values are context-dependent. A careful usage of variables such as $@ and positional parameters ($1-9) saves you lots of bug hunting.

The next section develops a class called unixServer. You create a class sunServer that inherits from unixServer and redefines the _reboot and _getWindow operations to perform correctly on Solaris machines. The next section present sunServer.cls first, as it demonstrates inheritance, and later presents its parent, unixServer, because it involves other advanced object concepts. That issue aside, Listing 4-7 shows sunServer.cls demonstrating inheritance as discussed previously.

Listing 4-7: sunServer.cls

```
#
# sunServer.cls
#
# This class inherits from unixServer.cls
#
# Construction
#
# . sunServer <ref> <host/ip address> [ip address]
#
##############################################################

#
# Inheritance must be done outside of constructor
# function
#
. unixServer $args

_sunServer()  {
  _unixServer $1 $2
}

_getWindow()  {
  arguments=${1:-/bin/ksh}
```

```
    eval remsh $_strHost \\
    '/usr/openwin/bin/xterm -display $DISPLAY -e $arguments'
}

_reboot() {
    reboot
}
```

unixServer Class

This entire book focuses on applying the shell object concepts to system configuration and management tasks. Scripting is widely used for these types of applications, and this area can also take advantage of object-orientation. For now, this section introduces the first iteration of the unixServer class—the class which represents servers on a network. This class provides operations on UNIX servers such as monitoring disk space and retrieving statistics for you. This version of the class is not distributed, but you can create a whole collection of objects with the class to represent the different machines distributed across your network.

Remote Machine Operation Commands

This version of unixServer uses the `r-utilities`. The `r-utilities` are a collection of commands that perform operations on remote machines. Although a bit of authentication overhead must be configured prior to using the command `remsh` (or `rsh`), many networks have these utilities readily available to users. If you're not familiar with the `remsh` command, you should give it a try (use `rsh` if your system doesn't have `remsh`):

```
remsh <remoteserver> uptime
```

The preceding code shows you the `uptime` on the remote machine you specified as <remoteserver>. If you don't have authentication set up, you might have received this rather disappointing output:

```
permission denied.
```

Three conditions are necessary for you to `remsh` into another network host. First, you must have an account under the same ID (on the remote machine). Second, you must have a file called `.rhosts` in your home directory on the remote server. This directory should contain a list of the servers from which you are allowed to `remsh`. If you usually work from the same workstation, you can get by with just putting your workstation's hostname in the file as follows:

```
chrisj  itchy
```

The first field is your login name, while the second field is the name of your workstation. You should change this file's permission to be readable only by you, as follows:

```
chmod 400 .rhosts
```

Lastly, the remote machine must be able to resolve your hostname; that is, if you are attempting to `remsh` into the host `abu` from `milhouse`, `abu` needs to know the identity of `milhouse`.

Getting the `rutilities` to work can be frustrating. Remember the three main rules: first, you must have an account under the same name on the remote machine; second, the remote machine must know the host from which you're coming (for example, an entry in /etc/hosts or DNS); third, you must have a file called `.rhosts` in your remote home directory that indicates you're allowed to perform remote operations.

Apart from these three constraints, the only other hindrance to using `remsh` is if your server administrator has removed the capability from your machines for security reasons. If so, perhaps you can do some social engineering to get it temporarily reinstated. Also, if you have a PC, you can run Linux (an excellent flavor of UNIX) and be your own server administrator. Because this last idea is completely under your control, it may be the best solution.

The unixServer class implementation uses `remsh` to execute commands on remote machines to query statistics. Subclasses of this class are intended to inherit and redefine functions with platform-specific code. This enables you to use your unixServer objects to easily create network-wide scripts that work in a similar manner, regardless of platforms. In addition to providing this functionality, the class unixServer implements some object concepts this book has not yet discussed.

Composition

The unixServer class actually contains other objects. A preceding section demonstrated how objects can know of other objects by name, and invoke methods upon those objects. In that case, the lives of the objects are not necessarily intertwined, and each object is free to go its separate way. The composition used here departs from that approach in several key ways. First, the unixServer class instantiates disk objects as it needs them. The lifetime of these disk objects is controlled by the lifetime of the server object that owns them. If configurations have changed and a file system is removed, the server object may drop a disk or two.

Second, these disk objects are not inherited, not referenced, and not publicly known or available. Although you can call a method on a disk object contained within a server object, their implementation is private and their existence is encapsulated behind the server object's published methods: `_getDiskUsage` and `_showDiskUsage`.

These methods use an object list to iterate through the server's disk objects, executing statistics-gathering methods on the disks. When you instantiate a unixServer object, you issue the `set` command to examine the server's current data members. For the first time, you see a composite object relationship in the shell. For example, a disk object instantiated at `disk1` may have a method of `_getKbAvail`. If you have instantiated an instance of `unixServer.cls` as `server1`, you can invoke an operation on the contained object in the following way:

```
server1_disk1_getKbAvail
```

This sort of technique for invoking methods on object-contained objects is used in other languages as well.

The following shows the output of the `set` or `env` command on a unixServer instantiation:

```
MyServer_dRef0_nCapacity=47%
MyServer_dRef0_nKbAvail=226483
MyServer_dRef0_nKbSize=452805
MyServer_dRef0_nKbUsed=202937
MyServer_dRef0_strMount=/
MyServer_dRef0_strName=/dev/hda2
MyServer_dRef1_nCapacity=59%
MyServer_dRef1_nKbAvail=801312
MyServer_dRef1_nKbSize=1947168
MyServer_dRef1_nKbUsed=1145856
MyServer_dRef1_strMount=/uranus
MyServer_dRef1_strName=/dev/hda1
MyServer_host=probing
MyServer_hostinfo=host.inf
MyServer_imp=unixServer
```

In your unixServer class, you won't be explicitly invoking operations on the contained disk objects. The actual names of the disk object instances won't be known until runtime, because every server to which your class is applied may have different disk configurations. Given this fact, your collection of disk objects is created dynamically at object instantiation, and placed into an object list. The object list class (see `objlist.cls`) holds all of a unixServer's disk objects, and has the capability to invoke operations upon them using the `objlist.cls?s _execute` method. Listing 4-8 shows the `unixServer.cls` implementation.

Listing 4-8: `unixServer.cls`

```
#
# unixServer.cls
#
# Methods
#
#   _getUsers
#   _getDiskUsage
#   _showDiskUsage
#   _getLoad
#   _getWindow
#   _reboot
#
# Data Members
#
#   string      _strHost
#   string      _strIP
#   integer     _nUsers
#   integer     _nLavg
#   objlist     _oDiskList
#   disk        _oDref
#
# Construction
#
#   . unixststem <ref> <hostname/ip address> [ip address]
#
################################################################

_unixServer() {
  if [ "$1" = "" ]; then
    return 1
  fi
  _strHost=$1
  _strIP=${2:-}
  #
  # If remote shell command is specified, use it
  _strRemsh=${_strRemsh:-remsh}
}

_getUsers() {
  _nUsers=$($_strRemsh $_strHost 'w|wc -l')
  ## write it to STDOUT, for now
  echo $_nUsers
}
_createDiskObjects() {
  #
  # shift out header information
  shift 7;
  #
  # create array with disk information
  set -A devArry $@
  ((c=0))
  #
```

Chapter 4: Using Shell Objects 103

```
   # create objects in loop
   #
   while (( c < ${#devArry[*]} ))
   do
      #
      # create a disk object
      #
      . disk _oDref${c} ${devArry[c]} ${devArry[c+1]} \
${devArry[c+2]} ${devArry[c+3]} ${devArry[c+4]} \
${devArry[c+5]}
      #
      # add to object list
      #
      _oDiskList_addItem _oDref${c}
      ((c=c+6))
   done
}

_getDiskUsage()  {
   if (( $# < 2 )); then
      _nHighDisk=${1:-90}
      _getDiskUsage $($_strRemsh $_strHost 'bdf||df -k' \
2>/dev/null)
   else
      _DeviceArgs=$@
      #
      # create a list object for devices
      #
      . objlist _oDiskList
      ## now You have arguments
      _createDiskObjects $_DeviceArgs
      _nTotalDevs=$x
   fi
}

_showDiskUsage()  {
   #
   # Call _getFullList on disk object array
   #
   _oDiskList_execute getFullList
}

_getLoad()  {
   LoadString=$($_strRemsh $_strHost 'uptime')
   LoadString=${LoadString##*:}
   ## write to STDOUT, for now
   echo $LoadString
   _nLavg=${LoadString%%,*}
}

_getWindow()  {
   arguments=${1:-"/bin/ksh"}
   eval $_strRemsh $_strHost \\
   '/usr/bin/X11/xterm -display $DISPLAY -exec $arguments'
```

```
}

_reboot() {
  shutdown -r now
}
```

By keeping the functionality of disk operations within disk objects, you insulate your unixServer class from any changes in disk object operations. If you had to give the unixServer class knowledge of how to obtain disk statistics itself, it would be a more rigid and less extensible object. These two classes are only coupled by the unixServer's dependency on disk objects implementing a method called _getPercentUsed or _getKbAvail. The loose coupling is advantageous to both classes and allows their implementations to be changed quite easily, thus allowing them to be adapted to other environments.

Class Factories

The final player in this version of the unixServer class arrangement is servFactory.cls. This class uses a factory technique to implement different subtypes of the class unixServer. Because you aren't yet using a distributed environment of UNIX objects, you will try to provide some of the same benefits that distribution would provide in your local classes.

EXAMINING DISTRIBUTED ADVANTAGES

Toward the end of this book, you adapt many of the objects you've created into a distributed systems management application. This application has objects representing UNIX servers distributed to the machines they represent. Likewise, these remote locations also contain the other objects associated with your application.

This architecture enables total encapsulation from the remote machine's details. All operations on remote machines are done through the unixServer's class interface. The object that sports this interface may implement them in any way necessary. Given this fact, the distributed servers themselves may be of any platform and can actually be non-UNIX machines, provided they have the right communication and implementation software installed.

Your object request broker (ORB) is the primary means of communication between your distributed objects and the pieces of distributed code that want to operate with them. The object request broker has a similar architecture to CORBA/IIOP, but is far less complex as it only deals with shell objects. Basically, object request brokers are distributed to the different servers that hold objects. These brokers listen for requests for object references, and upon receiving one, return an interface definition back to the caller. The client proxy code you write translates these interface definitions into a skeleton object that exists on the client side. This skeleton object looks and feels just like the distributed one, and the client codes with it just as though it were coding with a local object, because the proxy is actually local. The proxy simply forwards all method invocations off to the implementing server and then listens for return results.

The implementing server on the other side of the request broker holds persistent and unique object instances for each client request. This architecture affords the most flexibility, as it requires you to program towards an interface and not an implementation. As long as the distributed objects adhere to the interface definitions, the implementation can change without regard to the clients.

This approach is ideal, but it is not what you have in this chapter!

FINDING LOCAL SOLUTIONS

The problem with instantiating instances of the unixServer class is that you have to know the type of remote system to instantiate the right subclass. For example, if the remote server is running Solaris, you need to create a local sunServer object to invoke methods on that machine. If the remote server is running Linux, you just use the unixServer object or a custom-tailored linuxServer object. Ideally, you would create subtypes to represent all of the varied flavors of UNIX on your network.

How can you create client code that doesn't have to know the remote machine's flavor of UNIX? The answer: use a class factory. A class factory decouples client code from having to instantiate a particular concrete class.

In your scenario, if you have several different subtype of the same class and don't want to sort out which object belongs to which class in your code, you could use this technique (so, of course, you will!). Because all remote servers are represented with local objects, the client machine must know the remote system's type. Instead of having to know every time you instantiate an object, you create a simple list and use it repeatedly.

This list, called `host.inf` in some of the examples, contains host names to OS mappings in a simple fashion, `hostname:OS`:

```
itchy:Linux
scratchy:SunOS
abu:HP-UX
wiggum:SunOS
milhouse:UNIX
```

This list is easy to maintain, and in many cases, you can create it once and forget about it for months. The class `servFactory.cls` uses this class to instantiate the correct subtype of unixServer. You instantiate server objects with this class in exactly the same way you instantiate server objects with the unixServer class:

```
. servFactory MyServer wiggum
```

In this case, however, servFactory turns around and looks up wiggum in host.inf. Upon seeing that wiggum is of type SunOS, servFactory implements an instance of sunServer on your behalf with all of the original arguments you placed.

This implementation relieves you of sorting out which machine is which in your scripts. You can treat every machine on your network as an instance of servFactory, and simply code with the provided interface. Figure 4-2 shows the relationships.

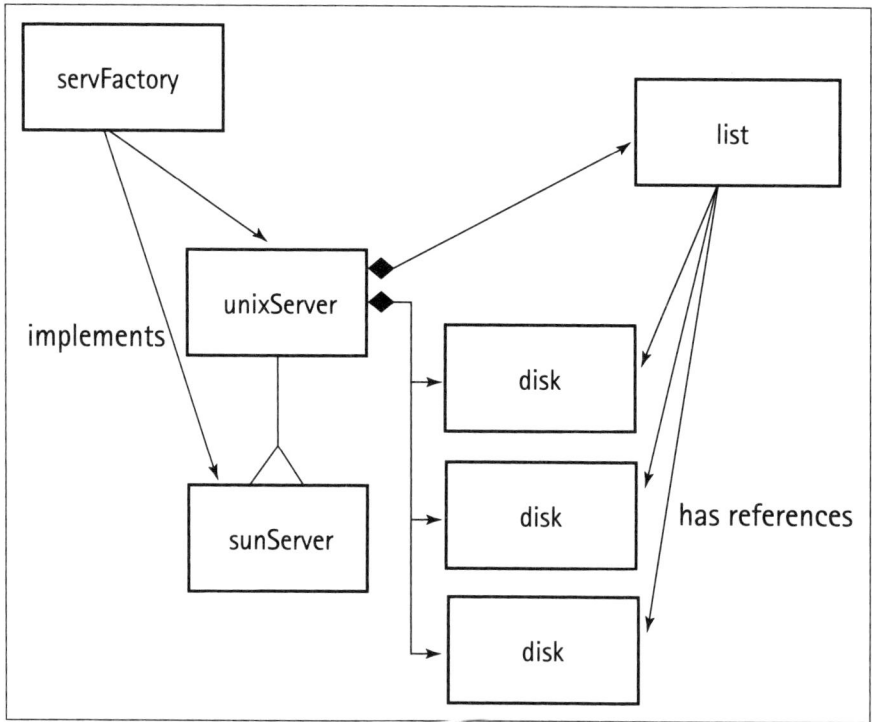

Figure 4-2: The relationship between servFactory, unixServer, disk, and list

The code to servFactory.cls is shown in Listing 4-9.

Listing 4-9: servFactory.cls

```
#
# servFactory.cls
#
# Implements correct subclass of unixServer.cls based
# on hostname provided. Hides knowledge of OS type from
# client code.
#
```

```
# Methods
#
# _servFactory   <hostname>
#
# Data Members
#
# _strHostinfo   filename of host-to-OS mapping
#
# Construction
#
# . servFactory <ref> <hostname>
#
########################################################################

_servFactory() {
  case $(uname) in        ## Some systems use rsh
    *inux)                ## others remsh...
      _strRemsh=rsh   ;;  ## (this is for the client,
  esac                    ## not the remote server...)
  _host=$1
  _IP=$2
  #
  # establish default hostinfo file
  _hostinfo="host.inf"
  #
  # retrieve host-to-OS mapping
  if ! mapping=$(grep $_host $_hostinfo); then
    mapping="UNIX"
  fi
  case ${mapping#*:} in
    SunOS)
      _imp=sunServer ;;
    HP-UX)
      _imp=hpServer  ;;
    Linux)
      _imp=unixServer ;;
    *)
      _imp=unixServer ;;
  esac
  #
  # implement object
  . $_imp $ObjectId $_host $_IP
}
```

Now, you create a simple script that attempts to instantiate a version of servFactory, and then call upon the unixServer methods that you receive back to check on disk usage. You need either to create a file called `host.inf` with your `hostname:OS` entry, or accept the default unixServer implementation that servFactory provides if it cannot resolve the hostname. Listing 4-10 shows `example2.sh`.

Listing 4-10: example2.sh

```
#!/bin/ksh
#
# A simple example to demonstrate aggregate objects
#

# instantiate a server object
# - substitute the name of your server here
# - also, this version of unixServer uses rsh, or remsh
#   so you need to have the authentication necessary
#   for using the "r" utilities
#
. servFactory MyServer probing

print "Calling _getDiskUsage..."
MyServer_getDiskUsage

print "Calling _showDiskUsage..."
MyServer_showDiskUsage
```

If all goes well, your output should be similar to the following:

```
Calling _getDiskUsage...

Calling _showDiskUsage...
Device: /dev/hda2 Mounted At: / Percent Used:47%
Device: /dev/hda1 Mounted At: /uranus Percent Used:59%
```

USING SERVFACTORY

The preceding examples are too simplistic and don't really demonstrate the full power of the classes and relationships developed thus far.

You should experiment with these objects from the command line and get a feel for their capabilities and strengths. The key to understanding the advantages of object containment is understanding its different capabilities. You can call any method of any contained object by referencing the object's name through its parent. An `objlist` instance belonging to unixServer can have its methods invoked as follows:

```
unixServer_objlist_getAllItems
```

You can also call all of the contained objects data members using the same `object_object_property` type expressions. You should try experimenting further with these objects, and then try applying them in solving problems. Some more examples of using `servFactory.cls` from the command line follow:

```
$> . servFactory server1 localhost

$> server1_getDiskUsage

$> server1_oDiskList_getAllItems
server1_oDref0 server1_oDref6 server1_oDref12

$> server1_oDref6_getKbAvail
763241

$> server1_oDref0_getPercentUsed
67%

$> print $server1_oDref12_strName
/dev/hdc
```

The preceding examples show how to use an embedded object's data members and methods through its parent.

Summary

Although this chapter is your first exposure to using classes to complete tasks, it also introduces some new and complicated object relationships. These relationships of object references, inheritance, and composition may be easy to grasp, but hard to apply at first. You may need some time to code and experiment in order to begin seeing the power of these relationships. This book attempts to cover a lot of ground — as a result, these topics are explained rather quickly. While this chapter should be enough for you to understand logistics and begin to see advantages, the greater part of a book could be spent describing these concepts.

The next chapter discusses the means for objects to intercommunicate, as well as the different mechanisms provided by the UNIX OS. These topics are followed by harnessing the power of Java API calls that don't have any representation from the shell. The next chapter enables you to create shell commands for sockets, message queues, and any other API you want to use — bringing you closer to creating distributed applications.

Chapter 5

Object Communication

IN THIS CHAPTER

- ◆ Understanding how messaging works
- ◆ Examining object to object communication
- ◆ Creating a message receiver
- ◆ Carrying out interprocess communication
- ◆ Using named pipes to communicate across shell processes

THUS FAR, THIS book has described how object-based programming differs from traditional, procedural-style programming. You've examined the various features of classes, the power of inheritance and polymorphism, and seen how objects' abstract processes and data encapsulate their properties behind distinct, reusable interfaces.

The concept of object communication is another departure from procedural programming in OOP. Objects don't always simply call each other's subroutines. Although an object may call another object's function, the encapsulation and distinction in place between objects serves to strengthen this object-centric view, which encourages abstraction and detachment.

Object-based programming is well-suited to what is commonly referred to as event-driven programming. By using objects instead of a long string of procedural commands, you give yourself the chance to model an application after the systems it intends to represent. In the real world, events happen. Machines crash, processes fail, and users end telnet sessions without typing `exit`. (Gasp!) By more closely modeling the systems that objects represent, event-driven techniques can provide great benefits to the object-oriented programmer. Events allow a program or dynamic system to respond to changes in the environment, and not necessarily follow a series of clearly linear instructions. Events allow for dynamic changes that affect systems as a whole.

Event-based programming is a means of coupling objects to events — instead of other objects — to complete tasks. As in everything demonstrated so far, objects tend to encapsulate the dynamic aspects of a system, allowing them to work in as many situations as possible. In this case, unforeseen changes in the environment are dynamic, and your objects should be able to deal with them in a variety of ways.

112 UNIX Shell Objects

One key aspect of event-based programming is not tying any particular object to the responsibility of handling an event. More than one object can register itself to handle an event. Likewise, all objects can ignore any event they please. Subclasses can pass an event off to their parent. The idea is that the events are bound to the objects, and the objects aren't bound to the events. This approach enables you with the flexibility of changing a system without affecting the objects involved.

Messages

Apart from all this nifty talk about mysterious messages bringing news of their world to objects, you may be wondering: Just how does messaging work?

Many different methods can implement a messaging system. As in all programming, you have to consider the scope of your communication. Will it cross process boundaries? Will it cross machine boundaries? If these are true, then special programming techniques need to be used. The following examples demonstrate both inprocess communication and interprocess communication. You will examine many different means of interprocess communication.

The first solution implements a message-handling object. This object is passed event messages and routes them to the particular object that is supposed to handle the message. Furthermore, the receiving object can do whatever it wants with the message, including passing it off to another object or its parent. Figure 5-1 shows a message-handling scheme. In this figure, messages that are raised are mapped to a receiving object.

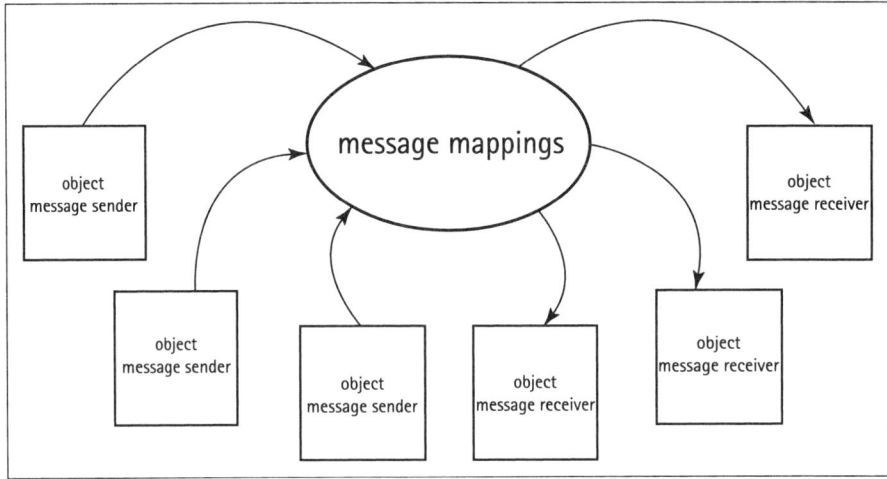

Figure 5-1: A message handling scheme

Several mechanisms exist for message handling. In the beginning, you use a reference to a central message handler to signal our events. You also register objects as receivers with the message handler, which works well for inprocess communication. The example branches out to use a named-pipe as a means of communicating across process boundaries. You also touch on different API level means of interprocess communication that aren't directly available to the shell.

Eventually, in your distributed application, you extrapolate the messaging technique into a larger context of networked servers.

Object to Object Communication

The simplest means of communication between objects is for one to invoke the methods of another, or for an application to decide when to invoke object methods based on the current state of the application. In the Chapter 4 examples, an account object sends a user object a _getFields message when it wishes to retrieve information. This approach is a tightly-coupled message implementation as the receiver and sender are intimately bound together. This implementation is acceptable in this situation; by design, accounts are entirely dependent on users and cannot exist without a reference to a user object.

While you may not consider an account's action on a user reference to be a message, this description is exactly the case. By viewing objects as encapsulated, detached, self-sufficient entities that operate upon themselves and interact with others, the notion that every interaction with an object is equivalent to sending a message to an object is real. The following code shows a tightly-coupled communication arrangement:

```
_checkDisk() {
  dRef=$1
  if (( $( ${dRef}_getPercentUsed ) > 90 )); then
    admin_alert "$(${dRef}_getName) is nearing capacity"
fi
}
```

In the preceding example, a class method is entirely dependent on two criteria: on being passed a reference to a disk object implementing _getPercentUsed; and an instantiated object named admin that supports an operation _alert, supposedly sending a message to the right place. This class is not that flexible. Dependencies on other objects should only exist when the objects are so closely bound together that one cannot exist without the other. The instantiated admin object is very rigid. Not only do you need to have an admin object in existence, you have to be able to reference it through the ID admin.

The next example shows the message removed from a class implementation and placed in the hands of a chunk of application code. After apparently instantiating a disk object, the code checks its available space, and sends an alert via an instantiated `admin` object. The explicit object instances are okay because they have been created within this application, but you still have a message explicitly bound to a receiver.

```
if (( $( oDref0_getPercentUsed ) > 90 )); then
fi
```

The generated message is okay, but coding in this way doesn't allow for that much flexibility. You've taken the message handling away from the class, and placed it in the hands of application code. This approach is fine, but you still have a hard-coded association for the message sender and the message receiver.

You want to create your objects to be able to signal messages, and to be able to respond messages. You want to avoid linking senders and receivers together, however. Of the many methods to achieve this approach, some methods take advantage of interprocess communication, while others take advantage of intermachine communication. Regardless of the scope of the messaging environment, the same structure can be used.

Events

While maintaining this object-centric view, you can refer to messages interchangeably as events. These events may occur in our system, or happen to the environment in which our application is running. Objects can handle or choose not to handle these events. The events can be forwarded to other objects, or not even handled at all. Your goal is to decouple sender and receiver.

Your first example is probably the simplest means of routing messages. If you've ever tried to program in Visual C++ for Windows, you may be familiar with the idea of message mapping. Message mapping is a feature provided to your programs to allow them to interface with the operating system and graphical user interface (GUI) events. In your Visual C++ program, you can pick and choose various events and then map them to a particular function within your class. You don't need to worry about how the event is generated – just make sure that you've set up your function to be a receiver of the message.

Your first message-handling object will be of a similar nature. It will achieve the goal of decoupling sender and receiver for greater flexibility. You'll create a message-handling class `msgHandler.cls` that takes care of mapping events to receivers. Any object with a reference to the message handler can raise an event, and the handler will forward the signal to the correct object, if it has a handler at all.

This solution works fine as is, for in-process applications; that is, as long as your objects exist in the same program or process space, they can use a message-handling object. You have flexibility in configuring the message mapping – even while

Chapter 5: Object Communication

the program is in execution. The classes themselves are decoupled from the receiving of messages or routing a message to the appropriate receiver, which allows for greater reuse of code.

As one trade-off to this approach, your application must instantiate a message-handling object, or the classes that depend on it for events won't be able to communicate. This instantiation isn't hard to insure, and mirrors the inclusion of a library such as events.h into your C++ program.

Updating the objlist Class

Before presenting the msgHandling.cls class, you need to update the objlist.cls class presented in the last chapter. You've changed the functionality to incorporate a _removeItem method that removes an individual element and renumbers the remaining events in sequence, thus adding flexibility in maintaining lists. The main change is that the _removeLastItem method has been replaced by a _removeItem method:

```
_removeItem() {
      Item=$1
      _list[Item]=""
      (( _lastItemUsed = _lastItemUsed-1 ))
      set -A _list $( _getAllItems )
}
```

This function sets the item that needs to be deleted to null, and then resets the internal array _list with new contents – thus realigning the element numbers.

You still haven't added a handy InsertItem method into the objlist class. Let's give it a try.

Listing 5-1 shows the modified version of objlist.cls.

Listing 5-1: objlist.cls

```
##############################################################
#
# objlist.cls - mod from Chp 4 to include per item removal
#
# Version Info:
# $Id: objlist.cls,v 1.4 1998/02/06 07:20:42 chrisj Exp $
# $Log: objlist.cls,v $
# Revision 1.4  1998/02/06 07:20:42  chrisj
```

```
#
# ----------------------------
#
# Methods
#
#_addItem
#_getItem
#_getAllItems
#_removeItem
#_execute <objref> <method> <arguments>
#
# Data Members
#
#_list[_lastItemUsed]
#
# Construction
#
#. objlist <ref>
#
###################################################################

_objlist()   {
 (( _lastItemUsed=0 ))
}

_addItem() { Item=$1
        _list[_lastItemUsed]=$Item
        (( _lastItemUsed = _lastItemUsed+1))
}

_getItem() { pos=$1
        echo ${_list[pos]}
}

_getAllItems()    {
 echo ${_list[*]}
}

_removeItem()  {
 Item=$1
 _list[Item]=" "
        (( _lastItemUsed = _lastItemUsed-1))
 set -A _list $( _getAllItems )
}

_execute() { method=$1 ARGS=$2
        for object in $( _getAllItems); do
                ${object}_${method} $ARGS
        done
}
```

Creating the msgHandler Class

The `msgHandler` class consists of a few simple functions and two list objects. The functions are responsible for adding an event-to-object mapping, deleting an event-to-object mapping, retrieving a list of handled events, and managing a function for raising an event to the attention of the message handler. The data members are the two list objects constituting messages and handlers, as shown in Listing 5-2.

Listing 5-2: `msgHandler.cls`

```
########################################################################
#
# msgHandler.cls - Shell Objects Message Handling
# $Id: msgHandler.cls,v 1.2 1998/02/06 07:16:25 chrisj Exp $
# $Log: msgHandler.cls,v $
# Revision 1.2  1998/02/06 07:16:25  chrisj
#
# ----------------------------
#
# Methods
# _msgHandler - constructor
# _addHandler - register new message-to-object mapping
# _deleteHandler - remove message-to-object mapping
# _getEvents - list all mappings
# _raise - signal an event
#
# Data Members
# nEvts - number of events registered
# events - list object of events
# handler - list object of handlers
#
########################################################################

_msgHandler() {
 ((nEvts=-1))
 #
 # env variable EVENTHANDLER will
 # provide reference for other objects
 #
 EVENTHANDLER=$ObjectId
 . objlist events
 . objlist handlers
}

_addHandler() {
 ((nEvts=nEvts+1))
 #
 # event name is first param
 #
 events_addItem $1
 #
 # handling object is second param
```

```
#
handlers_addItem $2
}

_deleteHandler()    {
 evt=$1
 ((c=0))
 while (( c <= nEvts ))
 do
        if [[ $(events_getItem $c) = "$evt" ]]; then
                events_removeItem $c
                handlers_removeItem $c
        fi
        ((c=c+1))
 done
}

_getEvents()   {
 events_getAllItems
 handlers_getAllItems
}

_raise()     {
 evt=$1
 sigObj=$2
 ((cnt=0))
 for obj in $(events_getAllItems)
 do
        if [[ "$obj" = "$evt" ]];  then
                hndlr=$(handlers_getItem $cnt)
                $hndlr $sigObj
        fi
        (( cnt = cnt + 1 ))
 done
}
```

You'll build this class with an application that has a couple of representative classes. Namely, a `controller`, `system`, and `newsystem` class will communicate through a message object. Because this is local to a process, any object needing to raise events can get a reference to the only message-handling object through the value of an environment variable $EVENTHANDLER. When a `msgHandler` is instantiated, it sets this variable to be equal to its current instantiation ID. Other classes within the application can get the reference through this variable.

Once a class has a reference to the `msgHandler` instance, it can begin raising events. The application designer must map raised events to receiver objects by calling the `msgHandler_addHandler` method. This method takes an event name and a receiver object method as a parameter. For example, if you want an object named `admin` to invoke its alert method whenever a critical event is raised, use the following:

```
msgHandler_addHandler critical admin_alert
```

Any object that subsequently raised a critical event has an `admin_alert` operation invoked with a reference to the invokee as a parameter. This technique moves event handling from the class level to the application level. It also can be reconfigured at runtime by deleting the handler and adding a new mapping, as follows:

```
msgHandler_deleteHandler critical
msgHandler_addHandler critical system_Shutdown
```

Now all critical events are handled by a `system` object's `shutdown` method. This is similar to how a message mapping might occur in Windows – although in Windows, the events are handled by the "message pump."

If you plan on using messaging extensively in your programs, you may want to enhance this scheme by creating an object to represent the message itself. Such an object could be easily passed across the network to enable distributed messaging (see KSOP in Chapter 8).

Demonstrating Messaging with Classes

Your example program, `example1.sh`, uses three classes to demonstrate messaging.

CONTROLLER CLASS

The first class, controller, obtains a reference to the `msgHandler` via the `EVENTHANDLER` variable, and subsequently begins raising critical and operational events. The application must add handlers for these messages, as shown in Listing 5-3.

Listing 5-3: `controller.cls`

```
######################################################################
#
# controller.cls
# $Id: controller.cls,v 1.1 1998/02/06 07:23:21 chrisj Exp $
# $Log: controller.cls,v $
# Revision 1.1  1998/02/06 07:23:21  chrisj
#
# -----------------------------
# Demonstration class for event handling
#
######################################################################
_controller() {
  #
  # Obtain reference to central event handling object
```

```
    if [[ ! -n $EVENTHANDLER ]]; then
          print -u2 "_controller: need event handler"
          return 1
    fi
    evtH=$EVENTHANDLER
    _nCtrlState=1
}
_isCritical() {
 ${evtH}_raise critical
}

_isOperational()     {
 ${evtH}_raise operational
}

_doControl()  {
  if (( _nCtrlState != 1 )); then
        _isCritical
  else
        _isOperational
  fi
}
```

SYSTEM CLASS

The second class, system, simply shuts the system down, or proceeds normally if everything is okay, as shown in Listing 5-4.

Listing 5-4: system.cls

```
##################################################################
#
# systems.cls
# $Id: system.cls,v 1.1 1998/02/06 07:22:51 chrisj Exp $
# $Log: system.cls,v $
# Revision 1.1  1998/02/06 07:22:51   chrisj
#
# -----------------------------
# Demonstration class for event handling
#
##################################################################

_system()      {
 echo "System started..."
}
_doShutdown() {
 echo "** SYSTEM SHUTTING DOWN **"
}
_doWork()      {
 echo "System status normal"
}
```

NEWSYS CLASS

The third class, newsys, is simply a replacement for system.cls to demonstrate that mappings can be changed while the program is running, as shown in Listing 5-5.

Listing 5-5: newsys.cls

```
##################################################################
#
# newsys.cls
# $Id: newsys.cls,v 1.1 1998/02/06 07:28:20 chrisj Exp $
# $Log: newsys.cls,v $
# Revision 1.1  1998/02/06 07:28:20  chrisj
#
# -----------------------------
# Demonstration class for event handling
#
##################################################################

_newsys()    {
 print "New system added..."
}
_doShutdown() {
 print "** NEW SYSTEM SHUTTING DOWN **"
}
```

This relationship enables you to code your class without regard for the messages they may receive, or who may respond to the messages they send. The only requirement is that an application instantiate a message handler for your objects to use. The point of dependency is that any class wishing to raise events must have a reference to the msgHandler. The application must subsequently map messages to instantiated objects to handle, as shown in Figure 5-2.

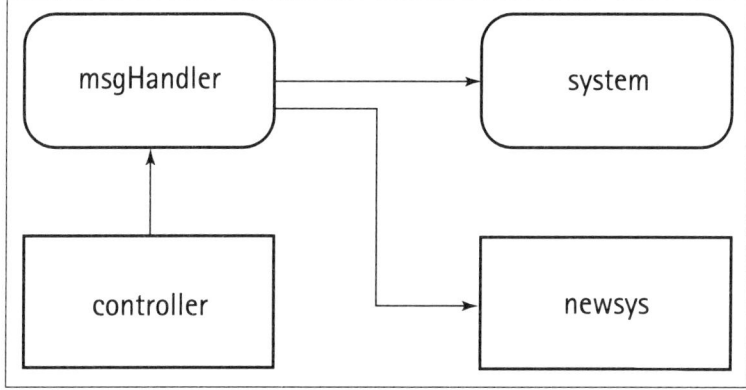

Figure 5-2: The relationships between messaging classes

Critical and Operational Events Example

The example program `example1.sh` simulates an environment where a controller controls the operations of various systems by raising critical and operational events. These events are then mapped by the application to one system, and then another system, as shown in Listing 5-6.

Listing 5-6: `example1.sh`

```ksh
#!/bin/ksh
######################################################################
# example1.sh
#
# Demonstrate use of simple message handling through a centralized
# messaging object
######################################################################

#
# instantiate a message object
  . msgHandler msg

#
# bring in class components
  . system sys
  . controller ctrl
  . newsys sys2

#
# configure message mapping
  msg_addHandler critical sys_doShutdown
  msg_addHandler operational sys_doWork

#
# begin system interactions
  ctrl_doControl
  sleep 1
  ctrl_doControl
  sleep 1
#
# change system state
  print "Changing System state..."
  ctrl_nCtrlState=2
  sleep 1
  ctrl_doControl
#
# change messaging arrangement
  msg_deleteHandler critical sys_doShutdown
  msg_addHandler critical sys2_doShutdown
```

```
#
# new system interactions
 ctrl_nCtrlState=1
 ctrl_doControl
 sleep 1
 ctrl_doControl
 sleep 1
 print "Changing System state..."
 ctrl_nCtrlState=2
 sleep 1
 ctrl_doControl
```

Event Handling Example

One way to use events successfully creates a series of relevant events and messages for your problem domain. In a windowing system, events can be user clicks and button actions. The context of the buttons and their location in the interface can determine their meaning. (Is OK on a Save dialog? Or a Load dialog?) The placement and resizing of windows and their scrollbars, menus, and buttons are good candidates for messages and events, thus allowing these GUI components to be used in a greater variety of situations. In a distributed network management system, good candidates may include the execution of critical applications, systems availability, and network and hardware status. When you've properly addressed the type of events within your system, you can begin developing your scheme for handling them.

In this section, you create a generic message receiver, signal.cls. This class adds to the previous example in that it can be used to handle the events of any object. If you don't have an exact corresponding action for the event, you can map events to signal.cls as a good default class.

signal.cls has one method, _alrtRcpnt, which calls _getState on the object that generates the message. The state information is then dumped into a log file, dated, and mailed to root (or anyone else relevant). This sequence requires that your objects implement a simple _getState method to provide signal.cls with proper information.

The two classes involved in this scheme, unixServer.cls and disk.cls, have been slightly modified from their initial debut. They both now incorporate a simple _getState method to dump their internal data, and a _this variable that holds the current instantiation ID of the object or a reference to itself. The _this data member can be used when your class's internal method needs to return or obtain a reference to the ID under which it's currently instantiated. For example, _getState searches through the environment variables of the current shell process for its particular class instantiation's data members. Your class cannot know the instantiated object ID prior to run time.

```
_getState()    {
  set | grep ^$_this
}
```

TIP The getState method and this property are very useful and should be incorporated into most objects you create. You may want to develop a broad, reusable base class that incorporates these methods and properties as well as necessary messaging functions.

When you develop your classes, you often find that you need a reference to the current object. When creating classes with shcc, you frequently use the variable ObjectId to reference the current object. This approach is fine, but won't be reliable among many different instantiated objects. The context in which you reference ObjectId returns different results, and in many cases only reflects the ID of the most recently instantiated class. The _this identifier solves this problem as it is initialized at construction, and is owned by the object that created it.

Improving the disk Class

The updated version of disk.cls is shown in Listing 5-7 and the CD-ROM.

Listing 5-7: disk.cls

```
################################################################
#
# disk.cls
#
# $Id: disk.cls,v 1.2 1998/02/07 06:28:39 chrisj Exp $
# $Log: disk.cls,v $
# Revision 1.2  1998/02/07 06:28:39   chrisj
# Added _getState function
#
# -----------------------------
#
# Methods
#   _disk - constructor
#   _getName
#   _getPercentUsed
#   _getKbSize
#   _getKbUsed
#   _getKbAvail
#   _getMount
#   _getFullList
#   _getState
```

```
#
# Data Members
#
#   _strName=$1
#   _nKbSize=$2
#   _nKbUsed=$3
#   _nKbAvail=$4
#   _nCapacity=$5
#   _strMount=$6
#
######################################################################

_disk(){
 if (( $# < 4 )); then
        print "Unable to construct disk object."
        return 1
 fi
 _strName=$1
 _nKbSize=$2
 _nKbUsed=$3
 _nKbAvail=$4
 _nCapacity=$5
 _strMount=$6
 _this=$ObjectId
}
_getName()     {
 echo $_strName
}
_getPercentUsed()    {
 echo $_nCapacity
}
_getKbSize()  {
 echo $_nKbSize
}
_getKbUsed()  {
 echo $_nKbUsed
}
_getKbAvail() {
 echo $_nKbAvail
}
_getMount()    {
 echo $_strMount
}
_getFullList(){
 print -n "Device: $_strName Mounted At: $_strMount"
 print " Percent Used:"$_nCapacity
}

_getState()    {
 set | grep ^$_this
}
```

This class has been improved with the addition of the _getState function and the _this data member. You may consider incorporating this class into all shell objects that you develop. The _getState function can be extremely useful in debugging and can also be modified to support serialization, which is used to store an object to disk or transport it across the network.

Improving the unixServer Class

The new version of unixServer.cls, as shown in Listing 5-8, has sustained similar changes.

Listing 5-8: unixServer.cls

```
############################################################
#
# unixServer.cls - modified for event handling
#
# $Id: unixServer.cls,v 1.5 1998/02/07 06:28:50 chrisj Exp $
# $Log: unixServer.cls,v $
# Revision 1.5  1998/02/07 06:28:50  chrisj
# Added _getState method, raising events now in _getLoad...
# Added _this operator
#
# ---------------------------
# Methods
#
#   _getUsers
#   _getDiskUsage
#   _checkDiskSpace
#   _getLoad
#   _getWindow
#   _getState
#   _reboot
#
# Data Members
#
#   string       _strHost
#   string       _strIP
#   integer      nUsers
#   integer      _nLavg
#   objlist      Dref
#   msgHandler   evtH
#
# Construction
#
#   . unixServer <ref> <hostname/ip address> [ip address]
#
############################################################
```

```
_unixServer() {
  if [ "$1" = "" ]; then
    return 1
  fi
  _strHost=$1
  _strIP=${2:-}
  #
  # Initialize device counter
  #
  _nTotalDevs=0
  #
  # If remote shell command is specified, use it
  #
  _strRemsh=${_strRemsh:-remsh}
  #
  # Try to obtain reference to event handler
  #
  if [[ ! -n $EVENTHANDLER ]]; then
    print -u2 "WARNING: Unable to reference event handler."
  else
    evtH=$EVENTHANDLER
  fi
  #
  # copy ObjectId
  #
  _this=$ObjectId
}

_getUsers() {
  _nUsers=$($_strRemsh $_strHost 'w|wc -l')
  ## write it to STDOUT, for now
  echo $_nUsers
}
_createDiskObjects() {
  #
  # shift out header information
  shift 7;
  #
  # create array with disk information
  set -A devArry $@
  ((c=0))
  #
  # create objects in loop
  #
  while (( c < ${#devArry[*]} ))
  do
    #
    # create a disk object
    #
    . disk _oDref${c} ${devArry[c]} ${devArry[c+1]} \
      ${devArry[c+2]} ${devArry[c+3]} ${devArry[c+4]} \
        ${devArry[c+5]}
    #
```

```
       # add to object list
       #
       _oDiskList_addItem _oDref${c}
       ((c=c+6))
       (( _nTotalDevs = _nTotalDevs + 1 ))
    done
}

_getDiskUsage() {
   if (( $# < 2 )); then
      _getDiskUsage $($_strRemsh $_strHost 'bdf||df -k' \
                  2>/dev/null)
   else
      _DeviceArgs=$@
      #
      # create a list object for devices
      #
      . objlist _oDiskList
      ## now we have arguments
      _createDiskObjects $_DeviceArgs
   fi
   #
   # Call _getFullList on disk object array
   #
   _oDiskList_execute getFullList
}

_getState() {
   set | grep ^$_this
}

_checkDiskSpace() {
   for object in $( _oDiskList_getAllItems )
   do
      #
      # If under 100 megs left, raise disk_alert event
      if (( ${object}_getKbAvail < 100000 )); then
         ${evtH}_raise disk_alert $ObjectId
      fi
   done
}

_getLoad() {
   LoadString=$($_strRemsh $_strHost 'uptime')
   LoadString=${LoadString##*:}
   ## write to STDOUT, for now
   echo $LoadString
   if echo $LoadString | grep "[0-9]\."; then
      ${evtH}_raise high_load $_this
   fi
}

_getWindow() {
```

```
  arguments=${1:-"/bin/ksh"}
  eval $_strRemsh $_strHost \\
  '/usr/bin/X11/xterm -display $DISPLAY -exec $arguments'
}

_reboot() {
  shutdown -r now
}
```

You have significantly changed the unixServer class to incorporate event handling. The class now raises events according to disk usage and load average. You've done away with the `_showDiskUsage` and placed that functionality within the `_getDiskUsage` method. You've also added a new method, `_checkDiskSpace`, that raises a `disk_alert` event to the `msgHandler` if disk space is too high. Also, the `_getLoad` method now raises a `high_load` event that is also mapped out to `signal.cls`.

The `_getState` and `_this` operators can easily be applied to every object you create. All objects need a reference to themselves, and all choose to dump their state at some point. Also, the `_getState` method can be further expanded into a function to store an object persistently to disk. A stored object can span application instances, and be reloaded and reused by any subsequent application. You can also create a base class, `shellobj.cls` or similar, to contain methods and data members relevant to all your shell classes. You have many options with this approach.

Your signal object can be used to map anything. Any raised event can be mapped to the signal class and have its internal state dumped to a log file. The `_alrtRcpnt` method receives an object reference and invokes `_getState` on the reference it receives. Listing 5-9 shows `signal.cls`.

Listing 5-9: `signal.cls`

```
#################################################################
#
# signal.cls - a simple object to handle system events
#
# $Id: signal.cls,v 1.3 1998/02/07 06:27:38 chrisj Exp $
# $Log: signal.cls,v $
# Revision 1.3  1998/02/07 06:27:38  chrisj
#
# ----------------------------
#
# Methods
#
# Data Members
#
#################################################################

_signal() {
  print -u2 "Signaler added..."
```

```
   _rcpnt=$1
}

_alrtRcpnt() {
  obj=$1
  cat << eom > log

  $(date)
  AUTOMATIC ALERT!

  This alert was triggered by $1...
  Retrieving statistics:
  $(${obj}_getState)
eom
  #
  # now e-mail it
  mail root < log
}
```

Now create an instance of unixServer.cls (using the factory class servFactory, of course), a msgHandler instance, and a signal instance. Map your two events that unixServer.cls raises to the signal's _alrtRcpnt function, as shown in diskalert.sh in Listing 5-10.

Listing 5-10: diskalert.sh

```
#!/bin/ksh
########################################################################
# diskalert.sh
#
# A message handling example.
# Signals alerts based on available disk space
#
########################################################################

#
# instantiate a message object
  . msgHandler msg

#
# bring in class components **use your own hostname!
  . servFactory srv localhost
  . signal sig chrisj

#
# configure message mapping
  msg_addHandler disk_alert sig_alrtRcpnt
  msg_addHandler high_load sig_alrtRcpnt

#
# begin system interactions
```

```
msg_getEvents
srv_getUsers
srv_getDiskUsage
srv_checkDiskSpace
srv_getLoad
```

Diskalert.sh shows an application for messages. You can add handlers and remove them at will or as the needs of your system change. In a larger, more dynamic system, event mappings can be assigned through a GUI application. For example, a manufacturing plant may have computer systems that automate every aspect of production. A production manager can use an application to map system events to the appropriate handler. The widget waxer can raise an "out of wax" event. The production manager can map this to either a signaling light to which a worker can respond, or an available wax dispensing robot.

Process Boundaries

In many shell scripts, interprocess communication (IPC) is carried out through coprocesses or named pipes. This section discusses both of these items briefly before moving on to operating system level IPC mechanisms, including message queues and semaphores.

This chapter concludes with a shell example using named pipes, and you'll eventually create a distributed application that uses a combination of named pipes and Internet socket connections for communication. You have to delve into a bit of Java coding to create your socket commands, and as result, demonstrate a basic way to wrap an API for use within the shell. Chapters 6 and 7 discuss these topics in greater detail.

Named Pipes

A named pipe is the easiest form of IPC to implement. A *pipe* is simply a file – or appears to look like a file, because it has permissions, ownership, and a location. A pipe is also written to in a similar fashion to writing to a file. When your process attempts to write to a pipe, it tries to write until another process opens the pipe for reading and takes the message. The opposite is also true: if you attempt to read a pipe, your process blocks until the pipe is opened by another process for writing. A pipe can be created using the mkfifo command as follows:

```
$> mkfifo mypipe
```

Now try writing to it as follows:

```
$> print hello >> mypipe &
```

An ampersand (&) placed after the command makes the process run in the background. Without this ampersand, the process won't return until the pipe is opened for reading. If you don't run the process in the background, you won't receive your prompt to type the following command:

```
$> read message < mypipe

$> print $message
hello
```

You also would have received an indication that your first process had completed, because when the pipe was opened for reading, the pending message was received, and the writing process was allowed to continue.

FIFO (First In First Out) implementations can behave slightly different from UNIX to UNIX, especially when you begin to layer your pipes across background and coprocesses. Always check for unexpected behavior when developing with named pipes.

Named pipes are handy in creating IPC – albeit with the following considerations. All processes must wait for their signals to be read on the opposite side of the pipe, which can limit your programs. If you have a process waiting for a signal to come across a named pipe, it cannot do any other processing until it receives the message. This arrangement is fine for your signal class, which waits to have events raised, but the arrangement is bad for the target of those signals, which need to listen to the signal object for any messages.

One way of beating the pipe problem breaks the functionality of your application down into more specific parts. In the Object Request Broker developed later in this book, the server process actually creates object instances tethered via named pipes. These instances are all unique to the remote process that invoke them, and remain persistent until released by their caller. The invoked instances are free to do any amount of processing, and only return back to the listening state when they are able. While they are dependent on the ORB to give them messages, they are not dependent on where the messages originate.

Named pipes can be very useful, and they occur frequently in later parts of this book.

Coprocesses

A *coprocess* is similar to a pipe, but is an actual background process spawned by your shell script that is capable of reading and writing from its parent process. A coprocess is not bound on reading and writing like a pipe. A coprocess simply runs in the background, with its STDIN and STDOUT attached to your shell script. Type in the following and save it as `cpsh.sh`:

```
#!/bin/ksh
while true
do
read myinput
print "I was sent: $myinput"
done
```

Be sure and `chmod +x` it so you can run it as follows:

```
$> ./cpsh.sh |&
```

You can now use `read` and `print` commands normally to communicate with the background process. Use the `-p` option with `read` and `print` to indicate that its input or output is to be directed at the coprocess:

```
$> print -p "My first message"
$> read -p var

$> print $var
I was sent: My first message

$> print -p "This is another message"

$> read -p var2

$> print $var2
I was sent: This is another message
```

While the coprocess performs tasks, its STDOUT can be read by your script, and you can pass information to the coprocess through its STDIN when the coprocess is ready to accept it.

Consider coprocesses (and their positive and negative attributes) when you need to communicate across processes.

API Level Solutions

This section discusses some of the more powerful means of interprocess communication available at the UNIX API level. While you don't implement C code for Message Queues or Semaphores, you should be familiar with their strengths and weaknesses. If Message Queues or shared memory makes or breaks your application, you should implement the small C/C++ wrapper to use them from the shell. To that end, you create Java shell commands for controlling sockets. The idea of wrapping an API is presented in a following chapter.

The UNIX operating system and development environment provides a rich set of APIs for use in application development. These APIs often take the form of C/C++ libraries that can be used in a variety of applications. These APIs usually address areas of programming that are difficult to implement, but used often – thus the need for a simple, reusable encapsulation.

Message Queues are similar to named pipes, but allow for greater flexibility. Message Queues can be used in an application that has several processes. Similar to named pipes, processes can insert messages into the queue with an associated ID number. Processes that need to read from the queue can pull the latest message corresponding to the ID they need, allowing for multiple processes to share the same message queue. This approach is ideal for application messaging and also offers persistent messages. Processes can die, applications can be restarted, and the queued messages persist because they are stored on disk.

Named Pipes for IPC

To demonstrate how to use named pipes to communicate across shell processes, let's expand on the first example, example1.sh. In your new version, you control the message mapping from a separate process, feeding the new mapping from a shell script called pipe.sh.

The only changes you've made to example1.sh is to put the control statements in an infinite loop and have the process check a named pipe for a new value to pass off to msg_addHandler. The code is quite simple, but it shows the steps of using a named pipe to communicate between processes.

Before you can use the two programs, you need to make a named pipe, or a FIFO named pipe:

```
$> mkfifo pipe
```

Now you can run the programs, as shown in Listing 5-11 and 5-12.

Listing 5-11: pipe.sh

```
#!/bin/ksh
while true
do
print "Enter the message mapping:"
read mapping
print $mapping > pipe
done
```

This script expects you to enter an appropriate message mapping to send down the pipe to the listening program example3.sh, which is shown in Listing 5-12. example3.sh then responds to the new mapping, adding the appropriate handler.

Listing 5-12: example3.sh

```
#!/bin/ksh
######################################################################
# example3.sh
#
# Demonstrate use of named pipes
######################################################################

#
# instantiate a message object
  . msgHandler msg

#
# bring in class components
  . system sys
  . controller ctrl
  . newsys sys2

#
# configure message mapping
  msg_addHandler critical sys_doShutdown
  msg_addHandler operational sys_doWork

#
# begin system interaction loop
while true
do
  ctrl_doControl
  sleep 1
  #
  # change system state
  print "Changing System state..."
  ctrl_nCtrlState=2
  sleep 1
  ctrl_doControl
  #
  # changing state back
  ctrl_nCtrlState=1
  #
  # adjust msg mapping
  msg_deleteHandler critical
  read newmap < pipe
  msg_addHandler $newmap
done
```

You should probably open two X-windows and run each process separately. If you are on a console or a terminal, you can simply run one process in the background. When you start example3.sh, it runs like the first version, but stops after one iteration. If you subsequently run pipe.sh and type in critical sys2_doShutdown, example3.sh starts moving again with alerts mapped to the sys2 object instance. If you type the following into the pipe.sh window at the next iteration, it continues once again, mapped to the original sys object.

critical sys_doShutdown

Figure 5-3 shows a shot of the two processes in action.

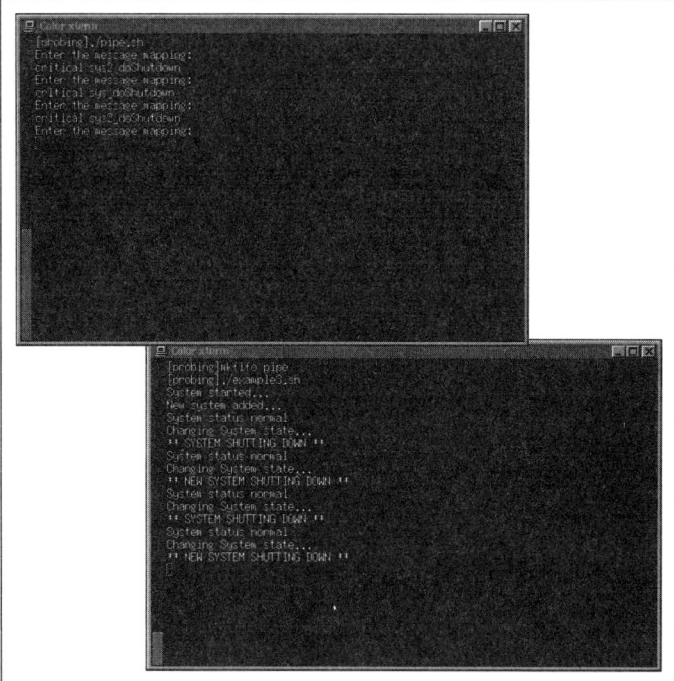

Figure 5-3: example3.sh **and** pipe.sh **in action on Linux**

Summary

In this chapter, you created some simple messaging applications. While simple, they demonstrate the power of decoupling events from the objects that need to act upon them. In procedural programming, a linear set of instructions are followed with each result and consequent action already mapped out. Such systems are rigid and cannot respond well to unforeseen changes in the environment.

By nature, object-oriented programming improves upon this model. In this chapter, you learned that objects try to model the systems in which they operate. In natural and mechanical systems, unforeseen events occur and components of the system react accordingly. In your programs, you can have your objects raise events without regard for how the system may respond. In turn, you can map the raised events to the appropriate response objects. As the system evolves and changes, your events can be remapped to different objects, thus affording great flexibility.

The next chapter discusses more of what the advanced APIs offer application developers before delving into the creation of socket commands.

Chapter 6

Using Java from the Shell

IN THIS CHAPTER

- Coding in Java
- Examining Java's syntax and object-orientation
- Exploring input and output
- Understanding Java's language features

THE SHELL IS a great scripting language. While many claim that it is not nearly as powerful as compiled languages, most of these people aren't familiar with the shell's finer points, and the ease and speed at which some tasks are accomplished. When it comes to system configuration, management, and maintenance, the shell is much more flexible than compiled code. You can slice and dice directories full of config files more easily with sed and awk than with C or C++.

While the shell is powerful in these respects, it does have some major drawbacks regarding sophisticated applications. First, the shell is an interpreted language, and as such, it is slower than compiled machine code. Also, the shell is single-threaded, only allowing one line of execution throughout an application. While you can have different processes communicating through IPC, threading is more powerful when it comes to certain operations, especially at the device and network level. The shell also has no support for sockets. Most powerful applications these days involve one form or another of a multithreaded socket listener. Most HTTP servers are multithreaded, with subsequent requests passed off to available threads. Anything that depends on multiple socket connections works well with a multithreaded implementation.

The shell is lacking in these areas, and is usually brushed aside for any large-scale software projects. Also, with emerging languages like Java, network and multithreaded programming are easier than ever. Despite these deficiencies, the shell still can be very powerful, and has strengths unequaled in any other language. For these reasons, it's worthwhile to write your own commands to support functionality that the shell doesn't ordinarily handle.

In this chapter, you explore the features of various advanced programming techniques and discuss feasible uses from the shell. You also learn to write your own commands in Java. While the chapter doesn't provide a full tutorial on Java programming, you should have no trouble following along if you're a skilled shell scripter who has dabbled in C or Perl.

Choosing Java

In most cases, if you wish to use an API or use advanced system concepts, you need to write them in Java or C/C++. The most widely-used programming language for systems development on the UNIX platform is C. The C programmer can choose from a vast array of libraries, frameworks, and toolkits. Java, however, is emerging as a powerful and flexible language. Coding in Java has many advantages over coding in C++, particularly ease of use and portability. Java provides an excellent set of networking tools and makes writing multithreaded networking applications a breeze. Much of the slowness associated with Java is not nearly as apparent in non-GUI networking components. Also, Java has a broad array of available ORB products and interoperability across the network can easily be achieved.

Java also has some advantages over C++ for both the less-experienced programmer and the programmer with other priorities. Java has built-in memory management and garbage collection, thus preventing pesky memory leaks and crashes that can bring a C++ application to its knees. Also, some of the more complicated aspects of C++ programming, such as pointers, don't exist in Java. Basically, Java is an excellent language for creating OO applications. Java is powerful, Java is portable, and most importantly, Java is fun!

Your familiarity with many object-oriented concepts only helps your exposure to Java in this chapter. Java can be a tough language in which to learn OO for the first time, and having some OO knowledge will make your Java experience much easier.

Applets and Applications

Most certainly, you will not be writing Java applets, which are small GUI-based programs that can execute within the context of a Web browser or applet viewer. While applets are fine and dandy, you will not be using these programs. Instead, you will create standalone applications in Java. You can run them on the command line by passing them off to the Java interpreter. Java applications do not have to follow the security measures required of applets. They can read STDIN and write to STDOUT, open files, and perform just about any task common to applications. With Java, your shell scripts will no longer be boxed in by the shell's lack of support for advanced programming techniques.

Portability

Java is emerging as the language of middleware and distributed systems, and its portability makes it ideal for distributed object architectures. The binaries included with this book for creating sockets can readily be executed under UNIX, Linux, and even Windows without a single modification.

The growth of the Internet and the conversion of systems from the client-server model to the distributed systems model is helping to fuel Java's popularity. Today's systems have an increasing desire to connect disparate Internet-based clients first to a middle tier of Web and directory servers, and finally to an array of distributed back-end systems for all sorts of data across an enterprise. A browser running on a Macintosh computer may connect to a Solaris machine running a Web server, which in turn pulls data from an array of UNIX, NT, and MVS machines. One approach to taming this large, distributed environment is through distributed objects. While object request brokers try to provide platform- and language-independent interfaces, there is still a need to deploy a vast number of objects and services on many different platforms. Java fills this need quite well. An object-based system written in Java can be distributed entirely independent of the hardware architecture, thus allowing for objects and application components to be truly portable and for hardware resources to be applied more freely. You'll see this portability in your distributed application. By creating your low-level networking components in Java, you allow the same components to be used on both Windows and UNIX machines. There are a variety of shell interpreters for Windows; using the architecture designed in this book, you could easily control distributed UNIX shell objects from an NT machine.

Also, the flexibility of Java as an Internet and networking language only encourages its use in this environment. Java has a rich set of classes for handling data streams, URLs, multimedia, and all other sorts of elements from today's applications. While many Internet-based applications can be written in C++, their Java counterparts are easier to create, maintain, and extend.

You'll incorporate some of Java's power in the next chapter as you code several commands for creating and using sockets as a means of communications between processes and servers. Sockets are virtual ports where machines can send and receive data streams. Similar to a named pipe, a socket connection is associated with a server and a port number. Once a connection is established, the parties on both sides can begin sending data to each other in a similar fashion to pipes. The low-level networking considerations are hidden from the programmer; you are free to simply send strings back and forth, and interpret them in your application as desired.

Other Java Features

Besides sockets, Java supports numerous APIs for advanced computing. The techniques used develop your socket commands can readily be applied to creating commands that support a variety of API functions in your shell scripts.

By writing your own commands, you can add the power of sockets, multithreading, IPC, and many other powerful techniques to your shell scripts.

Examining Java's Syntax and Object-Orientation

Before writing socket commands in the next chapter, you should familiarize yourself with some Java syntax. As mentioned earlier, you can adapt the preceding object-oriented techniques to Java, with the syntax constituting the only significant barrier.

When programmers decide to move to Java, they are faced with a double challenge. First, Java incorporates some of its own language features, but the main stumbling block is learning object-orientation. OO is a world apart from linear C programming, and can be a rather daunting undertaking.

Java syntax is really not that difficult; at the character level, it mimics C/C++. This section doesn't go into great detail explaining the syntax, because it exceeds the scope of these few pages and is not the topic of this book. You should be able to pick up a great deal just by completing the examples, however, as this section illustrates how to create simple objects in Java. All of the same techniques that you've applied in the shell can be applied within a Java application.

As a departure from the shell, Java syntax is not line-dependent. Commands are divided in Java in a similar manner to C/C++ — with a semicolon. A statement can span as many lines as necessary in your text editor; only the semicolon is significant to the compiler. The following two lines are equivalent:

```
if ( x > 3 ) doThisFunction();
if ( x > 2 )
doThisFunction();
```

Comments are another notable syntax difference between Java and the shell. Java accepts both the // style and /* ... */ style of comments as in C/C++:

```
// Java comment
/**
Another Java Comment
**/
```

If you're familiar with C/C++, you will find Java syntax to be identical, except for importing classes and declaring functions. The base character-level syntax is the same.

Java also supports nested operations. In the shell, for example, use the following if you want to use the output of another function or command within an evaluation or test:

```
if (( ${uRef}_getAge > 25 )); then
print "Older than 25... "
fi
```

Java also supports nested operations, but the syntax is a little cleaner. To do the exact same operation, use the following:

```
if ( uRef.getAge() > 25 )
System.out.println("Older than 25... ");
```

You can be flexible with your nested operations:

```
while ( ( c = System.in.read() ) != '\n' )
```

The preceding example is the beginning portion of a `while` statement. The inner parentheses assign c the value of `System.in.read()`, and then that value is compared with `'\n'`.

You can pick up most of the syntactic particulars by examining code examples. The main difference between Java and other languages is in data typing, function declaration, and public and private specification.

Java supports the keywords `public` and `private` (as well as others) to indicate whether an object's data and functions are directly available to other objects. You have not yet implemented this feature in the shell. By declaring something as private, you ensure that only your class can alter that data. The private specifier can be used to enforce encapsulation by cutting off all access to the object's internal implementation. Both functions and data can be declared private. To declare an internal data member as private, you need to provide access functions if you want other objects to be able to alter the value. This enables you to change how your object internally represents data by shielding the implementation. You can change the data types or even the location of the data without breaking the interface already used. In contrast to C/C++, you declare a property's access rights at declaration:

```
public void setName(String newname)
{
strName = newname;
}
```

This function is declared and defined at the same time: the keyword `public` initially describes its access, and `void` specifies its return type. This function returns nothing — it only takes a parameter `newname` as a string and assigns the object's internal data member `strName` to the new value. Prior to this function, `strName` could have been declared as follows:

```
private String strName;
```

By declaring the data member private, all operations on the property have to be done by the class. All class methods could alter the data, but any other external object or entity wishing to change or retrieve it need to use the access function. You could define a retrieval function as follows:

```
public String getName() {
return strName;
}
```

With this information, you should be able to start coding some simple routines. You'll construct a few objects and write a couple of examples to illustrate how a standalone application can function. In a departure from other languages, all Java files must be a class, and as such, they must be class definitions providing methods and data members. To create a standalone application, make the main executive part of your program a class, and the Java interpreter will call the `main` function offered by your class. You may import any other available class files into this program. Your main declaration could look like the following:

```
public static void main( String Args[] )
{
// do stuff
}
```

As you can see, this function takes an array of `Strings` as an argument, just as any command line program.

Getting Started

Java is easy and you can get started right away. This program will be a standalone application that you can run from the command line – provided you've installed the JDK. For easiest use, you should add the JDK directory to your path:

```
PATH=$PATH:/usr/local/java/bin
```

Now you can pass any class off to the Java interpreter. For instance, if your class was named `myServer.class`, you could execute it as follows:

```
java myServer
```

Armed with this knowledge, you're ready to begin coding.

Your first class simply has a couple of methods and writes a message to the screen. This should help familiarize you with the basic requirements to get an executable program. Listing 6-1 is an OO version of "Hello World."

Listing 6-1: `Hello.java`

```
public class Hello
{
  public String message;

  public Hello()
  {
```

```
    message = "Hello World!";
  }

  public void printMessage()
  {
    System.out.println(this.getMessage());
  }

  private String getMessage()
  {
    return message;
  }

  public static void main (String Args[])
  {
    Hello h = new Hello();

    h.printMessage();
  }
}
```

To compile your first Java class, make sure that your CLASSPATH variable contains the default Java installation class directory as well as the current working directory (.). The command used to compile Java is javac:

```
$> javac Hello.java
```

You can run the newly created Hello.class as follows:

```
$> java Hello
Hello World!
```

The Hello class is defined within brackets, and public and private specifiers are used to declare what can be altered and accessed by other objects. Basically, you created one public function, printMessage, and one private function, getMessage. These functions mainly illustrate the use of public and private properties. The message that your Hello class contains is a private member; as such, other objects cannot alter its value directly. Rather, you have to provide an access function to deal with the private member. Also, the private function can only be called by other internal functions of the class. Use private functions to accomplish internal workings of your object that you want to keep encapsulated. Also, you have to declare your variables before using them. In the shell, everything is a string. Java has an assortment of basic types, and of course, a plethora of user- and application-created types (objects).

Typing in Java is fairly simple and more flexible than the strict typing presented in C++. For example, C++ doesn't readily have a String type, while Java initially provides this type. Although both of these languages are object-oriented, you could also create an identical type of String in C++.

Java takes care of memory allocation and reallocation for you, which can be quite a relief when your programs grow more complex. One of the biggest challenges of developing a sophisticated C++ application is tracking down memory leaks.

Class Interaction Example

The second example illustrates the interaction between three objects: two instantiations of a class human and one instantiation of a class vendor. These three objects interact in a way that leaves the humans penniless, and the vendor holding all of their money.

The first class, human, is an object representing a consumer. This object has a certain amount of money, and can spend with money. You pass the object off to an instance of vendor, which in turn calls the `takeMoney` interface on your human. At this point, the human's cash is decremented by one hundred dollars. If the human does not have enough money to pay, the vendor indicates accordingly. The process continues until both humans are broke. This is one example where objects closely resemble real life! Listing 6-2 demonstrates `human.java`.

Listing 6-2: human.java

```
// human.java
//
public class human
{
  private int money;
  private String name;

  public human(String nm, int m)
  {
    money = m;
    name = nm;
  }

  public void takeMoney(int m)
  {
    money -= m;
  }

  private void setMoney(int m)
  {
    money = m;
  }

  public int getMoney()
  {
    return money;
  }

  public String getName()
```

```
{
  return name;
}
}
```

As you can see, the private specifier protects the human's primary asset: money. For any changes to be made to this internal figure, another object has to call an access function. The human provides the functions setMoney and takeMoney for dealing with money. The first method gives the human a certain amount, and the second taketh away.

The vendor class has some narrowly focused methods as you might expect. The vendor supports one particular operation, makeSale, which takes a human as a parameter. The vendor object then seeks to invoke the takeMoney method of the human. This sequence is followed by an increment in the vendor's profit total, and so forth. Listing 6-3 demonstrates vendor.java.

Listing 6-3: vendor.java

```
// vendor.java
//
import human;

public class vendor
{
  public vendor(){}
  private int profitTotal;

  public void makeSale(human h)
  {
    if (h.getMoney() < 100)
    {
      System.out.print(h.getName());
      System.out.println(" doesn't have enough" +
        " money, Approved for Credit!");
    }
    h.takeMoney(100);
    profitTotal += 100;
  }

  public int getProfit()
  {
    return profitTotal;
  }
}
```

Finally, you put these two objects together in prog.java, as shown in Listing 6-4. prog.java is a simple class that only implements a main function to begin the interaction of your other two objects.

Listing 6-4: prog.java

```java
// prog.java

import vendor;
import human;

public class prog
{
  public prog(){}

  public static void main( String Args[] )
  {
    human h1 = new human("Fred", 150);
    human h2 = new human("Sam", 300);
    vendor v1 = new vendor();

    for (int c = 0; c < 4; c++ )
    {
      v1.makeSale(h1);
      v1.makeSale(h2);
      System.out.println("Human " + h1.getName()
        + " has:" + h1.getMoney());
      System.out.println("Human " + h2.getName()
        + " has:" + h2.getMoney());
      System.out.println("Vendor profits: " +
        v1.getProfit());
    }
  }
}
```

References

Notice that objects can be freely passed to each other in prog.java. This characteristic is similar to your approach in the shell. If you've instantiated an object, you can pass it off for another object with which to play. In the shell, this book frequently refers to passing an object "reference" back and forth between objects. This statement can be confusing if you're experienced in C++ or with pointers. When an object has a reference to another object in the shell, this statement means that it "knows" of an object instance by name. In reality, the object is not moving anywhere – it simply shares the same process space as other objects and by default is accessible to them. The term "reference" indicates when an object knows another object instance by name, but doesn't actually contain or own the object. This slight difference has been referred to as containment or aggregation. For example, you've been calling the following example a "reference" in the shell:

```
_getUserName() {
  uRef=$1    # Pass object name as parameter

  ${uRef}_getName  # Invoke method on object
}
```

You've been calling the following example "aggregation" or "containment" in the shell:

```
_getUserName() {
  # user object already exists within this class
  # so you can just call the function
  _usr_getName
}
```

The preceding account class example is a good example of shell references. The account class knows of a separate user object, but does not contain or own it. The unixServer class is a good example of containment, because this class contains various disk objects, as well as a list object to organize references to disk objects further.

In Java, objects are passed by wholesale. This works essentially the same way as in the shell. For example, you can write the same functions as follows:

```
_getUserName(user uRef) {
  # Object passed in as parameter
  uRef.getName();
}
```

You can also have a contained object:

```
_getUserName() {
  # user object already exists within this class
  user.getName();
}
```

Using objects in Java won't be much different than how you've been using them in the shell. If you're a C++ programmer and you take "reference" to mean literally the reference operator (&) or a pointer to an object instance in memory, the process can be confusing. This function is usually expressed in syntax as follows:

```
_getUserName(user* uRef)  {
  # Object pointer passed in as parameter
  uRef->getName();
}
```

You won't have to deal with pointers in the shell or in Java.

Exploring Input and Output

Because you will use Java applications as components among shell objects, you need to become familiar with Java's mechanisms for reading and writing standard output and standard input, commonly referred to as STDOUT/STDIN. The most convenient way for shell scripts to talk to Java programs is by launching the Java application as a coprocess to your shell application, thus attaching the read and write ends of the Java program to your shell application.

If you have dabbled with Java applets or are expecting a GUI created with the Java AWT (Abstract Window Toolkit), this section is completely different from those forms of input and output. This application will be basic command line I/O, similar to a compiled C++ routine.

The first concept is reading and writing from the command line. Your first program reads input from the command line, and then immediately spits out what was just typed. This sequence follows a routine that can accept parameters from the command line. Both of these concepts will probably be the basis for any sort of Java application you want to integrate with shell objects.

You can read STDIN in a Java program by first importing the basic I/O routines:

```
import java.io.*;
```

Then, you can use the I/O objects. The `System` and `DataInputStream` classes have many routines for dealing with I/O. The first routines you learn are the following:

```
DataInputStream.readLine();
```

and

```
System.out.print("Words!\n");
```

You will first read input and output with these routines. Java also presents some other objects for reading and writing in streams. These include the obvious `InputStream` and `OutputStream`, as well as their close cousins, `DataInputStream`/`DataOutputStream`.

Listing 6-5 demonstrates reading and writing STDOUT/STDIN.

Listing 6-5: `inout.java`

```
// inout.java - read from the command line
//

import java.io.*;

public class inout
{
```

```
  public inout(){}
  public String wurdz;

  public void run()
  {
    DataInputStream in = new DataInputStream(System.in);

    while (true)
    {
      try {
        wurdz = in.readLine();
      } catch (IOException e) {
        System.out.println(e);
      }

      System.out.println(wurdz);
    }
  }

  public static void main (String Args[])
  {
    inout io = new inout();

    io.run();
  }
}
```

This program creates a simple loop that executes forever, by reading keystrokes off the command line and then writing them back to the screen. While useless as an application, this program demonstrates how to read and write data from the command line, which is exactly what your socket application will need to do.

You can also pass parameters to your Java application via the command line. This approach is similar to your technique in the shell with positional parameters. Instead of using $1 to reference the command line arguments, you use the String array Args[] that you've indicated in your main function. You can use the elements of this array as your command line arguments. You will need to take advantage of when creating your own standalone Java programs. Listing 6-6 demonstrates getargs.java.

Listing 6-6: getargs.java

```
import java.io.*;

public class getargs
{
  public getargs(){}

  public static void main (String Args[])
  {
    for (int c = 0; c < Args.length; c++ )
    {
```

```
      System.out.println(Args[c]);
   }
   System.exit(0);
  }
}
```

As you can see, the code is pretty simple. A simple loop is created against the array length. You then iterate through the elements of the array, printing each one to STDOUT.

Understanding Java Language Features

Java features some nifty features lacking in other languages. Aside from the vast array of networking classes, Java uses a few other bells and whistles to make programming easier.

In object-oriented terms, Java supports separate interface inheritance, as opposed to class and interface inheritance as in the shell and C/C++.

Interfaces

When you inherit from a class, you inherit all of the methods and data members that the class implements. By nature, you inherit the interface that the parent class was using. If you want to only inherit the interface without the underlying data members, you need to create an abstract base class. An abstract class is a class that describes methods, but does not actually implement them. The implementation is left to classes that inherit from this base, abstract class. Interface inheritance occurs in C++ in the same way, and the process happens in a similar way in the shell. You create a reusable base class with little or no implementation and derive subclasses from it, thus inheriting the interface and allowing for polymorphism.

For example, you can describe a method in the shell as follows:

```
_myMethod() {
   _myVar = $1
}
```

Subsequently, you can have another class inherit this method and redefine it as follows:

```
_myMethod() {
   _myVar = _myNewVar
}
```

You inherit interfaces in the shell with this method. This works fine, but requires you to create an actual base class with implementation, as opposed to just an interface.

Java enables you to create a separate interface to be implemented by other classes. This clean separation lets you focus on interface creation and provides a safe way of publishing documentation for your object code. You can distribute an interface definition with your class to be used by developers, but you don't have to divulge your precious source code, which is implemented in a compiled class file.

Similar to a class, an interface is declared within brackets:

```
public interface unixServer
{
  public abstract int getUsers();
  public abstract void checkDiskUsage();
  public abstract String getUptime();
}
```

This interface definition would be implemented in a class as follows:

```
public class sunServer implements unixServer
{
// method implementation here
}
```

This implementation allows several different classes to implement the unixServer interface — you provide for other parties to use your class without distributing the source code.

You create a simple interface, called PersonInfo. Its specification is in the file PersonInfo.java. This file holds an interface definition for retrieving human attributes such as name and age (this is familiar territory, right?). This interface is implemented by class Person, which provides the implementation code. The Person class is in the file (you guessed it) Person1.java. Listing 6-7 demonstrates PersonInfo.java.

Listing 6-7: PersonInfo.java

```
// Interface PersonInfo.java
//

public interface PersonInfo
{
  abstract void setName(String s);
  abstract String getName();
  abstract void setAge(int i);
  abstract int getAge();
}
```

Your person class uses this extraordinarily simple interface, as shown in Listing 6-8.

Listing 6-8: Person1.java

```java
// Person1.java - Person1 class file
//
public class Person1 implements PersonInfo
{
  public String name;
  public int age;

  public Person1()
  {
    name = "Bill";
    age = 25;
  }

  public String getName()
  {
    return name;
  }

  public void setName(String nm)
  {
    name = nm;
  }

  public int getAge()
  {
    return age;
  }

  public void setAge(int i)
  {
    age = i;
  }

  public static void main(String Args[])
  {
    Person1 p = new Person1();

    System.out.println(p.getName());
    System.out.println(p.getAge());

    p.setName("Roger");
    p.setAge(69);

    System.out.println(p.getName());
    System.out.println(p.getAge());
```

```
    System.exit(0);
  }

}
```

You can see the main function in action:

```
$> javac PersonInfo.java
$> javac Person1.java
$> java Person1
```

Inheritance

Java implements inheritance with the `extends` keyword, which enables you to override any functions and inherit any code. You can reference a superclass function within a subclass via the `super` keyword. For example, if you have a class that implements an `add` function that adds two numbers, you can execute the function in derived classes as `super.add()`. This is similar to scope resolution in C++ and can be done in the shell on functions that aren't overridden. If you override a function in the shell, you cannot access the superclass implementation unless you create a separate instance of the superclass. When a function is overridden in the shell, the superclass implementation no longer exists. By contrast, if you choose not to implement a function in a derived shell class, you can still call on the superclass implementation.

You'll now create a `Customer` class that inherits from the preceding `Person` class. You need to remove the `main` method from `Person1.java`, and use the new version included in `Customer1.java`. You can also create a separate class just to use the two Person and Customer objects. Regardless, the code for `Customer1.java` is shown in a following section. No implementation whatsoever is done except for the addition of a `balance` data member and its access functions. All the other functionality is inherited, or extended, from the Person class. Listing 6-9 shows the modified version of `Person1.java`, in which the main function has been removed.

Listing 6-9: `Person.java`

```java
// Person.java - Person class file
//

public class Person implements PersonInfo
{

  public String name;
  public int age;

  public Person()
  {
    name = "Bill";
```

```
    age = 25;
  }

  public String getName()
  {
    return name;
  }

  public void setName(String nm)
  {
    name = nm;
  }

  public int getAge()
  {
    return age;
  }

  public void setAge(int i)
  {
    age = i;
  }

}
```

Listing 6-10 shows the first version of the Customer class, Customer1.java.

Listing 6-10: Customer1.java

```
// Customer1.java customer class
//
public class Customer1 extends Person
{
  public int balance;

  public Customer1(){
    super();
    balance = 0;
  }

  public void setBal(int b)
  {
    balance = b;
  }

  public int getBal()
  {
    return balance;
  }

  public static void main(String Args[])
  {
```

```
    Customer1 c = new Customer1();

    System.out.println(c.getName() + " " + c.getBal());
    c.setName("Freddy");
    c.setBal(1000);
    System.out.println(c.getName() + " " + c.getBal());

  }
}
```

You can use `java Customer` to watch execution.

```
$> java Customer1
```

Threads

Java makes multithreading simple. You can create an instance of a Thread class, and hand your object off to the thread that runs with it. As such, you need to implement the `Runnable` interface, and provide a `run` method for your class.

The Thread class provides the functionality needed for managing your thread. You do not need to delve into hundreds of lines of system code to manage threading in your program. In the simplest way, you just pass an acceptable class off to the Thread constructor, and then call `Thread.start()`.

You add the run method to your Customer class, and let the customer do some work. You create a new file, `Thrd.java`, which instantiates a customer and pass the instance off to a thread for execution.

Listing 6-11 shows the modified version of `Customer1.java`, `Customer.java`:

Listing 6-11: `Customer.java`

```
// Customer.java
//

public class Customer extends Person implements Runnable
{
  public int balance;

  public Customer(){
    super();
    balance = 0;
  }

  public void setBal(int b)
  {
    balance = b;
  }

  public int getBal()
  {
    return balance;
```

```
   }

   public void run()
   {
     Customer c = new Customer();

     System.out.println(c.getName());
     c.setName("Freddy");
     System.out.println(c.getName());
   }
}
```

As you can see, `Customer.java` implements a run method that does some operations on the class. `Customer.java` also implements the `Runnable` interface, which is what the Thread class expects. (This is just for demonstration.) In the socket application you develop in Chapter 7, you may want to do socket listening and handling with these threaded techniques.

The file `Thrd.java` (Listing 6-12) creates an instance of the Customer class and the Thread class. It then hands the Customer off to the Thread, which runs the class and produces the output you see on the screen.

Listing 6-12: Thrd.java

```
// Thrd.java - demonstrates threading
//
import java.net.*;

public class Thrd
{
  public static void main (String Args[])
  {
    Customer c = new Customer();

    Thread t = new Thread(c);

    t.start();
  }
}
```

To run:

```
$> javac Customer.java
$> javac Thrd.java
$> java Thrd
```

Java's support for threading is unparalleled. In C/C++ application development, threading is by far the most complex topic, with IPC mechanisms close behind. Java has successfully encapsulated threading within a thread object. Note the ease at which you can implement threading in your programs – simply give your class a `run` method. This ease should encourage you to explore how threading can solve complex programming problems, thus making your applications more responsive and efficient.

Other Features

Java supports the notion of packages. Type and objects can be scoped at a package level and referenced within your applications. You can create whole collections of object classes and interfaces, and include them into a package. This enables you to give your collection a common name and import it wholesale into source files that need to use it.

Packaging has several benefits. First, you may often create collections of objects that need to work together. If you simply import each class by hand into your source file, you have to insure that every class exists somewhere within your class path. Also, another class may exist with the same name that the compiler may grab first, ignoring the class you intended to include.

Packages insure that classes that work together can stay together. To declare a particular class or package, just issue the following within your source file:

```
package myclasses;
```

With the preceding, the class or interface you subsequently define will be included in the package. When you wish to use the classes together in a related application, you can simply import the whole package as follows:

```
import myclasses.*;
```

This sort of statement should be familiar from many of your classes.

Java also supports exception handling between `try` and `catch` blocks. Certain operations can be arranged to handle or "throw" various exceptions.

When performing your input operations from command line text, you threw `IOException`. If there was an IO problem, you could have written your function to catch to `IOException` as an object instance, and call an operation on the exception object:

```
try {
System.in.read();
} catch (IOException e) {
Systen.err.println(e);
}
```

Exceptions are a form of error handling that enables you to handle errors or to pass them off to another part of your program. If no one handles the error, the program simply exits (or refuses to compile). The idea behind Java's implementation of exception handling is to create an exception object and decouple error handling from the other parts of your programs.

The main ingredients for exception handling are the exception objects. Certain classes that you create and many of the classes included in the JDK are wired to generate exceptions when certain runtime conditions aren't met. When an exception is raised, the runtime environment begins searching for someone to catch or throw the exception. If an exception is caught, methods can be invoked on the caught object, indicating what may have gone wrong. If the exception is simply thrown, and no one else chooses to catch it, the program simply exits.

The classes included with the JDK provide many different types of exceptions — unless you write your own packages, you may never to stray beyond these provided classes.

Summary

Java is a rich language to explore for application development. Take some of the ideas here and adapt them to support any shell application. By harnessing the power of Java, your shell scripts can easily reach out across the network, create threads, and perform advanced tasks that would otherwise be unavailable to your scripts.

The next chapter delve into Java network programming, which is the basis for your shell object request broker. As you will see, Java has an excellent networking object model.

Chapter 7

Encapsulating the Network with Components

IN THIS CHAPTER

- Java networking objects
- Internet sockets
- Java networking with the shell

NETWORK TRANSPARENCY IS one of the key features of distributed objects. You've been coding with objects that exist on the same machine, and the techniques you've been learning and applying have demonstrated their usefulness. In this chapter, you will see these object techniques pay off. The network can be the most difficult variable with which to deal when creating an application, and if you can abstract it with an object, you can allow your objects to cross machine boundaries.

To those who write network-aware scripts, this chapter will surely be a blessing. Personally, I was a systems administrator with a large credit card company. We had well over two hundred UNIX servers. The platforms ranged from HP-UX, AIX, DEC, and Solaris, in addition to a Vax and an MVS thrown into the mix every so often. We tried to standardize our system configurations in an effort to minimize hassles and troubleshooting, but we still couldn't finalize a ubiquitous configuration. Because the machines were being used in different environments with different user and application needs, the system configuration could not be standardized. As a result, widespread changes in policy usually meant that files were going to have to be updated by hand.

In one particular instance, we had to disable a certain Internet service for security reasons. Although we were on a private network, integration with the rest of the world was inevitable, and we decided to begin tightening the loose ends. This particular change involved editing the `inetd.conf` file on over 200 machines, and then triggering the reinitialization of Inet services by invoking the appropriate command (`inet -d`, on many of the systems).

As an industrious shell scripter, I quickly wrote out a plodding routine to `remsh` into each of the machines, slice and dice the file with `sed`, and then kick off the reinitialization. Simple enough, huh? Unfortunately, the main problem was that `inetd.conf` wasn't located in exactly the same place on each machine. Also, different flavors of UNIX had different commands to restart Inet services.

One approach to this task would be to create `case` statements for each type of UNIX host on the network. You could then determine the remote OS type, and tailor the location of `inetd.conf` and the command to restart the services accordingly. This method also would have worked, but on some of the machines, `inetd.conf` was still in a different place on the same flavor of UNIX. Poor system configuration? Maybe, but it still didn't change the problem.

As you can imagine, the first few times I ran my script, I was successful on about 80 percent of the machines. On some of the others, either the file wasn't edited, or I issued the wrong command to restart Inet services. In a few cases, I actually managed to disable Inet services altogether, in which case I got to hop in my car and drive out to the machine's location to deal with it on console terms (a really fun part of being a system administrator).

This chapter should help remedy some of those problems. While nothing beats a standardized system configuration, a way of representing remote systems locally would be ideal. You construct this representation in the coming chapters, but for now, you try to encapsulate the network, rendering it virtually transparent to your shell scripts. Wouldn't it be nice to communicate between machines as easily as using a named pipe? That's exactly what you create in this chapter, and you also create a shell object wrapper around our socket command to provide an appropriate interface for our other shell objects.

Understanding Networking

Hardly any UNIX machines exist by themselves. In fact, hardly any computers exist by themselves. Even home PCs communicate on a regular basis with network hosts to retrieve e-mail, as well as URLs in the form of Web pages. These days, you cannot escape the network.

While working on one machine seems complicated enough, trying to deal with a remote host is akin to trying to string a couple of tin cans across the Atlantic. To communicate from the shell level with another machine, you have to either open a Telnet session or issue a remote shell command. Using a utility like `remsh` involves considerable overhead and preplanning. You need to have an account on the remote machine, and the remote host needs to be able to resolve the hostname of the machine from which you're coming. These contingencies alone make using `remsh` implausible for any highly-distributed shell program. Also, you may want to integrate non-UNIX hosts into your network. How would you `remsh` into them? Fortunately, you can use many other ways of contacting a network host.

TCP/IP

TCP/IP (Transmission Control Protocol/Internet Protocol) is the most widely accepted networking protocol in existence. While TCP/IP is absolutely ubiquitous now, a few years ago many systems didn't care about TCP/IP. Any number of PCs were linked through Novell software using the beloved IPX protocol. Windows didn't really start acknowledging the TCP/IP stack until the release of Windows 3.1. TCP/IP can thank the Internet for much of its popularity.

TCP/IP is a reliable protocol. Information is sent via TCP/IP in the form packets. The data you send from your Web browser across the Internet to a Web server is broken down into packets. These packets are transmitted and reassembled on the receiving side. TCP/IP is much more involved, but you only really need to be concerned with how things work at the application level.

When you open a Telnet, FTP, or HTTP connection, you are using TCP/IP as your transport layer. When an application creates a connection to a database to stream information, it is most likely communicating over TCP/IP. All of these modes of communication have TCP/IP as their meat and potatoes, with sockets are the application interface. Sockets are represented at the machine level with a port number. This is virtual port, and not an actual plug in the back of the machine! If you want a demo, try the following. Pick your favorite (or not-so-favorite) Web site. From your Internet-connected machine (this works on Windows 95 as well), open a Telnet connection to port 80, and then simply hit return. You are effectively Web surfing without a browser, as the following demonstrates:

```
$> telnet www.microsoft.com 80
[ press return ]
HTTP/1.0 400 BAD REQUEST

Content-type: text/html

<body><h1>HTTP/1.0 400 BAD REQUEST
</h1></body>
```

The returned first lines constitute the HTTP header. These lines tell the browser the status of the request (400), and what type of information the server is returning (in this case, `text/html`). Other content types could be `image/gif`, `zip`, `jpg`, and so forth. The blank line between the header and the HTML content is HTTP's way of telling the browser that the header is complete. When you code in CGI in a following chapter, you will probably make the mistake of leaving out the blank line a few times. You'll wonder why the browser can't display your program's output – but you'll discover more about this topic at the end of the book.

 When coding CGI, you must always print a blank line (carriage-return) after sending the HTTP header. Without this blank line, your CGI scripts will never work and you will give up frustrated!

You will probably never code with TCP/IP directly; rather, you will use an API to make network connections for you. These APIs are far richer than what you can accomplish with `remsh` or trying to massage a telnet session through your application.

The Sockets API

With API features, you will primarily be taking advantage of sockets. Sockets establish a data stream with a remote host. In fact, almost all the UNIX utilities you use for communicating with remote servers use sockets, including Telnet, FTP, HTTP, and the r-utilities (`remsh`, `rsh`, `rcp`, and so forth). Several different types of sockets exist, but you will be using plain old TCP sockets. These sockets are connection-oriented – as opposed to connectionless sockets such as UDP, which require the expense of establishing a connection.

A handshaking routine is conducted between the machines before a socket connection is established. Once connected, your communication should be pretty snappy. Other types of sockets, such as UDP, are not connection-oriented. A UDP socket connection forwards your message off to the remote host, but you may never hear anything back. UDP is often referred to as being an unreliable protocol, but it can be useful. For example, if you need to send logging messages over the network to a remote host rapidly and frequently, you may not be too concerned if .001 percent of those messages are scrambled or arrive out of sequence.

TCP sockets, however, are reliable and good for communicating small or large portions of exact data; that is, you type in one message or string of characters on one end, and the exact same sequence comes out the other side. You'll be using sockets in this fashion.

To harness the socket's API, you use objects from the Java package `java.net.*;`. You'll import this package into your main socket routines. The first step in creating a socket relationship establishes a server to manage your connections. The server socket will be the persistent process that hangs around on a machine, waiting for client connections to the socket. Client sockets attempt to establish a connection to the server, and once connected, trade various amounts of information before eventually disconnecting. Once disconnected, the path is clear for other clients to connect and exchange data with the server. Figure 7-1 shows client and server sockets.

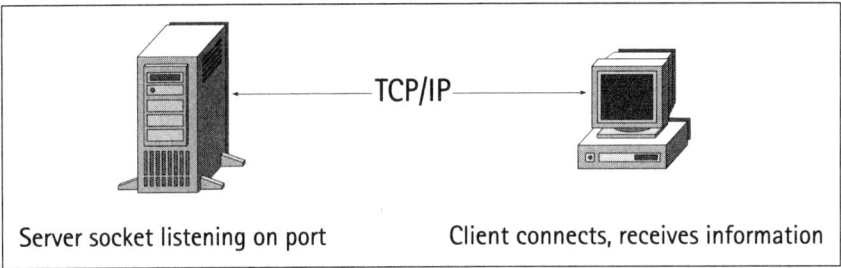

Figure 7-1: Client and server sockets

When you've established a connection between client and server, you can send data back and forth between the sockets using the same type of stream functions you used in the preceding chapter for STDIN and STDOUT.

The Java code for creating and reading from a socket connection looks similar to the following:

```
sock = new socket("localhost", 2112);
DataInputStream in =
   new DataInputStream(sock.getInputStream());
String stuff;
stuff = in.readLine();
System.out.println(stuff);
```

As you can see, using sockets is as easy as the other tasks you've done with Java.

Pipes Revisited

You use your socket connections in similar method to pipes. If you were creating a Java-based application, you might do well to create a multithreaded server, create objects to code and decode your messaging protocol (KSOP, to be explained in the following chapter), and to implement your local and remote objects. This approach is a good Java method, but you will be doing something different.

Instead, you use your sockets exactly like pipes. You create a socket server that simply prints all client requests to STDOUT, and then waits for something to be written to its STDIN. Upon receiving input, the server forwards that information straight back to the client. The client Java process then also simply writes its message to STDOUT, and waits for another message on STDIN. You are essentially extending the pipe metaphor across the network. With this simple approach, you are trying to establish interprocess communication among distributed shell scripts. You are creating a base-level communications interface that you can adapt with shell object wrappers for use in your shell applications.

 By linking your socket commands to FIFOs, you can swap in network connectivity into any existing shell script that uses named pipes!

The Shell Architecture

Much of your use for sockets will be demonstrated in the following chapters when you develop an object request broker. The basic unit consists of a socket class in the shell. This class instantiates a FIFO system pipe and also creates a Java client as a coprocess. This coprocess is the wormhole to the network. Whatever you write into your socket class's pipe will be instantly grabbed and sent down the tubes. On the server end, the message will be extracted, acted upon, and any return result sent back to you. In this way, you can keep a minimal dependency on Java. You can add additional features and sophisticated socket arrangements in the socket class that wraps the Java command. Too much intelligence built into your Java routines makes them less applicable to a variety of situations, and forces you to create several slightly-different versions of the command. When you create your ORB, you actually create a Connection Manager that tracks all of your socket connections to various distributed servers. This Connection Manager actually maintains and instantiates socket classes on your behalf. By consolidating all of your connections to different servers, you reduce the amount of time spent creating new connections.

For now, you can simply concern yourself with making sockets, and developing a shell interface for your Java program.

Using Sockets

To start your socket programming, create a simple client and a simple server. The client connects to the server and the server responds with a greeting. The client writes the message out to the screen and then closes the connection.

You can start by examining some of the operations of the socket class. You are instantiating a member of the socket class as `sock` with `"localhost"` and port 2112 as parameters. You then create an object of `InputStream` and call the socket's method to return its input stream:

```
Socket sock = new Socket("localhost", 2112);
InputStream in = sock.getInputStream();
```

Once you have the socket's input stream, you can begin reading what is being sent. You read in one byte at a time and echo them to the screen:

```
while ( (ch = (char) in.read()) != '\n' )
System.out.print(ch);
System.out.println("");
```

In the preceding case, you create a `while` loop that reads byte by byte from the socket's input stream. By default, `InputStream.read()` returns an integer (`int`), so you are casting it as a character (`char`) for display. *Casting* is the method in which you take a variable of one type and effectively alter its type for a particular operation. When you're finished reading the message, you close the connection as follows:

```
sock.close();
```

Listing 7-1 shows the completed version of `client1.java`:

Listing 7-1: `client1.java`

```
import java.net.*;
import java.io.*;

public class client1
{
  client1(){}

  public void run()
  {
    try {
      Socket sock = new Socket("localhost", 2112);
      InputStream in = sock.getInputStream();

      char ch;

      while ( (ch = (char) in.read()) != '\n' )
        System.out.print(ch);
      System.out.println("");

      sock.close();
    } catch ( IOException e ) {
      e.printStackTrace();
    }
  }

  public static void main ( String Args[] )
  {
    client1 c = new client1();

    c.run();
  }
}
```

UNIX Shell Objects

The server portion of your application simply accepts connections, and returns one message: "This is the default server message." You create a `ServerSocket` in basically the same way, but you specify the port number. The hostname is assumed to be the machine on which the process is running:

```
ServerSocket servso = new ServerSocket( 2112, 100);
Socket so = servso.accept();
```

The `accept` function of the `ServerSocket` class returns an instance of a connected socket. Basically, when a client hits the server for a connection, the connection can be handed off via the `accept()` method. Your program actually pauses at `servso.accept()` until a connection comes in. When you finally get a connection, you try to get access to its `OutputStream`:

```
OutputStream out = so.getOutputStream();
```

After getting an instance of the connected socket's output stream, you can send your default message, and then close the connection:

```
String st = "This is the default server message!\n";
for (int c = 0; c < st.length(); c++)
ps.write( (int) st.charAt(c) );
so.close();
```

The complete listing of `server1.java` appears in Listing 7-2.

Listing 7-2: `server1.java`

```
import java.net.*;
import java.io.*;

public class server1
{
  server1(){}

  public void run()
  {
    ServerSocket servso;
    Socket so;
    OutputStream os;
    String st;

    try {
      servso = new ServerSocket( 2112, 100 );

      so = servso.accept();

      os = so.getOutputStream();
```

```
    st = "This is the default server message!\n";

    for (int c = 0; c < st.length(); c++)
      os.write( (int) st.charAt(c) );

    so.close();

  } catch (IOException e) {

    e.printStackTrace();
  }
}

public static void main ( String Args[] )
{
  server1 s = new server1();

  s.run();
}
}
```

With Java, these files compile and run on any hardware that supports a Java VM. To try the example, first launch the server process (run it in the background from the shell), and then try connecting the client:

```
$> java server1 &

$> java client1
This is the default server message!
```

By running the server as a background process, you don't have to open a new window to run the client. As as you can see, the process of creating sockets is pretty simple in Java.

You can also try your original Telnet trick again. Just start the server, and then telnet to the machine at port 2112:

```
$> java server1 &

$> telnet localhost 2112
This is the default server message!
Connection Closed...
```

In programming sockets, connections are expensive to create; that is, they take a long time. If you need to create a new connection to a server every time you send or receive information, your application will crawl. The next example addresses this problem.

`Client2.java` and `Server2.java` are essentially the same as our first examples, but with a couple notable changes. First, our server will be receiving messages instead of sending them. When it receives a message from a client, it will write it out to the screen. The server will also stay up indefinitely. Once started, you will have to manually end the server process. It will continue to accept client connections all day long.

Your client process starts from the command line with a message as a parameter. The client then connects to the server, sends the message, and then disconnects. You see exactly how long it takes to create a connection. In another example, you maintain client and server connections and examine the increased speed of your data transfer.

Be sure and run `client2.class` with your message as a parameter: `java client2 HELLO`.

At first, your client creates a socket instance directed at `"localhost"` and port 2112 again. As a slight change, you get an instance to the socket's output stream as a `PrintStream` object instead of an `OutputStream` object. The `PrintStream` object features the `println()` function, which makes it easier to write a line of text to the server:

```
Socket sock = new Socket("localhost", 2112);
PrintStream out = new PrintStream(sock.getOutputStream());
```

As another difference, your `run` method takes a string as an argument. This argument is passed in from the command line to your main function, which then passes it off to the `run` function.

```
public static void main ( String Args[] )
{
client2 c = new client2();

c.run(Args[0]);
}
```

When you've obtained the output stream for your socket, you write the string to it as follows:

```
out.println(message);
```

Then you close the connection as follows:

```
sock.close();
```

Listing 7-3 shows the full listing of `client2.java`:

Listing 7-3: `client2.java`

```
import java.net.*;
import java.io.*;

public class client2
{
  client2(){}

  public void run(String message)
  {
    try {
      Socket sock = new Socket("localhost", 2112);
      PrintStream out =
        new PrintStream(sock.getOutputStream());

      out.println(message);

      sock.close();
    } catch ( IOException e ) {
      e.printStackTrace();
    }
  }

  public static void main ( String Args[] )
  {
    client2 c = new client2();

    c.run(Args[0]);
  }
}
```

Your server process has also changed. First, the server is persistent and always exists until explicitly shut down. It takes a connection, reads in the message, writes the message to the screen, and then terminates the connection. To keep the process up indefinitely, enclose the key features within a `while` loop:

```
while (up)
{
so = servso.accept();
is = new DataInputStream(so.getInputStream());
st = is.readLine();

System.out.println(st);
so.close();
}
```

Also, in the preceding, you switch to using the `DataInputStream` object to provide operations on your socket connection's input stream. These operations enable you to read one line of text from the stream without having to do a `for` loop as before and wait for the newline (\n) character. Assign the result of `DataInputStream.readLine()` to your instantiated String object `st`:

```
st = is.readLine();
```

Because you're mainly interested in actual strings of text from your socket command, you can safely use the `println` and `readLine` methods.

You've also encountered the `boolean` type for the first time. An instance of this type can either be true or false. If you set `up` to `false` within your loop, the loop exits.

Listing 7-4 shows the complete listing of `server2.java`:

Listing 7-4: `server2.java`

```java
import java.net.*;
import java.io.*;

public class server2
{
  server2(){}

  public void run()
  {
    ServerSocket servso;
    Socket so;
    DataInputStream is;
    String st;
    boolean up = true;

    try {
      servso = new ServerSocket( 2112, 100 );

      while (up)
      {
        so = servso.accept();

        is = new DataInputStream(so.getInputStream());

        st = is.readLine();

        System.out.println(st);
        so.close();
      }

    } catch (IOException e) {
```

```
      e.printStackTrace();
    }
  }
  public static void main ( String Args[] )
  {
    server2 s = new server2();

    s.run();
  }
}
```

Exploring the Socket Command

Your socket command will be simple. You want to make the least common denominator socket command for use in your shell programs. By keeping the socket command simplistic, you can use it in the widest variety of situations. You can build more intelligence into your networking component, and even make your object request broker a multithreaded Java server, but the focus of this book is the UNIX shell – not so much Java. Therefore, your socket command should simply be a reusable component among your shell objects.

Figure 7-2 shows the architecture of your socket commands. You want to emulate the UNIX FIFO pipe structure, which is flexible for your shell scripts. Both of these components are tied to their STDIN and STDOUT for their basic operation. They basically behave exactly like a pipe, except what goes in is forwarded across the network to the receiving process. These implementations are actually slightly more complicated than presented so far.

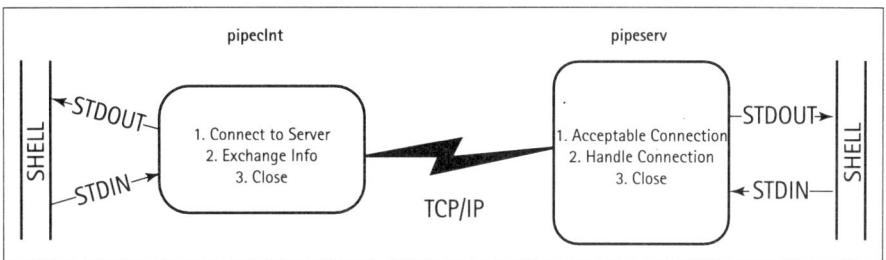

Figure 7-2: Java client and server components

The Client

The client needs to be able to connect to a server, attach its STDIN and STDOUT to a shell process, and then disconnect. The server needs to be able to accept such a connection, and handle it accordingly until the client wishes to disconnect. The server then needs to drop the connection and be ready to obtain another connection.

You should note that your server only handles one remote connection at a time, due to your shell-centric design. While you can instantiate countless objects on a machine's behalf and attach these objects to several different remote processes, a server can only communicate with one machine per time. To clarify, you can have eighteen different processes running on host A that instantiate eighteen different objects that live on server B, but host C will not be able to communicate with object instances on server B until host A is finished. You are trying to emulate a pipe, and the pipes used by shell scripts are certainly single-threaded and can only handle one connection at a time. The architecture presented in this book is primarily instructional, and if you want your object request broker to handle simultaneous connections, you can easily build that intelligence into your Java server. Actually, the overhead is fairly small. You only need to add an additional field to your communication protocol indicating where the message originated. Currently, any message sent to the server is routed back to the same connection. If you add many simultaneous connections, you only need to allow the Java server to route messages back to the appropriate connection. Regardless of the server implementation, if you're trying to attach the server to shell scripts, you need to bridge the process and language boundary with a named pipe that cannot determine where a message is coming from or where it is going. For brevity, your implementation only allows single connections. Note, however, that many different clients can connect in a matter of seconds, but only one can communicate at a time. If you need the additional connections, you can expand on this section's contents.

 Although a server can only entertain one client at a time, you can disconnect from the server, leaving your object instance still intact. You can then reconnect later and perform additional operations. Also, on the client side, you can create *n* number of server objects from the same client host, even across several processes. One client host may also establish connections with any number of servers.

Your client process differs from your earlier implementations. This version of the client takes a command line argument indicating the server with which to make a connection. This string value needs to be either the abbreviated or fully qualified domain name of the server. For example, to connect with a machine named jupiter.venus.com, you could use either:

```
$> java pipeclnt jupiter
```

or

```
$> java pipeclnt jupiter.venus.com
```

Chapter 7: Encapsulating the Network with Components

You can use any name to which the server will answer through DNS. Basically, the name you use to telnet is the name you use here. This value is passed off to our class's main function, which in turn, hands it off to the run method as follows:

```
public static void main ( String Args[] )
{
  pipeclnt wormhole = new pipeclnt();

  wormhole.run(Args[0]);
}
```

The run method is ready to accept this variable as a string:

```
public void run(String server)
{
try {
....
```

You use a PrintStream object for your socket connection's output stream and DataInputStreams for both STDIN and the socket's input stream. STDOUT is handled by the default System.out object. When your class's run method is called, all of your necessary stream objects are constructed as follows:

```
/* Create socket connection */
Socket sock = new Socket(server, 2112);

/* Create PrintStream object for socket output stream */
PrintStream out =
new PrintStream(sock.getOutputStream());

/* Create DataInputStream for stdin */
DataInputStream stdin =
new DataInputStream(System.in);

/* Create DataInputStream for socket's input stream */
DataInputStream in =
new DataInputStream(sock.getInputStream());

/* Create boolean variable for infinite loop */
boolean connected = true;

/* Create string object for messages */
String st;
```

The default port for your connection is 2112 – this is the port used by your object request broker. If you want to use a different port, you only need to change it in the client and server Java programs. The shell components of your system have no knowledge or interest as to which port is used. Your choice of port may depend on whether you'll be running your server as root, or if there are other applications on your machine that may already be using the port. Certain ports, usually lower numbered ports, are reserved for use by applications running under the superuser ID. Unless you are root, you won't be able to have your server listen on these ports. Also, other applications may be using the port already. Certain popular ports are 80 (http), 25 (smtp), and 1561 (some CORBA implementations), but any of these applications can be configured to run at a different port. Regardless of your port choice, the application still functions accordingly. You should try to standardize the port number across every instance of your application, however, to avoid confusion.

The rest of your client process is a loop that sends and receives messages. The shell object that launches your client as a coprocess explicitly controls the lifetime of your connection. At disconnection, the client sends a message with the server who closes the connection, and the client then closes itself and exits. The loop follows:

```
while (connected)
{
/* read stdin and write to socket connection */
st = stdin.readLine();
if (st.compareTo("disconnect") == 0) {
 out.println(st);
 sock.close();
 System.exit(0);
}
out.println(st);

/* get response and write to STDOUT */
st = in.readLine();
System.out.println(st);
}
```

The full listing of `pipeclnt.java` is shown in Listing 7-5.

Listing 7-5: `pipeclnt.java`

```
// pipeclnt.java
// $Id: pipeclnt.java,v 1.1 1998/02/23 00:52:20 chrisj Exp $
// $Log: pipeclnt.java,v $
// Revision 1.3 1998/02/23 00:52:20 chrisj
//
// Client process connects to server, maintains connection
// and sends STDIN to server, waits for response, then writes
// response to STDOUT.
//

import java.net.*;
import java.io.*;

public class pipeclnt
{
  pipeclnt(){}
```

```java
public void run(String server)
{
  try {
    /* Create socket connection */
    Socket sock = new Socket(server, 2112);

    /* Create PrintStream object for socket output stream */
    PrintStream out =
      new PrintStream(sock.getOutputStream());

    /* Create DataInputStream for stdin */
    DataInputStream stdin =
      new DataInputStream(System.in);

    /* Create DataInputStream for socket's input stream */
    DataInputStream in =
      new DataInputStream(sock.getInputStream());

    /* Create boolean variable for infinite loop */
    boolean connected = true;

    /* Create string object for messages */
    String st;

    while (connected)
    {
      /* read stdin and write to socket connection */
      st = stdin.readLine();
      if (st.compareTo("disconnect") == 0 ) {
        out.println(st);
        sock.close();
        System.exit(0);
      }
      out.println(st);

      /* get response and write to STDOUT */
      st = in.readLine();
      System.out.println(st);
    }
  } catch ( IOException e ) {
    e.printStackTrace();
  }
}

public static void main ( String Args[] )
{
  pipeclnt wormhole = new pipeclnt();

  wormhole.run(Args[0]);
}
}
```

The Server

Your server implementation significantly differs from your previous versions. Your server process needs to accept a connection, exchange information with the client for as long as the client wishes, and then terminate the connection when told to do so. It then needs to listen, and accept any future connections. This approach enables your server process to remain running indefinitely, providing services to clients as needed.

The server process doesn't need command line parameters. The server is assumed to have started on the machine on which it is intended to run. Obviously, you cannot create a server socket on a remote machine. The main function of your `pipeserv` class simply constructs an instance of itself, and then calls its own `run` method:

```
public static void main ( String Args[] )
{
  pipeserv wormhole = new pipeserv();

  wormhole.run();
}
```

The `run` method first constructs the objects that will be reused through connections, which are a string object for the messages and a Boolean value indicating the connection state:

```
/* Create string object for messages */
String st;
/* Boolean variable for infinite loop */
boolean up = true;
```

You then enter the try block in which you create your server socket and your input stream for STDIN – these are also reused across connections:

```
try {

/* Create the server socket */
ServerSocket servso =
new ServerSocket( 2112, 100 );

/* Create input stream for STDIN */
DataInputStream stdin =
new DataInputStream(System.in);
```

The first parameter passed to `ServerSocket` is the port number, and the second is the queue length. Now that you constructed your objects, you're ready to deal with connections. The main loop of our program is quite small, but includes a call to `handleConnection`, which actually does all the work:

Chapter 7: Encapsulating the Network with Components 179

```
while (up)
{
  Socket s = servso.accept();

  this.handleConnection(s, stdin);
}
```

After you've handled the connection, and your call to handleConnection has returned, the loop starts over again with the following:

```
Socket s = servso.accept();
```

This line of code actually pauses until a connection is established. You can think of the accept function as the starting point to socket interaction. This concept describes the program flow, although the handleConnection function does most of the work. The function takes a socket object and a DataInputStream object as parameters:

```
public void handleConnection(Socket so, DataInputStream stdin)
{
 try {
```

These objects represent the recently connected socket, and STDIN from the shell. The server is also handled as a coprocess by a shell object.

Once handleConnection has received a socket, it can construct input and output stream objects based on the socket:

```
/* Create input stream for socket */
DataInputStream is =
new DataInputStream(so.getInputStream());

/* Create output stream for socket */
PrintStream out =
new PrintStream(so.getOutputStream());
```

Next you read the first message in from the socket connection:

```
// get input from socket

String st = is.readLine();
```

You then enter your processing loop, in which you extract messages from the socket and display them to STDOUT for processing by the shell object. The server then waits for a message back from the coprocess via STDIN, and sends that back to client connection. You are notified that the client wishes to disconnect when it actually sends the disconnect message. You are limited in flexibility with your Java socket processes, because they are intrinsically tied to STDIN and STDOUT, and the shell coprocesses that control them. Therefore, you have to make the socket processes simple. Ordinarily, a server and a client can both be aware of when their connection has ceased, and the server can call the close method. You actually let the client indicate its desire to end the connection by notifying you with the "disconnect" string:

```java
while (st.compareTo("disconnect") != 0 )
{
  System.out.println(st);

  /* Read input from STDIN, write to socket */
  st = stdin.readLine();
  out.println(st);
  st = is.readLine();
}
```

Once the client has indicated that it wishes to close the connection, the loop is broken and the connection is closed:

```java
// close connection
so.close();
```

At this point, `handleConnection` returns and the accept function acts again as the wait point for future connections. Listing 7-6 shows the full listing of `pipeserv.java`.

Listing 7-6: `pipeserv.java`

```java
// pipeserv.java
// $Id: pipeserv.java,v 1.3 1998/02/23 00:52:55 chrisj Exp $
// $Log: pipeserv.java,v $
// Revision 1.3 1998/02/23 00:52:55 chrisj
//
//   Server process waits on socket 2112 and
//   writes all incoming messages to STDOUT, then waits for
//   return input, which it sends back to the client
//

import java.net.*;
import java.io.*;

public class pipeserv
{
  pipeserv(){}

    public void run()
    {
      /* Create string object for messages */
      String st;
      /* Boolean variable for infinite loop */
```

```java
    boolean up = true;

    try {

      /* Create the server socket */
      ServerSocket servso =
        new ServerSocket( 2112, 500 );

      /* Create input stream for STDIN */
      DataInputStream stdin =
        new DataInputStream(System.in);

      while (up)
      {
        Socket s = servso.accept();

        this.handleConnection(s, stdin);
      }

      servso.close();
      System.exit(0);


    } catch (IOException e) {

      e.printStackTrace();
    }
  }

public void handleConnection(Socket so, DataInputStream stdin)
{
  try {
    /* Create input stream for socket */
    DataInputStream is =
      new DataInputStream(so.getInputStream());

    /* Create output stream for socket */
    PrintStream out =
      new PrintStream(so.getOutputStream());

    // get input from socket

    String st = is.readLine();

    while (st.compareTo("disconnect") != 0 )
    {
      System.out.println(st);

      /* Read input from STDIN, write to socket */
      st = stdin.readLine();
      out.println(st);
      st = is.readLine();
    }
```

```
    // close connection
    so.close();
  } catch (IOException e) {
    e.printStackTrace();
  }

    return;
  }
  public static void main ( String Args[] )
  {
    pipeserv wormhole = new pipeserv();

    wormhole.run();
  }
}
```

Investigating Shell Examples

Now you can communicate across machine and process boundaries with an ordinary shell script.

As previously discussed, the `print -p` and `read -p` commands communicate with a coprocess. The STDIN and STDOUT of the coprocess are attached to the controlling script. In the following example, you essentially have a coprocess relationship distributed across the network. After you issue a `print -p`, a shell process residing on an entirely different machine issues a `read -p` and receives your message. This approach is an excellent means of interprocess communication for shell scripts!

Compared to the Java programs you've just created, the example shell scripts that control these Java programs are quite simple. You create a coprocess by applying the |& symbol after command name, as follows:

```
# create java server as co-process
java pipeserv |&
```

You can then control the `pipeserv` command's STDIN and STDOUT. By design, `pipeserv` simply forwards its STDIN and STDOUT off to its client connection. Now you can see the benefits of keeping your Java processes simple.

Your first script, `test1.sh`, launches your server process and waits for connections. In the following example, you create a greeting server in the shell script. Basically, your script waits for input from the coprocess, interprets the message, and routes back the appropriate greeting:

```
read -p message
```

Chapter 7: Encapsulating the Network with Components

Once you've obtained the message from the coprocess, compare it against your list of known greetings:

```
case $message in

"Hello")
output="Hello yourself!"
;;

"How are you?")
output="I'm fine, and you?"
;;

"Goodbye")
output="Goodbye!"
;;

*)
output="Unknown phrase."
;;
esac
```

You assign the variable output to be equal to your response string. Once you've set up your response, you send it back to the coprocess:

```
# write message back to socket
print -p $output
```

As you can see, this example is a simple shell script. Upon closer examination, notice that the coprocess is actually forwarding your messages across the network to a similar socket-shell symbiosis on the other side. Listing 7-7 shows the complete listing of test1.sh.

Listing 7-7: test1.sh

```
#!/bin/ksh
#
# Create a java server and trade message with a client

# create java server as co-process
  java pipeserv |&

while read -p message
do
  case $message in

    "Hello")
      output="Hello yourself!"
      ;;
```

```
        "How are you?")
          output="I'm fine, and you?"
          ;;

        "Goodbye")
          output="Goodbye!"
          ;;
        *)
          output="Unknown phrase."
          ;;
      esac

      #
      # write message back to socket
      print -p $output
done
```

The client side is completed by an equally simple script, test2.sh. This script launches your Java client as a coprocess with the server name as a parameter:

```
# create java client as co-process
java pipeclnt $1 |&
```

Once your connection has been established, you line up your messages to be sent to the coprocess, and eventually across the network. Each of your messages is phrased to elicit a kind response from the server, resulting in a polite conversation:

```
for messg in "Hello" "How are you?" "Goodbye" "disconnect"
do

print -p $messg

read -p output

print $output

done
```

Your last message to the server is the disconnect string, which causes the server to close your connection. The shell's coprocess is now free to exit. Listing 7-8 shows the full listing of test2.sh.

Listing 7-8: test2.sh

```
#!/bin/ksh
#
# Create a java client and trade message with a client


# create java client as co-process
```

Chapter 7: Encapsulating the Network with Components

```
  java pipeclnt $1 |&

#
# read messages from STDIN, and write to server

for messg in "Hello" "How are you?" "Goodbye" "disconnect"
do

  print $messg
  print -p $messg

  read -p output

  print $output"\t* REMOTE *"

done
```

Try these shell scripts by opening two windows on your machine. You can put the server and client on different machines, or keep them on your local machine. Regardless of location, you'll need to start the server first:

```
$> ./test1.sh
```

You won't see anything after this command – in fact, the process won't ever come down. You need to explicitly control-C it, and even then you may have to kill the `pipeserv` process running underneath! This example is just a simple demo, and the server is meant to last a long time; therefore, the process that spawns the server also determines its demise.

The client, however, is a little friendlier. Because it cleans up after itself, you can run it repeatedly. The client also shows you the available quickness of communication across processes. In this simple example, you are actually crossing four processes and the TCP/IP network. Still, the results are pretty snappy after the initial connection lag. Connections are slow to create, and as you develop your object request broker, you'll see how to economize your connections by sharing them and keeping them persistent as long as possible. To try the client script, you need to indicate the machine on which your server is located, even if it's the local machine:

```
$>./test2.sh localhost
Hello
Hello Yourself!   *REMOTE*
How are you?
I'm fine, and you?   *REMOTE*
Goodbye
Goodbye!    *REMOTE*
```

You're done – a simple conversation is conducted between two individual shell scripts running on completely different machines. A little more than you expected from the shell? Probably not if you've read this far!

 To terminate, your Java server process must be explicitly killed. Its primary job is to be a listener, and as such, it must try to stay available all of the time. You could pass a string from the outside indicating for the server to terminate, but that task could allow rogue users to kill your server. If you're uncomfortable killing UNIX processes, you can create a starter script to log the PID of the server. You can also create a stop script, which reads the PID and issues the kill command.

This section describes how your socket commands coexist with your shell objects. You actually use coprocesses to attach your Java commands to UNIX FIFO pipes, thus allowing any number of processes running on the machine to use the services of the Java connection. If you keep all of your connections solely as coprocesses, only one shell process can communicate at any given time. By attaching the Java commands to FIFOs, you can maintain one connection to a server to be used by any number of shell objects.

Creating a Socket Class for the Shell

You need to create a reusable object to represent socket connections. You'll use this object in every shell script that needs access to the network. You'll also use one instance of your class across multiple objects, thus minimizing your network connections.

Your class basically bridges a FIFO pipe with a Java socket coprocess. The class accepts a server as a parameter and creates a FIFO pipe with the same name as the server. It then instantiates a network connection to the target. Finally, your class then goes to work, bridging all input and output from your pipe across the network via the Java coprocess. Figure 7-3 shows socket.cls wrapping a Java process.

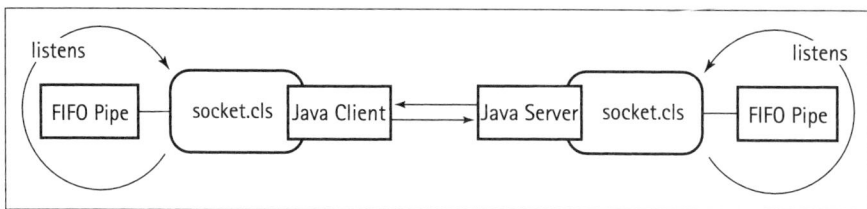

Figure 7-3: Socket.cls wrapping a Java process

As a result, you can do the following:

Chapter 7: Encapsulating the Network with Components 187

```
$> print "message" > miles

$> read result < miles
```

In the preceding, `miles` is not only a FIFO in the current directory, but all messages sent to that location are magically transported across the network to the host `miles`, who has a shell process ready to act upon these messages.

The `socket.cls` constructor takes care of contacting the remote server and creating the local FIFO, as follows:

```
_socket()      {
       _strTarget=$1

       mkfifo $1

}
```

You use the `mkfifo` command to generate a pipe with the same name as the server you attempt to contact with the `pipeclnt` command.

An instantiated socket object has its `sendrecv` method called to start communication. This function basically enters an infinite loop of communication with the server, as follows:

```
#
# read input from pipe
read mesg < $_strTarget

#
# write input to socket
print -p $mesg

#
# read result from socket
read -p rez

#
# write result to pipe
print $rez >> $_strTarget
```

The same sort of behavior used in your Java processes is exhibited here, with one exception to the shell client. The `sendrecv` method also checks the STDIN for a disconnect message. If it receives this message, it notifies the server to close the connection and then cleans up, as follows:

```
if [[ $mesg = "disconnect" ]]; then
#
# disconnect from server process,
# exit shell process
```

```
print -p "disconnect"

#
# remove FIFO pipe

rm $_strTarget
return
fi
```

You can have also build this functionality into the Java client itself. Listing 7-9 shows the complete listing of socket.cls.

Listing 7-9: socket.cls

```
##############################################################
#
# socket.cls
#
# This object creates a bridge from a FIFO pipe to a
# network socket connected to a remote server. A socket client
# is instantiated as a co-process, and effectively attached
# to a FIFO for access from multiple, local processes.
#
# Methods
# _socket
# _sendrecv
#
# Data Members
# _strTarget  - remote machine to connect with
# _pPid       - PID of Java co-process
#
##############################################################
_socket() {
  _strTarget=$1

  mkfifo $1
}

_sendrecv() {
  #
  # This function puts the object into a loop, listening
  # on the FIFO for incoming messages, forwarding those to
  # the co-process. It then listens on the co-process for
  # the result, which it writes back out to the FIFO.
  #
java pipeclnt $_strTarget |&
#
  while true
  do
    #
    # read input from pipe
    read mesg < $_strTarget
```

```
    if [[ $mesg = "disconnect" ]]; then
      #
      # disconnect from server process,
      # exit shell process

      print -p "disconnect"

      #
      # remove FIFO pipe

      rm $_strTarget
      return
    fi

    #
    # write input to socket
    print -p $mesg

    #
    # read result from socket
    read -p rez

    #
    # write result to pipe
    print $rez >> $_strTarget
  done
}
```

The architecture of the socket class is meant to optimize connectivity. You can instantiate one socket class per remote machine with which you wish to communicate. Any process running on the local machine can use the pipe created by the socket class. This approach enables us to create several different object instances existing on the remote machine that are controlled by several different local processes. You only have to create one connection, and your throughput should be pretty snappy.

Summary

In this chapter, you learned how to use Java's convenient object model to create client and server Internet sockets. Until now, this powerful API for use in distributed computing hasn't readily been available to shell programmers. By tying a socket-capable binary executable to a shell script as a coprocess, you can communicate not only across machine and network boundaries, but across programming boundaries as well. By letting a shell object connect a static FIFO pipe to a network socket, and eventually to another FIFO pipe on another machine, you allow for Internetworking of shell scripts, which should be of great utility.

The next chapter uses these Java commands by creating an object request broker for the shell. To facilitate object-to-object communication, the chapter develops a Korn shell object protocol (KSOP).

Chapter 8

Distributed Objects

IN THIS CHAPTER

- The Korn shell object protocol
- Proxies for clients
- Connection management
- The object request broker server
- Distributed architectures

DISTRIBUTED OBJECTS ARE the wave of the future. As applications and services become more distributed across the network, the need to access these services easily from a variety of different applications is essential. Connecting disparate, detached, standalone entities is the province of distributed objects.

Exploring Distributed Services

If you consider the concepts discussed and used in the code thus far, you realize that object-orientation is about small, self-contained components that are as independent as possible. This level of detachment allows for the most reuse. Encapsulation helps to conceal object implementation from those who need its services, thus furthering the capability to reuse the object and forcing you to think in terms of interfaces – not implementation. These ideas work great for developing applications from components. But until now, all of these components have more or less been assembled at design time. You take different pieces of code and link them together to form an application. You can reuse these components in other applications you develop. This strategy has proved its worth, and now you will extrapolate it across the network level. Why should the objects and services you reuse exist on one machine? Why should applications that are used across a network not take advantage of distributed services?

The Advantages of Distribution

In this chapter, you discover a mechanism for deploying the objects you've developed across the network, and how to use these distributed objects in code that executes on any machine. You can create a `unixServer` object that represents a host on your network, and code with it as if it were local. In fact, you'll be able to create objects that represent every host on your network, and use one script on your workstation to control them all. Best of all, coding with a remote object is virtually no different than coding with a local object. Previously, you used syntax like the following to create an object within your script:

```
. unixServer myServer localhost
```

Afterwards, you could code with the `myServer` object. Use the following code to implement the same object to reside on a remote machine:

```
. proxy.sh remotemachine unixServer myServer
```

In this case, you pass off the location and type of object you want to the proxy object, as well as the name you wish to use locally. After this call, you can code with the `myServer` object as if it were local.

Access functions and encapsulation pay off the most in this instance. By keeping all internal data encapsulated, you can completely hide the implementation of this object. In fact, this object could reside on a non-UNIX machine or be written in an entirely different language, provided the communications are set up properly. Because you are writing your networking components in Java, you could easily use one of the commercially available shell interpreters on a Windows machine to interact with distributed UNIX servers.

How does this work? In this chapter, you design an object request broker (ORB). The Common ORB Architecture (CORBA) is an industry standard created by the Object Management Group to facilitate network and distributed development. CORBA is an extremely robust set of services and a common protocol IIOP (Internet InterORB Protocol) supported by many different vendors. Objects can be written in C++, registered with an ORB, and used by Java applets residing on someone's Web page. Likewise, objects can be written in Java, registered with an ORB, and used by clients written in C++ running on Windows. Other object models exist, including the Microsoft Windows COM and DCOM models, as well as the Java Beans component models, but CORBA is the most fully developed, tested, and widely-used distributed object architecture today. Unlike the others, CORBA is used in powerful manufacturing applications. The Boeing company uses IONA's Orbix ORB to integrate its many applications and platforms used in the manufacturing of airplanes via its famed DCAC/MRM system. Distributed objects are here to stay, and CORBA and DCOM/COM architectures are paving the way. Figure 8-1 shows a simple distributed object architecture.

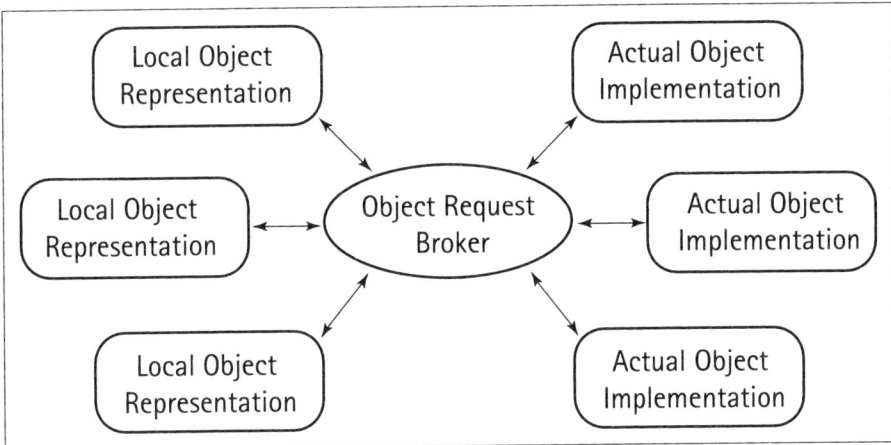

Figure 8-1: A simple distributed object architecture

Regardless of the ORB, the concepts remain the same. An application that uses objects should be able to do so, regardless of their location. This capability is the power of distributed computing. The ORB you develop in this chapter, however, is not CORBA-compliant. While it would be great to control CORBA objects with Korn shell scripts, developing a language mapping for the Korn shell is no small task and a little outside the scope of this book. Instead, you develop your own simple way for objects to communicate. Your architecture will be interface-driven and have its own wire protocol: KSOP (Korn Shell Object Protocol), which is really just a string representation of an object. You'll take an object's name, location, and methods and pack it into a compact string for transport across the network. Senders and receivers will have facilities for coding and decoding your object representations.

Distributed Interfaces

Because interfaces are crucial in object-oriented programming, especially distributed object programming, much of this book discusses this topic. The interface is what an object presents to the world — it is the front end to the encapsulated data the object contains. One of the primary ways that you share objects across the network is through an interface definition of the object. When a client needs a remote object, it asks a proxy or some sort of network liaison for the remote object. The proxy queries or indicates to the ORB that it wishes to use a remote object. Upon receipt of an object reference, the client can begin to use the remote object. Every method invocation is reflected in the remote object. Parameters and messages are passed off to the ORB, which then passes the name of the method and the accompanying arguments to the object instance. Likewise, the method's return results are routed back to the caller. The effect is transparent to the client. When a client using a remote `person` object issues a `myPerson_getName`, the result almost instantly returns, just as if the method call had been local.

The interface allows this process to work. You don't need to know the behavior (or method of behavior) of a person object, even if it is a gigantic COBOL process running on a VAX machine (ew!). You just need to ascertain your client knows the methods that a person object supports. The ORB handles your method invocation, and makes sure that the actual object instance receives your method invocation. You only need connectivity to the ORB. You begin coding with a remote object in the language in which your program is written; you don't know or care about the language in which the remote object was constructed.

If you were to write CORBA objects, you would actually use a language called the IDL (Interface Definition Language) to create object skeletons. These IDL skeletons could then be used to construct objects in any language of your choice. IDL is the language of CORBA and allows different programming languages to talk to each other. The IDL can be considered the common ground between languages. IDL is fairly simple and contains no implementation – only interfaces. As a result, there are no conditional expressions, evaluations, arithmetic sections, logical operators, or other factors that are very language-dependent. IDL only has a few simple data types. This simple language provides a middle ground as any language that wishes to implement CORBA-compliant objects can simply provide a translation from IDL to native code. A variety of IDL compilers can generate skeleton object code in a native language from IDL. From the same piece of IDL code, you can generate a C++ object skeleton as well as a Java object skeleton. If you are ambitious, you can even generate a Korn shell skeleton from IDL. While this book does not work in CORBA, it certainly takes advantages of interfaces.

Distributed Servers

By now you're probably wondering what is involved in this seemingly complex programming procedure. This chapter dissects every nook and cranny in due time, but let's continue with the overview. On the server side, you have the ORB process – although in distributed object programming, "server" and "client" roles are sometimes indistinguishable, because many times an object plays the role of a server and then suddenly plays the role of a client. In most of this book's examples, the objects controlled by the ORB reside on the same machine as the ORB, but this condition is not a requirement. If you want to place ten objects on host *A* that you want to control from ten different machines on your network, you just need to put an ORB server process on host *A*, and those objects would then be available to the world. Objects, however, don't necessarily need to be on the same machine as the ORB that controls them. Given the Java-pipe components you developed in the preceding chapter, anytime you use a pipe to communicate across shell processes, you could just as well cross machine boundaries. This situation is quite a powerful development for script writing. In all of your existing shell code, any FIFO can be substituted with your networking commands – effectively distributing your application. These network pipes are the backbone of your distributed development in the shell.

 In many CORBA implementations, you can register any object with an ORB regardless of its location. For example, a particular Web server software package allows for plug-ins to be generated from CORBA IDL. The objects can then be registered with the Web server as an application, even if they are on a completely different server from the Web server. This approach is great for Internet applications that need access to distributed services.

Most ORB implementations have an object repository where their registered objects and interfaces are kept. The ORB server basically listens for network connections, supplies the location of object implementations to solicitors, and implements method invocations on behalf of client requests. The ORB server also sees that any return messages are routed back to the caller, and the ORB server process may take care of cleaning up object instances that it controls when the client no longer wishes to use them.

Distributed Clients

As previously discussed, the programmer need not concentrate on the client side. Instead of creating an object from a file that exists on the same machine, you ask the remote server for the object. This call, depending on the language, may return a pointer or some form of reference to the remote object that you can use locally.

Creating an instance of a remote object is similar to employing the factory object used earlier to encapsulate you from different types of `unixServer` objects. Previously, you used a `servFactory` class to instantiate subtypes of `unixServer` objects. The factory actually looked up the server's hostname in a table to determine the server's type of UNIX. The factory then instantiated the appropriate object, which enabled to worry not about which subtype you were implementing, but only that the subtype implemented the desired common interface. Unfortunately, all of the objects that represented remote servers were actually implemented locally and used the `rutilities` to bridge the network. With local object implementation, the main problem was the required knowledge of the target server's UNIX flavor. You certainly couldn't use an HP-UX object on a Solaris machine.

The ORB relieves the need for the factory class (in that particular situation). You can now simply ask for a `unixServer` interface without knowledge of the machine that implements the object. As far as your clients are concerned, the remote machine could be a Windows NT server. Your clients do not have to deal with network connections either. The client only needs to ask the proxy stub code for the remote object — the proxy takes care of everything else. In the architecture developed in this chapter, you actually use a connection manager to handle your connections to remote machines. You may have a local script that uses remote objects located on three servers. You may want to run multiple instances of this script at the same time. You don't want every object to open its own connection to a remote server. Creating connections is time-consuming, especially using the method of bridging FIFOs and Java. Once a connection is established, however, communication is pretty snappy. To make your calls more efficient, a connection manager maintains one connection per remote server. When a proxy seeks to retrieve a remote object for a client, it first checks that the connection has been created — if not, it asks the connection manager to create it. Likewise, the connection manager notes when a connection is being used and lets the connection drop when no local clients are using it, which helps optimize your performance. Using this scheme, you can have ten different scripts reference ten different objects across a few network hosts, and only maintain one connection per host.

 If you use one particular machine to house most of your remote objects, you don't need to use the connection manager. In this case, you can simply create one connection when needed and use it throughout the client program.

Distributed Proxies

The proxy or stub is the real workhorse on the client side. In the scheme you develop, the proxy actually takes care of requesting a network connection from the connection manager, retrieving a remote interface, decoding, and building a virtual object from the interface that it returns to the client. Surprisingly, the code for the proxy, as well as the ORB server, is quite small. You can configure your proxies to your needs, but this proxy depends upon you to set up a connection. You can also use the connection manager to create the connection and call the proxy for you.

The proxy then attempts to locate the ORB server, and asks for the requested interface. If the server does not hold the interface, the proxy exits and indicates that condition. You can also configure your proxies to start querying other hosts on your network at your discretion.

Provided that the proxy locates an ORB and successfully retrieves the interface, it then has the rather daunting task of constructing a virtual object on your behalf.

Examining Distributed Architecture

This section discusses in greater detail the distributed architecture you design in this chapter. Your design has two main components: objects and connections. In your local, single-threaded scripts, you can combine objects, raise events, and code with objects directly. You'll be adding the distributed network to this scenario, which complicates matters considerably. The main side effect: the need for seamless connections to all of these remote machines.

A Word about Pipes

This architecture is entirely dependent on named pipes for its operation. Your clients send information down a pipe and immediately attempt to read results back. Normally, a write or read to a pipe causes your program's execution to pause until another process opens the other side of the pipe for reading or writing. For example, examine the following code:

```
print "hello" > mypipe
read answer < mypipe
print $answer
```

You should expect your program to pause after the `print` statement until another process opens the pipe and extracts your message: `hello`. Your program could then continue on to the `read` statement, in which it pauses until another program opens the pipe for writing. This sequence allows the second program to act on your message: `hello`, and then write a response to you. On some operating systems, your message would be immediately extracted out of the pipe by your `read answer` statement before any other process would have a chance to extract it. This condition defeats the purpose of pipes for IPC, but it does occur on some flavors of UNIX. Thankfully, this is not the case on Linux.

If your flavor of UNIX exhibits this behavior, in which a `write` to a pipe followed by an immediate `read` results in your process extracting the very data it just put into the pipe, you need to incorporate some sort of timing mechanism to allow another process to read the information.

This scenario may not be the case from the command line, and it may appear to work. To test, you need to create two programs. The first program attempts to read from a pipe, does something with the variable it receives (for good measure), and then sends a message back into the pipe. You need to create another routine just like the preceding "hello" example that prints to a pipe and subsequently reads from it. Start with the first program. If your second program writes hello and then immediate extracts hello, and your first program ends up reading a blank line or null character, you need to implement timing.

Timing can be as simple as doing some processing in between reads and writes, or in the extreme, actually inserting a `sleep` statement. Usually a mere fraction of a second is a long enough pause for another process to read from the pipe.

Connections and Objects

You've done a few clever things so far to help yourself along. A named pipe, or FIFO, is the principal means of interprocess communication within the UNIX shell. This approach is a well-established practice and many people are used to coding with pipes – therefore encapsulating the network via the named pipe mechanism was a logical step. By creating a FIFO attached to a Java coprocess, you can easily snap your network component into place anywhere a named pipe is being used. In itself, this approach can revolutionize the way you write shell programs.

The second task you need to accomplish before you can distribute your objects is to develop a protocol for representing objects (or at least their interfaces) in a format appropriate for transport across the network. Furthermore, this format needs to be both translated back into an object once it reaches its destination and easily converted into the format when it's about to be transported.

Your connections are based on pipes. When a client script wishes to establish a connection with a remote server, it can use a socket object (see `socket.cls`) to establish the connection. Any process running on the client machine that needs to communicate with the object broker can use this one connection. Once the connection is established, it can remain intact as long as needed. In fact, you'll design a connection manager that maintains server connections so that client scripts requesting remote objects need not be considered with managing connections. If script A needs an object on host B, it first sees if a pipe exists for this server; if not, it can either create the connection itself, or signal the connection manager to create one. If you're writing standalone scripts that complete their work and then exit, you can easily manage your own connections. If you intend to run several different scripts or several instances of the same script, you may want to use a connection manager to keep track of things.

A following section discusses the connection manager in depth; for now, let's examine more of the connections involved in your application.

THE CLIENT

You'll probably be most concerned with the client script at first. A client script can instantiate any type of local or remote object. You've coded many examples already where your scripts have accomplished a variety of tasks by instantiating objects, using their interfaces, and then cleaning up when the work is done. You can instantiate remote objects virtually the same way. The only difference between local and remote object creation is that you have to ask for a remote object from the server that owns it. You'll develop a script, `proxy.sh`, that will take care of asking a server for an object instance and creating the appropriate interface for you on the client side. The syntax for `proxy.sh` follows:

```
proxy.sh <servername> object myObject
```

As you can see, this approach is fairly straightforward. The only extra information you need to supply is the host name where the object is implemented. If done locally, this same instantiation would be as follows:

```
object myObject
```

Once you've obtained a reference, you can code normally, as follows:

`myObject_method arguments`

Method invocations are exactly the same for both local and remote objects. The only difference required of the client is the utilization of the proxy script to retrieve and emulate the remote object.

As a side effect of this architecture, you cannot reference a member variable of an instantiated remote object. Internal data is encapsulated; if you need to know the value of an internal data member, you need to call its access function. This caveat needs to be considered when designing your distributed objects. You'll need to supply access functions for every data member with which a client may need to deal. While you may think this step is a hindrance, it actually forces you to encapsulate your data. Little performance overhead exists, and in most cases, you design your objects in this manner anyway. At this point, representing remote objects locally, even down to each specific data member, is not particularly difficult. With a few modifications to the KSOP protocol, you could add fields for marshaled data. This step slightly complicates matters, and these changes need to be designed into your code/decode routines. For the most part, however, this approach is not impossible.

THE PROXY

As described in a preceding section, the proxy retrieves remote object interfaces on your behalf and constructs a virtual object for you to use. Notably, the proxy defines a `_release` method as opposed to the `_delete` method. Because your objects' data is located on a remote machine, you cannot delete it locally. Therefore, when you're done with a remote object, you call its `_release` method. The release method informs the server that you are finished with the object and that the server can drop its instance. The connection used to contact the server, however, is not affected. You'll use a different approach to sever a Java socket connection.

In terms of the client, the proxy plays the most important role. The proxy completes all of the secret work that must be done in order to let your client think that its dealing with a real object. When you give `proxy.sh` the name of an object to retrieve, it turns around and asks the ORB server for instructions on how to construct the correct interface. For example, if you ask for a person object, the ORB returns a KSOP string with the following encoded version of a person interface:

`394598374958734:setName:getName:setAge:getAge`

The `proxy.sh` script decodes this version into an interface. It then iterates through the definition, creating ghost implementations of every method contained in the string. `proxy.sh` creates each method with the same basic implementation. The method takes parameters, encodes them in KSOP, and then sends them off to the ORB. The method then listens for the return results, and presents back to you in an appropriate way. This effect is transparent for you, because the object behaves as intended. The subtle difference: there is no real implementation on the client side.

THE OBJECT BROKER

The object broker sits between a client and a distributed object instance. The object broker process listens on port 2112 for requests. Once a request is received, the ORB acts upon it appropriately. The ORB services the following main types of requests: request, method, and release.

As you may guess, the request type of method is a client's initial ask for an object interface definition. The object broker decodes the KSOP string to determine which object the client is after. A KSOP request may look like the following:

```
request:person
```

The ORB decodes this request and begins looking for a person object in the repository. The repository is a directory beneath the ORB server's home that contains interface definitions for all of the objects registered on the server. The ORB finds the correct definition, loads it, and returns the KSOP string to the client. Just prior to returning the interface, the ORB server launches an instance of the object as a separate process tethered via a uniquely named pipe. This process stays intact until the caller eventually calls the release method, at which point the tethered process exits. This sequence enables you to create countless instances of the same object on the server, with each one keeping its own private data.

As you might expect, the method request is an invocation of a method on an instance object. The method request usually looks like the following:

```
39475938745345345:setName:Fred
```

The ORB decodes this string and determines the proper object instance, and then forwards the method and arguments to the tethered object instance. Whatever the instance returns to the ORB is also returned back to the client.

The release request is the third type of request that the ORB handles. The relcase request is the client's means of telling the server that a particular object can be destroyed. Actually, the ORB hands this information over to the object itself and lets it conduct its own exit. The ORB then removes the unique pipe from which the object was tethered.

The ORB's main purpose is to provide a single point of access to distributed objects. The ORB also maintains standalone object instances on behalf of client requests.

THE OBJECT INSTANCE

The final piece of your distributed architecture is the actual remote instance. As previously noted, when the ORB server process gets a request for an interface, it locates the interface within the repository. If the ORB server process finds the interface, it sends it back to the client and then calls the following:

```
instance $UniqueIdentifier $Object $args &
```

The preceding launches the instance script in the background, passing it the name of the object. The instance script then instantiates this object with the given parameters and waits for subsequent requests from the ORB.

The first argument passed to your instance script is the UniqueInstance Identifier, which is the approximately 18-digit random integer that the ORBserver generated when it launched the instance. This number is used to identify this specific instance for the ORB based on client requests. Every method invocation and operation that a client wishes to perform on a remote object will have this random digit ID number associated with it. This approach ensures that every object requested by a client has its own unique instance, and keep its data encapsulated and secure.

When the instance receives this ID number, it listens on a named pipe with the same name as the ID. If you look in the ORBserv's directory while it's executing, you'll see a named pipe created for each active instance. When the ORB receives a request, it breaks apart the KSOP string to retrieve the unique ID, and then sends the method invocation into the pipe named after that ID.

When the instance script receives the release message, it tears down its object instance. Then the ORB removes the named pipe, and the instance finally exits.

The Big Picture

As you can see, you use a pipe every time you need to communicate across processes. Every time you need a "thread" of execution that takes care of its own operation, you launch either a coprocess or a background process, and tie it to your application with a named pipe. As shown in Figure 8-2, you can bridge the network in every place you're using a pipe.

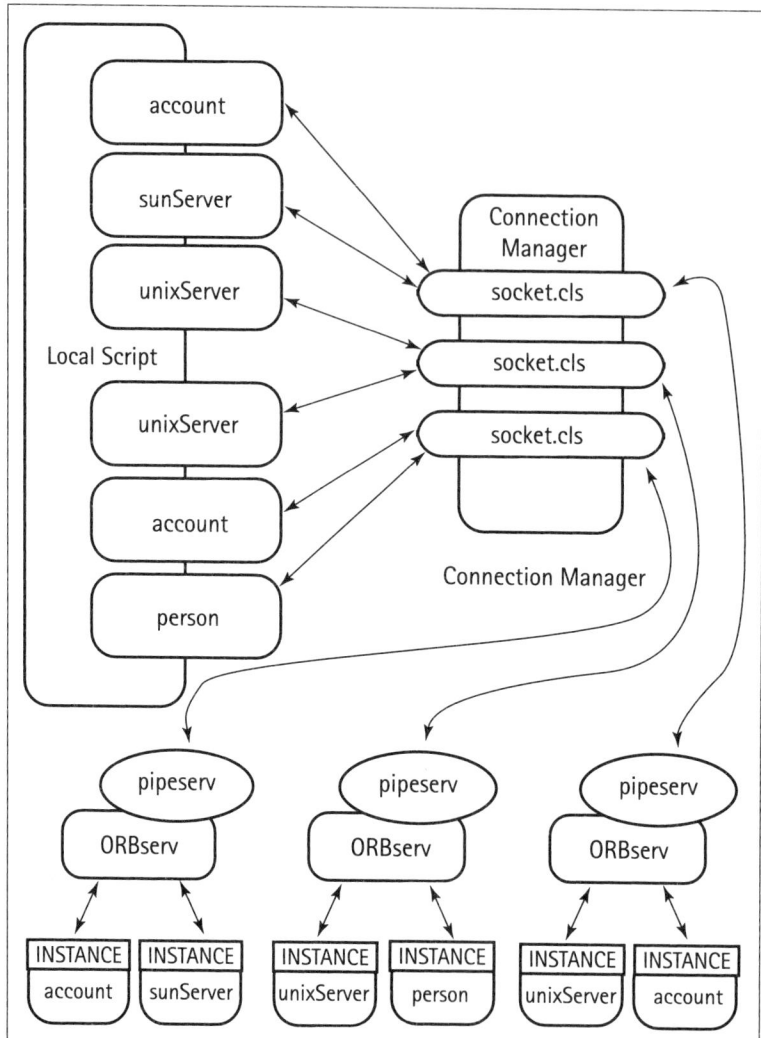

Figure 8-2: An overview of the distributed object architecture

Understanding Korn Shell Object Protocol

When you package up your object interfaces and send them floating across bit space, you package them in your own custom protocol. This method enables you to pack your interfaces into a concise string format that is less likely to be corrupted or misplaced during transport. As mentioned previously, the basic format of Korn

Shell Object Protocol (KSOP) is a colon-delimited string, with different types of requests coded slightly differently. In all cases, however, the first field indicates the type of request.

Requesting an Interface

To request an interface in KSOP, you simply put `request` in the request type field, and the object name that you wish to use as the second field:

```
request:person
```

This particular KSOP string causes the ORB server to look up the interface definition for a `person` object in the repository. If successful, the string returns the interface to you and spawns an instance process for the object.

Defining the Interface

After you've requested an interface, a definition is packaged up and sent back to you. The key ingredients are the Unique Identifier, followed by every method that the object implements:

```
345937898374597345:setName:getName:setAge:getAge
```

You would never see this string unless you turn on debugging within your proxy or server, or delve into expanding the capabilities of KSOP. The proxy process on the client side expects this string immediately following an object request, and knows how to decode it. The first field is used in all subsequent transactions with the server throughout the life of this object. The server uses this field to figure out which pipe controls the actual object instance. The client-side proxy then iterates through each method name until no names remain. With each method name it discovers, the proxy creates a skeleton function that simply forwards the Unique Identifier, the method name, and any parameters off to the server. It then listens for whatever return results are generated.

Invoking a Method

When you call a method on your object, the skeleton code that `proxy.sh` generates for you is put to use, converting your method call and parameters into KSOP format to ensure the server routes it to the correct object instantiation. A method call using the preceding definition you received looks like the following:

```
345937898374597345:setName:Bob
```

The server decodes this message and forwards it to the pipe that connects your particular person object with the server. The instance takes care of calling `_setName` on the real object, and the success or failure of the call is routed back to you.

Releasing an Object

Once you're finished using an object on the client side, you should call its `release` method. In fact, if you fail to call `release`, the server leaves your object instance running. If you foresee a problem with stale instances lingering about, you could easily modify the ORB server process to occasionally "reap" instances that haven't received any requests during a given time frame. The KSOP format generated when you call an object's `_release` method follows:

```
release:345937898374597345
```

The preceding can destroy the remote object. The ORB server process forwards this onto the object instance that exits, removing its pipe link to the ORB.

If you lose your local copy of an object, or your local program crashes while objects are still active on the remote server, they will have to be torn down manually. Also, if a client causes things to get totally hosed up on the server, you can always `telnet` to the server and issue the `killserver` command, in which the ORB cleans up all of its instances and then exits.

Coding the Client Proxy

The client workhorse, `proxy.sh`, is fairly simple to code. As previously explained, `proxy.sh` has the job of retrieving an interface definition from the ORB and building a virtual object on the client side based on the interface.

Before you can begin coding with the `ORBserv` toolset on the CD-ROM, you need to make sure that the `java` binary, as well as all of the scripts used by the client and server components of the ORB, are in your `PATH` variable. Consult the installation program and `README` file on the CD-ROM for details.

Launching the Request

You launch `proxy.sh` with the name of the remote server, the object you want to use, the local name of the object, and any construction arguments:

```
proxy.sh devgate person MyPerson Bob 40
```

In this case, the remote server is a machine called `devgate`, the object is a person object called `MyPerson` locally, and the construction parameters are `Bob` and `40`. After issuing this request, you could call the following:

```
$>MyPerson_getName
Bob
```

Of course, this call executes quickly, depending on the network connection to the remote server, the distance involved, other traffic, and so forth. Overall, the effect is transparent to the client.

Always source `proxy.sh` into the current shell; that is, always execute `proxy.sh` with a dot (.). This way, the object is available in your current shell process. Without a dot, `proxy.sh` creates a local object and then exits, taking the object with it!

Directly using `proxy.sh` assumes that you've created a connection using the socket class:

```
$> . socket sock devgate

$> sock_sendrecv &
[1] 12396
```

After you've created an instance of the socket class and called its `_sendrecv` method as a background process, you can use `proxy.sh` directly. You'll have to send the disconnect string to the server pipe in order to close the socket connection. If you use the connection manager (`connectionMgr.sh`), you don't have to manage connections at all. The connection manager dynamically creates and destroys socket connections, based on your needs.

When `proxy.sh` first receives your request, it contacts the ORB, as shown in the following code:

```
#!/bin/ksh
#
# proxy.sh - remote object retriever
#
```

UNIX Shell Objects

```
sPipe=$1
serverObject=$2
localInstance=$3
shift 3
init_arguments=$@

# check for connection
if [[ ! -p $sPipe ]]; then
    print "no connection to $sPipe"
    return 1
fi

#
# retrieve interface from server
#
print req:$serverObject:$init_arguments > $sPipe
read Interface < $sPipe
```

Proxy.sh first identifies the remote server as sPipe, the remote object as serverObject, and your local name as localInstance. It then shifts these positional parameters out of the way and grabs whatever construction arguments you are passing as init_arguments. Afterwards, proxy.sh checks to see if a connection exists for the required server – if not, it exits with an error message. Provided you have a connection, proxy.sh sends a KSOP interface request off to the server, and listens for the server to respond.

All of the code in this chapter, as well as the functionality of the ORB server in general, depends on pipes, and more precisely, the fact that a call to a pipe pauses until another process reads or writes to the other side (synchronous pipes). Some operating systems allow your script to write to a pipe and immediately read from it. If you have a similar situation, you will need to incorporate some sort of pausing mechanism between pipe reads and writes, in which you give the other process enough time to act on the pipe before your process reads or writes from it again.

Building the Object

When proxy.sh has an interface for your object, it constructs all the methods indicated in the interface definition – a difficult task.

proxy.sh starts by parsing out the KSOP definition, and noting the unique instance identifier and the methods that the object implements. It creates an array, inAr, that contains all of this information:

```
#
# construct object from interface based on instance name
#
oldIFS=$IFS
IFS=:
set -A inAr $Interface
IFS=$oldIFS
```

You temporarily alter the IFS character to be a colon to parse the KSOP string easily. Afterwards, you set IFS back to its original state, which is normally a white space or carriage return.

Next, proxy.sh goes into a loop, iterating through the methods indicated in the definition, and creating a skeleton implementation of each method:

```
#
# do loop implementing methods
#
usvID=${inAr[0]}

(( ct = 1 ))
while (( ct < ${#inAr[*]} ))
do

   eval "${localInstance}_${inAr[ct]}()
   {
       print
meth:$usvID:${inAr[ct]}:\$1:\$2:\$3:\$4:\$5 >> $sPipe
   read result < $sPipe
   print \$result
   }"
   (( ct = ct + 1 ))
done
```

You grab the unique identifier from the first position in the array. A counter is initialized at one (to skip the identifier at position 0 in the array) and loops until the counter has reached the total number of elements in the definition. The skeleton method you implement creates a long KSOP string that will be sent back to the server every time your method is called. The basic format of the implementation string follows:

```
meth : unique ID : method name : colon delimited arguments
```

The ORB serv receives this string no matter what method you invoke on your local object. After this has been defined, the counter is incremented, and the next method in the KSOP definition string is implemented.

Creating the Release Method

`proxy.sh` also creates a release method that essentially does the same thing as a local object's delete method. This release method tells the server that you finished with the object and its instance may be destroyed. You must call this method when you are finished using an object; otherwise, you will leave a remote instance lingering about on the server.

The release method checks to see if the object was created using the connection manager. This condition is indicated by the existence of a `server.connections` file with the remote server name. If so, the release method notifies the connection manager that the object is no longer using a connection to the remote server. When the connection manager determines that no local objects are using a connection to a particular server, it tears down the connection, thus eliminating the need for you to do any socket management.

```
#
# create release method to let go of remote instance
eval "${localInstance}_release()
  {
    print release:$usvID > $sPipe
    read result < $sPipe
    print \$result
    #
    # If you're using the connectionMgr, let it know you are exiting
    if [[ -f $sPipe.connections ]]; then
      connectionMgr.sh release:$sPipe
    fi
  }"
```

You can also implement this method as `delete` instead of release. As a result, client scripts that use objects would not have to know if they were deleting a local object, or releasing a remote one. Listing 8-1 shows the complete listing of `proxy.sh`:

Listing 8-1: `proxy.sh`

```
#!/bin/ksh
#
# proxy.sh - remote object retriever
#

sPipe=$1
serverObject=$2
localInstance=$3
shift 3
init_arguments=$@

# check for connection
if [[ ! -p $sPipe ]]; then
```

```
      print "no connection to $sPipe"
      return 1
fi

#
# retrieve interface from server
#
print req:$serverObject:$init_arguments > $sPipe
read Interface < $sPipe

#
# construct object from interface based on instance name
#
oldIFS=$IFS
IFS=:
set -A inAr $Interface
IFS=$oldIFS

  #
  # do loop implementing methods
  #
  usvID=${inAr[0]}

  (( ct = 1 ))
  while (( ct < ${#inAr[*]} ))
  do

    eval "${localInstance}_${inAr[ct]}()
    {
print meth:$usvID:${inAr[ct]}:\$1:\$2:\$3:\$4:\$5 > $sPipe
    read result < $sPipe
    print \$result
      }"
    (( ct = ct + 1 ))
  done

  #
  # create release method to let go of remote instance
  eval "${localInstance}_release()
  {
    print release:$usvID >> $sPipe
    read result < $sPipe
    print \$result
    #
    # If you're using the connectionMgr, let it know you are exiting
    if [[ -f $sPipe.connections ]]; then
      connectionMgr.sh release:$sPipe
    fi
  }"
```

When using the `proxy.sh` script, consider whether you're going to be using the connection manager. If you use the connection manager, you should never directly code with `proxy.sh`. When using `proxy.sh`, however, you are responsible for creating and destroying your own connections.

If you have an existing connection to a remote server, you can sever that connection by sending a disconnect string to the remote server. For example, if you have a socket object connected to a remote server named `devgate`, you would have a local pipe name `devgate`. You could sever the connection as follows:

```
print disconnect > devgate
```

Using the connection manager eliminates this concern.

Dissecting the Connection Manager

The connection manager eases the use of distributed objects by dynamically creating and destroying connections to remote servers based on the number of local clients requiring connections to any remote ORB.

Creating Persistent Connections

The connection manager enables you to write client code without concern for or the expense of creating server connections. Creating connections is time-consuming — if your client scripts had create connections for every object instance, your scripts would crawl. The connection manager holds onto persistent connections until no clients are using them, allowing your scripts to execute faster.

The syntax to use the connection manager is identical to `proxy.sh`, except you call `connectionMgr.sh` instead of `proxy.sh`. For example, you use the following to create a remote person object on the server `devgate`:

```
connectionMgr.sh devgate person MyPerson Bob 40
```

The connection manager creates a connection if one does not exist, and then calls upon `proxy.sh` to retrieve the object for you. If a connection is already established to `devgate` by another process, it uses this existing connection, and increments the reference count of connections to that server. As mentioned previously, when the reference count reaches zero, the connection manager drops the remote connection. This process is illustrated in the following code:

```
server=$1
.....
object=$2
shift 2
arguments=$@

if [[ -p $server ]]; then
```

```
    #
    # pipe already exists, you can just increment the reference count
    read rc < $server.connections
    rc=$((rc + 1))
    print $rc > $server.connections
    . proxy.sh $server $object $arguments
else
    #
    # create the connection, launch proxy
    id=$RANDOM
    . socket sock${id} $server
    sock${id}_sendrecv&
    print "1" > $server.connections
    . proxy.sh $server $object $arguments
fi
```

Creating Multiple Connections

The connection manager enables you to create as many connections to as many remote machines as necessary, without any prompting from you. It consolidates all client connections to remote servers, maintaining only one connection per server. The script maintains a reference count, and dynamically manages your connections.

To use the power of the connection manager, simply create your objects via connectionMgr.sh instead of proxy.sh. The connectionMgr.sh script maintains a .connections file for each server. If you create a remote object and list the directory in which the connection manager is located, you may see a file such as the following:

devgate.connections

Likewise, you see a file for each remote server on which you currently have object instances. If you view the contents of the file, you see a digit indicating the number of local objects that use the connection. When an object is released, the number drops by one. Obviously, when the number reaches zero, the connection is zapped.

When you call your remote object's release method, the connection manager is notified. It decrements the reference count or destroys the connection:

```
if [[ $server = @(release*) ]]; then
    #
    # delete a reference
    spipe=${server#*:}
    read refcnt < $spipe.connections
    refcnt=$((refcnt - 1))
    print $refcnt > $spipe.connections
    if (( $refcnt < 1 )); then
        #
        # tear down this connection
        print disconnect > $spipe
```

```
    rm $spipe.connections
  fi
  exit
fi
```

The connectionMgr.sh script cleans up after itself by removing the .connections file. Listing 8-2 depicts the entire code listing.

Listing 8-2: connectionMgr.sh

```
#!/bin/ksh

server=$1
if [[ $server = @(release*) ]]; then
  #
  # delete a reference
  spipe=${server#*:}
  read refcnt < $spipe.connections
  refcnt=$((refcnt - 1))
  print $refcnt > $spipe.connections
  if (( $refcnt < 1 )); then
    #
    # tear down this connection
    print disconnect > $spipe
    rm $spipe.connections
  fi
  exit
fi

object=$2
shift 2
arguments=$@

if [[ -p $server ]]; then
  #
  # pipe already exists, you can just increment the reference count
  read rc < $server.connections
  rc=$((rc + 1))
  print $rc > $server.connections
  . proxy.sh $server $object $arguments
else
  #
  # create the connection, launch proxy
  id=$RANDOM
  . socket sock${id} $server
  sock${id}_sendrecv&
  print "1" > $server.connections
  . proxy.sh $server $object $arguments
fi
```

Creating the Object Request Broker

The crux of the distributed development is the ORBserv.sh script, which is the central part of any distributed shell application you develop. The ORBserv.sh is responsible for entertaining client connections, instantiating and maintaining server objects, and looking up object interface definitions in the object repository.

The ORB is actually two distinct server processes. The first, of course, is the ORBserv.sh itself; the second is the instance script that manages and maintains instantiated objects.

Examining the ORB Process

When the ORB first starts, it tries to create a listening server Java process on port 2112. If you need to configure this number, you can do so in the pipeserv.java file presented in Chapter 7.

EXPLORING INITIALIZATION
The ORB server launches its Java socket listener, pipeserv.java, in the background as a coprocess. It notes the PID (process ID) and also initializes a variable bg_instances, which is a reference to how many instances the ORB currently supports:

```
# create server co-process for communication|binds to port 2112 by
  default
java pipeserv |&
jPid=$! ## copy of background PID string
bg_instances=1 ## Number of active background processes
#
```

CREATING INSTANCES
After these events are completed, the ORB is basically ready to go. The functionality is broken into a couple of functions and one main executive loop. The first function presented in code is createInstance():

```
createInstance() {
  #
  # create a persistent instance of the object
  #
  mkfifo $UqId   # make a fifo of the unique id
  #
  # launch the instance script with object and fifo
  instance $object $UqId $arguments &
  ((bg_instances = bg_instances + 1))
  return
}
```

This routine is called whenever the ORB has successfully retrieved an interface definition from the repository and is ready to instantiate an object. As you can see, all of the work is handed off to the instance script. The ORB just creates a named pipe based on the unique instance identifier, and increments its `bg_instances` reference count. The unique instance identifier is generated when a request is first received, and is used by clients, instances, and the ORB to identify any particular object instance. The unique identifier is also the named pipe that serves as the tether between the ORB and the instance.

FORWARDING METHOD INVOCATIONS

The next function presented in code is `forwardMethodArgs()`. This function is called when the ORB receives a KSOP request beginning with `meth`:

```
forwardMethodArgs() {
  shift
  UniqueIDfifo=$1
  while (( $# > 0 ))
  do
    methInvoc_Args=${methInvoc_Args:-}$1:
    shift
  done
  #
  # send method information to instance
  print $methInvoc_Args >> $UniqueIDfifo
  methInvoc_Args=""
  #
  # read result of method invocation
  read retResult < $UniqueIDfifo
  return
}
```

First, `forwardMethodArgs` shifts out the first element in the KSOP string: the actual keyword `meth`. It grabs the unique identifier as `UniqueIDfifo`, and then begins building a string to represent the method call and the method arguments. Once this construction is complete, the string `methInvoc_Args` is sent to the tethered instance via the `UniquedIdfifo`. The result is then read back, and the main executive loop takes care of forwarding the result back to the client.

CREATING THE MAIN EXECUTIVE LOOP

The main loop of `ORBserv.sh` listens on the socket for client requests. Based on the type of KSOP string received, it can do a number of things. These different possibilities are indicated in a `case` statement that covers all of the KSOP possibilities. The loop is started as follows:

```
while true
 do
  #
  # get request from socket
```

Chapter 8: Distributed Objects

```
if ! read -p rawRequest; then
  print -u2 "ORBserv.sh: co-process dead, exiting."
  exit
fi
```

The ORB checks for the existence of the coprocess before attempting to read from it. If the coprocess doesn't exist, you would generate an error, and the loop would continue infinitely trying to read from a coprocess that doesn't exist. Therefore, ORBserv exits if it cannot read from the coprocess.

After the KSOP string has been pulled from the socket as rawRequest, you can begin the case selection:

```
case $rawRequest in

  #
  # retrieve interface definition, or forward method
  # request off to object instance
  #
```

Currently, the ORB server expects five different types of KSOP requests. Let's examine each of these types in detail and see how they are implemented in code.

UNDERSTANDING INITIAL OBJECT REQUEST
The KSOP string for an initial request begins with req:

```
#
# KSOP object request
#
@(req*) )
  UqId=$RANDOM$RANDOM$RANDOM
  oldIFS=$IFS
  IFS=:
   set -A reqArray $rawRequest
  IFS=$oldIFS
  object=${reqArray[1]}
   reqArray[0]=""
   reqArray[1]=""
   arguments=${reqArray[*]}
   _def=$(< repository/$object.def)
   interface=$UqId:$_def
  print -p $interface
  createInstance
  ;;
#
```

First, you generate a unique identifier. You can use a combination of the string RANDOM automatically generated by the shell. Most Korn shell implementations return a different string for RANDOM every time it is referenced. Some shells, however, only generate a new value for RANDOM every second, or some other predefined interval.

Once you've determine the unique identifier, you can break apart the KSOP string to determine which object the client desires. You again alter the IFS variable to decode the KSOP string and are left with the object variable and a series of construction parameters, if any. ORBserv.sh then attempts to find the appropriate .def file within the repository and send it back to the client. Finally, the createInstance function is called to launch the object.

EXAMINING OBJECT METHOD INVOCATION

The second possibility in your case statement is for method invocations, which begin in KSOP with the string meth.

```
#
# KSOP object method invocation
#
@(meth*))
    # send off to forwardMethodArgs without :'s
    oldIFS=$IFS
    IFS=:
    forwardMethodArgs $rawRequest
    IFS=$oldIFS
    #
    # send back result
    #
    print -p $retResult
    ;;
#
```

Here, you again alter IFS in order to parse the KSOP string. This time, however, you simply forward the string off to the forwardMethodArgs function. When this call returns, the retResult variable is defined by the method invocations return result, which may be a number indicating failure or success (1 or 0), a simple string, or a long list of data. forwardMethodArgs does not need to output or return explicitly the retResult variables. All variables have global scope within a shell script, and you can reference retResult from anywhere. Again, use print -p to send the string back to the Java coprocess.

LEARNING KSOP OBJECT RELEASE

When a client wishes to release an object, it sends the KSOP release string, which begins with release.

```
#
# KSOP object release
#
@(release*))
    # Change IFS to : in order to set array
    oldIFS=$IFS
```

```
    IFS=:
    # define array
    set -A tempArray $rawRequest
    IFS=$oldIFS
    print "release" >> ${tempArray[1]}
#
# remove FIFO
#
    rm ${tempArray[1]}
    if [[ ! -p ${tempArray[1]} ]]; then
      print -p OBJECT_RELEASED
    #
    # decrement bg_instances
    #
      (( bg_instances = bg_instances - 1 ))
    else
      print -p OBJECT_MAYBE_RELEASED
    fi
    ;;
#
```

This particular `case` item does more of its own work. Again, you parse the KSOP string using `IFS` to determine which instance to release. You define an array, `tempArray`, and can retrieve the unique identifier from the second element of the array. Once this has been accomplished, you can send the release notice to the instance via the tether, and then remove the unique identifier pipe. Afterwards you can decrement or `bg_instances` reference count, and indicate to the client whether or not you were successful eliminating the object instance. If `ORBserv` still has the unique identifier FIFO, it indicates this condition to the client by sending the message `OBJECT_MAYBE_RELEASED`; otherwise, your local object call to `_release` results in the message `OBJECT_RELEASED`.

KILLING THE ORB

In this newfound world of distributed shell programming, you may find yourself with many unwanted object instances on a server with no local connection. You may still have a socket connection, but you'll have no method of releasing them. How could this possibly happen? Imagine that you have a client script that creates fifteen objects on a remote server, does some operations, and then releases them and exits. If your program crashes before it releases the server objects, two things happen. First, your local representations are destroyed when your program exits. Second, all fifteen objects are still active on the server. Ouch!

A number of safeguards can be implemented to avoid this situation. You can go to elaborate extremes to guarantee that all remote objects are destroyed in the event your local program crashes. For example, if you can successfully identify many points of failure in your code, you can call a `_releaseObjects` function to destroy all server objects in the event of an impending crash.

For the immediate situation of having untethered objects rampant on your server, this section includes the `killserver` command. You can send the `killserver` command either from a connected socket or by telneting directly to port 2112.

```
telnet devgate 2112
trying devgate.uranus.com...
Connected to devgate.
Killserver
Connection closed.
```

You can also send this command down a connected pipe. Here is the `killserver` code on the server side:

```
#
# KSOP Kill ORBserv
#
killserver)
    #
    # Tear down java co-process
    #
    kill -9 $jPid
    #
    # Tear down any instances
    #
    while (( bg_instances > 1 ))
    do
       kill %$bg_instances
       (( bg_instances = bg_instances - 1))
    done
    #
    # exit the server
    #
    exit
    ;;
```

First, the `killserver` section destroys the Java coprocess referenced through `jPid`. Second, you determine the number of `bg_instances` and use the Korn shell's job control facility to eliminate them one by one, decrementing `bg_instances` as you go. Finally, the `ORBserv.sh` can exit.

INVESTIGATING KSOP UNKNOWN
For all other KSOP requests, this version of `ORBserv.sh` simply responds with "Unknown Interface":

```
#
# KSOP Unknown
#
*)
```

```
        def="Unknown interface"
        if ! print -p $def; then
          print -u2 "ORBserv.sh: co-process dead. exiting."
          exit
        fi
        ;;
```

Once again, the ORB checks for the existence of the coprocess before writing to it. The complete listing of ORBserv.sh is shown in Listing 8-3.

Listing 8-3: ORBserv.sh

```
#!/bin/ksh
#
# ORBserv.sh
#
# $Id: ORBserv.sh,v 1.1 1998/02/05 07:14:55 chrisj Exp chrisj $
#
# $Log: ORBserv.sh,v $
# Revision 1.1  1998/02/05 07:14:55  chrisj
#
# Uncomment following line for debugging output!
#set -vx
#
# !!!!!!!!!
#  Make sure PATH contains the java binary and
#    the instance script (./instance)
# !!!!!!!!!
#
# create server co-process for communication|binds to port 2112 by
 default
java pipeserv |&
jPid=$! ## copy of background PID string
#
# Set trap to kill Java co-process on exit
trap 'kill -9 $jPid' TERM QUIT INT HUP STOP
#
bg_instances=1 ## Number of active background processes
#
# createInstance()
#  This function is used to create an object
#  instance on behalf of a
#  client. The instance is assigned a unique id, used
#  by the client and ORB to communicate with the
#  instantiated object that is tied to the ORB
#  via a named-pipe.
#
createInstance() {
  #
  # create a persistent instance of the object
  #
  mkfifo $UqId  # make a fifo of the unique id
```

```
    #
    # launch the instance script with object and fifo
    instance $object $UqId $arguments &
    ((bg_instances = bg_instances + 1))
    return
}
#
# forwardMethodArgs()
#   This function is used to forward a
#   client method invocation to the
#   the appropriate object instance.
#   The unique identifier is pulled from
#   the request and the information is
#   forwarded to the correct object via
#   the named pipe.
#
forwardMethodArgs() {
  shift
  UniqueIDfifo=$1
  while (( $# > 0 ))
  do
    methInvoc_Args=${methInvoc_Args:-}$1:
    shift
  done
  #
  # send method information to instance
  print $methInvoc_Args >> $UniqueIDfifo
  methInvoc_Args=""
  #
  # read result of method invocation
  read retResult < $UniqueIDfifo
  return
}
#
# Main Loop
#   This loop blocks on I/O while
#   reading from the co-process. The co-process
#   will send client requests and object instance
#   requests from whatever
#   clients attach to port 2112.
#
while true
 do
 #
 # get request from socket
 if ! read -p rawRequest; then
  print -u2 "ORBserv.sh: co-process dead. exiting."
  exit
 fi

 case $rawRequest in

  #
```

```
# retrieve interface definition, or forward method
# request off to object instance
#
#
# KSOP object request
#
@(req*) )
  UqId=$RANDOM$RANDOM$RANDOM
  oldIFS=$IFS
  IFS=:
   set -A reqArray $rawRequest
  IFS=$oldIFS
  object=${reqArray[1]}
   reqArray[0]=""
   reqArray[1]=""
   arguments=${reqArray[*]}
   _def=$(< repository/$object.def)
   interface=$UqId:$_def
  print -p $interface
  createInstance
  ;;
#
# KSOP object method invocation
#
@(meth*))
  # send off to forwardMethodArgs without :'s
  oldIFS=$IFS
  IFS=:
  forwardMethodArgs $rawRequest
  IFS=$oldIFS
  #
  # send back result
  #
  print -p $retResult
  ;;
#
# KSOP object release
#
@(release*))
  # Change IFS to : in order to set array
   oldIFS=$IFS
   IFS=:
    # define array
    set -A tempArray $rawRequest
   IFS=$oldIFS
   print "release" >> ${tempArray[1]}
  #
  # remove FIFO
  #
  rm ${tempArray[1]}
  if [[ ! -p ${tempArray[1]} ]]; then
    print -p OBJECT_RELEASED
    #
```

```
      # decrement bg_instances
      #
      (( bg_instances = bg_instances - 1 ))
    else
      print -p OBJECT_MAYBE_RELEASED
    fi
    ;;
  #
  # KSOP Kill ORBserv
  #
  killserver)
    #
    # Tear down java co-process
    #
    kill -9 $jPid
    #
    # Tear down any instances
    #
    while (( bg_instances > 1 ))
    do
       kill %$bg_instances
       (( bg_instances = bg_instances - 1))
    done
    #
    # exit the server
    #
    exit
    ;;
  #
  # KSOP Unknown
  #
  *)
    def="Unknown interface"
    if ! print -p $def; then
      print -u2 "ORBserv.sh: co-process dead. exiting."
      exit
     fi
    ;;
  esac

  done
#
# eof
```

Creating the Instance Script

The ORB server works in tandem with the instance script. The instance script is called upon for each object that the server wishes to create. If fifteen objects are being used by your ORB, you will have fifteen separate processes running the instance script, each tethered back to the ORB via a uniquely named pipe.

The ORB server calls the instance script during the `createInstance` function. The instance script determines several items from the parameters that it is passed:

```
# Initial parameters
#
# $1: The object to create
# $2: The tether pipe to ORBserv.sh
#
_object=$1
_IDpipe=$2
_strArguments="$3 $4 $5 $6 $7"
```

It grabs the object and tether pipe from the first two parameters, and then concatenates the remaining positional parameters to form the `_strArguments` string. You are using this primitive concatenation method, instead of the $@ variable, because of the sourcing of shell objects into your script. The nature of shell classes is heavily dependent on $@, and use of it in different parts of your code may result in strange behavior. You can safely copy $@ right at the beginning of the instance script to another name, and use that as your argument string. Regardless of your method, the same results are achieved.

The instance script then creates an instance of the object, located within the repository directory:

```
#
# Implement the object from the repository
#
. repository/$_object thisInstance $_strArguments

#
# Main loop
#  Here, we listen on the tether pipe
#  for method invocations, or
#  the instructions to terminate.
#
while true
do
  read methodInvocations < $_IDpipe
  if [[ $methodInvocations = "release" ]]; then
    exit
  fi
  invoke $methodInvocations
done
```

Name the instance `thisInstance`, because it will be the only object used in this process. A separate instance process is created for each object created on a client's behalf. After creating the object, the instance script goes into a main loop, reading ORB messages from the unique ID tether and acting upon them. The ORB server parses the KSOP request into a more natural form, and the instance script can more easily invoke the proper method on the object via the `invoke` function.

```
#
# invoke()
#   This function invokes a method on the object instance
#
invoke() {
  method=$2
  #
  # Concatenate arguments, the quick and easy way
  args=$3$4$5$6
  result=$(thisInstance_${method} $args)
    thisInstance_${method} $args >> instance.log

  echo $result >> $_IDpipe

  return
}
```

The invoke function grabs the method from the second positional parameter. It then invokes the method on the instantiated object, collecting the results in a `result` variable. This information is then sent back through the tether pipe to ORB, who ultimately returns it to the client. Listing 8-4 shows the complete version of instance.

Listing 8-4: instance

```
#!/bin/ksh
#
# instance.sh - create and maintain persistent object instance
#
#
# uncomment following line for debugging output
#set -vx
#

# Initial parameters
#
# $1: The object to create
# $2: The tether pipe to ORBserv.sh
#
_object=$1
_IDpipe=$2
_strArguments="$3 $4 $5 $6 $7"

#
# invoke()
#   This function invokes a method on the object instance
#
invoke() {
  method=$2
  #
  # Concatenate arguments, the quick and easy way
  args=$3$4$5$6
```

```
    result=$(thisInstance_${method} $args)
    thisInstance_${method} $args >> instance.log

    echo $result >> $_IDpipe

    return
}
#
# Implement the object from the repository
#
. repository/$_object thisInstance $_strArguments

#
# Main loop
#  Here, we listen on the tether pipe for method invocations or
#  the instructions to terminate.
#
while true
do
   read methodInvocations < $_IDpipe
   if [[ $methodInvocations = "release" ]]; then
     exit
   fi
   invoke $methodInvocations
done
```

Registering Interfaces with the Server

Once your ORB server is up and running, you can place any object you've created within the repository. The repository is simply a directory beneath the ORB server script, `ORBserv.sh`. This directory contains both ready-to-run classes (already "compiled" with `shcc` — see Chapter 3), and definition files that just contain the KSOP definition string.

Under the `tools/ORBserv` directory on this book's CD-ROM, the `repository` directory holds several classes and definition files. Take a look at `person.def`:

```
setName:getName:setAge:getAge
```

The preceding is a simple definition. Basically, any method that your class implements should be included in this definition. The ORB server process looks for this file when a client requests an object instance, and is coupled with a unique instance identifier and sent back to the client. For example, the class `objlist.cls` has a class file like the following:

```
_objlist() {
  (( _lastItemUsed=0 ))
```

```
}
_addItem() { Item=$1
        _list[_lastItemUsed]=$Item
        (( _lastItemUsed = _lastItemUsed+1 ))
}
_getItem() { pos=$1
        echo ${_list[pos]}
}
_getAllItems()      {
  echo ${_list[*]}
}
_removeItem()  {
  Item=$1
  _list[Item]=" "
        (( _lastItemUsed = _lastItemUsed-1 ))
  set -A _list $( _getAllItems )
}
_execute() { method=$1 ARGS=$2
        for object in $( _getAllItems); do
                ${object}_${method} $ARGS
        done
}
```

If you create a definition file for this class, you simply include one line into the `objlist.def` file:

```
addItem:getItem:getAllItems:removeItem:execute
```

Except for the constructor, each method is indicated once. You don't need to include the constructor because all classes are required have to have this element. Also, when you initially request the object, the constructor is called for you with your arguments.

You must place both the definition file and the ready-to-run "compiled" class file. If the class file does not exist, the ORB server will not be able to find it.

Creating ORB Examples

Now that you've completed so much ORB shell programming, it's time to give it a try. If you've installed the material off the CD-ROM, the README file indicates various PATH assignments and items for the ORB to function correctly. The following section is a quick synopsis.

Starting the Server

For the ORB server to function correctly, you need to create a directory named repository underneath `ORBserv.sh` and place your class and class definition files there. Once this is completed, the only requirements involve the user who is running `ORBserv.sh`. Basically, the `ORBserv.sh` should be started in a separate window or logon session, and left alone. You can run it in the background, but you should instead run it by itself. For `ORBserv.sh` to execute correctly, you need to make sure that the `java` command is in your path, and that a dot (.) is placed as the last element in your `PATH` so that `ORBserv.sh` and `instance` can source and execute files. The dot should be the last element in your `PATH` for security reasons. If you have a serious aversion to putting the dot in your `PATH`, you can simply go through `ORBserv.sh` and `instance` "pathing-out" the location of all dependent scripts and so forth.

After accomplishing these tasks, you can go to the directory in which the server lives, (/usr/local/uso/tools/ORBserv if you installed the default installation from the CD-ROM) and type the following:

```
$> ./ORBserv.sh
```

This process remains active until the server is shut down. To enable debugging, uncomment the following line in your `ORBserv.sh` file:

```
#set -vx
```

With the preceding, you should begin to see copious debugging output as the ORBserv executes.

Starting a Client

Now you can try a client application. You can proceed from any other machine on your network, or if you're trying it for the first time, you may want to try it directly on the machine where you're running the ORB server. If you've accepted the defaults from the CD-ROM's install script, you should have client code located at /usr/local/uso/tools/ORBserv/client. This directory contains some examples as well as the dependency files `pipeclnt.class`, `proxy.sh`, `socket`, and `connectionMgr.sh`.

To get things started from the command line, try the following:

```
$> . socket sock localhost
```

```
$> sock_sendrecv&
```

The preceding starts a socket connection to the server, `localhost` (which you should substitute for the host that is actually running `ORBserv.sh`). Be sure and run the _sendrecv method in the background or you'll have to open another window or start another login session. Once this method is running, you can get an object from the server:

```
$> . proxy.sh localhost person myPerson Me 25
```

Now begin using the object:

```
$> myPerson_getName
Me

$> myPerson_getAge
25

$>myPerson_release
OBJECT_RELEASED
```

You should also be able to run the demo programs located in the same directory.

 Both the ORBserv.sh and any client scripts need to have both the Java binary and the ORB shell object directories in their PATH environment variables in order to function.

RUNNING the Examples

The example scripts show how to use both proxy.sh directly and the connection manager. The first example in Listing 8-5 nearly matches the events from the preceding command line.

Listing 8-5: demo.sh

```
#!/bin/ksh

# example.sh
#    Creates connection to server,
#    uses object, release object, closes
#    connection

#
# create socket to servername: probing
  . socket sock localhost
  sock_sendrecv &

#
```

```
# get person interface from server
  . proxy.sh localhost person aperson

#
# use object
  aperson_setName Chris
  print "Calling get name:"
  aperson_getName

  aperson_setAge 25
  print "Calling get age:"
  aperson_getAge

  print "Releasing object:"
  aperson_release

  print "Closing connection"
  print disconnect > localhost
```

This example uses the socket class and `proxy.sh` directly. `_sendrecv` is executed in the background, and `proxy.sh` is sourced directly into the current shell. Also, make sure to release the object and close the connection!

The second example (in Listing 8-6) shows how to use the connection manager, which eliminates the need for creating or closing connections.

Listing 8-6: `demo2.sh`

```
#!/bin/ksh

# example.sh
#   Creates connection to server,
#   uses object, release object, closes
#   connection

#
# get person interface from server
  . connectionMgr.sh localhost person aperson

#
# use object
  aperson_setName Fred
  print "Calling get name:"
  aperson_getName

  aperson_setAge 23
  print "Calling get age:"
  aperson_getAge

  print "Releasing object:"
  aperson_release
```

You use the connection manager in the exact same fashion as `proxy.sh`, except you don't give any thought to what is occurring in the background. You still have to release the object after using the connection manager, but you don't need to concern yourself with the connections.

Summary

In this chapter you've covered an extensive amount of material. A comparably detailed explanation of CORBA would run about a thousand pages longer than this chapter, because as CORBA tries to provide language mappings and solutions for everything under the sun.

This chapter should be a good foundation for building distributed applications. Even if you decide not to use an ORB, creating shell scripts with the capability to communicate with each other across the network should change your shell programming forever. If you decide to start using the benefits of the ORB, you can easily adapt the techniques presented here to suit your needs. All of the shell coding involved in the ORB server and the client- and server-side support scripts is fairly simple. The only complicating factor is the tangled complex of pipes that link together all of your processes for IPC – by far, this element is the most difficult thing to manage and can cause the most problems. Distributed programming opens a can of worms unknown by the likes of single machine applications.

In the next chapter, you start designing an application to manage user accounts and track system statistics on distributed servers across the network.

Chapter 9

Designing an Object-Oriented System

IN THIS CHAPTER

- Object-oriented design issues
- Application goals
- Required services
- High-level to low-level designs
- Object integration

CLASSES, METHODS, AND properties are the work of the object-oriented programmer, but these concepts are meaningless unless applied within a well-crafted object-oriented design. Far too easily, you can use mechanisms of object-orientation without using the design patterns. To get the most out of objects, you must use them wisely.

Grasping the Goals of an Object-Oriented System

Building systems with objects and components is very hot these days. Almost every product that hits the market has somehow managed to string together every conceivable buzzword and tackle every conceivable problem. You can only imagine the befuddlement of those who are tasked with choosing software for an organization. An IT director may ask: How will this software meet my company's needs? The marketer replies: Why, this software is robust, scaleable, component-based, object-oriented, cross-platform, dynamic, and extensible. Who can argue with that? Separating the buzzwords from what they really mean is difficult.

What is scalability? Let's say you can create an application that meets the needs of 100 users. This same application can also meet the needs of 10,000 users with little or no modification. While this example may sound scaleable, the word is still applied within every conceivable context. What about component-based, object-oriented, and cross-platform? How are these goals met?

Unfortunately, the definition of these words is determined by the marketers that choose to use them, and as a result, they can mean many different things.

Using the tools developed so far in this book, you begin working on an application in this chapter. I can assure you that this application will be component-based, object-oriented, cross-platform, dynamic, and extensible. You will bridge *n*-tiers and have distributed components throughout the enterprise. Of course, there will be lots of code reuse as well an extensible and independent series of interfaces, allowing for easy scalability!

Building Components

Realistically, today's object-oriented and distributed systems have some real and painstakingly crafted concepts that actually give meaning to the barrage of buzzwords.

The idea of components is not new, however. Even back in the days of yore, when the programmer wielded a C compiler, components were a part of every large system. The usage of components, however, has changed slightly.

Components are the building blocks of a larger application. A component can be anything from an interchangeable library of functions to a runtime component that can bind from across the network. A component is really just a part of a system. There always have been, and always will be, lots of components.

When you write C code, you often import libraries of functions. These functions take difficult, frequent tasks and provide a function to accomplish these tasks. As an application programmer, you can simply include the appropriate function definitions into your code to reap the benefits of someone else's work. Tasks such as the pesky details of networking, graphics devices, and handling common data structures such as strings are better left to a function library. Why should you have to repeat the same tedious tasks over and over? Eliminating costly rework is often a goal of components. For example, if you were centering text on the screen, you would be wasting your time if you determined the length of the screen, determined the length of the text, subtracted the length of the text from the length of the screen, divided the result by two, and eventually placed text *n* spaces into the line every single time you wanted to center a piece of text. Consider the following code:

```
#!/bin/ksh
# center.sh
# center text - a really hard and tedious method
screen=80
text=$1     # pass text in as first parameter
ltext=${#text}  # length of text
spaces=$(( screen - ltext ))
tablength=$(( spaces / 2 ))
(( x = 0 ))
#
# Tab over correct amount, then print string
#
```

Chapter 9: Designing an Object-Oriented System   233

```
while (( x != tablength ))
do
  print -n " "  # -n, no carriage return
  (( x = x + 1 ))
done
print $text
```

While the preceding example is simple, this is a lot of work just to center a piece of text. Would you want to code this every time you had to center a string of text? Of course not, and instead you should create a function to do this work for you:

```
#!/bin/ksh
# center.fn
# center text - a function
center() {
  screen=80
text=$1       # pass text in as first parameter
ltext=${#text}  # length of text
spaces=$(( screen - ltext ))
tablength=$(( spaces / 2 ))
(( x = 0 ))
#
# Tab over correct amount, then print string
#
while (( x != tablength ))
do
  print -n " "  # -n, no newline character
  (( x = x + 1 ))
done
print $text
}
```

The previous example is at least more efficient. Every time you need to center a piece of text you could use a command like the following:

```
#!/bin/ksh
# report.sh - a big report

# first, source in the function
. center.fn
# now we can use it....
center "Today's Big Report"
```

Isn't this easier? These exact types of repetitive tasks lead programmers to create reusable pieces of code. Perl programmers liberally use Perl modules. Java programmers import packages. As a cutting-edge shell programmer, you can reuse objects within your code.

The function library or command toolkit is the most basic form of components and modularity. Today's systems often desire runtime components and even network-based components. These components become more complicated, but their existence stems from similar motives.

Apart from reusing code in toolkits and function libraries, you often want to use components and building blocks to carry out certain parts of your application's functionality. You can write data access code and reuse it in many of your applications that need access to database systems. You may write certain routines that adapt a graphics library to work with different display adapters. The goal is to be able to reuse parts of your application in other applications. Figure 9-1 shows an application component shared by more than one application.

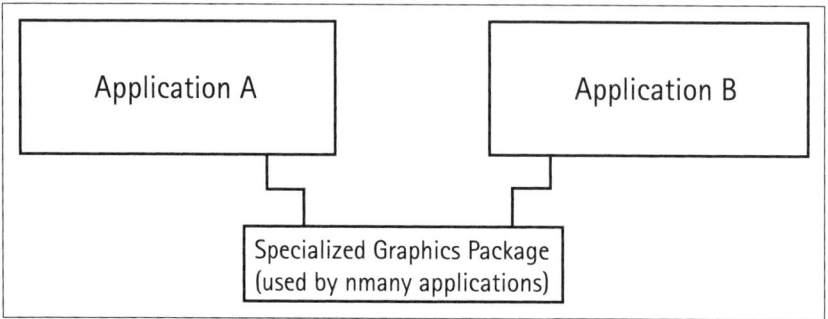

Figure 9-1: Application components can be reused by different applications.

Breaking Apart the Application

As an application becomes more complicated, tries to run on more platforms, or becomes distributed, the application needs to be broken into smaller pieces. You may create an application that needs to do certain little tasks differently according to the platform on which it runs or the environment in which it exists.

For example, you previously created networking components that appeared to your shell code to be a named pipe, but you cleverly constructed them to shoot the data across the network to another named pipe, which also appeared to another shell program as a typical, plain-old pipe.

Using named pipes in the beginning enabled you to create more than one shell script as part of your application. You could have one script accomplish certain tasks, and then pass off a task such as looking up data or maintaining a network connection to another script, connecting it via a pipe. This approach enables you to change out the functionality of your application without necessarily redistributing the entire application. If you have an application for computer-aided design and architecture, you may want the application to work with a variety of display hardware on various systems. By keeping the parts of your application that handle graphics modular, you can swap in function libraries and so forth for each different display configuration you support.

Breaking apart an application is a great way to make your application extensible, but it's definitely required for a distributed application. When you're developing a distributed application, you often use components that aren't mixed together until the application is actually running. This approach introduces new problems and advantages.

Examining Runtime Components

Apart from application pieces, there is another type of component building block used at runtime. These types of components are more difficult to manage, and must be carefully constructed to promote reuse. Your application may need access to a database. Although there are many different types of database management systems (DBMSs), a common interface like Open Database Connectivity (ODBC) or Java Database Connectivity (JDBC) accesses them. Therefore, for your application to work in a variety of environments, you must use the correct interface for the database management system in use. The specific type of DBMS is not known until runtime. Thus, the DBMS interface can be considered a runtime component, as shown in Figure 9-2.

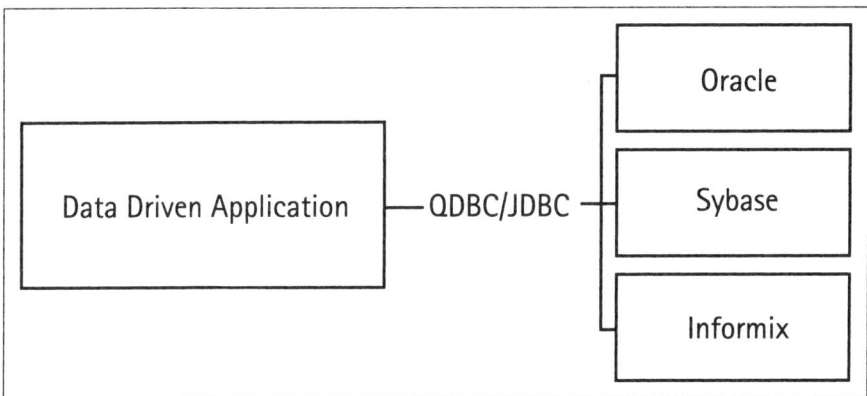

Figure 9-2: An application can use many different DBMS via ODBC and JDBC.

Linking together components at runtime is a necessity in distributed applications. If you create an application to manage distributed systems, you may need to bind across the network to a component that your application has never seen before. Provided the component writer bestowed upon his piece of code the necessary "hooks" for your application to connect with, you still need to set up the proper communications medium so the application pieces can talk to each other.

Using runtime components presents more of a challenge for compiled code, but is a snap in the shell. If your application has sources in different function libraries, using runtime components can be as easy as swapping out a file before your application starts. For this scheme to work, the function libraries must implement the same functions so that your application can work with all of them. This process leads you to object-orientation, and particularly, encapsulation.

Saving the Day with Object-Orientation

As you can see, reusing code throughout the development process is a great start. This approach lets you consolidate your efforts and try to cover only new ground programming, without backpedaling and reimplementing the same features over and over again. In addition, creating your application in different pieces gives you the ability to integrate your application quickly into different environments and run on many more platforms. Furthermore, the ability to link to components at runtime enables you to distribute your application physically across machine boundaries, providing even greater power.

As a result, a mass of distributed, disparate entities need to be integrated for your application to get off the ground. This situation is an ideal place for object-orientation. In fact, it would be quite painful to try and develop many of today's systems without the benefit of objects. Can you imagine the difficulty in developing a distributed systems management application in C with the most basic of socket commands?

The rise of the Internet and distributed programming has helped to usher in the object-oriented paradigm. Object-orientation has been around for decades, but its primary use was for the realistic modeling of complex systems. OO languages like Ada were used by embedded systems engineers to create missile guidance systems. Lately, object-orientation's other benefits have come of age in the light of today's demanding development environment.

A few key features of object-orientation ease the development and management of distributed systems. Object-oriented techniques surpass modules, function libraries, and simple packages. At the code level, inheritance enables you to reuse code used across many different types of tasks. As mentioned earlier, inheritance can be thought of as similar to using a function library.

Inheritance differs from function libraries in a couple of important ways. You write objects to carry out the tasks of data and operations that you believe to be related. You can use inheritance when objects are similar to each other. You wouldn't derive a text-editing object from a text-centering object just to get the capabilities of centering text. Instead, you first create objects for handling text, and then for editing text. Ultimately, you may want to create different types of word processors and text editors, all of which can have objects derived from your text-editing object (which may implement a centering function). Using objects has many benefits, as covered in the preceding chapters, with code reuse as a prominent example.

When you seek to create a function library, you are consolidating reusable code to save time and effort. Reuse is not just a hodge-podge of snazzy tools that makes putting together software like throwing together omelets at a diner. Object-oriented reuse is based on carefully designing your objects to factor out base behavior that can be shared by the most components. Furthermore, the nature of designing with objects enables you to think of your application in terms of what it does and what its intellectual point, as opposed to viewing it as a series of linear instructions, executed methodically. Object-orientation enables you to model real-world processes, and isolate and factor out common functionality that can be reused.

Exploring Application Objects

The preceding section discussed reusing code within function libraries as well as the importance of reusing pieces of your application within other applications. This latter concept often involves deciding on a common interface so that all applications have some form of common ground with which to use the application component. Object-orientation excels at this work by forcing you to write code that lives behind an interface. The nature of encapsulation helps minimize the necessity of complex function calls and advanced knowledge of how the component is going to carry out the tasks that you request.

When you encapsulate functionality behind an interface, you strive to simplify the interface so that it can be reused in the most situations. You also accomplish polymorphism with this process. This is a perfect solution for writing data access code or graphics routines that can work with a variety of display hardware.

Objects tend to triumph over function libraries and modules in its strong sense of encapsulation. Using object-oriented techniques, you can easily incorporate logic into your components. For example, you write a banking application that uses data from several different data servers on the bank's and another company's network. Some of the products and services that the bank offers have been created quickly to meet customers needs and as a result, need to be flexible and pull data from different sources across the Internet. This situation creates a nightmare for data management. One of the application goals may be to allow the customer to sign up for a particular "Snazzy-Guard" or some other form of account protection. For a monthly fee, the bank protects the customer's charge account from over-limit fees, fraud, and offers "value-added" traveler's insurance, rental insurance, and so forth. Your bank lets another company, GrossCo, offer all of the insurance and antifraud benefits, and the bank itself only waives the over-limit fees.

When a customer signs up for this service over the Internet, three events occur. First, all sorts of wonderful marketing metrics are thrust into one particular data server. Second, the user needs to have their billing account updated reflecting the new fees. Finally, the company that provides the insurance and other "value-added" services, GrossCo, has provided an interface for you into their data network, and you need to let them know that your customer is now using their services. This last step introduces some serious problems. What if your application is successful at marking the customer's account with the additional fee on the bank's data server, but fails when trying to register the customer with the GrossCo database? Would you undo the information in the bank's database? Would you keep trying GrossCo's data interface, attempting to register the customer?

Object-orientation can help in this situation. By writing the business rules into an object, you can allow for these contingencies without affecting any data. One particular object, called SnazzGuard, can provide an interface such as _signUpSnazzyGuard that confirms the customer gets that particular service. This object lives on a network server and encapsulates the many transactions necessary to update all of the data servers. If any one of these particular processes fails, the object can abandon the whole process, indicating the `_signUpSnazzyGuard` has returned a value of 1.

This process provides a much more flexible way of providing this service to the bank's customers. Any time an application wishes to apply Snazzy-Guard to a customer's account, it simply loads that particular object, and calls the `_signUpSnazzyGuard` method.

This example not only illustrates the break up of an application's functionality, but also demonstrates the use of a distributed runtime component.

Understanding Distributed Runtime Components

The SnazzGuard object can be used by multiple applications. This capability requires that the object be available at runtime to these applications, and support any type of communications protocol that the other applications may use to integrate the component. One method of accomplishing this requirement is to make SnazzGuard more or less a port-listener; SnazzGuard then sits at some particular location on the network, listens for carefully formatted requests, and indicates back to these callers the success or failure of transaction. This approach works, but requires every application that wishes to use the SnazzGuard object be aware of the particular protocol that the port-listener uses, as well as the exact location of the machine and port number where the listener is located. Also, this approach prevents applications from using the service as if it were a part of their own code.

The object request brokers solve this problem. ORBs communicate across IIOP (Internet InterORB Protocol), a well-known and agreed-upon protocol; hence, ORBs don't need to burden you with the details. Apart from the benefits of the common communications protocol is the runtime method in which the ORB works. When the SnazzGuard object is deployed onto an object broker, it becomes a piece of distributed code that applications can incorporate as their own. The application may believe it's dealing with native code, carefully conjoined at runtime with the application; in reality, the object is sitting across the network. This situation enables you to use truly distributed code, and not just distributed services. Also, you do not need to know the specific machine and data port where the SnazzGuard service lives. The object request broker can assign the object into a name-space; that is, an agreed-upon portion of the network in which any request by any machine for a SnazzGuard object results in an instance of your particular SnazzGuard object returned to the caller, and integrated into the caller's code as if it is native.

The object request broker can also accommodate many different languages. This capability allows for native code to integrate the SnazzGuard object intimately, even if the native code is Win32 C++ and SnazzGuard is a Java binary compiled on Solaris. The ORB provides a language mapping for various native languages, and the SnazzGuard object is written to subscribe to an interface – not necessarily the logical mechanics of any one language. Again, interfaces are key in allowing your distributed components to interoperate. The interface provides the encapsulation necessary to surpass any type of logical language construct and provide operations that reflect a real-world task. Figure 9-3 shows the network availability of such an object.

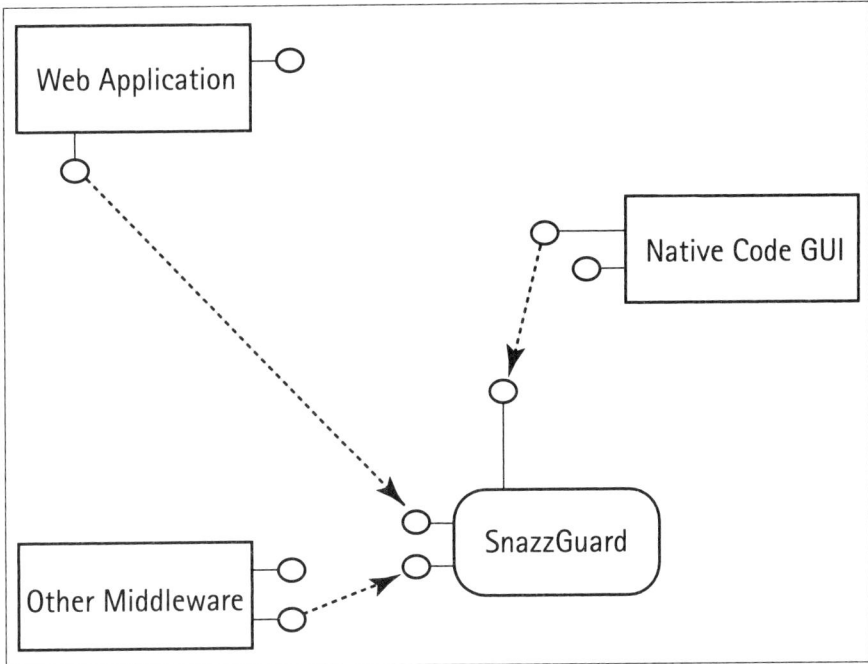

Figure 9-3: A SnazzGuard object available to the network

Using Interfaces to Facilitate Scalability

Interfaces are also a path to scalability. By breaking up your application into components, you give yourself the ability to take a weaker part and replace it with a more high-powered version that can take advantage of different hardware or new network services. With traditional techniques, you'd still have all of the preceding configuration and communication problems spoken. As you may have guessed, object-orientation's use of interfaces is a great solution for this situation.

By using a network-based, distributed component, you offer yourself the greatest encapsulation and distributed power. A distributed object can run on different kinds of hardware, be tightly wed with native client code, and also carry all of the benefits that object-orientation offers design-time components. Also, you can design a thought-out interface that can be used far into the future. This approach allows for scalability, as the interface encapsulates any additional processing power or resources that the object acquires to support scaling.

Identifying Application Goals

In this chapter, you design an object-oriented, distributed application. You need more than grammar skills to link together these buzzwords, because you're actually going to complete this application in code. Actually, much of the code is already written (well, at least the hard stuff), so you can concentrate on the tasks at hand.

Providing Features

What would an application be without features? A conglomeration of data and bugs? Disk fodder? Your application is going to be chock-full of features to make your life easier. At a minimum, it will automate some repetitive tasks and provide some system maintenance utilities. Primarily, this application is a lesson that teaches you how to break a program up into distributed, functional pieces with many different runtime options. You develop a set of objects representing high-level operations in your application, and you can develop both a shell- and Internet-based front end.

Your application, dubbed SMU (System Management Utility), has several key uses for maintaining UNIX servers:

- Adding, deleting, and managing users and groups
- Tracking key systems resources
- Monitoring critical applications
- Rebooting servers

SMU is similar to a system administrator's assistant, providing routine maintenance functionality coupled with distributed power. For example, under normal circumstances, a system administrator must manually copy the /etc/passwd file or use a distributed service like NIS (Network Information Services) to allow for consistency between user accounts across machines. Using SMU, you can easily create accounts on a variety of different machines using the same localized information.

Exploring User Management

In Chapter 4, you developed account and user objects, which enable you to add a user to the password and accounting files with relative ease. They also demonstrate how objects cannot interoperate, as the account object always has a reference to a user object.

Creating a user on one machine is not difficult, but the process becomes more complicated when you want to maintain consistent information across servers. A variety of schemes exist for this process, but your method will be elegant. First, some systems use the NIS, also known as the Yellow Pages, to distribute password and host information. The YP commands (named after ypbind, ypwhich, and so forth) are used to control NIS on a machine. If you have ever been involved in a system or network that used NIS, you are probably intimately familiar with the headaches caused by this scheme. A server must bind to an NIS server with the ypbind process to use NIS. This configuration can possibly create a situation where users cannot log in if the `ypbind` process isn't running. Also, the `ypmaps`, as they are sometimes called, can become corrupted; often, the system administrator scrambles to figure which part of the incredibly complex process has failed and how to rectify it so that users can use the system. An amazingly bad situation can occur when someone decides to "push" the `ypmaps` out from the wrong server. This situation distributes useless or corrupt maps across the network, bringing everything to a halt.

None of these problems associated with NIS occur if a user is kept in a server's local accounting files. In this process, users are always able to log onto the server, even if their network peers crash and burn into a heap of plastic and flames. The burden with maintaining local system files is keeping them all synchronized and up-to-date.

Many administrators have written snazzy shell scripts that copy `/etc/passwd` and `/etc/shadow` from host *A* to all the other hosts on the network. The administrators may have even put this sequence into the `crontab`, so that any changes made on host *A* are eventually distributed out to the network nightly. Although this process can create problems, it is a better alternative to NIS. What if the files of host *A* are goofed, and then distributed across the network? What if someone makes local changes on host *X* that are erased when your script runs? Some of these mishaps are the price of automation. You can choose to have everything centrally located and override local configurations, or have everything distributed and do all of the changes manually. Computers can be both a blessing and a curse.

The scheme you develop enables you to manage the accounting files (and anything else) remotely. Without automation, the scheme easily manages all of the servers from one central place.

Using the ORB you created in the last chapter (or the unixServer objects from Chapter 4), you can create account and user objects locally that are actually on a remote server. This configuration enables you to construct a user object using local information, and then create an account on the remote server. The interface you develop for SMU enables you to input user data from a Web-based form, and then creates the user on any machine fitted with an ORB.

Tracking Disk Space

Disk space is often easy to track and certainly easy to manage. The only real concern is when a system is used by many people, and you're not sure of the importance of certain large files that hog all the disk space. More often than not, you go out of your way to contact the owner, who is usually oblivious to the existence of the files and tells you to go ahead and erase them.

Disk space can create enormous problems, however. Often, a server can crash if it runs out of disk space. On some systems, this situation can be particularly bad, because the operating system will refuse to mount a full disk. For example, you have a UNIX server with a gigabyte of disk space, and you've split that space across a few file systems (UNIX supports the notion of logical volumes — "disks" that can be spread across or contained within multiple "physical" devices). When you normally configure your UNIX server to have a few file systems, you keep the root files system fairly small and give more space to the areas where applications will live, such as /usr, /var., and /opt. A configuration may look like the following:

```
Filesystem      kbytes      avail      capacity    mount
/dev/disk0      239855      36000      83%         /var
/dev/disk0      49155       0          102%        /
```

Problems can arise when a file system becomes full, and the operating system refuses to mount it. A typical scenario: the root file system becomes full during some everyday operations. As a result, the server flails, and goes down for reboot. On its trip back up, while proceeding through the boot process, it refuses to mount a full file system; in this case, the root file system /. The server attempts to skip this file system but cannot manage to bring itself to a multiuser state. Giving up, it decides to reboot again. The process starts anew. Sound like a nightmare? Imagine the frustration of system administrators who are standing by the console, waiting ten minutes for the machine to boot, only to realize they have a couple of quick seconds to do some maintenance before the system crashes back down. In addition, when you're first trying to figure out what's wrong, you actually miss a couple of cycles and can only sit staring at a monochrome screen for about an hour.

A good configuration is the best cure for file system space. Don't place log files in the root file system. Log files are usually the culprit for full disks. Also, don't place user directories within the root file system. Users also tend to fill up disks, especially developers who seem to accumulate core files within their directories.

 Core files are usually large files generated when a program unexpectedly ends. Core files can be used to aid in debugging and determining the source of failure for an application. More often than not, core files simply accumulate throughout directories, gathering dust and acting as a black hole for disk bytes.

SMU will let you examine disk space on distributed servers from your Web browser. This configuration should at least provide a heads-up on possible problems, and let you quickly browse statistics.

Rebooting Servers

SMU will also enable you to reboot a server through the `unixServer_reboot` method. While enabling someone to reboot your server from the Web causes potential security considerations, you can minimize these risks if they are of concern to you. Also, while you will develop a browser-based interface for SMU, you can also use SMU's services in your own applications. This architecture is described in a following section; in this section, you're only examining the features. The Web interface can be password-protected, and you can also choose to leave something like a server reboot out of your application.

A routine reboot schedule is usually part of maintaining a server. Many places choose to implement an automated reboot of machines on a weekly basis, or task a system administrator with the effort. Regardless, rebooting is a common way of keeping a server running smoothly. Many applications tend to get lethargic and bloated if left running unchecked. This condition is usually due to the application's design or poor coding, and it almost always occurs sooner or later. Some server processes can be left running for an entire year and stay well-behaved. Other times, the server process begins hogging the machine after only a few hours.

SMU will enable you to browse through the processes running on a server, and let you reboot the server at will.

Although security is an issue in Web-based applications, a number of measures can be taken to ensure that only authorized personnel are able to access the SMU Web forms. Consult your Web server's documentation on setting up security.

If you use your UNIX objects within other applications that you create, the reboot method is a blessing. If you want to reboot a collection of servers, you can line up objects representing all servers, and call the reboot method for each one. This approach enables you not to ignore the remote flavor of UNIX and the particulars of the shutdown or reboot command, as these details are encapsulated within the object.

Tracking Applications

SMU also enables you to browse the processes running on the server. This browsing is routinely done to make sure that critical processes are running, that they are not taking up too much CPU time, and for taking general stock of the server's utilization.

Understanding Required Services

For the application to behave, you need to provide some common operations besides the preceding features. This application's core components are designed to be used both by a Web-based interface and any other applications that require its services. A client to SMU can be a Web-based interface, a shell script, or any other type of distributed client you want to develop. The goal here is maximum reuse.

The architecture that you build around SMU will be primarily a Web server-based collection of middleware and logic objects that use distributed server objects to control the network, and HTML served to browsers as a client interface. This three-tier architecture houses most of the logic and operations on the Web server.

To support this architecture, the middleware application (which lives on the Web server) needs operations to start and stop it, as well as the capability to keep it loosely coupled with the server objects it uses to accomplish requests and operations forwarded by its clients. This capability enables you to change the functionality of the third-tier components without affecting the other aspects of your distributed application.

Creating a Comprehensive Design

Now you can delve into SMU's architecture. Most of the dirty work will be done by objects you wrote in Chapter 4. You will revamp and improve upon some of these objects, as well as rework the interface of your unixServer object. You will try to provide two versions of unixServer object implementations that sport the same interface: the first is managed by an ORB, while the second is responsible for reaching across the network on its own. These implementations enable you to design the application, even if you choose not to (or server constraints disallow you to) use the ORB.

Grasping Server Details

From now on, this chapter refers to all of the working objects as if they are distributed. When reference is made to a distributed object, that same object can live with the rest of the application if it reaches across the network on its own. You have to make this decision when writing the application. As previously mentioned, the primary location of SMU will be on the Web server. All of the operations and logic will appear to reside at this location, even if the actual workhorses are distributed.

For example, if someone using a browser-based client wants to add a user to a remote machine, they first enter the information into a Web form, and then hit the submit button on the Web page. The Web server sends this information to SMU's CGI-based application, which seeks to invoke the correct object to create the account on the remote machine. You select the type of object that the application uses. The CGI application looks to invoke an object to control the remote machine, and uses the object as if it were local. You decide whether the object is really located on the remote machine and the object's services are provided via an ORB, or if the object truly is local and reaches out to the remote host on its own.

The third-tier objects consist of accounts, users, disks, and servers, and handle requests that originate from the first tier. They are handled by the object request broker, and appear to be local objects to the Web application.

Creating a UNIX Server Facade

You create a new version of the unixServer object in Chapter 10 that provides an interface for almost all of the operations you want to perform. In turn, this object is composed of many of the smaller objects, which actually perform operations on the different aspects of the UNIX system. The unixServer acts as a sort of facade, presenting a false front and encapsulating you from the different tasks that have to be accomplished in order to perform various operations.

For example, you create account and user objects and use them together to add new accounts to a UNIX system. The unixServer interface provides an operation along the lines of _createAccount, which takes user information as a parameter. This interface encapsulates you from the details. The unixServer class knows it needs to create both user and account objects, as well as pass along the right information in order to create the account. Likewise, the unixServer class takes care of invoking the right methods on these objects to complete the work.

An object of this type is very useful for providing a common set of operations that need to be performed upon a particular entity. Because all of your account, disk, user, and other objects have something to do with a UNIX machine, you can conveniently wrap them up with a facade – an object that appears to be one, single large entity, when in reality it's composed of many other objects. The facade enables you to provide the operations needed by a complex object without coding a complex object. While the components that make up a unixServer are useful in many other types of objects, a large object called unixServer would not be very flexible, because it would try to be everything for everyone. Factoring out behavior into least common-denominator objects is the way to maximize reuse and efficiency. If you give the unixServer class intimate knowledge of all its tasks, it would be impossibly rigid, unextensible, and useful only in the context of the application using it.

The facade is a design pattern that affords the convenience of a simple, useful interface that encapsulates a collection of complex objects working together.

Examining the Object Request Broker

The ORB will be the link from your third-tier objects to your second-tier logic application. If you view the ORB as yet another piece of middleware, you actually have a four-tier system, but because it resides on the server and maintains the actual unixServer instance, the ORB is considered part of the same process on the third tier.

The object request broker is really not that complicated. It consists of one server process that manages instances of client-invoked objects. The ORB takes advantage of your Java and shell-based socket classes to accomplish much of its operations. The ORB is also tightly dependent on synchronous, named-pipe communications, which may cause problems if your operating system does not fully support true synchronous pipes (for example, if you write to a pipe and your process is allowed to continue without another process reading the other end of the pipe).

For SMU to work, the ORB will need to be deployed onto every machine that you wish to control, which should be relatively easy to implement. If you install the ORB collection from the CD-ROM onto each machine you wish to control, you can just stick the right objects into the repository and launch the ORB process. You can then control objects anywhere TCP/IP reaches; that is, all across the Internet. The ORB process itself is fairly lightweight, and only carries a Java socket process as baggage. Instances are dynamically created and destroyed based on client utilization, and the whole process usually takes minimal CPU utilization. Therefore, the ORB should not pose a threat as interference for machines busy doing other types of work.

If you want to implement a minor, but broad-sweeping design change, you can create object instances that are tethered to your ORB but reside on a separate machine. In your ORB, you create an instance every time a client requests an object the ORB knows. This instance is really just a background process tethered to the ORB via named pipe. Because you created your Java network components to appear as named pipes, your object instances can be located on a different server from the ORB.

By converting the ORBserv.sh to register objects remotely, you can create a name resolution space in which a collection of machines can all register objects with the ORB. Clients can ask the ORB for objects by name, and the ORB takes care of locating and using them. You can also create other namespaces and bridge them together.

The primary way that separating objects from their brokers changes matters is that your objects basically need to run themselves, and tether themselves back to the ORB. CORBA works in this manner, and you could fairly easily implement this process in your architecture. The ORB would have to be modified to accept connections from objects that want to be registered. The ORB could then spawn an instance process in the background that simply opens a shell-based socket object as a connection with your distributed object. Your distributed object would have to run the Java server socket component and listen for requests. If you plan on controlling many distributed objects and want their location to be transparent, this type of architecture is worth the implementation effort. If, however, you want to allow a collection of objects on a few particular servers to be used by the entire network, the architecture described here works fine.

Dissecting the Network

Ideally, the unixServer composite object lives on the server that it represents. This object is managed by the ORB, meaning that no network awareness needs to be built into the object itself. The ORB takes care of networking for you by holding references to objects, and providing interfaces to these objects for clients across the network.

This implementation can be powerful. Because TCP/IP runs just about everywhere, you can deploy objects onto your servers, start the ORB process, and have these objects available to the Internet via port 2112. Provided your network is connected to the Internet, this sequence is possible. You can also build a gateway application. Because the main logic-oriented part of your application runs as middleware on a Web server, it's really the only machine that needs to be available to your Web browser. As long as it can maintain a network connection to the servers it wishes to control, you can still do maintenance from a Web browser. Figure 9-4 shows the three-tier architecture in simple, network terms:

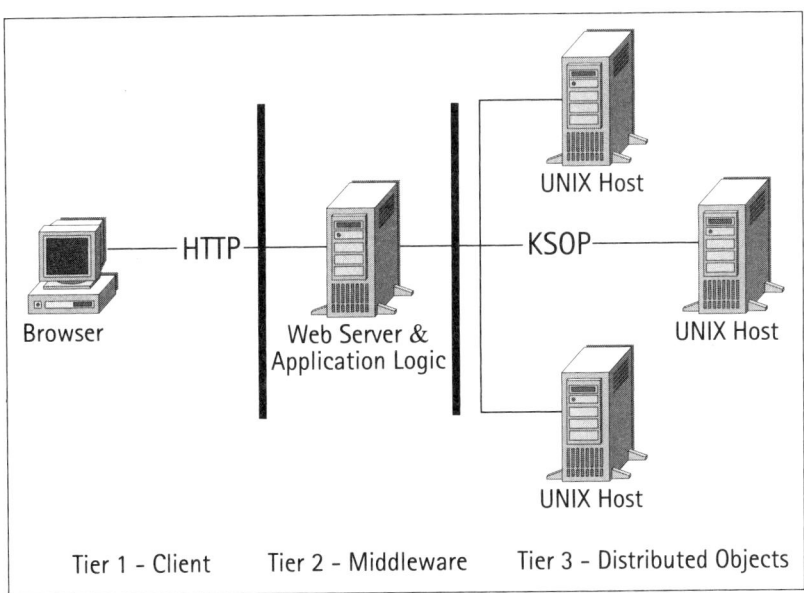

Figure 9-4: A three-tier networked architecture

In your application, clients and servers use the Java socket processes and the shell-based socket objects to handle and encapsulate networking. By coding your network components to function as named-pipes, they can easily be snapped into any application that uses pipes, thus bridging TCP/IP.

Hooking Up Commands

To create more than one type of interface for your application, you should try to encapsulate its functionality behind a series of operation objects. This approach will be used with SMU. The command scheme that you create will have applications as clients. These applications may be other programs, a Java-based GUI interface, or as in the example you create in Chapter 13, a browser-based set of forms.

Without creating a series of operation objects to encapsulate the functionality of your application, every interface you create would need to couple itself directly to your objects. While most of the functionality would be included in the unixServer façade interface you created, your end-user applications would still need to bind to a unixServer object and have knowledge of how it completed tasks. This situation would slightly vary the wiring of each interface – an undesirable outcome.

By creating operations like 'add user', 'reboot system', and so forth, you allow for easy integration with any type of interface you choose to create. As long as all of the objects you want to use on a remote server are within the PATH of the ORBserv.sh process, you only need to bind to operations objects across the network. These operation object instances take care of instantiating the unixServer and any other server objects as you need them, which makes hooking up interfaces a breeze. You simply load the operation objects from the ORB and then start using them. You can easily create a menu system in the Java AWT, a command line driven series of scripts, or a CGI program.

Figure 9-5 shows how a operation object can use its knowledge of other classes to complete tasks on a caller's behalf. In your client script, you could reboot a UNIX host just by typing the following:

```
# Reboot a server
#
. rebootCMD aCmd
aCmd_execute
```

You just call the _execute method of an operation object to complete its task. All operation objects implement the execute method, which enables you to use any type of operation easily. The operation class is be a base class, and all of your specific operations derive from it, thus overriding the _execute method with their specific functionality. For example, the preceding operation object's execute method may look like the following:

```
# rebootCMD::execute

_execute() {
  serverRef_reboot
}
```

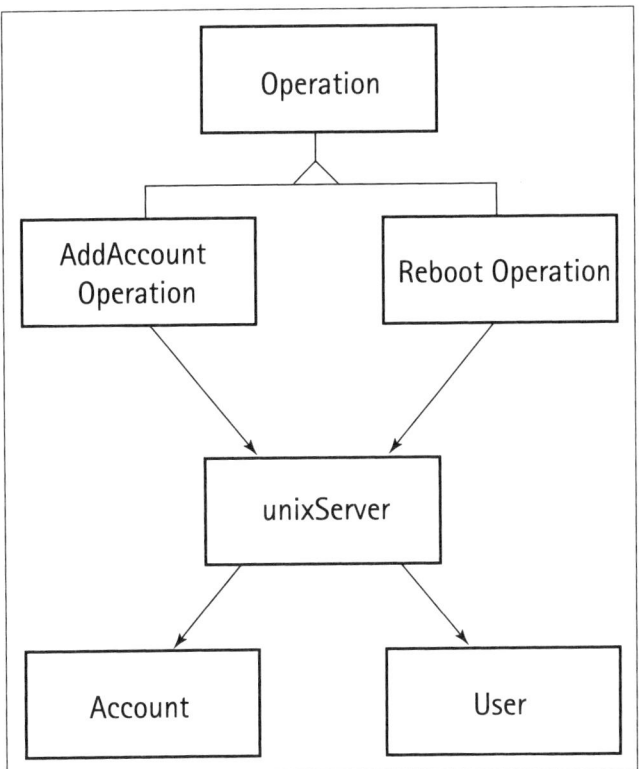

Figure 9-5: An operation object knows which methods to call from other objects

You only have to call reboot on the particular server object within your execute method. The server reference can be obtained at construction, and saved until use. This sequence raises another architectural design issue: whether to instantiate operations on the remote servers via the ORB, or to create them along with the logic of your application and let them take care of retrieving particular server objects from the ORB. In the first scenario, the application just loads all of its operation objects at startup, and uses them throughout its execution (you complete these steps in the following chapter). The second option, however, enables you to create a few remote server objects, and use them by your local operation objects. This option involves creating remote object instances and keeping them persistent, and providing a reference to them in your operation objects, which places more responsibility on your application. Both techniques have benefits, but for simplicity on the middle tier, you should choose the first approach: loading remote operation objects.

Understanding the Web Server and CGI Application

Most of the work occurs on the Web server. You will create a CGI-based application in the Korn shell that handles client browser requests, and construct the logic that translates these requests into operations handled by an ORB and a distributed server object.

This process is relatively easy because you're creating operation objects to encapsulate all of the remote server operations. The CGI application just loads an operation object for whatever server it needs to perform an operation. You'll create CGI objects to break apart HTTP requests and format HTTP responses, which makes quick work of parsing an HTTP request to determine what the user wishes to do. Then you can just load the appropriate operation from the server and call its execute method.

For those of you familiar with scripting but unfamiliar with Web programming, this approach opens up a whole new world. You'll be surprised at the ease of creating a Web interface. While Perl is a popular language for CGI development, you can use any type of executable code, and your Korn shell CGI works just as well as any other solution.

You create a main action script, name it something like `smu_action.cgi`, and provide Web forms for the browser that enable the user to do data entry and select command options. When they hit the submit button, their information is posted to your `smu_action.cgi`, which parses apart the request and invokes the appropriate actions. You also create some other CGI to help with displaying correct information to the user; your HTML pages won't be static, and CGI is really the only way to include server-side information.

To create the CGI application, you need to have a Web server installed on your machine. The recommended Apache package is included on the CD-ROM, but any CGI-capable server should work. If you are creating this application primarily on a Linux box, you probably already have all the tools you need, as most installations of Linux come bundled with a Apache.

Exploring the Interface

The interface is the user experience. The CGI application provides an HTML form-based interface for performing operations on your distributed servers. As presented in the book, the interface is fairly basic, but you can easily embellish and improve upon its features.

Understanding the Big Picture

Now that you've completed the high-level, comprehensive design, take a step away and look at the overall plan. This complex application involves many pieces.

Chapter 9: Designing an Object-Oriented System   251

If you are committed to completing the application as presented in the book, it is strongly suggested that you do so on a Linux machine. Most of the tools are already installed, and you can run the application straight off the CD-ROM with minimal configuration effort. After you decide what's right for your environment, you can begin coding a distributed application that runs on 200 servers, if you like.

Figure 9-6 shows the integration of every object in the application, and a general process flow.

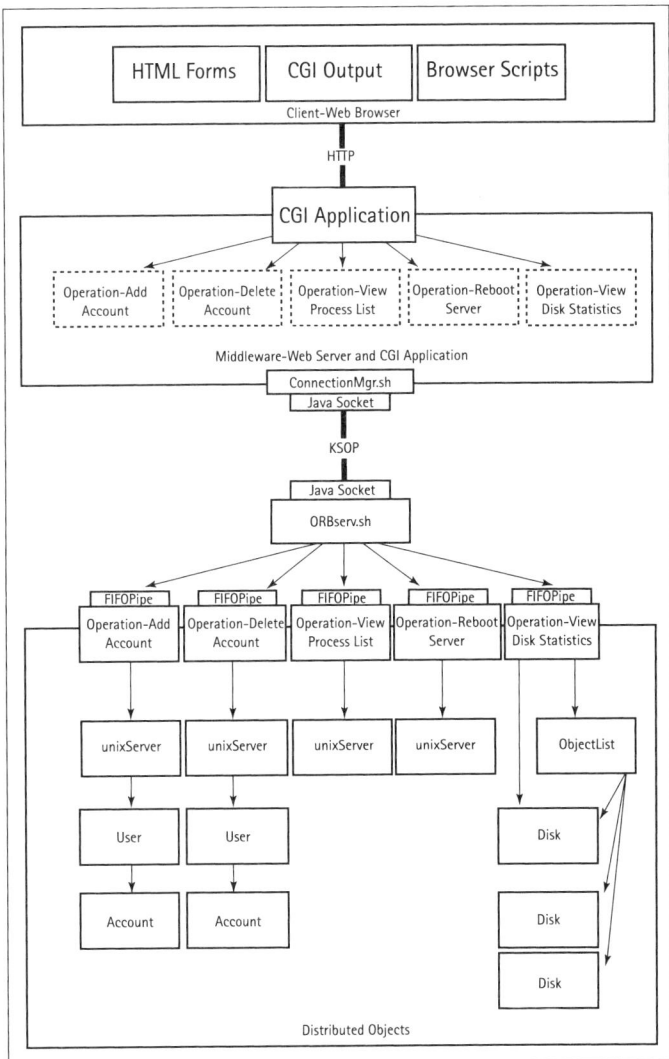

Figure 9-6: SMU in its distributed entirety

Summary

This chapter describes a complicated, distributed application. The most difficult aspect of SMU is connecting all the different run-time pieces together. Creating a distributed application requires careful planning, and in most cases, an object-oriented design to support a high level of encapsulation and to decouple key components from each other, thus allowing for greater flexibility. While your feature list may not be ideal, it's a good start; the features are the easiest items to incorporate into the application. The object-based architecture and distributed connectivity are by far the most difficult to incorporate.

In the next chapter, you begin to implement your objects. While some are brand-new, others are quick rehashes of existing interfaces you created in preceding chapters. You hold off on the CGI interface until Chapter 13, but what you create in the next chapter can be used by any type of application, and you can create quick shell scripts to demonstrate its power.

Chapter 10

Creating a Shell-Based Distributed Application

IN THIS CHAPTER

- Creating a base operation class
- Revamping the unixServer class
- Encapsulating complex operations
- Deploying new objects into the repository
- Creating a distributed client application

IN CHAPTER 9, you created an extremely complicated diagram and outline for a distributed application. In this chapter, you build this distributed application.

You start by creating a base Operation class to encapsulate complicated operations behind a simple, ubiquitous interface. From the base Operation class, you derive several more classes, each implementing a variety of complex operations behind its _execute interface. As you'll see, this sequence makes hooking up distributed clients a breeze.

Creating the Core Base Classes

The base operation class is simple. This is an abstract class, but because the shell has no support for complete abstraction or null functions, you should implement some baseline functionality here to avoid worrying about it in derived classes. On that note, operation simply implements the _getState method, along with defining _this in the constructor method. These tasks should be performed for every object, and you might as well complete them now.

Discovering the Operation Base Class

You derive all of your complex operation commands from `operation.cls`, which is shown in Listing 10-1:

Listing 10-1: `operation.cls`

```
#
# operation.cls
#
# Methods
#
# _execute    <virtual>
#
###############################################################


_operation() {
  _this=$ObjectId
}

_execute() {
  echo
}

_getState() {
  set | grep ^$_this
}
```

The base class is pretty thin, which is good because you're after the interface, not necessarily the implementation. In this case, you're using inheritance primarily to get the interface. In this case, you cannot create pure virtual functions in the shell, so you might as well incorporate some truly baseline functionality.

Before you proceed too far in creating operation classes, you should revisit the unixServer class. Originally, you created this class in Chapter 4 to reach out across the network to the different machines represented by the object. This process worked well, and you created a factory class to relieve you of the burden of knowing the remote system's UNIX flavor at runtime by keeping a small `host.inf` file. Now the objects that represent UNIX servers are actually distributed out to the servers they represent. In a way, this situation is much better, because it completely encapsulates the specifics of the remote machine.

As a result, you'll somewhat change the unixServer class. The new class will be called `uServer.cls`, and provides the same type of operations, but the code has changed.

Creating the New uServer.cls Class

Some items in the original constructor have been removed, and now you start with the following:

```
_uServer() {
  #
  # Initialize device counter
  #
  _nTotalDevs=0
  #
  # copy ObjectId
  #
  _this=$ObjectId
  #
  # retrieve hostname
  #
  _strHost=$(hostname)
}
```

Now the constructor only initializes a few variables, and sets the server's hostname based on local execution of the hostname command. Previously, you set up your commands for remote command execution (remsh), and you also abandoned the message handling implemented in Chapter 5. The _nTotalDevs string represents the number of disk devices; at first, you initialize it to zero until the object takes stock of its file system information. You also define the _this operator — because this operator comes in handy, you should define it as part of your standard procedure.

Most of the original methods are still intact, although you lost a few data members, including _strIP, which represented the IP address. Because the object now resides on the remote machine it represents, much of the network-based code from the original version could be discarded.

The _getUsers method is basically the same, albeit with networking code removed:

```
_getUsers() {
  _nUsers=$(w|wc -l)
  #
  # write it to STDOUT, for now
  #
  echo $_nUsers
}
```

The code is much cleaner without the clumsy networking commands. You use the what command (w), and pipe its output to wc -l to count the lines. This approach is a quick way of determining the number of user sessions active on the machine (real or unreal) and serves your purpose.

The _createDiskObjects method is essentially unchanged, and still creates disk objects by iterating through a device output listing as follows:

```
_createDiskObjects() {
  #
  # shift out header information
  shift 7;
  #
  # create array with disk information
  set -A devArry $@
  #
  # Initialize counter variable
  ((c=0))
  #
  # create objects in loop
  #
  while (( c < ${#devArry[*]} ))
  do
    #
    # create a disk object
    #
    . disk _oDref${c} ${devArry[c]} ${devArry[c+1]} ${devArry[c+2]} \
        ${devArry[c+3]} ${devArry[c+4]} ${devArry[c+5]}
    #
    # add to object list
    #
    _oDiskList_addItem _oDref${c}
    #
    # Increment counter
    #
    ((c=c+6))
    #
    # Increment device count
    #
    (( _nTotalDevs = _nTotalDevs + 1 ))
  done
}
```

The preceding is an excellent example of aggregation; in fact, you should instantiate a uServer or unixServer object and simply call _getState after a call to _getDiskUsage. You can then see the relationship of the contained objects, and also call their methods as follows:

```
MyUNIXServer_oDref6_getKbAvail
```

The preceding calls _getKbAvail on the contained oDref6 object. Building objects from other objects is always a wise decision.

Chapter 10: Creating a Shell-Based Distributed Application 257

The _getDiskUsage function has changed slightly. Apart from the removal of networking code, you've cleaned up the recursive call to ensure that events proceed smoothly:

```
_getDiskUsage() {
  if (( $# < 2 )); then
    #
    # Recursively call _getDiskUsage(), this
    # time with a higher argument count
    #
    _getDiskUsage $((bdf||df -k) 2>/dev/null)
    #
    # Make sure you return, or fall through function
    # again
    #
    return 0
  else
    #
    # Now you have a higher argument count
    #
    _DeviceArgs=$@
    #
    # create a list object for devices
    #
    . objlist _oDiskList
    #
    # Call createDiskObjects
    #
    _createDiskObjects $_DeviceArgs
  fi
  #
  # Call _getFullList on disk object array
  #
  _oDiskList_execute getFullList
}
```

This function also takes advantage of containment, as the information is first sent to _createDiskObjects to be constructed and then placed within an object-list. You can then call the _execute method of your list object to iterate through the list, invoking the appropriate method on each referenced object within the list.

In the _checkDiskSpace method, the 100 megabyte warning zone has been lowered to 50 megabytes. This method still uses the object list to retrieve a list of objects, and then does some evaluation with each object. The _execute method of the object list class is not appropriate here because you need to test the individual results of each method call. Objlist_execute simply executes a method on each object in a linear fashion without a chance to pause and evaluate the result. Using a for-each loop in association with Objlist_getAllItems enables you to do whatever you like with each object instance within your for loop:

```
_checkDiskSpace() {
  #
  # Iterate through disk objects
  #
  for object in $( _oDiskList_getAllItems )
  do
    #
    # If under 50 megs left, print error message
    #
    if (( $(${object}_getKbAvail) < 50000 )); then
      print -u2 "Disk Nearing Capactiy!Object::${object}"
    fi
  done
}
```

The _getLoad method now retrieves load information without networking, as follows:

```
_getLoad() {
  #
  # Retrieve Load String
  #
  LoadString=$(uptime)
  LoadString=${LoadString##*:}
  #
  # write to STDOUT, for now
  #
  echo $LoadString
  if echo $LoadString | grep "[0-9]\." > /dev/null; then
    print -u2 "Warning: High Load!!"
  fi
}
```

This version of the unixServer class, uServer, is improved from the original implementation, but still provides the same interface. Listing 10-2 shows uServer.cls in its entirety:

Listing 10-2: uServer.cls

```
##############################################################
#
# uServer.cls - modified for event handling
#
# $Id: uServer.cls,v 1.5 1998/03/31 17:51:32 chrisj Exp $
#
# ----------------------------------------
# Methods
#
#   _getUsers
#   _getDiskUsage
#   _checkDiskSpace
```

```
#    _getLoad
#    _getWindow
#    _getState
#    _reboot
#
# Data Members
#
#  string      _strHost
#  integer     _nUsers
#  integer     _nLavg
#  objlist     _oDiskList
#  disk        _oDref
#
# Construction
#
#   . uServer
#
#####################################################################

_uServer()  {
   #
   # Initialize device counter
   #
   _nTotalDevs=0
   #
   # copy ObjectId
   #
   _this=$ObjectId
   #
   # retrieve hostname
   #
   _strHost=$(hostname)
}

_getUsers() {
  _nUsers=$(w|wc -l)
   #
   # write it to STDOUT, for now
   #
   echo $_nUsers
}
_createDiskObjects() {
   #
   # shift out header information
   shift 7;
   #
   # create array with disk information
   set -A devArry $@
   #
   # Initialize counter variable
   ((c=0))
   #
   # create objects in loop
```

```
    #
    while (( c < ${#devArry[*]} ))
    do
        #
        # create a disk object
        #
        . disk _oDref${c} ${devArry[c]} ${devArry[c+1]} ${devArry[c+2]} \
            ${devArry[c+3]} ${devArry[c+4]} ${devArry[c+5]}
        #
        # add to object list
        #
        _oDiskList_addItem _oDref${c}
        #
        # Increment counter
        #
        ((c=c+6))
        #
        # Increment device count
        #
        (( _nTotalDevs = _nTotalDevs + 1 ))
    done
}

_getDiskUsage()  {
    if (( $# < 2 )); then
        #
        # Recursively call _getDiskUsage(), this
        # time with a higher argument count
        #
        _getDiskUsage $((bdf||df -k) 2>/dev/null)
        #
        # Make sure you return, or fall through function
        # again
        #
        return 0
    else
        #
        # Now you have a higher argument count
        #
        _DeviceArgs=$@
        #
        # create a list object for devices
        #
        . objlist _oDiskList
        #
        # Call createDiskObjects
        #
        _createDiskObjects $_DeviceArgs
    fi
    #
    # Call _getFullList on disk object array
    #
    _oDiskList_execute getFullList
```

Chapter 10: Creating a Shell-Based Distributed Application 261

```
}

_getState() {
  set | grep ^$_this
}

_checkDiskSpace() {
  #
  # Iterate through disk objects
  #
  for object in $( _oDiskList_getAllItems )
  do
    #
    # If under 50 megs left, print error message
    #
    if (( $(${object}_getKbAvail) < 50000 )); then
      print -u2 "Disk Nearing Capactiy!Object::${object}"
    fi
  done
}

_getLoad() {
  #
  # Retrieve Load String
  #
  LoadString=$(uptime)
  LoadString=${LoadString##*:}
  #
  # write to STDOUT, for now
  #
  echo $LoadString
  if echo $LoadString | grep "[0-9]\." > /dev/null; then
    print -u2 "Warning: High Load!!"
  fi
}

_getWindow() {
  #
  # Argument to window is first parameter
  #
  arguments=${1:-"/bin/ksh"}
  /usr/bin/X11/xterm -display $DISPLAY -exec $arguments
}

_reboot() {
  #
  # override this in derived class
  #
  shutdown -r now
}
```

Deriving a sunUserver Class

As before, you can derive a subtype of uServer to represent the specifics of your particular UNIX flavor while at the same time keeping the convenient uServer interface. The `sunUserver.cls` class overrides two methods of its parent, uServer, that are appropriate for a Sun Solaris machine.

First, the `_getWindow` method is changed to reflect the Solaris location of X-Window utilities:

```
_getWindow() {
  #
  # Argument to window is first parameter
  #
  arguments=${1:-"/bin/ksh"}
  /usr/openwin/bin/xterm -display $DISPLAY -exec $arguments
}
```

Also, the `_reboot` method has been changed to reflect something that works on Solaris. At first, you issue a `sync` command just for safety. The `sync` command takes all memory currently swapped out or in the midst of paging, and places it back onto the disk. Because it minimizes the chances of losing data, complete this process before rebooting the server, as follows:

```
_reboot() {
  #
  # Sync disks, issue reboot command
  #
  sync
  reboot
}
```

Listing 10-3 shows `sunUserver.cls` in its entirety.

Listing 10-3: `sunUserver.cls`

```
################################################################
#
# sunUserver.cls - modified for event handling
#
# $Id: sunUserver.cls,v 1.1 1998/03/31 19:01:12 chrisj Exp $
#
# -------------------------------------
# Methods
#
#   _getUsers
#   _getDiskUsage
#   _checkDiskSpace
#   _getLoad
#   _getWindow
#   _getState
```

```
#    _reboot
#
# Data Members
#
#    string      _strHost
#    string      _strIP
#    integer     _nUsers
#    integer     _nLavg
#    objlist     _oDiskList
#    disk        _oDref
#
# Construction
#
#    . uServer
#
########################################################

#
# Inherit from parent uServer class
#
. uServer $args

_sunUserver() {
  _this=$ObjectId
}

_getWindow() {
  #
  # Argument to window is first parameter
  #
  arguments=${1:-"/bin/ksh"}
  /usr/openwin/bin/xterm -display $DISPLAY -exec $arguments
}

_reboot() {
  #
  # Sync disks, issue reboot command
  #
  sync
  reboot
}
```

Creating the Operation Classes

With some of the fundamentals out of the way, you can begin coding the various operation classes that will represent your application. These operation classes will allow for the easy attachment of different kinds of interfaces to your system. As you'll see, these classes are fairly simple. Their main function is to decouple operations and commands from the collections of objects needed to implement them. If you don't create command objects, you have to obtain references to several different objects in order to create an account. Furthermore, you would have to do this in the code for each type of interface you create: HTML, Java, or native client code. The operation classes only require a reference to the desired operation. The instantiated operation subtype on the remote server takes care of creating the objects it needs to complete tasks.

This process is highly flexible and also easy to implement.

Add Account Operation

The first operation class creates accounts on a UNIX server. It directly uses the services of both the user object and account objects. Earlier, in Chapter 4, you created accounts using scripts that used these two objects. Here, you create an object to perform the operation wholesale, providing the simplest interface for client applications.

The constructor, derived from your base operation class, does nothing, but the execute method has a lot of power:

```
_execute() {
  #
  # Test argument count
  #
  if (( $# < 7 )); then
    print -u2 "$0: does not take less than seven arguments."
    return 1
  fi

  _login=$1
  _passwd=$2
  _uid=$3
  _gid=$4
  _gecos=$5
  _dir=$6
  _shell=$7

  #
  # Construct a user object
  #
  . user _u nobody
  #
  # Initialize with new data
  #
  _u_setFields $_login $_passwd $_uid $_gid $_gecos $_dir $_shell

  #
  # Create account object
  #
  . account _acc _u
  if ! _acc_createAccount; then
    print -u2 "$0: createAccount failed."
```

Chapter 10: Creating a Shell-Based Distributed Application

```
      return 1
  fi
}
```

First, you verify arguments, as you do not need to proceed unless you have exactly seven arguments. Next, you break apart the fields into their respective properties, and then move onto actually instantiating a user object. At first, the user object is initialized with the user `nobody`, and then you reassign the data fields to reflect the data passed to the _execute method.

If the user ID nobody does not exist on your system, you should replace this call with an equally docile account that can't actually log in. The logic of the user object requires an existing user ID in order for the constructor to work, so in this case you reassign the values when you want to create a new user.

After you create a user object, you create an account object and pass the user as a parameter. Error checking is done during the account creating process to indicate the success or failure of the operation to the caller. Listing 10-4 shows opAddAccount.cls in its entirety:

Listing 10-4: opAddAccount.cls

```
###############################################################
#
# opAddAccount.cls
#
# $Id: opAddAccount.cls,v 1.1 1998/03/30 21:42:39 chrisj Exp $
#
# -------------------------------------
#
# opAddAccount.cls
#
# Methods
#
# _execute <login> <passwd> <uid> <gid> <gecos> <dir> <shell>
#
###############################################################
#
# Inheritance of ::operation
#
. operation $args

_opAddAccount() {
  echo
}
```

```
_execute() {
    #
    # Test argument count
    #
    if (( $# < 7 )); then
      print -u2 "$0: does not take less than seven arguments."
      return 1
    fi

    _login=$1
    _passwd=$2
    _uid=$3
    _gid=$4
    _gecos=$5
    _dir=$6
    _shell=$7

    #
    # Construct a user object
    #
    . user _u nobody
    #
    # Initialize with new data
    #
    _u_setFields $_login $_passwd $_uid $_gid $_gecos $_dir $_shell

    #
    # Create account object
    #
    . account _acc _u
    if ! _acc_createAccount; then
      print -u2 "$0: createAccount failed."
      return 1
    fi
}

### eof
```

Delete Account Operation

Of course, side by side with creating accounts is deleting accounts. This operation follows the same logic as the preceding operation, but takes an existing account as a parameter at construction. The constructor for this object checks for the correct number of parameters, and initializes some internal data that represents the account's login ID.

```
_opDelAccount() {
    #
```

Chapter 10: Creating a Shell-Based Distributed Application

```
    # Test argument count
    #
    if (( $# != 1 )); then
      print -u2 "$0: constructor takes 1 parameter"
      return 1
    fi

    #
    # existing login ID as first parameter
    #
    _uiD=$1

}
```

If the user does not pass the correct number of parameters, the constructor exits. The _execute method for this object is also fairly straightforward. No confirmation message or other type of warning occurs before deleting the account. That type of logic is dependent on the interface being used. You want your operations to work equally well with both client GUIs and other distributed applications. Having an error message pop up is unwise if the client to your operation is simply a distributed process with no user actually running it. Such an error message just makes the operation unusable. Therefore, that type of logic is left to the client, and not in the operation's _execute method:

```
_execute() {

    #
    # Construct a user object
    #
    . user _u $_uiD

    #
    # Construct an account object with user object
    #
    . account _acc _u

    #
    # Delete the account
    #
    if ! _acc_deleteAccount; then
      print -u2 "$0: deleteAccount failed."
      return 1
    fi
}
```

In the preceding, you just create a user object with the given ID, and pass it off to the account. Barring any unexpected errors, you simply call account_deleteAccount. Listing 10-5 shows all of opDelAccount.cls.

Listing 10-5: opDelAccount.cls

```
##############################################################
#
# opDelAccount.cls
#
# $Id: opDelAccount.cls,v 1.2 1998/03/30 22:17:12 chrisj Exp $
#
# -------------------------------------
#
# opDelAccount.cls
#
# Methods
#
# _execute <login>
#
##############################################################

#
# Inheritance of ::operation
#
. operation $args

_opDelAccount() {

  #
  # Test argument count
  #
  if (( $# != 1 )); then
    print -u2 "$0: constructor takes 1 parameter"
    return 1
  fi

  #
  # existing login ID as first paramter
  #
  _uiD=$1

}

_execute() {

  #
  # Construct a user object
  #
  . user _u $_uiD

  #
  # Construct an account object with user object
  #
  . account _acc _u

  #
```

```
# Delete the account
#
if ! _acc_deleteAccount; then
  print -u2 "$0: deleteAccount failed."
  return 1
fi
}
```

Operation for Rebooting Servers

The next operation is a straightforward wrapper for uServer_reboot. This class simply provides the common _execute interface that your client applications want to use. In the constructor, you instantiate a uServer class (or subtype depending on your environment):

```
_opReboot() {
  #
  # Create a uServer object
  #
  . uServer us
}
```

In the _execute method, as you guessed, you call uServer_reboot:

```
_execute() {
  #
  # call Reboot method
  #
  if ! us_reboot; then
    print -u2 "$0:_reboot method failed."
  fi
}
```

Of course, check to make sure the call succeeded — otherwise, if someone calls the reboot operation, the system is dropped rather quickly with no questions asked!

The operation classes do not ask questions. The _execute method performs exactly as intended. Be careful not to reboot the server accidentally when initially testing your objects, or delete important accounts such as root.

Listing 10-6 shows opReboot.cls as it appears on the CD-ROM.

Listing 10-6: opReboot.cls

```
##################################################################
#
# opReboot.cls
#
# $Id: opReboot.cls,v 1.1 1998/03/31 17:17:33 chrisj Exp $
#
# -----------------------------------------
#
# opReboot.cls
#
# Methods
#
# _execute
#
##################################################################

#
# Inheritance of ::operation
#
. operation $args

_opReboot() {
    #
    # Create a uServer object
    #
    . uServer us
}

_execute() {
    #
    # call Reboot method
    #
    if ! us_reboot; then
      print -u2 "$0:_reboot method failed."
    fi
}
```

Operation to View Disk Space

As you may have noticed, most of these operation classes are simple wrappers for object methods that you've already established. The key reason for creating these operation classes is to provide an interface and encapsulate any object-specific functionality that may be required, regardless of its simplicity. Therefore, the _execute method of your opViewDiskSpace class really just uses the uServer class, which it creates at construction as in the preceding example:

```
_execute() {
    #
    # call getDiskUsage first on uServer object
    # then _checkDiskSpace
    #
```

Chapter 10: Creating a Shell-Based Distributed Application

```
    us_getDiskUsage > /dev/null
    us_checkDiskSpace
}
```

You must call _getDiskUsage prior to checking for disk space problems because _getDiskUsage instantiates all of your disk objects. If disk objects are only created when their information is needed, the information will be as current as possible. You also could have created disk objects at construction in uServer_uServer. Regardless, the call to getDiskUsage should always reprobe the disks for the most up-to-date information. In the preceding example, you redirect the output of _getDiskUsage to /dev/null, because it has no bearing on checking disk space. Listing 10-7 shows opViewDiskSpace.cls in full.

Listing 10-7: opViewDiskSpace.cls

```
#################################################################
#
# opViewDiskSpace.cls
#
# $Id: opViewDiskSpace.cls,v 1.1 1998/03/31 21:10:01 chrisj Exp $
#
# -------------------------------------
#
# opViewDiskSpace.cls
#
# Methods
#
# _execute
#
#################################################################

#
# Inheritance of ::operation
#
. operation $args

_opViewDiskSpace() {
    #
    # Create a uServer object
    #
    . uServer us
}

_execute() {
    #
    # call getDiskUsage first on uServer object
    # then _checkDiskSpace
    #
    us_getDiskUsage > /dev/null
    us_checkDiskSpace
}
```

View Disk Statistics Operation

Actually viewing the file system statistics that exist on the machine is similar to checking for disk space. The opViewDiskStats class take care of this function. This implementation is as straightforward as the preceding reboot operation. The constructor instantiates a uServer object, and the execute method calls uServer_getDiskUsage. Listing 10-8 shows opViewDiskStats.cls.

Listing 10-8: opViewDiskStats.cls

```
##################################################################
#
# opViewDiskStats.cls
#
# $Id: opViewDiskStats.cls,v 1.1 1998/03/31 21:05:01 chrisj Exp $
#
# ----------------------------------------
#
# opViewDiskStats.cls
#
# Methods
#
# _execute
#
##################################################################

#
# Inheritance of ::operation
#
. operation $args

_opViewDiskStats() {
   #
   # Create a uServer object
   #
   . uServer us
}

_execute() {
   #
   # call getDiskUsage on uServer object
   #
   us_getDiskUsage
}
```

Load Average Operation

SMU will also provide an operation for simply retrieving the load average of the host in question. The _execute method of opViewLoadAvg.cls calls uServer_getLoadAvg, and tailors the output slightly, as follows:

Chapter 10: Creating a Shell-Based Distributed Application

```
_execute() {
  #
  # retrieve load average from uServer instance
  #
  _lv=$(us_getLoad)
  #
  # format an output string
  #
  _lvStr="Current Load Average on $us_strHost is: $_lv"
  #
  # send it to STDOUT
  #
  print $_lvStr

}
```

The rest of the class is pretty straightforward and follows the pattern of the preceding operations. Listing 10-9 shows `opViewLoadAvg.cls`.

Listing 10-9: `opViewLoadAvg.cls`

```
#########################################################
#
# opViewLoadAvg.cls
#
# $Id: opViewLoadAvg.cls,v 1.1 1998/03/31 21:15:01 chrisj Exp $
#
# --------------------------------------
#
# opViewLoadAvg.cls
#
# Methods
#
# _execute
#
#########################################################

#
# Inheritance of ::operation
#
. operation $args

_opViewLoadAvg() {
  #
  # Create a uServer object
  #
  . uServer us
}

_execute() {
  #
  # retrieve load average from uServer instance
```

```
#
_lv=$(us_getLoad)
#
# format an output string
#
_lvStr="Current Load Average on $us_strHost is: $_lv"
#
# send it to STDOUT
#
print $_lvStr

}
```

View Process Table Operation

The operation to view a process table is slightly more complicated. These operations are designed to be distributed, and as a result, prefer to send their data back in a compacted string format. Therefore, when dealing with large quantities of data, you must decide how that information is to be formatted prior to sending it. In creating the view process table operation, you had the choice of sending the data as plain text, with a delimiter specifying line breaks, or another other format. Because the front end to the application you develop is going to be HTML-based, use opViewProcessTable.cls to return data in HTML format. If you plan to use the scripts within other applications, you can adjust the field delimiter accordingly.

Be sure to use the correct version of the ps command in your opView ProcessTable class. A good Linux version is ps -aux, while a System V Release 4 machine (as in Solaris) works better with ps -ef.

The constructor for opViewProcessTable.cls defines two internal data members: one initializes the delimiter, and the other initializes the string that actually holds the process table:

```
_opViewProcessTable() {
  #
  # Define line separator, we'll use HTML
  #
  _ml="<br>"
  _procString=""
}
```

In the preceding, you define _ml to be the HTML code <br>, which represents a line break. This definition ensures that the process table appears properly formatted on the browser screen. You can also change the formatting to your preference. Any complicated parsing should be done on the client side, but there is no set pattern to the process string, and parsing it after the fact can be difficult.

The _execute method retrieves the process string and writes the contents to a file. You can then use the read command to read each line in from the file, and append the HTML delimiter to the string. Once formatted, the string can be concatenated with the rest of the process string, in order to build one complete HTML-based string representing the entire process table. This string is returned to the client:

```
_execute() {
  #
  # use the version of ps for your system
  # and taste (i.e., Linux: ps -aux, SVR4: ps -ef)
  #
  if ! ps -aux > _.processtemp; then
    print -u2 "$0: could not create temporarily file"
    return 1
  fi

  #
  # Load ps output into string with your formatting
  #
  while read line
  do
    #
    # format string with _ml marker
    #
    _procString=${_procString}${_ml}${line}
  done < _.processtemp
  #
  # Dump temporary file
  #
  rm _.processtemp
  #
  # print to STDOUT
  #
  print $_procString
}
```

Listing 10-10 shows the complete version of opViewProcessTable.cls.

Listing 10-10: opViewProcessTable.cls

```
#################################################################
#
# opViewProcessTable.cls
#
# $Id: opViewProcessTable.cls,v 1.1 1998/03/31 21:39:31 chrisj Exp $
#
# -------------------------------------
#
# opViewProcessTable.cls
#
# Methods
#
# _execute
#
#################################################################

#
# Inheritance of ::operation
#
. operation $args

_opViewProcessTable() {
  #
  # Define line separator, you'll use HTML
  #
  _ml="<br>"
  _procString=""
}

_execute() {

  #
  # use the version of ps for your system
  # and taste (i.e, Linux: ps -aux, SVR4: ps -ef)
  #
  if ! ps -aux > _.processtemp; then
    print -u2 "$0: could not create temporarily file"
    return 1
  fi

  #
  # Load ps output into string with your formatting
  #
  while read line
  do
    #
    # format string with _ml marker
    #
    _procString=${_procString}${_ml}${line}
  done < _.processtemp
  #
```

```
# Dump temporary file
#
rm _.processtemp
#
# print to STDOUT
#
print $_procString
}
```

Deploying Operation Objects in the Repository

Now that you've created a whole collection of operation objects, you can deploy them into your ORBs repository and make them available to the network.

Taking Care of Dependencies

For your operation commands to function correctly, they'll need access to the objects that they use. As a result, you have to move the user, account, and uServer objects into the repository as well. Also, you need to ensure that the user ID with which you run the ORBserv has the repository in its path. For example, if you use the default installation off of the CD-ROM, you may want to include the following in your path before starting the `ORBserv.sh` program:

```
$> PATH=$PATH:/usr/local/uso/tools/ORBserv/repository
```

The preceding is in addition to making sure the Java executable is in your path. Also, if you use the operation objects to create and delete accounts, you need to run the `ORBserv.sh` as root and affirm that root's path has all the needed directories.

Creating Object Definition Files

For remote clients to use your operation objects from the network, you need to provide .def files within the repository. Because the goal was to provide a uniform interface for the operation suite, these files are extremely simple. In each case, you can suffice with the following:

```
execute:getState
```

Your objects support the preceding two operations. For example, to create the definition file `opViewDiskStats.cls`, you create a file called `opViewDiskStats.def`, that has only the following line:

```
execute:getState
```

You can then create definitions files (or just copy and rename your existing one) for each operation you've deployed into the repository.

 A valid definition (.def) file must exist for every object published in the repository; without a valid definition file, the ORB cannot provide the interface on the network.

After creating the definition files and providing the right path environment for your ORBserv user, you can begin using your objects from the network.

Creating a Distributed Client Application

Now you're ready to begin using the operation objects you've spent so much time creating. You create two versions of the demo application — the first is nondistributed and should be executed in the same directory as your operation objects (or at least have them in your PATH). This configuration enables you to confirm the operation of your objects and their dependencies prior to using them from across the network. Using objects across the network opens the possibility for an exponential increase in potential errors, and you should ascertain that everything works on the server before branching out.

Creating a Nondistributed Client

The script you use, OpDemo.sh, is simple but performs powerful tasks. OpDemo.sh is meant to be a menu-driven, command line program to test your operation object. The same structure used here can be imported with little modification into any type of client interface you wish to create. The CGI application created in Chapter 13 uses a structure virtually identical to this script to accomplish its operations.

The script starts by printing a menu in the form of a "here" document, and then reads input from the user:

```
#!/bin/ksh
#
# opDemo.sh
#
# Use operation objects...
#

#
```

Chapter 10: Creating a Shell-Based Distributed Application   279

```
# Print menu screen
#
cat << EOTxT
    MENU SYSTEM
***********************************************
    1) Create An Account on This System
    2) Delete An Account on This System
    3) Reboot the Server
    4) View Disk Statistics
    5) Check for High Disk Usage
    6) View Current Process Table
    7) View Load Average
    8) Quit

EOTxT
    #
    # read selection
    #
    print -n "Your Choice==>"
    read selection
```

This basic approach was also presented in Chapter 2. After retrieving the user's selection, you descend into a case statement to perform the different tasks presented in the menu:

```
#
    # Selection case switches
    #
    case $selection in

    1)
        #
        # Create Account
        #
```

The operations in the menu are numbered one through eight, and they are marked as the same within the case statement. The operations are all handled identically, except for delete account and create account, which add some client-side logic to the operation to prevent accidental misuse. The Create Account menu option is executed in code as follows:

```
    1)
        #
        # Create Account
        #
        print "Enter LoginID, UserID, GroupID, FullName, Dir, Shell"
        print "separated by spaces."
        print -n "ENTER FIELDS==>"
        read fields
        . opAddAccount opaa
        opaa_execute $fields
        ;;
```

You first instruct the user on the arrangement of the fields and how to separate them. After you retrieve their input, you instantiate the operation, and call the execute method passing the fields the user provided.

The Delete Account menu option has more built-in logic. It pauses before committing the deletion and confirms with the user. The user should notice he is about to delete root before he actually does it, and avert disaster:

```
2)
  #
  # Delete Account
  #
  print -n "LoginID of Account:"
  read name
  print "Confirm deletion of account $name? [y/n]"
  read answer
  if [[ $answer = "y" ]]; then
    . opDelAccount opda $name
    opda_execute
  fi
  ;;
```

After you retrieve the login ID they wish to delete, you confirm their intention, construct the appropriate operation object, and call the _execute method.

The remainder of the operations are all implemented in the same way, which proves the concept of your interface and the ease at which you can hook client applications to your code. The following shows how menu option 4, "View Disk Statistics" appears in code:

```
4)
  #
  # View Disk Statistics
  #
  . opViewDiskStats opvds
  opvds_execute
  opvds_Delete
```

The key parts in the preceding: you instantiate the operation, call the execute method, and then delete your reference so that it does not take up any more space. Listing 10-11 shows the complete version of opDemo.sh.

Listing 10-11: opDemo.sh

```
#!/bin/ksh
#
# opDemo.sh
#
# Use operation objects...
#
```

```
#
# Print menu screen
#
cat << EOTxT
   MENU SYSTEM
*******************************************
  1) Create An Account on This System
  2) Delete An Account on This System
  3) Reboot the Server
  4) View Disk Statistics
  5) Check for High Disk Usage
  6) View Current Process Table
  7) View Load Average
  8) Quit

EOTxT
  #
  # read selection
  #
  print -n "Your Choice==>"
  read selection

  #
  # Selection case switches
  #
  case $selection in

  1)
     #
     # Create Account
     #
     print "Enter LoginID, UserID, GroupID, FullName, Dir, Shell"
     print "separated by spaces."
     print -n "ENTER FIELDS==>"
     read fields
     . opAddAccount opaa
     opaa_execute $fields
     ;;
  2)
     #
     # Delete Account
     #
     print -n "LoginID of Account:"
     read name
     print "Confirm deletion of account $name? [y/n]"
     read answer
     if [[ $answer = "y" ]]; then
       . opDelAccount opda $name
       opda_execute
     fi
     ;;
  3)
     #
```

```
      # Reboot the Server
      #
      . opReboot opr
      #
      # bye bye...
      #
      opr_execute
      opr_Delete
      ;;
   4)
      #
      # View Disk Statistics
      #
      . opViewDiskStats opvds
      opvds_execute
      opvds_Delete
      ;;
   5)
      #
      # Check for High Disk Usage
      #
      . opViewDiskSpace vie
      vie_execute
      vie_Delete
      ;;
   6)
      #
      # View Process Table
      #
      . opViewProcessTable opvpt
      opvpt_execute
      opvpt_Delete
      ;;
   7)
      #
      # View Load Average
      #
      . opViewLoadAvg opvla
      opvla_execute
      opvla_Delete
      ;;
   8)
      exit
      ;;
   esac
exec $0
```

Creating a Distributed Client

If you were successful with the first demo, you can rest assured that your objects are in order, and you're ready to give it a whirl from the network. As previously mentioned, the only additional requirements are that the definition files are in place, and that the user who runs `ORBserv.sh` has the repository in their path prior to any other shell object paths. You don't want your operation object to load the wrong version of a user class or account class. As a means of reliability, only include the repository in the `ORBserv.sh` user's path — not in any other object paths. This approach ensures that only the correct versions of objects are loaded by any distributed instance. As a result, however, all object dependencies need to be place in the repository.

The `opDemoDist.sh` application you create basically mimics the preceding application, but you change the way in which you instantiate objects. You call on the connection manager to create objects, and call the `_release` method when you are finished using them. You need to have the client support scripts in your PATH when you run this application. The `chp10` directory on the CD-ROM contains everything you need to run the client portion of this application.

The change in how you create objects is pretty basic. Instead of proceeding as before, you use the following code to view the disk statistics:

```
4)
    #
    # View Disk Statistics
    #
    . connectionMgr.sh localhost opViewDiskStats opvds
    opvds_execute
    opvds_release
    ;;
```

The rest of the operations follow the same model. Listing 10-12 shows the full version of `OpDemoDist.sh`:

Listing 10-12: `OpDemoDist.sh`

```
#!/bin/ksh
#
# opDemo.sh
#
# Use distributed operation objects...
# Remember to call _release on distributed objects!!!!!!!
#

    #
    # Print menu screen
    #
cat << EOTxT
    MENU SYSTEM
```

```
	***********************************************
	1) Create An Account on This System
	2) Delete An Account on This System
	3) Reboot the Server
	4) View Disk Statistics
	5) Check for High Disk Usage
	6) View Current Process Table
	7) View Load Average
	8) Quit

EOTxT
	#
	# read selection
	#
	print -n "Your Choice==>"
	read selection

	#
	# Selection case switches
	#
	case $selection in

	1)
	   #
	   # Create Account
	   #
	   print "Enter LoginID, UserID, GroupID, FullName, Dir, Shell"
	   print "separated by spaces."
	   print -n "ENTER FIELDS==>"
	   read fields
	   . connectionMgr.sh localhost opAddAccount opaa
	   opaa_execute $fields
	   opaa_release
	   ;;
	2)
	   #
	   # Delete Account
	   #
	   print -n "LoginID of Account:"
	   read name
	   print "Confirm deletion of account $name? [y/n]"
	   read answer
	   if [[ $answer = "y" ]]; then
	     . connectionMgr.sh localhost opDelAccount opda $name
	     opda_execute
	     opda_release
	   fi
	   ;;
	3)
	   #
	   # Reboot the Server
	   #
	   . connectionMgr.sh localhost opReboot opr
```

Chapter 10: Creating a Shell-Based Distributed Application

```
      #
      # bye bye...
      #
      opr_execute
      opr_release
      ;;
   4)
      #
      # View Disk Statistics
      #
      . connectionMgr.sh localhost opViewDiskStats opvds
      opvds_execute
      opvds_release
      ;;
   5)
      #
      # Check for High Disk Usage
      #
      . connectionMgr.sh localhost opViewDiskSpace opvdsp
      opvdsp_execute
      opvdsp_release
      ;;
   6)
      #
      # View Process Table
      #
      . connectionMgr.sh localhost opViewProcessTable opvpt
      opvpt_execute
      opvpt_release
      ;;
   7)
      #
      # View Load Average
      #
      . connectionMgr.sh localhost opViewLoadAvg opvla
      opvla_execute
      opvla_release
      ;;
   8)
      exit
      ;;
   esac
exec $0
```

Summary

In this chapter, you created the first shell-based distributed application. This application can be a foundation from which you create more complex applications. By creating operation objects to encapsulate complex procedures, you simplify the process of hooking up client interfaces.

The next chapter explores enhancements to your object paradigm, including callbacks. Callbacks enable you to have a remote object invoke a method on a client object, which is a more robust solution and promotes distribution. It requires more overhead and programming effort at the ORB level, however. After that, you move onto creating CGI objects, and eventually hook up an HTML interface to the operations you created in this chapter.

Chapter 11

Rethinking an Object-Oriented System

IN THIS CHAPTER

- Modifying object-oriented systems
- Improvements for the SMU
- KSOP improvements
- Implementing object callbacks
- Updating existing software

THIS CHAPTER DISCUSSES methods and strategies for improving object-oriented systems. One of the main selling points of object-orientation is its easy extensibility and efficient reuse. While covering this topic, this chapter also covers improvements to your system that are wholly original, and as a result, do not involve much reuse. Original enhancements include object callbacks, or the capability for a remote, proxied object to call on the methods of its client. Quick and simple enhancements that illustrate reuse and efficiency in object-orientation include runtime changes, and the discussion of how object-oriented reuse changes the developmental process of software development.

Modifying an Object-Oriented System

The object press and advocates often tout the great developmental advantages of object-oriented software. They speak of efficiency and reuse, of reduced software lifecycles, and of increased flexibility and extensibility. While most of these statements are true, the cost and implementation factors in converting existing systems into object-oriented ones are often not mentioned. Also, a poorly executed object-oriented design seldom yields these developmental advantages. Many times, a system is rewritten more or less from scratch when the original implementation is poor. Such an occurrence nullifies any advantages that object-orientation may have brought to the development cycle. Frequently, development hours are lost as programmers and system architects go through the process of learning good object-oriented design techniques. Once these initial steps are taken, however, the benefits become apparent and quickly surpass traditional development efforts.

The Magic of Interfaces

The preceding chapter discussed an imaginary application created by an imaginary credit card bank. The key difficulty in that system involved integrating a few of the bank's key systems with a third-party service provider in an effort to provide SnazzyGuard credit and fraud protection to the bank's customers. The solution was to implement the business logic as a series of distributed interfaces with which network-aware applications could bind at runtime.

The benefits of object-orientation will stand out in this application. When the preceding chapter last discussed SnazzyGuard network implementation, a diagram depicted a SnazzGuard object publishing its interfaces to the network. The concept: an object broker such as CORBA or COM would take care of retrieving a SnazzGuard object and integrate it tightly with client code so that the SnazzGuard object appeared to be local code to the clients.

CHANGING THE CODE BEHIND THE INTERFACE

As with any company, the bank decides it needs to change the business logic slightly for the SnazzyGuard service. The bank is going to integrate yet a few more databases and "marketecture" data-gleaning services into the mix with the SnazzGuard application. This situation requires changes to the business logic of the network object. Thankfully, the interface to the SnazzGuard object is simple and functional, and provides good encapsulation from the inner workings of the object. All changes proposed by the bank's marketing department can be handled behind the scenes, and the interface does not have to change, because you did not mix it with the mechanics of your object. The SnazzGuard was written to provide the simplest interface possible to support the business logic in the most general way.

Now that the bank wants to change things, you as a programmer can go in and start recoding part of the object. You start by recoding the implementation of the interface that registers customers with the third-party company. The third party provides insurance and other aspects of the SnazzyGuard service. Within the interface, you add some code to dump user information into another one of the bank's network databases. This process leaves the interface for registering users intact. The original code written by the bank and the code written by the third-party service company remain unaffected. In fact, the new SnazzGuard object can be slipped into place without interrupting the system, which enables you to integrate the object at runtime, as opposed to shutting down the system.

DISCOVERING THE ADVANTAGES OF RUNTIME INTEGRATION

Apart from the business processes that go unaffected, there are many benefits to runtime integration. The idea of creating code that fits seamlessly with existing components illustrates a successful design — the result of successful encapsulation and a well-crafted object model.

In distributed, complex systems, many different pieces may require the services of a component during the operation of a system. Tracking down all of the systems and processes that are dependent on the use of one particular network component can become a project in itself. In these cases, runtime integration can be far more advantageous than bringing down the system.

SAVING THE BUSINESS PROCESS

Perhaps the greatest benefit to runtime integration and component development is not bringing down business processes due to system constraints. Often, one small piece of a system can delay all operations during an outage period. As with the preceding reasons, behind every distributed process that has a dependency on your object are the business reasons and processes that created that dependency in the first place. Countless hours are lost when a system has to be brought down, and a maintenance window has to be scheduled to determine the best time to bring down the system. These delays can lead to customer impact, and eventually, company losses.

In the SnazzGuard example, the bank not only has 24-hour dependency on the business object, but the third-party company probably also has dependencies. This situation creates a nightmare because downtime, outages, and impact have to be determined between two organizations that simply want to share in a joint venture.

By dropping the new version of the component into the system without shutting it down, you completely avoid the need for outages, scheduled downtime, and the endless miscommunication that can happen between two organizations. It's hard enough to get people to attend meetings, not to mention scheduling a system outage across organizations.

Suggestions for Your System

Now you can start thinking of ways to improve your system. While it meets many needs now, some additional improvements that update both the KSOP protocol and the server and client stub software.

The code developed here is not used when you complete your SMU application. This chapter introduces future directions in which you can take KSOP and SMU. The application you complete in the next two chapters builds on the system you created in Chapter 10. Therefore, you may want to keep the code from this chapter separate.

ONE-WAY OBJECT IMPLEMENTATION

SMU and KSOP currently only allow for one-way object communication; that is, you can load a remote object and use it locally, but the remote object cannot invoke methods on its client.

Using a remote object as if it were local increases network programming capabilities tremendously. To represent distributed objects and provide for network transparency, however, you should be able to pass objects to other objects, allow for an object to take a reference to the object that's calling it, and invoke methods on it.

Earlier, you created two objects that worked with each other: account and user. In your current system, you could easily create a remote user object and pass it to a local account object, but you would have difficulty creating a remote account object and passing a local user object to it. For this reason, you created the operation commands to encapsulate creating an account. You could make a local user object, call its `_getFields` method, and pass the result off to a remotely instantiated `opAddAccount_execute` method. This sequence achieves the same result, but differs from the first version. Figure 11-1 shows a local account object using a remote user object.

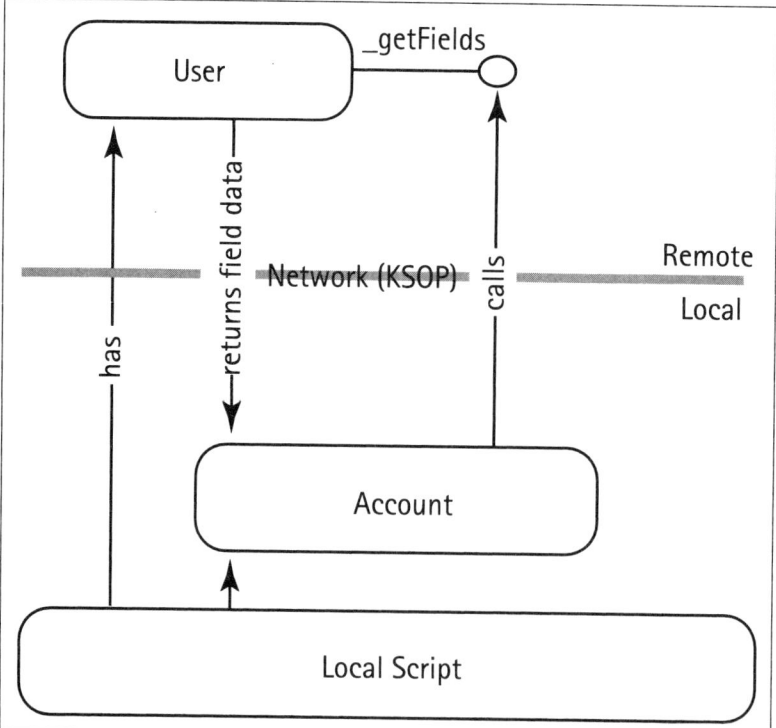

Figure 11-1: A local account object using a distributed user object

With this system, an account object needs to invoke methods on a user object. In a way, the account is a client of the user. In your scheme, a local account can use a distributed user because it only needs to invoke operations on the user and use the returned results. KSOP supports this procedure. The problem arises if the account object is a client of the user object, and in turn, the user object seeks to become a client of the account object. In this case, KSOP has no way of supporting a means for the remote user object to invoke methods on the local account. Conversely, a remote account object cannot invoke methods on a local user as shown in Figure 11-2.

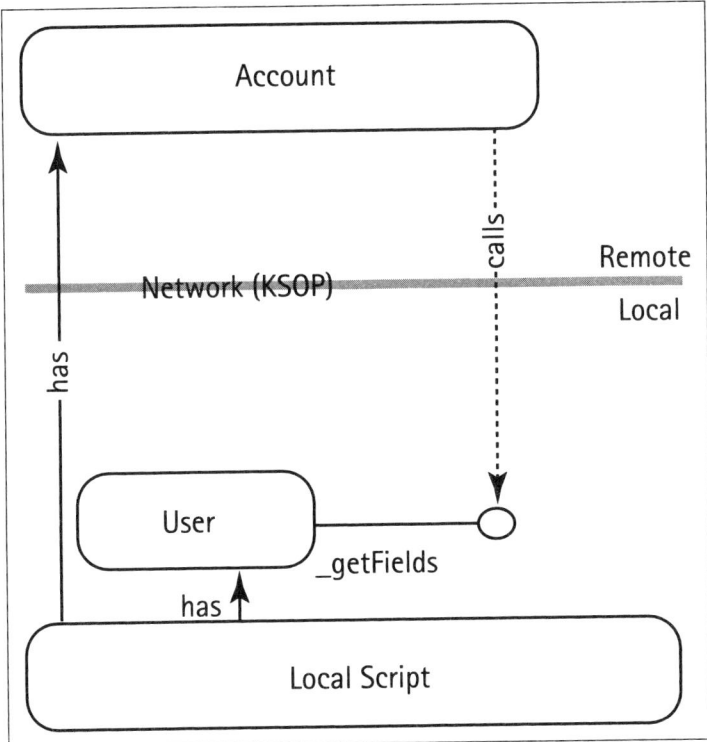

Figure 11-2: A remote account object can't invoke methods on a local user object.

You're able to circumvent this problem by providing for facades that encapsulate the details of complex operations. As previously mentioned, you can easily use a local user object with an opAddAccount object. Figure 11-3 shows a local user object being used with a remotely instantiated opAddAccount object to create a remote account.

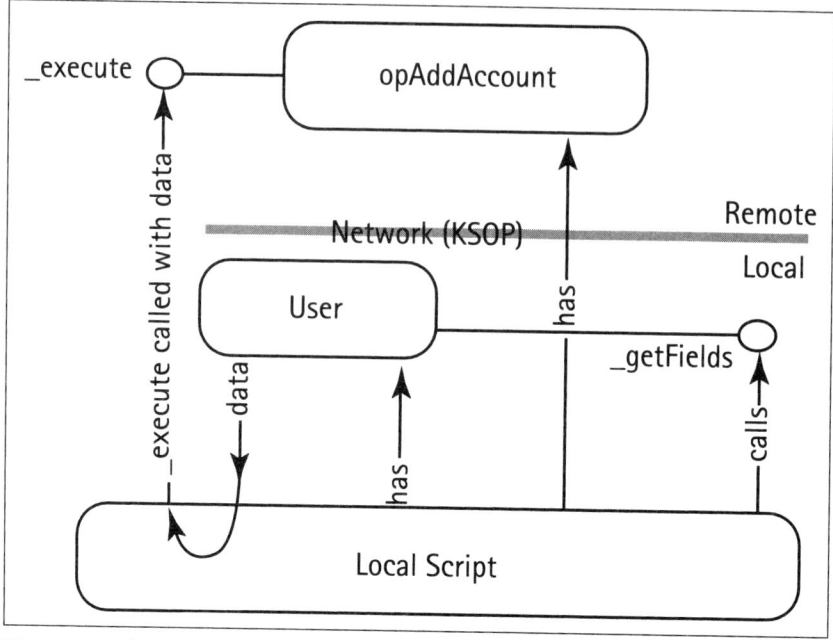

Figure 11-3: A local user object used with a remote `opAddAccount` object

This solution solves the problem, but it would be nice if remote objects could invoke methods on local objects that are using them as clients. Wouldn't it?

TWO-WAY DISTRIBUTED OBJECTS

The most flexibility in network programming occurs in implementing two-way communication. That way, applications created using existing account and user implementations can become distributed without substantial effort. As demonstrated in previous chapters, retrieving an object from a network broker is identical to local instantiation.

This approach frees you to develop applications purely with objects in mind, without regard for the physical and distributed systems to which they are farmed out. An object model needs to take into account the physical nature of entities and processes it represents; more often than not, however, the network is one entity that should become transparent.

OBJECT CALLBACKS

This section refers to the process of a remote object calling methods on a local object as an object "callback."

The goal of callbacks is to create two objects that call each other's methods interchangeably, and to distribute them onto two different machines. Figure 11-4 shows this relationship.

Chapter 11: Rethinking an Object-Oriented System

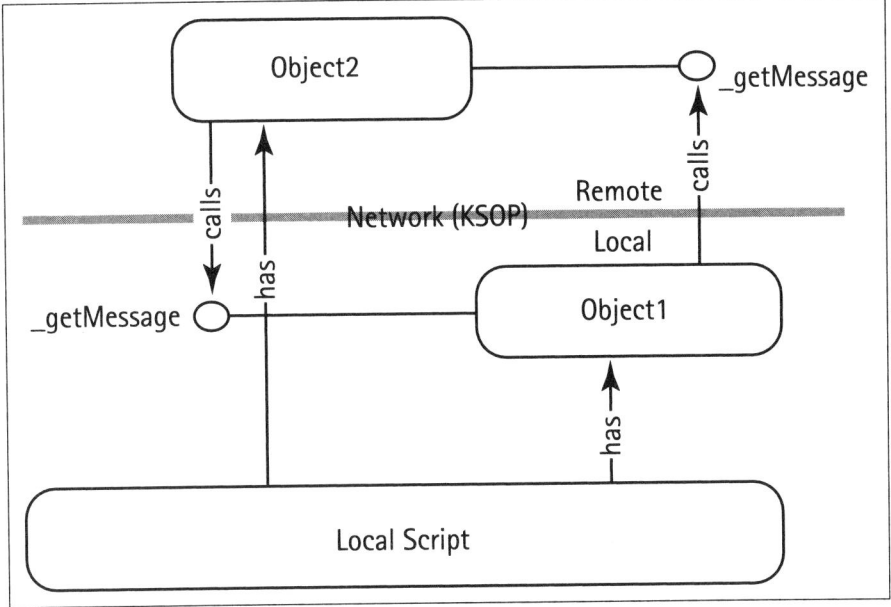

Figure 11-4: Object1 and Object2 holding references to each other across the network

The crux of the implementation is modifying the KSOP protocol, and the functionality of both the `proxy.sh` script and the `ORBserv.sh` program to support the additional functions. As previously mentioned, you should view this chapter as an exercise in process improvement, and not as an overhaul of the SMU application or KSOP protocol. In the following two chapters, you build on KSOP and SMU as presented in Chapter 10, and complete CGI objects and a Web-based GUI for using SMU. Therefore, this section strongly suggests that you leave your existing ORBserv setup intact, and create a new directory for your experiments. If you've installed the material off the CD-ROM, you can use the `chp11` directory as your playground for this chapter's experiments.

 When running the `ORBserv.sh` and `proxy.sh` scripts, pay close attention to what object directories and repository directories are in your path. If you create two ORBs on one machine, you don't want one ORB loading objects from the repository of the other.

Implementing Object Callbacks

Now you can begin creating this new type of functionality. Your shell objects located on the server can call methods on their clients. These methods may return anything to the server, such as information about the client machine or user information. For the ORB to handle callbacks correctly, you'll need to develop a KSOP string for them, modify the client- and server-side KSOP support software, and code your objects with callbacks in mind.

Callback Overview

This implementation of callbacks places the burden on both the client and the server. Obviously, the server needs to know which method on the client it wishes to invoke – that is the server's requirement. Also, the server object must derive itself from `clientCb` in order to use the callback functions. The client, on the other hand, must give a local object as a reference when it creates the server object. For instance, if a local script needs to create an account object on a remote server, and provide a local user object as a reference for pulling user information, it passes a reference to an instantiated user object to `proxy.sh` when asking for the server object:

```
$> . user MyUser chrisj
$> . proxy.sh MyUser localhost account MyAccount
```

This example creates a local user object that contains local data for the user `chrisj`, and also asks `proxy.sh` (assuming a connection has already been established) for a reference to a remote instance of an account object. Using the callback mechanism, the server-instantiated account can call `_getFields` on the user object, which is local. This call returns the `_strFields` data member back to server, which uses the information to create an account. Conversely, if you use the connection manager to retrieve the server object instance, you can use the following:

```
$> . connectionMgr.sh localhost MyUser account MyAccount
```

The server object needs to know what to do with the reference, and it will actually be the first parameter passed into `instance` when the server object is created. The server object invokes a method on the local object, in this case `MyUser`, by passing the method it wishes to use off to the `_clientCall` method that the server object would have inherited from `clientCb`.

 **TIP** You must support callbacks in your server code in order to use them. On the client side, you must always give a local object reference to the proxy so the server has something on which to callback.

Server Object Responsibilities

This scheme requires that you take callbacks into consideration when designing your objects. A server object must call a client through the clientCb::clientCall method. For example, if a remote account object needs to invoke the _getFields method on a local user object, it must do so through _clientCall:

```
_createAccount() {
  _userFields=$( _clientCall getFields)
  .
  .
  # Account creation code....
}
```

As the preceding snippet of code shows, _clientCall is used as opposed to a direct invocation on the user's method (user::getFields), because the user object is located on a different machine, and not in the same address space as the account object. In Chapter 4, an account object could invoke a user object's methods directly as follows:

```
_createAccount() {
  _userFields=$( {uRef}_getFields)
  .
  .
  # Account creation code...
}
```

The callback scheme also requires that you test the results of your callbacks, as a client may not have given a valid client-side object as a reference when it invoked the server object.

Client Object Responsibilities

On the client side, most of the work is done by proxy.sh, but you aren't off the hook. When you pass a reference off to proxy.sh or the connection manager, you are ensuring that the object is currently instantiated, and not just a local class. The proxy.sh program seeks to invoke live methods via the reference you've provided. As a result, the instantiated object must be present in the same address or process space as whatever server object you've created via `proxy.sh`. In the preceding example, you would have needed to create a valid user object before the server could invoke `_clientCall` with the `getFields` method as a parameter:

```
# local script code
#
. user au chrisj
# au is now a valid, active reference implementing the getFields method

# Create a connection to localhost
. socket sock localhost
sock_sendrecv&

# instantiate remote server object
. proxy.sh au localhost account acc

# call _createAccount on server, to start callback process
acc_createAccount

# clean up
acc_release
au_Delete
print disconnect > probing
```

As this example shows, the callback process is transparent to the client and goes on behind the scenes. The server's `_createAccount` method actually invokes `_clientCall` with `getFields` as a parameter. The special handling code that you build into `proxy.sh` intercepts this call, invokes the method on the instance it is handed, au, and returns the results back to the server. The server then completes its tasks and return any information necessary to the client, which appears as the result from the `_createAccount` call.

The initial callback from the server to the client is transparent to the ORB – it thinks it is just returning a result to the client. This return result is actually a formatted KSOP string that the `proxy.sh` interprets as a callback, however. After doing the necessary invocation on the client, `proxy.sh` sends another KSOP string back to the ORB that routes it back to the appropriate instance. The instance then formats a correct response, which it sends back to the client, and is handled by the ORB and the proxy as a simple return.

Modifying the KSOP Protocol

The format is basic and handled in much the same way as a method invocation. You actually need to handle a callback twice: once when the server initiates the call and once when the client returns a result back.

Formatting the Server String

You can actually shortcut the ORB's parsing utility when you first initiate a callback by placing the logic on the proxy side. The `proxy.sh` handles the result and checks to see if it is the KSOP callback key. The callback key handed by the server to the client looks like the following:

```
callback:setProperty:argument1:argument2:argument3
```

The `proxy.sh` takes care of parsing the preceding out into the KSOP key, the method to be called, and any and all arguments that should be sent to the method.

Formatting the Client String

The `proxy.sh` takes the return result of the method invocation and packages it up into another KSOP string, which the ORB needs to interpret:

```
returncallback:364827634872:callback_result_information
```

The format for the proxy generate KSOP string is first the KSOP key, the unique server instance ID used to identify each server instance to the ORB, and then whatever stringified information generated by the local call.

Modifying proxy.sh

First examine the modifications made to `proxy.sh` to support callbacks. You can start by adding code to copy the name of the passed-in local object reference:

```
# The local object client (capable of handling callback from server)
#
clientRef=$1
```

Recoding the Virtual Function

Also, you can add code within the implementation of each method to handle the possible callback key that may be passed back by a server object as a parameter:

```
#
# do loop implementing methods
#
usvId=${interfaceArray[0]}

(( ct = 1 ))
while (( ct < ${#interfaceArray[*]} ))
```

```
do
  eval "${localInstance}_${ifAry[ct]}()
  {
     print meth:$usvId:${ifAry[ct]}:\$1:\$2:\$3:\$4:\$5:\$6:\$7 >>
$serverPipe
     read result < $serverPipe
     if [[ \$result = @(callback*) ]]; then
       #
       # Attempt to execute callback method on
       # client object
       #
       r_string=\$(echo \$result | tr : \ )
       doCallBack \$r_string
       #
       # Return callback result to server
       #
       echo \$cb_result > $serverPipe
       #
       # get Result from server, again
       #
       read nResult < $serverPipe
       print \$nResult
       return 0
     fi
     print \$result
  }"
  (( ct = ct + 1 ))
done
```

You test the value of result to see if it contains the KSOP callback key; if so, you parse it. A different type of parsing occurs in the example, which abandons the use of the IFS (Internal Field Separator) and opts out for the tr command. The translate command (tr) can translate character patterns into other character patterns. For example, if you want to change every instance of a shell comment into a capital X, you could use tr in the following fashion:

```
tr \# X < source.sh > source.txt
```

The translate command reads its standard input, performs the pattern substitutions, and writes the results to standard output. The preceding works quite well at replacing instances of colons with spaces in a KSOP string. One drawback to this particular use of tr is that it can't always be used to prepare an argument string for use by a function. While the xargs command can be used to prepare argument lists from STDIN, many items are system-dependent and your mileage will surely vary. In this case, you should use tr to prepare a string that you can pass to a function.

You prepare a string with tr, and name it r_string. You then pass r_string off to the doCallBack function, which is the other major addition to proxy.sh to support callbacks.

Completing a Callback

The `doCallBack` method first takes stock of the parameters it was passed:

```
doCallBack()
{
  #
  # First arg is "callback" KSOP key
  #
  toss=$1
  #
  # Method is arg 2
  #
  method=$2
  #
  # Args is 3-9 (unpack 'em the easy way)
  #
  args="$3 $4 $5 $6 $7 $8 $9"
```

The first argument is the KSOP key that can be tossed, the second argument is the actual method to invoke, and the remaining arguments, if any, are the parameters to be given to the method. You invoke the method as follows:

```
    #
  # Invoke the method
  #
  if ! ${clientRef}_${method} $args > temp_rz; then
    cb_result="callbackfailure:$usvId"
    return 1
  fi
  read cb_result <  temp_rz
```

You invoke the method with the accompanying arguments and write to a file. pdKsh 5.2.12 does not support one critical aspect of shell programming: the capability to complete a statement such as `echo thing | read var`. Common shell programming sense leads you to think that `var` is now be equal to "thing", but this is not the case. The only other way to phrase an expression might be as follows:

```
var=$( echo thing )
```

The preceding example is okay, but `echo thing` is being executed in a subprocess and may not produce the expected results if your operation is more complex. This problem may not be an issue with your version of the Korn shell, but because this book is tailored more to pdKsh and Linux, it provides situations work on those machines. The easiest approach simply writes the result to a file and then assigns the value of `cb_result` to the contents of the temporary file.

If the local method call doesn't succeed, you can format a KSOP callback error. Because you haven't implemented this error handling in `ORBserv.sh`, you'll get an "Unsupported Interface" response from the server:

```
#
# Give KSOP format to callback result
#
cb_result="returncallback:$usvId:"$cb_result
#
# exit OK
#
return 0

}
```

If you choose to implement callbacks, you can complete the callback failure string as an exercise. If everything is okay, the function returns normally, and the result is sent back to the server as shown in the preceding code for creating the virtual functions. Listing 11-1 shows the full, updated version of `proxy.sh`.

Listing 11-1: `proxy.sh`

```
#!/bin/ksh
#
# proxy.sh - modified for callbacks
#
# $Id: proxy.sh,v 1.2 1998/04/06 00:38:30 chrisj Exp chrisj $
#
#

#
# The local object client (capable of handling callback from server)
#
clientRef=$1
#
# The rest: server pipe, remote object,
#    local reference name, arguments...
#
serverPipe=$2
serverObject=$3
localInstance=$4
#
# Shift out args to get to variable parameters
#
shift 4
init_arguments=$@

#
# doCallBack - invoke a client method on behalf of
#    the server object
#       **Must be internalized as a function to support multiple
```

```
#       callbacks.
#
doCallBack()
{
  #
  # First arg is "callback" KSOP key
  #
  toss=$1
  #
  # Method is arg 2
  #
  method=$2
  #
  # Args is 3-9 (unpack 'em the easy way)
  #
  args="$3 $4 $5 $6 $7 $8 $9"
  #
  # Invoke the method
  #
  if ! ${clientRef}_${method} $args > temp_rz; then
    cb_result="callbackfailure:$usvId"
    return 1
  fi
  read cb_result <  temp_rz
  #
  # Give KSOP format to callback result
  #
  cb_result="returncallback:$usvId:"$cb_result
  #
  # exit OK
  #
  return 0

}

# check for connection
if [[ ! -p $serverPipe ]]; then
    print "unable to contact connection manager"
    return 1
fi

#
# retrieve interface from server
#
print req:$serverObject:$init_arguments > $serverPipe
read Interface < $serverPipe

#
# construct object from interface based on instance name
#
oldIFS=$IFS
IFS=:
set -A interfaceArray $Interface
```

```
IFS=$oldIFS

  #
  # do loop implementing methods
  #
  usvId=${interfaceArray[0]}

  (( ct = 1 ))
  while (( ct < ${#interfaceArray[*]} ))
  do

  eval "${localInstance}_${ifAry[ct]}()
  {
     print meth:$usvId:${ifAry[ct]}:\$1:\$2:\$3:\$4:\$5:\$6:\$7 >>
  $serverPipe
     read result < $serverPipe
     if [[ \$result = @(callback*) ]]; then
       #
       # Attempt to execute callback method on
       # client object
       #
       r_string=\$(echo \$result | tr : \  )
       doCallBack \$r_string
       #
       # Return callback result to server
       #
       echo \$cb_result > $serverPipe
       #
       # get Result from server, again
       #
       read nResult < $serverPipe
       print \$nResult
       return 0
     fi
     print \$result
  }"
  (( ct = ct + 1 ))
  done

  #
  # create release method to let go of remote instance
  eval "${localInstance}_release()
  {
    print release:$usvId >> $serverPipe
    read result < $serverPipe
    print \$result
    #
    # If you're using the connectionMgr, let it
  # know you are exiting
    if [[ -f $serverPipe.connections ]]; then
      connectionMgr.sh release:$serverPipe
    fi
  }"
```

The `doCallBack` function is global, and therefore only works for one object instantiation. If you want to use multiple callback objects within the same process space, you need to internalize the `doCallBack` function in the same way you created the `_release` method. The `doCallBack` method needs to be unique for each object, and only pass that particular remote object's unique ID as a parameter when doing a callback. Without internalizing this method, each callback object supersedes the previous callback object.

Modifying the ORB Server

The smallest amount of changes actually happens to the `ORBserv.sh` program. The callback process is a one-time, two-way call between the proxy and ORB server. The initial call to the proxy appears as a simple return result to the ORB, and the subsequent return from the proxy is the only communication that needs to be distinguished.

The return message must contain the unique ID that identifies the instantiated object to the ORB, and inform the ORB of the message type. Therefore, you create a "KSOP Object Callback" section within the `ORBserv.sh` process. This section appears in a similar way to the method invocation, as it needs the same sort of handling:

```
    #
    # KSOP object callback
    #
    @(returncallback*))
      # send off to forwardMethodArgs without :'s
      oldIFS=$IFS
      IFS=:
      forwardMethodArgs $rawRequest
      IFS=$oldIFS
      #
      # send back result
      #
      print -p $retResult
      ;;
```

The ORB looks for the "returncallback*" string, with the initial KSOP key coming first in whatever string is returned. You then alter the IFS character to parse the string (remove the colons), and call `forwardMethodArgs` to send the information into the object instance, which can act accordingly. As usual, whatever response the instance sends back is propagated back to the client.

Add a hook for a `callbackfailure` string within the `proxy.sh` code, and you could also easily create a section for handling callback failures by the ORB. You can complete these tasks as an exercise.

If you're unsure where to insert this snippet of code or want to see a complete version, Listing 11-2 details `ORBserv.sh` as it appears in this chapter.

Listing 11-2: `ORBserv.sh`

```ksh
#!/bin/ksh
#
# ORBserv.sh
#
# $Id: ORBserv.sh,v 1.2 1998/02/05 07:14:55 chrisj Exp chrisj $
#
# $Log: ORBserv.sh,v $
# Revision 1.1  1998/02/05 07:14:55  chrisj
#
# Uncomment following line for debugging output!
set -vx
#
# !!!!!!!!!!
#  Make sure PATH contains the java binary and
#    the instance script (./instance)
# !!!!!!!!!!
#
# create server co-process for communication|binds
# to port 2112 by default
java pipeserv |&
jPid=$! ## copy of background PID string
bg_instances=1 ## Number of active background processes
#
# createInstance()
#  This function creates an object instance for a
#  client. The instance is assigned a unique
#  identifier, which is used by the client and ORB to
#  communicate with the instantiated object which
#  is tied to the ORB via a named-pipe.
#
createInstance() {
  #
  # create a persistent instance of the object
  #
  mkfifo $UqId   # make a fifo of the unique id
  #
  # launch the instance script with object and fifo
  instance $object $UqId $arguments &
  ((bg_instances = bg_instances + 1))
  return
}
#
# forwardMethodArgs()
#   This function is used to forward a client method
#   invocation to the appropriate object instance.
#   The unique identifier is pulled from the request
#   and the information is forwarded to the correct
#   object via the named pipe.
#
forwardMethodArgs() {
  shift
```

Chapter 11: Rethinking an Object-Oriented System   305

```
  UniqueIDfifo=$1
  while (( $# > 0 ))
  do
    methInvoc_Args=${methInvoc_Args:-}$1:
    shift
  done
  #
  # send method information to instance
  print $methInvoc_Args >> $UniqueIDfifo
  methInvoc_Args=""
  #
  # read result of method invocation
  read retResult < $UniqueIDfifo
  return
}
#
# Main Loop
#   This loop blocks on I/O while reading from
#   the co-process. The co-process
#   will send client requests and object
#   instance requests from whatever
#   clients attach to port 2112.
#
while true
 do
 #
 # get request from socket
 if ! read -p rawRequest; then
  print -u2 "ORBserv.sh: co-process dead. exiting."
  exit
 fi

 case $rawRequest in

   #
   # retrieve interface definition, or forward method
   # request off to object instance
   #
   #
   # KSOP object request
   #
   @(req*) )
     UqId=$RANDOM$RANDOM$RANDOM
     oldIFS=$IFS
     IFS=:
      set -A reqArray $rawRequest
     IFS=$oldIFS
     object=${reqArray[1]}
      reqArray[0]=""
      reqArray[1]=""
      arguments=${reqArray[*]}
      _def=$(< repository/$object.def)
      interface=$UqId:$_def
```

```
        print -p $interface
        createInstance
        ;;
    #
    # KSOP object method invocation
    #
    @(meth*))
        # send off to forwardMethodArgs without :'s
        oldIFS=$IFS
        IFS=:
        forwardMethodArgs $rawRequest
        IFS=$oldIFS
        #
        # send back result
        #
        print -p $retResult
        ;;
    #
    # KSOP object callback
    #
    @(returncallback*))
        # send off to forwardMethodArgs without :'s
        oldIFS=$IFS
        IFS=:
        forwardMethodArgs $rawRequest
        IFS=$oldIFS
        #
        # send back result
        #
        print -p $retResult
        ;;
    #
    # KSOP object release
    #
    @(release*))
        # Change IFS to : in order to set array
         oldIFS=$IFS
         IFS=:
          # define array
          set -A tempArray $rawRequest
         IFS=$oldIFS
         print "release" > ${tempArray[1]}
        #
        # remove FIFO
        #
        rm ${tempArray[1]}
        if [[ ! -p ${tempArray[1]} ]]; then
          print -p OBJECT_RELEASED
          #
          # decrement bg_instances
          #
          (( bg_instances = bg_instances - 1 ))
        else
```

```
           print -p OBJECT_MAYBE_RELEASED
      fi
      ;;
  #
  # KSOP Kill ORBserv
  #
  killserver)
      #
      # Tear down java co-process
      #
      kill -9 $jPid
      #
      # Tear down any instances
      #
      while (( bg_instances > 1 ))
      do
        kill %$bg_instances
        (( bg_instances = bg_instances - 1))
      done
      #
      # exit the server
      #
      exit
      ;;
  #
  # KSOP Unknown
  #
  *)
      def="Unknown interface"
      if ! print -p $def; then
        print -u2 "ORBserv.sh: co-process dead. exiting."
        exit
       fi
      ;;
  esac

 done
#
# eof
```

Modifying the Instance Process

The instance process does not need much modification, but you need to give the server object's code the name of the pipe that tethers the server object back to the ORB. The server stub code, `clientCb`, from which all server objects need to derive in order to support callbacks, sends message directly into the ORB pipe for routing back to the client.

When a callback-capable server object is first created, the instance passes the name of the server pipe as a parameter. First, however, the information is taken from the ORB pipe and formatted:

```
#
# Insert name of pipe back to ORB as first argument
#
_strArguments=$_IDpipe" "$_strArguments
```

You already are passing the name of the pipe to the instance script – you just need to reformat the creating string to include the name of the pipe as a parameter. This process requires you to code your server objects to expect the name of the pipe at construction.

Also, this version of the instance program alters how the `invoke` method works. It writes object output to a file, and then reads the results back in for greater shell compatibility:

```
invoke() {
  #
  # First arg is KSOP, second is method
  #
  method=$2
  #
  # Concatenate arguments, the quick and easy way
  #
  args="$3 $4 $5 $6 $7 $8 $9"
  #
  # Invoke method, retrieve result
  #
  thisInstance_${method} $args 2>&1 > tI_r
  read result < tI_r

  #
  # Return result back to pipe
  #
  echo $result >> $_IDpipe

  return
}
```

Listing 11-3 shows the new version of `instance` in its entirety.

Listing 11-3: `instance`

```
#!/bin/ksh
#
# instance.sh - create and maintain persistent object instance
#
#
# uncomment following line for debugging output
```

Chapter 11: Rethinking an Object-Oriented System 309

```
#set -vx
#
# Initial parameters
#
# $1: The object to create
# $2: The tether pipe to ORBserv.sh
#
_object=$1
_IDpipe=$2
_strArguments="$3 $4 $5 $6 $7 $8 $9"
#
# Insert name of pipe back to ORB as first argument
#
_strArguments=$_IDpipe" "$_strArguments

#
# invoke()
#  This function invokes a method on the object instance
#
invoke()  {
  #
  # First arg is KSOP, second is method
  #
  method=$2
  #
  # Concatenate arguments, the quick and easy way
  #
  args="$3 $4 $5 $6 $7 $8 $9"
  #
  # Invoke method, retrieve result
  #
  thisInstance_${method} $args 2>&1 > tI_r
  read result < tI_r

  #
  # Return result back to pipe
  #
  echo $result >> $_IDpipe

  return
}
#
# Implement the object from the repository
#
. repository/$_object thisInstance $_strArguments

#
# Main loop
#  Here, you listen on the tether pipe for method
#  invocations, or the instructions to terminate.
#
while true
```

```
do
  read methodInvocations < $_IDpipe
  if [[ $methodInvocations = "release" ]]; then
    exit
  fi
  #
  # Call invoke function
  #
  invoke $methodInvocations
done
```

Modifying the Connection Manager

You can also use the connection manager when using callbacks. The syntax is a little different than using `proxy.sh`, but the same results are accomplished. To invoke a server object with the connection manager, you must supply the local object instance as the second parameter, and the remote server name as the first:

```
$> . connectionMgr.sh localhost localObject serverObject localRef
```

This example assumes that an object called `localObject` has been instantiated and is within the same process or address space as the rest of the application. The rest of the parameters follow along the lines of previous use of the connection manager and should be self-explanatory.

The main changes support the callback reference. You take this reference as the second parameter and call it `callbackRef`:

```
callbackRef=$2
```

Other than that element, this example only modifies how you call `proxy.sh`, including the necessary local object reference:

```
  #
  # Call proxy to instantiate object
  #
  . proxy.sh $callbackRef $server $object $arguments
```

As you would expect, the connection manager works in the same manner. Most of the burden for creating and using callbacks resides in the construction of server objects and the construction of applications to take advantage of the architecture. Most of the work done to KSOP and the ORB is minor. Listing 11-4 shows the complete, updated version of the connection manager.

Listing 11-4: connectionMgr.sh

```ksh
#!/bin/ksh

server=$1
if [[ $server = @(release*) ]]; then
  #
  # delete a reference
  spipe=${server#*:}
  read refcnt < $spipe.connections
  refcnt=$((refcnt - 1))
  print $refcnt > $spipe.connections
  if (( $refcnt < 1 )); then
    #
    # tear down this connection
    print disconnect > $spipe
    rm $spipe.connections
  fi
  exit
fi

callbackRef=$2
object=$3
shift 3
arguments=$@

if [[ -p $server ]]; then
  #
  # pipe already exists, we can just
  # increment the reference count
  #
  read rc < $server.connections
  rc=$((rc + 1))
  print $rc > $server.connections
  #
  # Call proxy to instantiate object
  #
  . proxy.sh $callbackRef $server $object $arguments
else
  #
  # create the connection, launch proxy
  #
  id=$RANDOM
  . socket sock${id} $server
  sock${id}_sendrecv&
  print "1" > $server.connections
  #
  # Call proxy to instantiate object
  #
  . proxy.sh $callbackRef $server $object $arguments
fi
```

Creating an Example Callback Application

Now that you've made most of the modifications to the supporting KSOP and ORB software, you can begin to see how callbacks affect your code. Perhaps the most significant effect is that you must write server code that takes into account the interfaces of its clients and its capability to invoke methods on those clients. The same effect occurs when a client object writes — you must realize the flexibility you give yourself when you allow a server object to invoke methods on a local object.

In this section, you create two objects that both implement the same interface: one is targeted for local deployment, the other behind an ORB. These two objects only differ subtly in their composition.

Creating object1

The first local object, object1, is a simple interface that supplies you with a _getMessage function. This function returns a cheerful message:

I am a local object, my name is $_this, and I am happy.

Obviously, the _this data member is substituted with the object's instance name.

> **TIP** When you pass a local reference to the proxy, it must be a local instance name — not a class name. If you have an instance of object1 as o1, you must pass o1 to the proxy program.

The _getMessage method is rather simple:

```
_getMessage() {
  #
  # Print out object's message
  #
  print "I am a local object, my name is $_this, and I am happy."
}
```

You can substitute any message; because this message will be used as a callback method by server, you can even include something snazzy like a hostname, date string, other information. Listing 11-5 shows object1.cls in full.

Listing 11-5: `object1.cls`

```
#
# object1.cls
#
# $Id: object1.cls,v 1.1 1998/04/06 00:36:05 chrisj Exp chrisj $
#
# The first object in our two-way KSOP project
#
_object1() {
  #
  # Assign '_this' member
  #
  _this=$ObjectId
}

_getMessage() {
  #
  # Print out object's message
  #
  print "Im a local object, my name is $_this, and I am happy."
}

_getState() {
  #
  # default getState function
  #
  set | grep ^$_this
}
```

To give `object1` a try, just create it from the command line after you've compiled it with `shcc`:

```
$> . object1 o
$> o_getMessage
I am a local object, my name is o, and I am happy.
```

Creating object2

`object2` is another local object that prints out a different message. With this object, you can use multiple local objects and server callbacks within the same application. `object2`'s `getMessage` prints:

```
I am an object who lives on the machine: $host
```

This example adds the hostname for spice. This method is also used in a callback operation by a server object. Of course, the `_getMessage` code is essentially the same as the preceding code:

```
_getMessage() {
  #
  # Print out object's message
  #
  host=$(hostname)
  print "I am an object who lives on the machine: $host"
}
```

And if you need it, Listing 11-6 shows `object2.cls` in its entirety.

Listing 11-6: `object2.cls`

```
#
# object1.cls
#
# $Id: object1.cls,v 1.1 1998/04/06 00:35:55 chrisj Exp chrisj $
#
# The second object in our two-way KSOP project
#
_object2() {
  #
  # Assign '_this' member
  #
  _this=$ObjectId
}

_getMessage() {
  #
  # Print out object's message
  #
  host=$(hostname)
  print "I am an object who lives on the machine: $host"
}

_getState() {
  #
  # default getState function
  #
  set | grep ^$_this
}
```

Creating the Server Component

The server code is practically the same, except this example also adds a function to call `object1`'s `_getMessage` function. This function is a simple callback that shows the communication has been successfully achieved.

You must remember a couple of key aspects in order for any server-side objects to implement callbacks successfully. First, the server must derive itself from `clientCb` (shown later). Second, the server object must invoke all client operations via the `_clientCall` function implemented in the class `clientCb`.

Chapter 11: Rethinking an Object-Oriented System 315

The inheritance is completed outside of any function body, although you can call the inherited construct within your derived class's constructor if necessary or for clarity. You derive from clientCb as follows:

```
#
# Inherit from clientCb (callback functions)
#
. clientCb $args
```

Within the constructor, you call the parent or super construct clientCb:: clientCb with your first parameter, and define your default data member: _message. The preceding section indicated that the first parameter passed to a server object implementing callbacks is the name of the pipe back to the server. This operation is handled for you in clientCb, so you only have to call the superclass constructor in your derived class:

```
_server1() {
  #
  # Call parent constructor with pipe name
  #
  _clientCb $1
  #
  # Define our default message
  #
  _message="I am the server object!"
}
```

You can define a _getMessage function to keep the compatibility of interfaces, but the following example merely prints the _message string:

```
_getMessage() {
  #
  # print server object's message
  #
  print $_message
}
```

This server object's _getClientMessage implements a callback to invoke the simple _getMessage function you created earlier on your local objects, object1 and object2.

_getClientMessage only invokes the clientCb_clientCall method with getMessage as a parameter, including any other parameters that may be included. You pass getMessage because you know it is an operation that is supported by the client. In reality, you could call any client-supported method; for now, the local objects can only do getMessage. The server object's _getClientMessage function follows:

```
_getClientMessage() {
```

```
    #
    # Attempt to invoke a method on whoever our client is
    # (clientCb::_clientCall)
    #
 cb_rez=$( _clientCall getMessage "$1 $2 $3 $4 $5 $6 $7 $8 $9")
    print $cb_rez >> callback.log
    #
    # Output result, for now, just a confirmation message
    #
    print "Finished with the callback."
 }
```

By now, you're probably longing to see how clientCb is implemented, but this topic is presented in a following section. As shown in the preceding, the server object use the result that getMessage returns — instead, it just prints a success message "Finished with the Callback" and the function exits. You see this message from the client side when you call _getClientMessage on a remote server object. For proof and so forth, write the result into a callback.log file on the server so you can see the results of the callback scheme. Listing 11-7 shows server1.cls in its entirety.

Listing 11-7: server1.cls

```
#
# server1.cls
#
# $Id: server1.cls,v 1.1 1998/04/06 00:33:03 chrisj Exp chrisj $
#
# A sample server object that will invoke functions on a client
#

#
# Inherit from clientCb (callback functions)
#
. clientCb $args

_server1() {
   #
   # Call parent constructor with pipe name
   #
   _clientCb $1
   #
   # Define our default message
   #
   _message="I am the server object!"
}

_getMessage() {
   #
   # print server object's message
   #
```

Chapter 11: Rethinking an Object-Oriented System

```
    print $_message
}

_getClientMessage() {
  #
  # Attempt to invoke a method on whoever our client is
  # (clientCb::_clientCall)
  #
cb_rez=$( _clientCall getMessage "$1 $2 $3 $4 $5 $6 $7 $8 $9")
    print $cb_rez >> callback.log
    #
    # Output result, for now, just a confirmation message
    #
    print "Finished with the callback."
}
```

Creating the clientCb Stub Code and Base Class

The clientCb class is quite simple. This class jumps the ORB server's pipe and send a message back to the client, which is interpreted as a callback. It subsequently does some error checking to verify the success of the sequence. The clientCb is used as a base class to reuse the callback code. Coding the _clientCall function every time you wish to use a callback is redundant. If you don't want to derive your server object from clientCb, you can optionally create and contain a clientCb object within the lifetime of your server object. This approach produces the same effect, but your server and clientCb objects are instantiated under different names.

```
The constructor to clientCb is pretty straightforward:
_clientCb() {
  #
  # Pipe (fifo) back to ORB must be given as first argument
  # at construction by derived classes
  #
  _ORBpipe=$1
}
```

Copy the instance pipe tether for a way back to the ORB server. This step is important, and you must always code server objects that derive from clientCb to take the pipe as a first parameter. If you choose to contain a clientCb object, you don't have to worry about this requirement.

The crux of clientCb is the method _clientCall. At first, check for the existence of the pipe, and then subsequently test your communication attempts:

```
_clientCall() {
  _method=$1
  _argArray="$2 $3 $4 $5 $6 $7 $8"

  #
  # Check for existence of ORB pipe
```

```
    #
    if [[ ! -p $_ORBpipe ]];then
      print -u2 "$_ORBpipe is not a FIFO."
      return 1
    fi
    #
    # Invoke client method
    #
    if ! print "callback:$_method:$_argArray" > $_ORBpipe; then
      print -u2 "$0: Unable to send message to $_ORBpipe"
      return 1
    fi
    #
    # Read client response
    #
    if ! read cb_result < $_ORBpipe; then
      print -u2 "$0: Unable to obtain result from $_ORBpipe."
      return 1
    fi
    print $cb_result
}
```

The important aspects here are the first parameter, which is the client method on which you wish to callback, and the KSOP-formatted string, which is sent back to the client. The client method is always the first parameter, and you copy it as _method. The KSOP string is critical for the client proxy to treat your response as a callback and not as a simple return result. The string uses the following format:

callback:$_method:$_argArray

In this case, _method and _argArray are: first, the method you wish to invoke (the first parameter to the _clientCall), and second, the array of arguments you want to pass back to the client. Listing 11-8 shows clientCb.cls in its entirety.

Listing 11-8: clientCb.cls

```
#
# clientCb.cls
#
# $Id: clientCb.cls,v 1.1 1998/04/06 00:29:55 chrisj Exp chrisj $
#
#  Stub code for invoking methods on clients by server objects
#
# Methods
#
#   _clientCall <method> <arguments> -
# invokes method on whatever object
# is referenced by the client **Client must give an object
# reference to its proxy to support callbacks.
#
_clientCb() {
```

```
    #
    # Pipe (fifo) back to ORB must be given as first argument
    # at construction by derived classes
    #
    _ORBpipe=$1
}
_clientCall() {
    _method=$1
    _argArray="$2 $3 $4 $5 $6 $7 $8"

    #
    # Check for existence of ORB pipe
    #
    if [[ ! -p $_ORBpipe ]];then
      print -u2 "$_ORBpipe is not a FIFO."
      return 1
    fi
    #
    # Invoke client method
    #
    if ! print "callback:$_method:$_argArray" > $_ORBpipe; then
      print -u2 "$0: Unable to send message to $_ORBpipe"
      return 1
    fi
    #
    # Read client response
    #
    if ! read cb_result < $_ORBpipe; then
      print -u2 "$0: Unable to obtain result from $_ORBpipe."
      return 1
    fi
    print $cb_result
}

_getState() {
    set | grep ^$_this
}
```

Creating the Object Repository .def Files

Before you can create a sample application, you need to create definition files for the server object and publish them within the repository. The definition file for server1.cls is quite simple, as the interface is not complex. Within the repository, you need to create a file called server1.def, which contains the following line:

getMessage:getClientMessage:getState

This interface is sent back to the proxy when you request a server1 object. You can enhance KSOP by describing more about each object within the definition string. For example, you can indicate whether the server object supports callbacks, and if so, the expected type of interface on the client side. Also, if you want to create an even more robust version of KSOP, you can try to support serialization of objects for transporting them across the network. The scheme depends mainly on interfaces known by distributed entities, with the actual object data encapsulated and located throughout the network.

If you choose to serialize KSOP objects, you can actually take the interface and the supporting data, and re-create the object on another server complete with its state. Many strategies accomplish this task in addition to additional considerations, such as whether the class of the object needs to exist in the environment into which it is serialized.

Running the Demo Script

Now you can run the demo script and see the beauty of callbacks in action. Take the your simple object and server classes and create a small demo, which uses the callback capability of the server object. The server expects a client that implements getMessage, and the clients must provide a reference to themselves or whatever local, instantiated object for which they wish to allow callbacks.

Before you can run the demo, you need to adjust your path. The user running the ORBserv.sh process in this chapter is strongly recommended to have only this chapter's repository in the path (PATH). Of course, the ORBserv.sh user also needs the Java executable in its path as before. If you have more than one object repository in your path, you run the risk of using the wrong version of a class with an ORB.

As an illustration of the process, note the creation of two local objects:

```
#
# Make a local object as "callback" victim
#
. object1 oa
. object2 ob
```

These objects show how one server object can callback multiple clients. Also, note that you create your connection manually, and that you are responsible for both calling release on the remote object and delete on the local objects. You also have to tear down the connection manually, as opposed to letting the connection manager complete this task. Listing 11-9 shows the full demo script.

Listing 11-9: demo.sh

```
#!/bin/ksh
```

Chapter 11: Rethinking an Object-Oriented System   321

```
#
# Make a local object as "callback" victim
#
. object1 oa
. object2 ob

print "Testing local object's _getMessage function:"

  oa_getMessage

print "Creating server1 object on remote server (localhost)"

  #
  # Set up socket connection
  #
  . socket sock localhost
  sock_sendrecv&

  #
  # Retrieve object with proxy
  #
  . proxy.sh oa localhost server1 sa

print
print "Testing server object's _getMessage function:"
print

  sa_getMessage

print "Invoking _getClientMessage on server object:"
print

  sa_getClientMessage

print
print "Check callback.log on server to verify!"
print
  sa_release

#
# Now try again with different local object
#

print "Testing local object's _getMessage function:"

  ob_getMessage

print "Creating server1 object on remote server (localhost)"

  #
  # Retrieve object with proxy
  #
```

```
. proxy.sh ob localhost server1 sb

print
print "Testing server object's _getMessage function:"
print

  sb_getMessage

print "Invoking _getClientMessage on server object:"
print

  sb_getClientMessage

print
print "Check callback.log on server to verify!"
print
  sb_release

print
print "Closing connection..."
print
print disconnect > localhost
```

Summary

In this chapter, you created objects to implement server callbacks. This approach is one of many options for enabling two-way communication between server- and client-distributed objects. The chapter also discussed options (such as serialization) that enable you to send an object and all of its data across the network, as opposed to just the interface. Obviously, platform and language boundaries come into play when considering those types of operations.

In the next chapter, you create objects for handling CGI and other UNIX operations. The CGI objects will be used in the final chapter as you hook up a Web interface to your SMU application.

Chapter 12

Using Shell Objects with CGI

IN THIS CHAPTER

- Examining practical uses for shell objects
- Discovering the fundamentals of HTTP
- Understanding CGI
- Creating CGI objects
- Exploring example CGI applications

UNTIL NOW, MOST of your work with shell objects has dealt with system-related activities. In creating an account or determining system status, everything created so far in this book has been closely connected to the operating system. In this chapter, you branch out and discuss some practical, application-oriented uses for shell objects. You also apply shell object techniques to a flexible and increasingly important area of development: the Common Gateway Interface (CGI).

Discovering Practical Applications for Shell Objects

Apart from CGI, you should be able to apply shell object techniques in a variety of situations. Let's examine other uses for the shell besides system administration.

Application Menus

Many powerful end-user computing systems run on UNIX machines. The shell is not the friendliest operative environment; for novice users, it may actually hinder their productivity. In these cases, you should wrap whatever application on which the user is trying to work with an application menu.

Your company may have a banking application that retrieves statistics on accounts. The software may run on distributed UNIX servers, with the quickest access from a terminal. Instead of developing a complicated, GUI-based client that runs on a PC, your company opts for users simply to open a terminal window to connect to the UNIX machines. In this place, you don't want the end-users hitting a shell prompt.

An application menu can take care of operations in a database, viewing account statistics, reading and sending e-mail, and printing reports. All of these tasks can be easily accessed from the shell. Also, with the code presented in this book, you can connect a CGI application to your shell menu and present a cross-platform solution via a Web browser.

Application Glue

Integrating applications together is another common use for shell scripts and shell objects. As a systems administrator in a large banking network, I often developed complex shell applications whose sole purpose was to integrate different distributed components of large-scale applications. By using a shell script, you can finely tune the performance of an application. You can automate complex tasks such as restarting listeners, rotating log files, and starting the right processes at the right time. Using shell scripts to connect larger software pieces often reduces the need to restart a system from scratch and can also eliminate the impact of partial failures, as the script can restart the failed components.

Many UNIX applications are launched and configured with shell programs. This approach occurs in large relational database systems, Web servers, and many other types of applications. Of course, the entire boot sequence of a UNIX machine is mapped out in shell code.

In modern, distributed systems, the shell can play a major part in the CGI. As more applications are broken apart with their components strewn across tiers, the integration of Web servers and object brokers is necessary to provide universal, cross-platform access to application logic and data. Traditionally, Perl has been a popular language for CGI development. Perl is a scripting language not unlike the shell, however, and the shell can match almost all of Perl's functionality (although Perl makes parsing strings and other tasks a little simpler). You develop objects to handle these tasks and reuse them in many situations, so the initial complexity should not be daunting.

Examining CGI

You've probably visited more than one Web page and filled out a form, registered for free software, shopped for a car, and so forth. These pages handled dynamic data and bring life to what is ordinarily static HTML. Regardless of the language, CGI programming works behind the scenes of these pages.

Uncovering CGI

When a Web server receives a request, it must determine what type of information the browser is requesting. Usually, it makes this determination via the file extensions associated with the URL (Universal Resource Locator). For example, when you type `www.server.com/file.html` into your browser window, the Web server knows that you're asking for an HTML file. If you type `file.txt` in your browser's window, the Web server sends back the file in plain text format. The server is not just limited to file extensions to determine how to proceed with a file. You can also create certain directories on the server, handle the contents in a certain way, or pass the contents off to another piece of software, such as an application server for handling.

In terms of file types (or mime types), this chapter is most concerned with CGI. When you give a file a `.cgi` extension, the Web server (if properly configured) knows to execute the file instead of sending the contents back to the browser. When the server executes the file, it provides a special environment in which the program can run. This environment consists of variables that can indicate information to your CGI program, including the address of the host requesting your document, the arguments they may have passed from a form, and information about the server. When your program is executed, the data your program sends to STDOUT is sent back to the browser. That's all there is to it. For example, if you had a program that simply wrote "Hello World!" to the screen, you just need to move the file into the right directory that the Web server can access, and name the file with a .cgi extension. When someone accesses your file, "Hello World" is printed on the browser. One small catch exists – because your information is being sent to the browser, you have to send the right header so the browser will know how to handle the incoming data. In the simplest example, if your program produces the following output, it would be valid CGI:

```
Content-type: text

Hello World!
```

The blank line between content-type and your text is very important – it is discussed in a following section – but for now let's examine how to configure your Web server to run CGI.

Configuring the Web Server

The CD-ROM included with this book has the Apache Web Server bundled in the directory `apache`. Just follow the instructions located in the CD-ROM's README file for unpacking and installing the server. While the server's documentation is fairly adequate, one small configuration detail must be changed to run CGI. This section shows the change for Apache; if you're using different software, you need to make a similar modification in your own Web server software.

Once installed, the Apache package has a `conf` directory, in which all of the configuration files are kept. While they can seem rather daunting, your changes are minor. The CGI applications you develop will be complex and involve many different scripts. For ease of development and use, you should enable the CGI mime-type in your server's main document root, or from wherever you're going to place the code in this and subsequent chapters. In most systems, the server root is usually something like `/var/lib/httpd/htdocs` or `/usr/public_html`. Regardless of the location, you want the ability to drop any file with a .cgi extension into that directory (and subdirectories) and have the Web server execute it.

The `conf` directory of your Apache directory contains a file called `access.conf`. This file details what types of operations are active on particular directory mappings in which the server is configured. Find your main document root (or wherever you want to place this chapter's code), and look at its information. If your server root had been configured as `/var/lib/httpd/htdocs`, you should find the following information in your `access.conf` file (as shown in Listing 12-1).

Listing 12-1: A section of `access.conf` detailing the server root directory

```
<Directory /var/lib/httpd/htdocs>

# This may also be "None", "All", or any combination of "Indexes",
# "Includes", "FollowSymLinks", "ExecCGI", or "MultiViews".

# Note that "MultiViews" must be named *explicitly* --- "Options
  All"
# doesn't give it to you (or at least, not yet).

Options Indexes FollowSymLinks

# This controls which options the .htaccess files in directories can
# override. Can also be "All", or any combination of "Options",
# "FileInfo", "AuthConfig", and "Limit"
AllowOverride None

# Controls who can get stuff from this server.

order allow,deny
allow from all

</Directory>
```

The Apache documentation exhaustively describes all of the meaning behind some of this cryptic notation, but only one line concerns you – the line that begins with `Options` describes what type of operations are permitted within this directory `/var/lib/htppd/docs`, as follows:

```
Options Indexes FollowSymLinks
```

The words `Indexes` and `FollowSymLinks` are enabled options for this directory. `Indexes` means that the files in the directory will be presented back to the browser in an index form if there is no default (`index.html`) file present. This sequence enables users to select any file they want to view. You may have seen this feature on various FTP servers. The `FollowSymLinks` option tells the server to follow linked files. For example, if the file `index.html` is really a link to a file named `information.html`, the Web server allows it and sends back `information.html` to the browser.

You want to add an option to this list that allows for the execution of CGI files. Within this file, you should change the `Options` line to look like the following:

```
Options Indexes FollowSymLinks ExecCGI
```

This line is a serious statement to the Web server. After making such a change, the Web server needs to be restarted. Most likely, your package does not have a start script.

TIP If you are running Netscape Enterprise Server, you can enable CGI everywhere by running the admin server and choosing "allow CGI as file type" as an option in the server configuration menu.

Within the `logs` directory of the Apache installation, find a file that ends with the `.pid` extension. The content of this file is simply the process ID of the parent HTTP process. If you kill this process with the UNIX `kill` command, the Web server stops. You can then relaunch the `httpd` listener with a command as follows:

```
$> /usr/bin/httpd
```

This command starts the Web server (obviously, you need to change the path to reflect the location of your HTTP daemon), and CGI is now enabled. If you are using Netscape Enterprise Server, you'll have start and stop scripts within your `https-<servername>` directory.

Revealing the Mysteries of HTTP

Your Web browser and your favorite Internet site's Web server communicate with a simple protocol known as HTTP (Hypertext Transfer Protocol). This simple, text-based protocol lets a Web server know what a browser is requesting; in turn, it lets a browser know what the server is sending back.

Creating an HTTP Request

When your browser hits `www.server.com` and asks for "index.html," the request looks like the following:

```
GET /index.html HTTP/1.0
```

This string is followed by a blank line that tells the server the request is over.

Receiving the HTTP Response

All of the contents of `index.html` come back, as follows:

```
HTTP/1.0 200 OK
Server: Roxen/Challenger/1.1
Last-Modified: Thu, 12 Feb 98 06:38:28 +0000
Content-type: text/html
Content-length: 1138

<html>
......more HTML...
```

The server's response header is formatted in a fashion similar to the browser's header. The header information first indicates the HTTP type, which is `200 OK` here, but could have been anything from `302 Redirect` to `404 Not Found`. This particular response provides information about the server software (`Roxen Challenger`), the last modification time of the file, the file's mime-type (`text/html`), and the file's length as content-length. The content-length variable tells the browser how much data to expect. This attribute is particularly useful if the requested file is binary data, such as an image, which may not contain any discernable end-of-file marker. The HTTP header ends with a blank line followed by the data itself. When the browser makes a more complex request such as sending a form, as you'll see in a following section, the browser header looks much more like this response.

Handling Forms

Most CGI programs are designed to take user input from an HTML form on the user's browser. Usually, you enter all sorts of information about yourself, including your e-mail address, and then hit the submit button. Of course, the server responds that it's received your information and then, suddenly, you start to receive junk e-mail from unknown places. The magic behind this transaction is the HTML form along with the CGI program that handles it. After you fill out all of the fields in the form, the browser formats a particular header when you hit the submit button. For example, if you have just entered your name into a couple of text boxes and pressed submit, the browser probably sends like the following to the Web server:

```
POST /cgi-bin/formhandler.cgi HTTP/1.0
User-Agent: Mozilla 4.03 / Linux [en]
Content-type: application/x-www-form-urlencoded
Content-length: 36

firstname=Christopher&lastname=Jones
```

As you can see, the header is typical HTTP, with a blank line between the header and the form data. The header also contains other parameters such as `Accept-type:`, which tells the server what types of data the browser can handle.

After the blank line, a strange string indicates that `firstname=Christopher` and `lastname=Jones`. This is a URL-encoded string generated by your browser when you pressed the submit button. The HTML form you loaded had particular names for the fields you filled out; when the submit button was pressed, the information was encoded, and sent off to the server. In a following section, you write CGI shell objects that care of decoding and interpreting the form data sent by the browser.

Understanding the CGI Environment

Before you can begin coding your own CGI scripts, you'll need to grasp the particulars of the CGI environment. First, you should note that the Web server process runs as a particular user on your system, and as such, has the rights of that user. Your CGI scripts execute under this user's name and also carry those rights. As a result, you should never run your server as root, unless you want to open potential security holes. Ordinarily, the Web server runs as the user "nobody" or another docile user created for that sole purpose, as in "Web".

The CGI User

The account under which the Web server runs does not have many rights on your system. Although rare, it's possible to slip commands into an HTML form and, if not handled correctly by the CGI program, execute those commands on the Web server. This situation is more of a problem for Perl programs that act as gateways and actually present a command line to be executed by the shell. For example, consider the following command:

```
Open myPipe, "| /usr/bin/mail $user";
print myPipe "Howdy!";
```

If this example is in your Perl script, it could become potentially dangerous if you don't verify the field `$user`. Perl expands this, substituting variables with their values, before presenting it to the shell for execution. This sequence could result in someone using a phrase like the following into the form for the field $user, and possibly result in extra commands being executed on the server by your CGI script:

```
chrisj@blarg.net; echo; cat /etc/passwd
```

Never expose a variable within a command string. You should always interpret what has been given to your script and act accordingly, executing commands only within your program. The preceding example is a problem for any type of CGI that intends to function as a gateway for other commands, whether they are written in the shell, Perl, or in C using a system call.

In one of the following examples, you enable a user to execute a variety of docile commands on the server and present the information back to them. Safety is ensured in these examples by interpreting their menu choice to figure out which command subroutine you should run – not by actually using the command name as a variable within a string of execution. Despite your best efforts, however, presenting an application on the Internet always presents a potential security problem. Unplugging your computer's Ethernet card is the only solution, but that answer wouldn't be fun.

CGI Variables

Apart from security holes, CGI gives your programs a deluxe assortment of variables from which to determine not only the context of the request, but also the context of the server environment under which it is running. If you've successfully enabled CGI on your Web server, you're ready to try the first example. This example simply prints a list of all the environment variables that your script is running. Listing 12-2 shows `test.cgi`.

Listing 12-2: `test.cgi`

```
#!/bin/ksh
#
# test.cgi - dump CGI environment
#

#
# print the HTTP header, and a blank line.
#
print "Content-type: text/html"
print
#
# now the data
#
print "<html><body bgcolor=#FFFFFF>"
print "<font face=helvetica,arial color=#000000>"
set | while read env_vars
do
   #
```

```
    # print the variable, and an HTML carriage-return <br>
    #
    print $env_vars"<br>"
done
#
# close out HTML
#
print "</font></body></html>"
```

Save the preceding program as test.cgi and place it within your document root on your Web server. You can then address the script with your Web browser's location box, as follows:

http://localhost/chp12/text.cgi

You can substitute localhost for your server name if you're running your Web browser from a different machine than your Web server. Listing 12-3 shows the results you should receive, although your results may be slightly different regarding items such as DOCUMENT_ROOT, SERVER_NAME, and HTTP_ACCEPT, which all are specific to your environment.

Listing 12-3: The output of test.cgi

```
DOCUMENT_ROOT=/var/lib/httpd/htdocs
GATEWAY_INTERFACE=CGI/1.1
HOME
HTTP_ACCEPT='image/gif, image/x-xbitmap, image/jpeg, image/pjpeg,
  */*'
HTTP_ACCEPT_CHARSET='iso-8859-1,*,utf-8'
HTTP_ACCEPT_LANGUAGE=en
HTTP_CONNECTION=Keep-Alive
HTTP_HOST=probing
HTTP_PRAGMA=no-cache
HTTP_USER_AGENT='Mozilla/4.03 [en] (X11; I; Linux 2.0.29 i586)'
IFS='
'
KSH_VERSION='@(#)PD KSH v5.2.12 96/10/29'
MAILCHECK=600
OPTIND=1
PATH=/bin:/sbin:/usr/bin:/usr/sbin
PPID=106
PS1='$ '
PS2='> '
PS3='#? '
PS4='+ '
PWD=/var/lib/httpd/htdocs/smu
QUERY_STRING=
RANDOM=10536
REMOTE_ADDR=127.0.0.1
REMOTE_HOST=localhost
REQUEST_METHOD=GET
```

```
SCRIPT_FILENAME=/var/lib/httpd/htdocs/smu/test.cgi
SCRIPT_NAME=/smu/test.cgi
SECONDS=0
SERVER_ADMIN=chrisj@blarg.net
SERVER_NAME=probing.uranus.com
SERVER_PORT=80
SERVER_PROTOCOL=HTTP/1.0
SERVER_SOFTWARE=Apache/1.1.3
SHELL
TMOUT=0
_=set<>
```

The proceding output shows you valuable information. All of these environment variables are available for your CGI program with which to work. From this output, you can tell you're running under Apache 1.1.13, the browser used for the request was Netscape (Mozilla 4.03 / X11/Linux 2.0.29 i586), and the document requested was /var/lib/httpd/htdocs/smu/test.cgi. Look over Listing 12-3 for a few minutes to get a feel for all the information given to your CGI code by default. The possibilities for custom-tailored output are endless. Based on the browser type, you can determine what client-side features are supported. You can also glean other statistics, such as the remote IP address and remote server name from where the request arrived.

Creating CGI Objects

As far as your CGI objects are concerned, you primarily deal with requests from the browser, their variables and information, and the response that you send back to the browser. Therefore, this section presents a request object and a response object, along with three examples that use these objects to create simple CGI applications.

This section uses a few key CGI variables repeatedly. These variables represent the type of HTTP request (the GET or POST methods), the client browser type, and whatever data the browser is sending. Due to the way that the shcc interpreter parses your class files, you must remove the underscores from these key HTTP variables before compiling them in your class (.cls) files. Therefore, this section creates an "include" file called cgi.sh, which copies key HTTP variables into a more normal-looking format that your shell objects can use more easily.

Every time you create a new CGI object class, you should source this file into your class at construction time. Listing 12-4 shows cgi.sh.

Listing 12-4: cgi.sh

```
#
# cgi.sh
#
# Copy CGI vars for use in shell objects with shcc
#
```

```
ServerName=$SERVER_NAME
ServerPort=$SERVER_PORT
ServerSoftware=$SERVER_SOFTWARE
HttpAccept=$HTTP_ACCEPT
HttpUserAgent=$HTTP_USER_AGENT
RequestMethod=$REQUEST_METHOD
QueryString=$QUERY_STRING
ContentLength=$CONTENT_LENGTH
```

From the whole slew of CGI variables represented in Listing 12-3, this section is only interested in the request method, the user agent, browser type, and of course, the data passed to your script. These items will be the variables that your CGI objects know about at construction. Keep in mind that your CGI scripts using these shell objects can use any HTTP variable, regardless of what the CGI object uses.

The shcc converter presented in Chapter 3 uses underscores as a reserved character when determining object relationships. Be careful using it in classes you wish to compile with shcc.

Creating a Request Object

The most complex aspect of writing a CGI program is handling and interpreting the URL-encoded information that the Web server hands your script. Thankfully, once you've coded these routines, you can begin reusing them.

You'll code a request.cls class, which handles and decodes all types of CGI information for you, and make accessing such information as simple as possible. Start with request.cls by sourcing in the cgi.sh variables described previously:

```
#
# request.cls
#
# $Id: request.cls,v 1.0 1998/04/09 00:36:05 chrisj Exp chrisj $
#
# Object for handling HTTP Requests and Decoding Forms
#
# Methods
#
# Data Members
#
################################################################

#
# Source in cgi.sh to copy vars
#
```

```
. ./cgi.sh
#
```

After this task, the variables are available to your object. You may be curious why you don't reference the CGI variables (like HTTP_ACCEPT) directly in your object code. shcc is dependent upon underscores to determine object ownership. You code in some more exceptions to shcc's parsing formula, but this task is an exercise for you. While you're free to reference CGI variables in your CGI scripts that use the request and response objects, you'll run into problems if those variables are used internally when "compiling" your object.

For good measure, and to maintain the ability to have several objects active within the same address space, internalize each particular request or response to each object that represents it. If a request object is created, and seconds later another request object is created, the instance variables for each object remains separate because each object makes the CGI variables internal data members. This approach also allows for encapsulation by enabling you to code access objects for CGI variables.

The request object's constructor takes care of internalizing CGI data as follows:

```
_request() {
  #
  # Assign _this data member
  #
  _this=$ObjectId

  #
  # Copy some common Server variables
  #
  _serverName=$ServerName
  _serverPort=$ServerPort
  _serverSoftware=$ServerSoftware

  #
  # Copy client header info
  #
  _clientAccept=$HttpAccept
  _clientAgent=$HttpUserAgent
  _clientReqMeth=$RequestMethod

  #
  # Parse the Query string....
  #
  _parseGetPost
}
```

In addition to the default _this data member, you copy over the CGI variables and finally call a method _parseGetPost.

DETERMINING THE REQUEST METHOD

The _parseGetPost method takes care of determining what sort of request method is used by the client, and then calls another method to parse the actual data. The method starts by determining if either acceptable request type is used:

```
_parseGetPost() {
  if [[ $_clientReqMeth != "GET" && $_clientReqMeth != "POST" ]]
  then
    print -u2 "Invalid HTTP request, please use GET or POST"
    return 1
  fi
```

If neither GET nor POST is used, the constructor exits and indicates the reason for the failure. If everything is okay, you retrieve the input data based on the request type, and then call _parseURLenc:

```
if [[ $_clientReqMeth = "GET" ]]; then
    #
    # The Request Method was "GET"
    #
    _parseURLenc $QueryString
  else
    #
    # The Request Method was "POST"
    #
    _contentLength=$ContentLength
    read input
    _parseURLenc $input
  fi
}
```

The important point in this example is to ascertain the location of the data, and then pass it off to the _parseURLenc function. If the request was a GET, the form data and whatever other information included as a parameter is encoded into the QUERY_STRING variable (or $QueryString as imported by cgi.sh). The QUERY_STRING can look like the following:

Name=Santa&nickname=%22Saint+Nick%22&lastname=Clause

The values to the left (lvalues) of the equal signs are variable names as indicated in an HTML form. The ampersand delineates each key=value pair. Also, you should note that all spaces have been converted to plus (+) signs, and any special character such as a quote, parenthesis, asterisk, and so forth has been converted to hexadecimal and prefixed with a percent sign (%). This approach eliminates any confusion that may occur when trying to parse the query string apart.

In a POST operation, the URL-encoded data is not assigned to the QUERY_STRING variable. Instead, it is simply fed to your program's STDIN. Therefore, in the preceding example, you read in the URL-encoded string with a single read statement and then pass it off to _parseURLenc, where you take apart the plus signs and the ampersands and decode the hexadecimal applied to your form data.

DECODING AND PARSING GET AND POST

The next function, _parseURLenc, decodes the nasty data sent to your program. While at first this process may seem daunting, it's really simple – the same code, once created, can be used over and over again.

First, your _parseURLenc function copies the string it's been handed, and then breaks the string up into key=value pairs delineated with an ampersand as follows:

```
_parseURLenc() {
  _parseString=$1
  _noAmps=$( echo $_parseString | tr \& \ )
```

You assign the list of key=value pairs to the data member _noAmps. For this example, the tr command translates all ampersands into blank spaces. Next, you iterate through the newly-created key and value pairs, performing a number of edits on each pair. If the data comes from a GET operation, you assign the keys as data members within a url object. If the data comes from a POST operation, you assign the keys within a form object. You can easily apply any data to both types of objects and use the same objects interchangeably between POST and GET forms. For one main reason, the example differentiates between the forms. Usually, form data uses the POST method; however, you can embed a GET operation within a URL itself. For example, you could create a hyperlink to particular page and indicate extra information within the link itself, as the following markup illustrates:

```
<a href="special.cgi?preference=blue">I prefer Blue</a>
```

This link appears as "I prefer Blue" in the user's browser, and actually uses the GET method to send the key value pair preference=blue to the receiving script: special.cgi.

You can also choose not to differentiate between POST and GET within your CGI objects.

To iterate through the key value pairs, you can perform a simple for each in loop, and perform operations upon each member. First, break the key and value pair on the leftmost equal sign, which results in a separation of the variable name and value:

```
for each in $_noAmps
  do
    #
    # Break pairs on = and assign as data members
    #
    if [[ $_clientReqMeth = "GET" ]]; then
      obj=url
    else
```

Chapter 12: Using Shell Objects with CGI   337

```
      obj=form
   fi
   key=${each%%\=*}
   value=${each#*\=}
```

The next operation replaces all of the plus signs with the original spaces:

```
   #
   # Translate +'s into spaces
   #
   value=$(echo $value | tr \+ \ )
```

Next, you can begin to decode the hexadecimal if it exists. Remember, hexadecimal is prefixed with a % sign; if you do not have percent signs in your value string, you don't have to decode the hexadecimal:

```
if [[ $value = @(*%*) ]]; then

      #
      # Decode hexadecimal
      #
      newstring=""
      t_string=""
      t_string=$(echo $value | sed "s/%[0-F][0-F]/|&|/g")
```

To begin decoding, take the value of $value and add the pipe character on either side of the hexadecimal patterns so you can delineate them. This sequence results in URL encoding that appears as follows:

```
My Quote is |%22| Hello World|%22|
```

You can easily traverse this newly-defined string in the shell, and replace hexadecimal values as you find them:

```
      #
      # Copy IFS
      #
      oldIFS=$IFS
      IFS="|"
      #
      # Traverse string
      #
      for each in $t_string
      do
        if [[ $each = @(%*) ]];then
          each=$(grep $each ./hex2char | cut -c7)
        fi
        newstring=${newstring}${each}
      done
      IFS=$oldIFS
```

```
            value=$newstring

        fi
```

By setting the IFS character to a pipe (|), you can then isolate each hexadecimal occurrence. By default, most UNIX systems have a file called `ascii`, which contains the ASCII character set and its representative ASCII and hexadecimal codes. This example copies the hexadecimal part of this file into the same directory as the CGI objects with a little tailoring. To use these objects, you need to bring the file `hex2char` with you. Once you've isolated the hex encoding, you can `grep` for it out of the file and replace its occurrence in the string with the literal character it represents. You then piece the original string back together.

After piecing your string back together, you're ready to create the assignment. The idea is to have every variable in your form or URL from your HTML page represented as an instance variable in your request shell object. For example, if you create an HTML form with a textbox marked as `name`, the resulting CGI script that receives the form's post has an instance variable named `name`:

```
print "The name is: $request_form_name "
```

No additional work is needed by your CGI script — the request object completes the task. This approach makes handling forms and URL data exceptionally easy. Listing 12-5 shows `request.cls` in its entirety.

Listing 12-5: `request.cls`

```
#
# request.cls
#
# $Id: request.cls,v 1.0 1998/04/09 00:36:05 chrisj Exp chrisj $
#
# Object for handling HTTP Requests and Decoding Forms
#
# Methods
#
# Data Members
#
##############################################################

#
# Source in cgi.sh to copy vars
#
. ./cgi.sh
#

_request() {
    #
```

```
   # Assign _this data member
   #
   _this=$ObjectId

   #
   # Copy some common Server variables
   #
   _serverName=$ServerName
   _serverPort=$ServerPort
   _serverSoftware=$ServerSoftware

   #
   # Copy client header info
   #
   _clientAccept=$HttpAccept
   _clientAgent=$HttpUserAgent
   _clientReqMeth=$RequestMethod

   #
   # Parse the Query string....
   #
   _parseGetPost
}

_parseGetPost() {
   if [[ $_clientReqMeth != "GET" && $_clientReqMeth != "POST" ]]
   then
      print -u2 "Invalid HTTP request, please use GET or POST"
      return 1
   fi
   if [[ $_clientReqMeth = "GET" ]]; then
      #
      # The Request Method was "GET"
      #
      _parseURLenc $QueryString
   else
      #
      # The Request Method was "POST"
      #
      _contentLength=$ContentLength
      read input
      _parseURLenc $input
   fi
}

_parseURLenc() {
   _parseString=$1
   _noAmps=$( echo $_parseString | tr \& \  )
   for each in $_noAmps
   do
      #
      # Break pairs on = and assign as data members
      #
```

```
       if [[ $_clientReqMeth = "GET" ]]; then
         obj=url
       else
         obj=form
       fi
       key=${each%%\=*}
       value=${each#*\=}

       #
       # Translate +'s into spaces
       #
       value=$(echo $value | tr \+ \ )

       if [[ $value = @(*%*) ]]; then

         #
         # Decode hexadecimal
         #
         newstring=""
         t_string=""
         t_string=$(echo $value | sed "s/%[0-F][0-F]/|&|/g")

         #
         # Copy IFS
         #
         oldIFS=$IFS
         IFS="|"
         #
         # Traverse string
         #
         for each in $t_string
         do
           if [[ $each = @(%*) ]];then
             each=$(grep $each ./hex2char | cut -c7)
           fi
           newstring=${newstring}${each}
         done
         IFS=$oldIFS

         value=$newstring

       fi

       #
       # Assign as object members
       #
       eval _${obj}_${key}='$value'
     done
}
```

The hexadecimal to literal character conversion will remain static, and you don't need to provide any type of algorithm to execute this task. Even though the example chose to use a small `sed` command, many approaches can break apart a URL-encoded string.

Every printable character (and some not so printable) has a hexadecimal equivalent. Listing 12-6 shows the file `hex2char` you can use to decode your form data.

Listing 12-6: Hexadecimal to literal character conversion

%00	nul	%2A	*	%55	U		
%01	soh	%2B	+	%56	V		
%02	stx	%2C	,	%57	W		
%03	etx	%2D	-	%58	X		
%04	eot	%2E	.	%59	Y		
%05	enq	%2F	/	%5A	Z		
%06	ack	%30	0	%5B	[		
%07	bel	%31	1	%5C	\		
%08	bs	%32	2	%5D	]		
%09	ht	%33	3	%5E	^		
%0A	nl	%34	4	%5F	_		
%0B	vt	%35	5	%60	`		
%0C	np	%36	6	%61	a		
%0D	cr	%37	7	%62	b		
%0E	so	%38	8	%63	c		
%0F	si	%39	9	%64	d		
%10	dle	%3A	:	%65	e		
%11	dc1	%3B	;	%66	f		
%12	dc2	%3C	<	%67	g		
%13	dc3	%3D	=	%68	h		
%14	dc4	%3E	>	%69	i		
%15	nak	%3F	?	%6A	j		
%16	syn	%40	@	%6B	k		
%17	etb	%41	A	%6C	l		
%18	can	%42	B	%6D	m		
%19	em	%43	C	%6E	n		
%1A	sub	%44	D	%6F	o		
%1B	esc	%45	E	%70	p		
%1C	fs	%46	F	%71	q		
%1D	gs	%47	G	%72	r		
%1E	rs	%48	H	%73	s		
%1F	us	%49	I	%74	t		
%20	sp	%4A	J	%75	u		
%21	!	%4B	K	%76	v		
%22	"	%4C	L	%77	w		
%23	#	%4D	M	%78	x		
%24	$	%4E	N	%79	y		
%25	%	%4F	O	%7A	z		
%26	&	%50	P	%7B	{		
%27	'	%51	Q	%7C				
%28	(	%52	R	%7D	}		
%29	)	%53	S	%7E	~		
		%54	T	%7F	del		

Creating a Response Object

In addition to the request object, you also create a response object that helps simplify printing HTTP headers to the browser, as well as setting cookies and other sorts of fun items.

As discussed previously, HTTP headers can perform a variety of tasks, such as redirecting the user's browser to another URL, setting a Netscape-persistent cookie to store data, or communicating an error message or content type. The constructor for your object sets up many internal data members:

```
_response() {
    #
    # _this datamember
    #
    _this=$ObjectId

    #
    # define default content type
    #
    _contentType="text/html"

    #
    # Cookie expiry
    #
    expires="Fri, 31-Dec-99 23:59:00 GMT"

    #
    # Cookie Domain
    #
    domain="localhost"

    #
    # Cookie Path
    #
    path="/"
}
```

The preceding defines the default content type to be `text/html` to spare the trouble of having to set it every time you create a response object. It also sets some default cookie values to be used or overridden when creating cookies to store on the client browser. *Cookies* are a means of storing key value pairs on a browser so they can be returned every time the browser visits your Web site. Although sort of a hack, cookies provide a means of maintaining state between client requests. Frequently, a Web site may store registration information or a login or password in the form of a cookie in your browser for identification when you return to their site.

This fairly simple object only handles the basic HTTP header information. The function you would most likely use is the _printHeader method, which prints the value of _contentType as the HTTP header for the browser:

```
_printHeader() {
  #
  # Prints standard HTTP header
  #
  print "Content-type: $_contentType"
  print
}
```

The "302 Redirect" header can redirect a browser to a new location. The _redirection method takes a URL as a parameter, and then sends the user's browser away to the new location:

```
_redirection() {
  #
  # Sends the browser to another place....
  #
  # _url can be either relative path ( /path/newdoc.html )
  # or full URL ( http://www.domain.com )
  #
  _url=$1
  print "Location: $_url"
  print
}
```

You can use the _redirection method in conjunction with other HTTP directives such as "Set-Cookie." The _setCookie method takes a key and a value as arguments and builds a cookie string to be sent to the browser:

```
_setCookie() {
  #
  # Sets a cookie for the current domain
  #
  cookkey=$1
  cookvalue=$2

  #
  # set the cookie
  #
  cookie="Set-Cookie: ${cookkey}=${cookvalue};"
    cookie="$cookie expires=${expires}; path=${path};"
    cookie="$cookie domain=${domain};"
  print "$cookie"
}
```

344 UNIX Shell Objects

The response object also has a _setHeader method that you can use to define the content type. If you send binary data for an image to the browser, you can set the content type to be image/gif, print a content-length header reflecting the image size, and then send the binary data itself. The _setHeader method takes the content type as the first parameter:

```
_setHeader() {
  #
  # Define a content type
  #
  _contentType=$1
}
```

While this object does the basics, you can easily enhance it to cover a wide range of HTTP possibilities. Listing 12-7 shows the full code.

Listing 12-7: response.cls

```
#
# response.cls
#
# $Id: response.cls,v 1.0 1998/04/10 03:45:05 chrisj Exp chrisj $
#
# Object for handling HTTP Responses
#
################################################################

_response() {
  #
  # _this datamember
  #
  _this=$ObjectId

  #
  # define default content type
  #
  _contentType="text/html"

  #
  # Cookie expiry
  #
  expires="Fri, 31-Dec-99 23:59:00 GMT"

  #
  # Cookie Domain
  #
  domain="probing"

  #
  # Cookie Path
  #
```

```
    path="/"
}

_printHeader() {
  #
  # Prints standard HTTP header
  #
  print "Content-type: $_contentType"
  print
}

_redirection() {
  #
  # Sends the browser to another place....
  #
  # _url can be either relative path ( /path/newdoc.html )
  # or full URL ( http://www.domain.com )
  #
  _url=$1
  print "Location: $_url"
  print
}

_setCookie() {
  #
  # Sets a cookie for the current domain
  #
  cookkey=$1
  cookvalue=$2

  #
  # set the cookie
  #
  cookie="Set-Cookie: ${cookkey}=${cookvalue};"
    cookie="$cookie expires=${expires}; path=${path};"
    cookie="$cookie domain=${domain};"
  print "$cookie"
}

_setHeader() {
  #
  # Define a content type
  #
  _contentType=$1
}
```

Developing CGI Examples

Now you can code some quick examples to discover the easy use of the CGI objects. These examples consist of simple forms and the CGI scripts that handle them. First, you create two simple HTML forms: one that uses the GET method to send data to the CGI file, and one that uses the POST method to send the data. The CGI script is the same for both methods: emp.cgi.

Completing a Simple CGI Program

The forms represent simple data entry for an employee's name, age, and salary. The first file, get.html, uses the GET method and is shown in Listing 12-8.

Listing 12-8: get.html

```
<html>
<form action=emp.cgi method=get>
<font face=helvetica>
name:<input type=text name="name" size=20><br>
age:<input type=text name="age" size=3><BR>
salary:<input type=text name="salary" size=20><br>
<input type=submit value=submit>
</font>
</form>
</html>
```

Create this file and place it in the same directory with the CGI objects and the eventual CGI script. You should be able to access this file from your Web browser without any problems before coding the CGI.

The second file is post.html and behaves in a similar fashion, except it uses the POST method. Listing 12-9 shows post.html.

Listing 12-9: post.html

```
<html>
<form action=emp.cgi method=post>
<font face=helvetica>
name:<input type=text name="name" size=20><br>
age:<input type=text name="age" size=3><BR>
salary:<input type=text name="salary" size=20><br>
<input type=submit value=submit>
</font>
</form>
</html>
```

Chapter 12: Using Shell Objects with CGI

Use `emp.cgi` for the CGI to interpret these forms. Compared to the objects that it uses, the script is simple. At first, you just need to create a request object:

```
#!/bin/ksh

. ./request req
```

Follow the preceding with a header (the example manually prints this example):

```
print "Content-type: text/html"
print
```

You must always print a blank line after your HTTP header and before your browser content. If you omit this line, your CGI generates an HTTP error in the Web server's log files.

After these prerequisites, you can start to reference the form data in the preceding HTML files as members of either the `url` or `form` objects within your instantiated request object `req`. Listing 12-10 shows the full version of `emp.cgi` and demonstrates how to reference the fully-decoded form variables easily in your scripts.

Listing 12-10: `emp.cgi`

```
#!/bin/ksh

. ./request req

print "Content-type: text/html"
print

print "<html>"
print "<h3>Post Information</h3>"
print "name: <b> $req_form_name </b><br>"
print "age: <b> $req_form_age </b><br>"
print "salary: <b> $req_form_salary </b><br>"
print "<h3>Get Information</h3>"
print "name: <b> $req_url_name </b><br>"
print "age: <b> $req_url_age </b><br>"
print "salary: <b> $req_url_salary </b><br>"
print "<b><a href=get.html>get.html</a> or "
print "<a href=post.html>post.html</a></b>"
print "</html>"
```

Just use `print $req_url_name` to display the variable defined as `name` in your HTML file.

Examining a Questionnaire

The next example demonstrates how to display a complex HTML form as easily as in the last example. The HTML file `questions.html` uses lots of table tags and some form elements — if you're not familiar with HTML, this example should be good basic learning experience. `questions.html` appears in Listing 12-11.

Listing 12-11: `questions.html`

```html
<html>
<head>
  <title>Shell Objects Questionnaire</title>
</head>
<body bgcolor=#FFFFFF text=#000000>
<font face=verdana,tahoma,arial,helvetica>
<h3>Welcome to the Shell Objects Questionnaire!</h3>
Please fill out the questions below and click <b>Finished!</b> when
 you're done. This will go on your permanent record. Thank
 you!</font>
<form action="questionnaire.cgi" method="post">
<table>
  <tr>
    <td align=right> Name:</td>
    <td align=left><input type=text name="name" width=20></td>
  </tr>
  <tr>
    <td align=right>Age:</td>
    <td align=left><input type=text name="age" width=4></td>
  <tr>
    <td align=right>Address:</td>
    <td align=left><input type=text name="address" width=40></td>
  </tr>
  <tr>
    <td align=right><b>Question 1</b><br>
      <i>What is your favorite color?</i></td>
    <td align=left><input type=text name=favcolor width=20></td>
  </tr>
  <tr>
    <td align=right><b>Question 2</b><br>
      <i>What is your favorite Operating System,
      and why?</i><br></td>
    <td align=left><textarea name="favOS" cols=40
      wrap=physical rows=5></textarea></td>
  </tr>
  <tr>
    <td colspan=2>
       <input type=submit value=" Finished! ">
    </td>
```

```
    </tr>
  </table>
</form>
</font>
</body>
</html>
```

This example uses a combination of text boxes and the `<textarea>` tag for data entry, and posts the whole series to questionnaire.cgi. The questionnaire.cgi script uses a response object to format the header:

```
#!/bin/ksh
#
# questionnaire.cgi
#
# - Uses request.cls to handle form data
#

. ./request req
. ./response resp

#
# Print the HTTP header
#
resp_printHeader
```

After this step, the example is just straightforward variable handling in the CGI script, which is shown in its entirety in Listing 12-12.

Listing 12-12: questionnaire.cgi

```
#!/bin/ksh
#
# questionnaire.cgi
#
# - Uses request.cls to handle form data
#

. ./request req
. ./response resp

#
# Print the HTTP header
#
resp_printHeader

#
# Now, show some markup
#
cat << END_OF_HTML
```

```
<html>
<head>
  <title>Questionnaire Confirmation</title>
</head>
<body bgcolor=#FFFFFF text=#000000>
<font face=verdana,tahoma,arial,helvetica>
<h3>Questionnaire Confirmation</h3>
Thank you for taking time to fill out our questionnaire, your
  results are shown
below. If we think you have the right stuff, we'll be contacting you
  soon
to join our expedition to Pluto!<br><br>
END_OF_HTML

#
# Begin Form processing
#
print "<b>Name:</b>     $req_form_name    <br>"
print "<b>Age:</b>      $req_form_age     <br>"
print "<b>Address:</b>  $req_form_address <br>"
print "<br>"
print "<b>Question 1: <i>My favorite color is:</i></b>"
print "   $req_form_favcolor <br>"
print "<b>Question 2: <i>My favorite OS"
print " is:</i></b> $req_form_favOS <br>"

cat << END_OF_HTML
</font>
</body>
</html>
END_OF_HTML
```

Creating a Gateway Application

Commonly, CGI links Web forms to other applications. In the following chapter, you build a CGI program that interfaces with distributed shell objects across the network, enabling you to perform complex operations on UNIX servers from a Web browser. To begin thinking along those lines, the next CGI example shows not only how to generate dynamic HTML pages, but how to run other applications from within a CGI script.

The example HTML page, custom.html, presents some questions asking you the color and font with which you want the next page to be displayed. custom.html also gives you a choice of commands to be executed on the server. The drop-down select boxes enable you to choose between showing the date, the systems uptime, and user currently logged on. This example is a good demonstration of how you can wire a Web application with UNIX utilities. Listing 12-13 shows custom.html.

Listing 12-13: custom.html

```html
<html>
<head>
  <title>Custom Page Setup</title>
</head>
<body bgcolor="#FFFFFF">
<font face=helvetica,arial>
 <h3>Page Customization!</h3>
 Select from the options below for a
more tailored browsing experience
</font>
<form action=custom.cgi method=get>
<table>
   <tr>
      <td width=50% align=right bgcolor=#DDDDDD>
         <font face=helvetica,arial color=blue>
            What color would you like your page to be?
      </font>
      </td>
      <td width=50% align=left>
   <select name=color>
    <option value="#FF0000">red
    <option value="#0000FF">blue
    <option value="#FFFFFF">white
    <option value="#DDDDDD">gray
    <option value="#CCFFFF">aqua
    <option value="#00FF00" selected>green
   </select>
      </td>
   </tr>
   <tr>
      <td width=50% align=right bgcolor=#DDDDDD>
         <font face=helvetica,arial color=blue>
            What font would you like your page to use?
      </font>
      </td>
      <td width=50% align=left>
         <select name=font>
    <option>arial
    <option>times
    <option>tahoma
    <option>verdana
    <option selected>courier
         </select>
      </td>
   </tr>
   <tr>
      <td width=50% align=right bgcolor=#DDDDDD>
         <font face=helvetica,arial color=blue>
            What simple utility would you like to run?
      </font>
      </td>
      <td width=50% align=left>
```

```
            <select name=util>
        <option selected value=date>Show Data and Time
        <option value=who>See Who's Logged On
        <option value=uptime>See Uptime
            </select>
        </td>
    </tr>
    <tr>
        <td>
            <input type=submit value="  Submit  ">
        </td>
    </tr>
</table>
</form>
</body>
</html>
```

The CGI to which this form posts is slightly more complex than the earlier examples; it uses both the response and request objects. At first, you just instantiate your objects, and pull in the selections the user has made for color and font:

```
#
# Instantiate CGI objects
#
. ./request req
. ./response resp

#
# Set design parameters
#
font=$req_url_font
color=$req_url_color
```

Next, you can grab the `util` variable from the request. You use a `case` statement to test its value and then execute the appropriate routine:

 Be careful never to expose any CGI variables directly to the shell. Anyone can post to your CGI script, thus leaving a dangerous opportunity for a unauthorized user to work on your Web server.

```
#
# determine specified utility
#
util=$req_url_util
```

Chapter 12: Using Shell Objects with CGI 353

```
case $util in

  date)
    #
    # Get date
    #
    util_info=$(date)
    ;;

  uptime)
    #
    # Get system's uptime
    #
    util_info=$(uptime)
    ;;
  who)
    #
    # Show who is logged on
    #
    util_info=$(who | awk '{print $1}' | sort -u)
    ;;
  *)
    #
    # Uknown
    #
    util_info="Invalid selection"
    ;;
esac
```

You assign the results of the different utilities to the variable `util_info`, and you can write these results back to the browser. Note that the example checks the value of `util_info` in a `case` statement and doesn't expose it as part of the command as follows:

```
util_info=$( $util | awk '{print $1}' | sort -u)
```

The preceding example constitutes a security hole because users could do their own POST to your CGI program, and put any command as `util`. Never directly expose a CGI variable to the shell. For the most part, this application generates fairly docile data. Figure 12-1 shows the appearance of this application on Linux.

UNIX Shell Objects

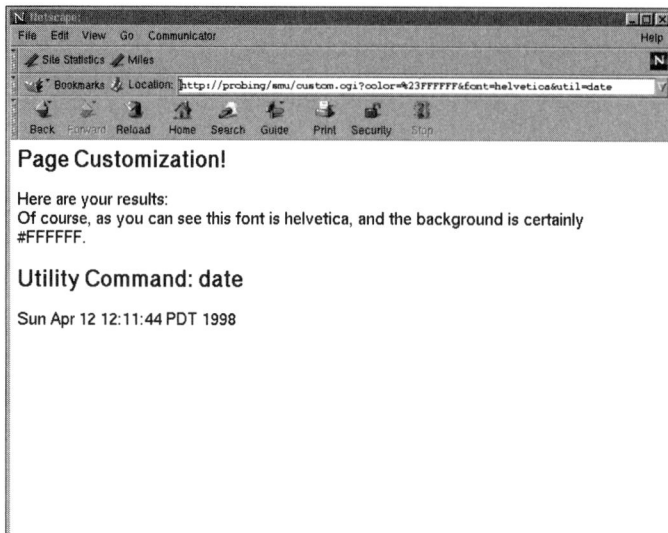

Figure 12-1: custom.cgi in action with Netscape on Linux

Listing 12-14 shows the full listing.

Listing 12-14: custom.cgi

```
#!/bin/ksh
#
# custom.cgi - display custom page design and execute a specified utility
#

#
# Instantiate CGI objects
#
. ./request req
. ./response resp

#
# Set design parameters
#
font=$req_url_font
color=$req_url_color

#
# determine specified utility
#
util=$req_url_util

case $util in

   date)
```

```
    #
    # Get date
    #
    util_info=$(date)
    ;;

  uptime)
    #
    # Get system's uptime
    #
    util_info=$(uptime)
    ;;
  who)
    #
    # Show who is logged on
    #
    util_info=$(who | awk '{print $1}' | sort -u)
    ;;
  *)
    #
    # Uknown
    #
    util_info="Invalid selection"
    ;;
esac

#
# Begin showing the page
#
resp_printHeader

cat << E_HTML
<html>
<body bgcolor=$color>
<font face=$font color=#000000>
   <h3>Page Customization!</h3>
   Here are your results:<br>
   Of course, as you can see this font is $font,
   and the background
   is certainly ${color}.
   <h3>Utility Command: $util</h3>
   $util_info
</font>
</body>
</html>
E_HTML
```

Summary

This chapter has exposed you to CGI programming and its simplicity once you've created some objects to encapsulate the dirty work. The request and response objects simplify CGI programming. The request object completely encapsulates URL encoding from your CGI, and provides a nice, object-oriented means of handling form and URL data.

The chapter also discussed how the CGI is a potential security problem, and that you should be more cautious as to how your form-handling CGI scripts handle the data they're passed. One common means of defense always checks passed-in data for unusual or unexpected characters, such as backslashes, semicolons, pipes, and so forth.

The concluding chapter shows how to connect a browser-based front end to your existing shell object architecture via CGI.

Chapter 13

Connecting from the Web

IN THIS CHAPTER

- Creating an HTML interface
- Serving HTML templates from CGI
- Creating Web forms
- Using distributed objects from CGI scripts
- Completing the SMU application

IN PRECEDING CHAPTERS, you created an object request broker, a whole slew of object-oriented shell code, and the underlying architecture for a systems management utility. In this chapter, you use your CGI knowledge to build an HTML front end to your systems application.

The application features Web forms for viewing processes on remote machines, viewing disk statistics and status, and creating and deleting user accounts. While these tasks may or may not match your desired tasks to complete from the Web, the application demonstrates how to connect some fairly complex operations across different servers. By the conclusion, you should be able to use the techniques presented here when developing your own applications.

Connecting the Components

The only new code in this chapter is a rather lengthy but simple set of CGI scripts that allows a browser-based HTML interface to connect to the distributed objects you created in Chapter 10.

In Chapter 10, you created a series of operation classes. These classes encapsulated the complex operations of other objects and acted as a facade, implementing the SMU application with a simple interface. The goal was to build all of the operations your application would need into objects, and simply supply an `_execute` method for those objects. This approach enables you to wrap any sort of GUI or user interface around the code easily. This chapter demonstrates the simplicity of this task. The most complex part of this chapter examines error checking and the display of the complex HTML tables that act as the GUI.

While the HTML and CGI are fairly simple with only a few new concepts, the overall code length is large because HTML tends to be long-winded and CGI has to complete lots of processing.

You start by developing a starting page for the whole application, followed by a series of CGI scripts to handle HTML forms. You code some error routines to help prevent object detachment across the Web, and then dive into some complex HTML.

Getting the Environment Ready

You need to be familiar with your Web server to implement the code in this chapter successfully. Primarily, you need to have CGI enabled on your Web server as an executable file type, and the user who runs your server (usually `nobody` or `Web`) needs their environment adjusted in order to run the ORB client components. As a result, the user needs to have the Java binary in their path, the `proxy.sh`, `connectionMgr.sh`, and supporting ORB client scripts, and the ability to read and write in the of the CGI scripts directory.

This version is developed in a directory named SMU under the server root. Use this location if possible to avoid unnecessary rework on the code. For example, if you've defined your server root as the following:

`/usr/public_html`

then your SMU directory follows:

`/usr/public_html/SMU`

You'll need to configure this directory; when you address this directory via a URL in your browser, it appears as `http://<servername>/SMU`.

Testing the Environment

Before you start CGI coding, try out the environment in which your CGI will be executed. This step minimizes the chance for errors generated while you're Web browsing, which are much harder to debug.

 You must have the `ORBserv.sh` running on the host from which you intend to import objects.

Chapter 13: Connecting from the Web

You should `su` to the user `nobody`, or whichever user your Web server runs as, and try out the following ORB commands:

```
$# su - nobody
$> cd /usr/public_html/SMU
$> ../connectionMgr.sh localhost opViewDiskStats myOp
1 [3619]
$> myOp_execute
......disk statistics......
```

The preceding must work without any problems if you expect your CGI scripts to work. In addition to this test, make sure the user `nobody` has write permission in the directory.

If the preceding works, you can be confident that your CGI debugging will be relatively easy — if even necessary.

When debugging CGI scripts, it's extremely helpful to do a `tail -f` on your Web server's log file, watching errors as they occur. The `tail` command displays the last ten lines of a file. If you use `tail` with the `-f` option, it continuously monitors the file, displaying new lines as they are added.

Creating the Interface

Now that everything is ready, you can begin creating the interface. Although the first page is actually static HTML, it offers an introduction to the application and serves as a home base, providing links to the various functional parts of the Web application.

Creating index.html

The CD-ROM contains an image file, `smu.jpg`, which is used repeatedly as the Web application's header. You can use this image or simply replace the image with a text heading. The HTML is shown in Listing 13-1.

Listing 13-1: `index.html`

```
<html>
<head>
   <!-- System Management Utility
        @(#) 1.0 - SMU
        A Demonstration of Distributed Shell Objects
   -->
```

```
        <title>System Management Utility (SMU)</title>
</head>
<body bgcolor=#FFFFFF text=#330088>
<p align=center>
    <img src="smu.jpg" alt="System Management Utility">
</p>
<center>
<table width=550 border=0 cellspacing=3>
    <tr>
        <td align=center>
          <font face=tahoma,arial,helvetica>
          <b>A Demonstration of Shell Objects</b>
          </font>
        </td>
    </tr>
    <tr>
        <td align=left>
          <font face=tahoma,arial,helvetica>
          <p align=left>
          Welcome to the System Management Utility
          demonstration. From here you can perform
          various operations on distributed UNIX servers that
          have been configured with a shell-based
          Object Request Broker.
          </p>
          <p align=left>
          If you've already configured a list of servers to be
          used in this application, follow the link marked
          <b>Server Maintenence</b> below. If this is your first
          time here, or you would like to edit your list of
          available servers, follow the link marked <b>Edit Server
          Configuration</b>
          </p>
          <p align=center>
           <a href="smuMain.cgi">Server Maintenance</a> ---
           <a href="smuServerConfig.cgi">Server Configuration</a>
           </p>
          </font>
        </td>
    </tr>
</table>
</center>

<p align=center>
<font face=tahoma,helvetica,arial>
 | <a href=index.html>SMU Home</a> |
<a href=smuServerConfig.cgi>Server
 Configuration</a> | <a href=smuMain.cgi>
SMU Operations</a> | <br>

</body></html>
```

Chapter 13: Connecting from the Web

When you address the URL, http://yourserver/SMU, you'll get the page index.html by default. Examine the series of links at the bottom of the page. The link marked "Server Maintenance" takes you to the form-based GUI that enables you to perform the different SMU operations on the distributed servers. Before you can begin using these operations, you first need to follow the other link, "Server Configuration." This link takes you to a form interface that enables you to create a list of the different servers with which you intend to use SMU. Each server needs to be outfitted with an ORBserv.sh setup in order for the CGI to import objects. Figure 13-1 shows a screenshot of the Server Configuration area.

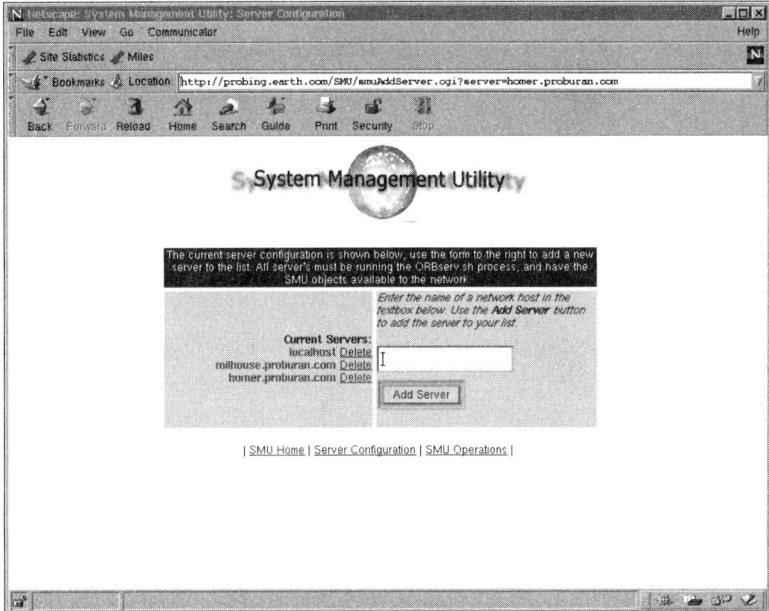

Figure 13-1: The SMU server configuration screen

The links at the very bottom are the same on every page. "SMU Home" simply returns you to index.html, while "Server Configuration" and "SMU Operations" take you to both the server configuration area and the form-based interface that you create for SMU.

Creating Template Files

Because this is a Web application, and not just a static collection of pages, you should create template files that can be reused to display similar types of messages and information. For example, instead of coding a separate, standalone HTML page for each possible error message, you can construct an error template and have a CGI program serve the same template, swapping in the appropriate error message.

The SMU application actually has several templates: one in particular for errors and a few to support the basic look and feel reused throughout the application.

These templates are used by all of the CGI scripts coded in this chapter. Listing 13-2 shows the first template, err.tmpl.

Listing 13-2: err.tmpl

```
<html>
<head>
    <!-- System Management Utility @(#) 1.0 - SMU -->
    <title>System Management Utility: Error </title>
</head>
<body bgcolor=#FFFFFF text=#330088>
<p align=center>
    <img src="smu.jpg" alt="System Management Utility">
</p>
<center>
<table width=550 border=0 cellspacing=3>
    <tr>
        <td align=center>
      <font face=tahoma,arial,helvetica>
      <b>There has been an error:</b>
      </font>
        </td>
    </tr>
    <tr>
        <td align=left>
      <font face=tahoma,arial,helvetica>
      <p align=left>
__MESSAGE__
      </p>
      </font>
        </td>
    </tr>
</table>
</center>

</body></html>
```

The only strange characteristic of this HTML is the __MESSAGE__ marking toward the bottom. With this marking, you can use the template for more than one type of error message. In your CGI script, you print out the template — grabbing the __MESSAGE__ string and replacing it with whatever error message fits the situation.

In addition to the error templates, two other templates support the general look and feel of the application. The first, smuTemplTop.tmpl, represents the first "half" of a Web page, and allows for the insertion of a dynamic title depending on which script is serving it. Listing 13-3 shows smuTemplTop.tmpl:

Chapter 13: Connecting from the Web

Listing 13-3: `smuTemplTop.tmpl`

```
<html>
<head>
   <!--- System Management Utility @(#) 1.0 - SMU --->
<title>System Management Utility:
__TITLE__
</title>
</head>
<body bgcolor=#FFFFFF text=#330088>
<p align=center>
   <img src="smu.jpg" alt="System Management Utility">
</p>
<center>
```

In the preceding example, you replace the __TITLE__ string with the particular title you want to use. The bottom half of SMU's typical Web page is shown in `smuTemplBottom.tmpl`, which has the global links you can use to navigate to different parts of the application. The bottom half of the template is shown in Listing 13-4.

Listing 13-4: `smuTemplBottom.tmpl`

```
</center>
<p align=center>
<font face=tahoma,helvetica,arial>
 | <a href=index.html>SMU Home</a> | <a
 href=smuServerConfig.cgi>Server
 Configuration</a> | <a href=smuMain.cgi>SMU Operations</a> | <br>

</body></html>
```

Creating CGI Error Scripts

Because of the complexity of the CGI scripts, your application consolidates some of the initial configuration and error handling. The file `smuErr.sh` defines a simple function that takes an error string as a parameter, and then displays the error template file, substituting the string into place. Listing 13-5 shows `smuErr.sh`.

Listing 13-5: `smuErr.sh`

```
#
# doError - prints message string in error template
#
doError()
{
  message=$1

  #
```

```
# Print header
#
resp_printHeader

#
# Display template and insert error message
#
while read text
do
   if [[ $text = "__MESSAGE__" ]]; then
      print "$message"
   else
      print "$text"
   fi

done < err.tmpl
}
```

As you can see, this function searches for the __MESSAGE__ string in the error template, and substitutes the string for whatever was passed in as an argument.

The file smuORBverify.sh checks the CGI environment for necessary dependencies – when these dependencies do not exist, the file reminds you. This feature can be a great aid for debugging. The script performs operations such as the following:

```
If ! which java 2>&1 > /dev/null; then
   ...error handling code
```

smuORBverify.sh checks for the existence of the Java binary executable, the connection manager, and a configured server list, as shown in Listing 13-6.

Listing 13-6: smyORBverify.sh

```
#!/bin/ksh
#
# Verifies that ORB client software is available
#

#
# Source in error code
#
. ./smuErr.sh

#
# Verify that you can use client ORB software
#
if ! which java 2>&1 > /dev/null; then
   error="SMU not configured. The <b>Java</b> binary can't be found."
   error=${error}" Make sure the user $(id) has <b>java</b> in its path."
   doError "$error"
   unset error
```

```
    exit
fi
if ! which connectionMgr.sh 2>&1 > /dev/null; then
  error="SMU not configured. The <b>connectionMgr.sh</b> is not
found."
  error=${error}" Make sure the user <font color=red>$(id)</font>
has "error=${error}"<b>connectionMgr.sh</b> in its path."
  doError "$error"
  exit
fi

#
# Verify you have a server.list
#
if [[ ! -f server.list ]]; then
  error="SMU not configured. You must first create a list of
servers"
  error=${error}"before you can begin SMU. To create a list, press"
  error=${error}"<a href=smuServerConfig.cgi> here</a>."
  doError "$error"
  exit
fi
```

 Although smuORBverify.sh tries to check your environment, not all of the CGI is sourced together, and you can lose your PATH variable across several CGI processes. Therefore, you should probably export and define the PATH in every CGI script with a dependency on Java or client ORB software.

Creating the Application

Apart from the initial page, index.html, the rest of your HTML interface is presented via templates and CGI. When you first begin the application, you should choose the "Server Configuration" link to set up a list of servers. The CGI smuServerConfig.cgi serves this link.

Server Configuration

This script serves up the basic template, swaps in the appropriate title, and builds a dynamic form enabling you to add and delete servers from your list. The advantages of the GET method over the POST method is shown in the section that enables you to delete a server:

```
for server in $( < server.list )
do
  print "<b>$server</b>"
```

```
          print "<a href=smuDelServer.cgi?server=$server>"
          print "Delete</a><br>"
done
```

While the `server.list` file is being dumped in the preceding section code, you grab each server listing and present the HTML link. You can place a variable within the link to indicate to which server you are referring, and this information is passed to the script `smuDelServer.cgi`. Listing 13-7 shows the full version of `smuDelServer.cgi`.

Listing 13-7: `smuDelServer.cgi`

```
#!/bin/ksh
#
# smuServerConfig.cgi
#
# - Maintains list of available UNIX servers for the SMU application
#


#
# Create cgi object
#
. ./response resp

#
# Source in error code
#
. ./smuErr.sh

#
# Print out top-half of template
#
resp_printHeader

while read HTML
do
   if [[ $HTML = "__TITLE__" ]];then
     print "Server Configuration"
   else
     print "$HTML"
   fi
done < ./smuTemplTop.tmpl

#
# Now display our server config form
#
cat << END_OF_HTML
<table border=0 cellspacing=4 width=500>
   <tr>
   <td align=center bgcolor=330088 colspan=2>
      <font face=tahoma,helvetica,arial color=white>
      The current server configuration is shown below, use the
```

```
          form to the right to add a new server to the list. All
          server's must be running the ORBserv.sh process, and have
          the SMU objects available to the network.
          </font>
      </td>
       <tr>
      <td align=right bgcolor=#DDDDDD width=50%>
          <font face=tahoma,helvetica,arial>
          <b>Current Servers:</b><br>
          <font color=red>
END_OF_HTML
if [[ ! -f server.list ]]; then
  print "<font color=red>No Servers Configured...</font><br>"
else
  for server in $( < server.list )
  do
    print "<b>$server</b>"
    print "<a href=smuDelServer.cgi?server=$server>"
    print "Delete</a><br>"
  done
fi
cat << END_OF_HTML
          </font>
          </font>
      </td>
      <!-- form for adding a server --->
      <td align=left bgcolor=#DDDDDD width=50%>
          <font face=tahoma,helvetica,arial>
          <i>Enter the name of a network host in the textbox below. Use
 the
          <b>Add Server</b> button to add the server to your
  list.</i><br>
          <form action="smuAddServer.cgi" method="GET">
          <input type=text size=20 name=server><br>
          <input type=submit value="  Add Server  ">
          </form></font>
      </td>
       </tr>
</table>
END_OF_HTML
#
# Print out bottom-half of template
#
cat ./smuTemplBottom.tmpl
```

Two supporting scripts carry out the operations indicated in smuServer
Config.cgi: smuAddServer.cgi and smuDelServer.cgi. Both of these scripts
expect the server to be passed as a parameter, and — as their names indicate — either
add or remove the particular server from the list. Listing 13-8 shows
smuAddServer.cgi.

UNIX Shell Objects

Listing 13-8: smuAddServer.cgi

```ksh
#!/bin/ksh
#
# smuAddServer.cgi
#
# Add entries to the server.list file
#
. ./request req
. ./response resp

#
# add server to file
#
print "$req_url_server" >> server.list

#
# Redirect browser to smuServerConfig.cgi
#
resp_redirection /SMU/smuServerConfig.cgi
```

Listing 13-9 shows smuDelServer.cgi.

Listing 13-9: smuDelServer.cgi

```ksh
#!/bin/ksh
#
# smuAddServer.cgi
#
# Add entries to the server.list file
#
. ./request req
. ./response resp

#
# Delete server from file
#
sed "s/$req_url_server//g" server.list > newlist
mv newlist server.list
#
# Redirect browser to smuServerConfig.cgi
#
resp_redirection /SMU/smuServerConfig.cgi
```

 Make sure to export your PATH variable to indicate where all dependency files are kept when creating the CGI scripts. The CGI "user" may not have all of the environment variables present or defined.

The Main Form

The main form in the SMU application is served from CGI. This CGI dynamically inserts your configuration list into a series of list boxes, so that you can choose upon which server you want to perform certain operations.

Most of the code is straightforward, but a lot of HTML markup is presented, as each form is slightly different than the last. The script starts by attempting to set up the environment:

```
#
# put ORBserv.sh client dependencies in PATH
#
PATH=$PATH:/usr/local/jdk1.1.1/bin:.
export PATH

#
# Import CGI objects
#
. ./response resp

#
# Source in ORB verification and error routines
#
. ./smuORBverify.sh
```

The following defines a function that retrieves the list of configured servers and displays the interior portion of a select box. This function is reused throughout the CGI script whenever a server select box is needed:

```
#
# Define a function to print out Server Names
# as select box contents
#
selectServers()
{
  for each in $(< ./server.list)
  do
    print "<option>$each"
  done
}
```

The remainder of the script, while lengthy, is quite straightforward. You alternate between displaying sections of HTML within a "here" document, and generating dynamic server select boxes. You should note that each form contains some of the same variables reflecting the targeted server, the requested object, and other fields. Figure 13-2 shows the section of markup that enables you to create new accounts.

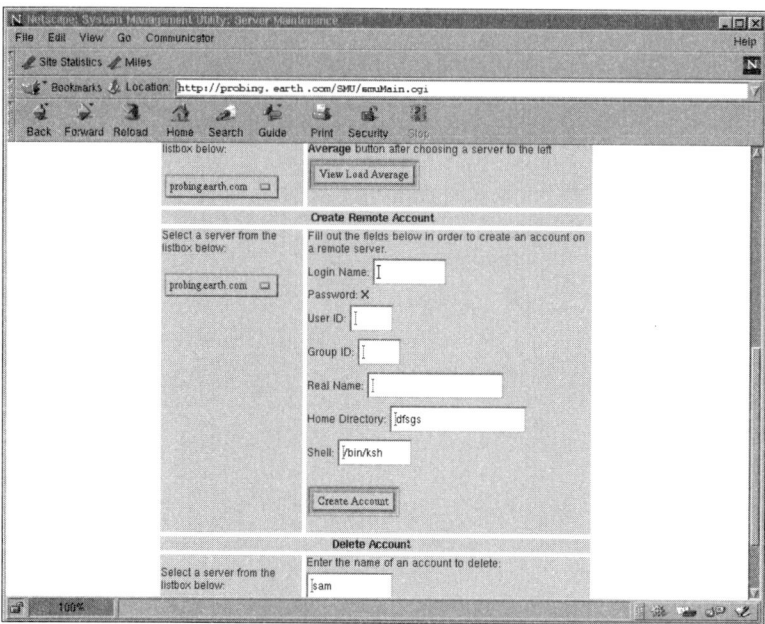

Figure 13-2: A screenshot of the Create Account section

The entire code listing for `smuMain.cgi` is shown in Listing 13-10.

Listing 13-10: `smuMain.cgi`

```
#!/bin/ksh
#
# smuMain.cgi
#
# Top level menu for performing operations on network hosts
#

#
# put ORBserv.sh client dependencies in PATH
#
PATH=$PATH:/usr/local/jdk1.1.1/bin:.
export PATH

#
```

```
#  Import CGI objects
#
. ./response resp

#
# Source in ORB verification and error routines
#
. ./smuORBverify.sh

c
#
# Finally, all is well, start HTML output
#
. response resp
resp_printHeader

#
# Print out first half of template
#
while read HTML
do
   if [[ $HTML = "__TITLE__" ]]; then
     print "Server Maintenance"
   else
     print "$HTML"
   fi
done < ./smuTemplTop.tmpl

#
# MAIN server maintenance area
#
cat <<END_OF_HTML
<table width=500 border=0>
   <tr>
   <td colspan=3 bgcolor=#330088 align=center>
      <font face=tahoma,helvetica,arial color=white size=+1>
       <b>System Operation Menu</b>
      </font>
   </td>
   </tr>
</table>
<table width=500 border=0 cellspacing=4>
   <tr>
   <td bgcolor=#DDDDDD align=center colspan=3>
      <font face=tahoma,helvetica,arial>
       <b>View Processes</b>
      </font>
   </td>
   </tr>
   <tr>
   <td bgcolor=#DDDDDD align=left width=33%>
      <font face=tahoma,helvetica,arial>
       Select a server from the listbox below:
```

```
            </font>
            <!---- ******************************
             View Processes Form
             ****************************** ---->
            <form action="smuORB.cgi" method=GET>
            <select name=server>
END_OF_HTML
#
# print out Server Names as select box contents
#
selectServers
#
# continue with HTML
#
cat <<END_OF_HTML
            </select>
        </td>
        <td bgcolor=#DDDDDD align=left width=66% colspan=2>
            <font face=tahoma,helvetica,arial>
             To View the current process tables press the <b>View Process
             Table</b> button after choosing a server to the left
            </font><br>
            <input type=hidden name=object value=opViewProcessTable>
            <input type=submit value=" View Process Table ">
            </form>
        </td>
         </tr>
END_OF_HTML
cat << END_OF_HTML
<br>
        <tr>
        <td bgcolor=#DDDDDD align=center colspan=3>
            <font face=tahoma,helvetica,arial>
             <b>View Disk Statistics</b>
            </font>
        </td>
         </tr>
         <tr>
        <td bgcolor=#DDDDDD algin=left width=33%>
            <font face=tahoma,helvetica,arial>
             Select a server from the listbox below:
            </font>
            <!---- ******************************
             View Disk Status Form
             ****************************** ---->
            <form action="smuORB.cgi" method=GET>
            <select name=server>
END_OF_HTML
#
# print out Server Names as select box contents
#
selectServers
#
```

```
# continue with HTML
#
cat <<END_OF_HTML
      </select>
  </td>
  <td bgcolor=#DDDDDD align=left width=66% colspan=2>
      <font face=tahoma,helvetica,arial>
       To View the current disk status press the <b>View Disk
       Status</b> button after choosing a server to the left
      </font><br>
      <input type=hidden name=object value=opViewDiskStats>
      <input type=submit value=" View Disk Status ">
      </form>
  </td>
    </tr>
<br>
    <tr>
    <td bgcolor=#DDDDDD align=center colspan=3>
       <font face=tahoma,helvetica,arial>
        <b>View Load Average</b>
       </font>
   </td>
    </tr>
    <tr>
    <td bgcolor=#DDDDDD align=left width=33%>
        <font face=tahoma,helvetica,arial>
        Select a server from the listbox below:
        </font>
        <!---- *****************************
        View Load Average Form
        ***************************** ---->
        <form action="smuORB.cgi" method=GET>
        <select name=server>
END_OF_HTML
#
# print out Server Names as select box contents
#
selectServers
#
# continue with HTML
#
cat <<END_OF_HTML
      </select>
  </td>
  <td bgcolor=#DDDDDD align=left width=66% colspan=2>
      <font face=tahoma,helvetica,arial>
       To View the current load average press the <b>View Load
       Average</b> button after choosing a server to the left
      </font><br>
      <input type=hidden name=object value=opViewLoadAvg>
      <input type=submit value=" View Load Average ">
      </form>
  </td>
```

```
        </tr>
<br>
   <tr>
    <td bgcolor=#DDDDDD align=center colspan=3>
       <font face=tahoma,helvetica,arial>
        <b>Create Remote Account</b>
       </font>
   </td>
    </tr>
    <tr>
    <td bgcolor=#DDDDDD align=left width=33% valign=top>
       <font face=tahoma,helvetica,arial>
        Select a server from the listbox below:
       </font>
       <!---- *****************************
        Create Account Form
        *****************************  ---->
       <form action="smuORB.cgi" method=GET>
       <select name=server>
END_OF_HTML
#
# print out Server Names as select box contents
#
selectServers
#
# continue with HTML
#
cat <<END_OF_HTML
       </select>
   </td>
    <td bgcolor=#DDDDDD align=left width=66% colspan=2>
       <font face=tahoma,helvetica,arial>
        Fill out the fields below in order to create an account on a
        remote server.<br>
        Login Name:
        <input type=text name=logID size=10><br>
        Password: <b>X</b><br>
        User ID:
        <input type=text name=uid size=5><br>
        Group ID:
        <input type=text name=gid size=5><br>
        Real Name:
        <input type=text name=gecos size=20><br>
        Home Directory:
        <input type=text name=hdir size=20><br>
        Shell:
        <input type=text name=shell size=10 value="/bin/ksh"><br>
       </font><br>
        <input type=hidden name=object value=opAddAccount>
        <input type=submit value=" Create Account ">
```

```
          </form>
       </td>
      </tr>
<br>
      <tr>
      <td bgcolor=#DDDDDD align=center colspan=3>
         <font face=tahoma,helvetica,arial>
          <b>Delete Account</b>
         </font>
      </td>
       </tr>
       <tr>
      <td bgcolor=#DDDDDD algin=left width=33%>
         <font face=tahoma,helvetica,arial>
          Select a server from the listbox below:
         </font>
         <!---- *****************************
          Delete Account Form
          ***************************** ---->
         <form action="smuORB.cgi" method=GET>
         <select name=server>
END_OF_HTML
#
# print out Server Names as select box contents
#
selectServers
#
# continue with HTML
#
cat <<END_OF_HTML
         </select>
      </td>
      <td bgcolor=#DDDDDD align=left width=66% colspan=2>
         <font face=tahoma,helvetica,arial>
          Enter the name of an account to delete:<br>
         <input type=text name=acct size=12>
         </font><br>
         <input type=hidden name=object value=opDelAccount>
         <input type=submit value=" Delete Account ">
         </form>
      </td>
       </tr>
<br>
</table>
END_OF_HTML

#
# Print out bottom half of template
#
cat ./smuTemplBottom.tmpl
```

Object Interface

The most important part of the Web application is the interface between the CGI scripts and the distributed shell objects. This critical script performs all of the actual work – actually, it imports the objects that are linked to the objects that perform the actual work. As far as the Web server is concerned, however, this script is where the action takes place.

This script instantiates remote operation objects on whatever server is passed in as a parameter. If you want to view the processes running on the host mickey, select mickey from the box on smuMain.cgi and press the "View Process Table" button on the form. That form posts to this script, smuORB.cgi.

The script determines the host and attempts to import the opViewProcessTable object from the host via the connection manager. If the call succeeds, the CGI calls the execute function on the object, and results are sent back to the Web browser. Figure 13-3 shows the result of a view processes call.

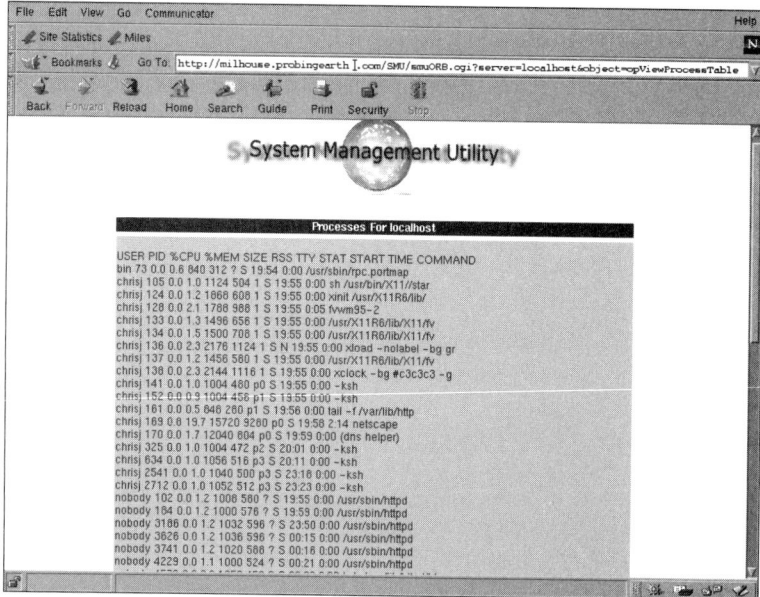

Figure 13-3: The result of pressing "View Process Table"

This script is the most complicated script in the application. In addition to the error handling functions that you import, this script defines several functions to consolidate reused functionality throughout the script. The doTopHalf function serves the typical template, swapping out the correct title:

```
doTopHalf()
{
  while read HTML
  do
    if [[ $HTML = "__TITLE__" ]]; then
      print "$1"
    else
      print "$HTML"
    fi
  done < ./smuTemplTop.tmpl
  return 0
}
```

You also have a simple `doBottomHalf` function and a `doConnectError`, which is a wrapper function around the `doError` specific to connection errors:

```
doBottomHalf()
{
  cat ./smuTemplBottom.tmpl
  return 0
}

doConnectError()
{
  object=$1
  server=$2
  error="Failure retrieving object: $object<br>"
  error=${error}" from host: $server<br>"
  doError "$error"
  exit
}
```

All of the results you present are shown in a gray table; the following function consolidates the effort:

```
doGreyTable()
{
  _greyMessage_=$1

  print "<table border=0 cellspacing=5 width=600>"
  print "<tr><td bgcolor=#330088 align=center>"
  print "<font face=tahoma,helvetica,arial color=white><b>"
  print "$_greyMessage_<b></font><tr><td bgcolor=#DDDDDD>"
  print "<font face=tahoma,helvetica,arial>"
}
```

The rest of the code primarily deals with performing the operations themselves. The architectural functionality is quite simple. You simply use a request form reference to determine which object the client wants to invoke, and upon which server:

```
opViewProcessTable)
    #
    # acquire object from server
    #
    if ! ../connectionMgr.sh "$server" "$object" myOp "$arguments"
    then
       doConnectError $object $server
    fi
```

Complete a `case` statement based on `$req_url_object` to determine which object has been requested. Next, call the connection manager to try and establish a connection, returning an error message if it fails. If this succeeds, try to begin the HTTP response, checking for failures and immediately releasing the remote object in the event something goes wrong:

```
    #
    # Prepare for output
    #
    if ! resp_printHeader; then
      myOp_release
    fi

    if ! doTopHalf "Process Table"; then
      myOp_release
    fi

    doGreyTable "Processes For $server"
```

You shouldn't leave a remote object hanging about for no reason, so it's always good practice to drop it if anything goes wrong. If your code has succeeded thus far, then you're ready to call the execute method and retrieve the remote data:

```
    #
    # print out process table
    #

    myOp_execute
    myOp_release
```

You can release the object as soon as the call returns – the object is no longer needed.

Chapter 13: Connecting from the Web 379

As the `instance` script used by the `ORBserv.sh` process runs, you may see error messages when trying to create and delete accounts. These errors are side effects and not bugs. The instance script, as presented in Chapter 8, executes its method once as a subprocess and once in a logging operation. To disable this behavior, you must write the results of a method invocation to a file and read the results back into the contents of a string, as shown in Chapter 11. This approach is due to pdKSH's inability to complete the statement `echo word | read var` and set the value of `var` to `word`.

If your operations are more complex, you can leave the reference up until receiving more feedback from the user. You can make subsequent calls on the object and release it only when finally finished with its services.

After you've used and released your object, close out the gray table you're using as follows:

```
#
# finish table
#
print "</font></td></tr></table>"

#
# close page
#
doBottomHalf

exit
;;
```

After the preceding, the case statement exits and the script is completed. Upon the next user selection from `smuMain.cgi`, the Web server runs the script again with the appropriate parameters. Listing 13-11 shows the full listing of `smuORB.cgi`.

Listing 13-11: `smuORB.cgi`

```
#!/bin/ksh
#
# smuORB.cgi
#
# @(#)1.0 - smuORB.cgi
#
# Executes operations on distributed objects and returns HTML
#
#
```

```
# put ORBserv.sh client dependencies in PATH
#
PATH=$PATH:/usr/local/jdk1.1.1/bin:.
export PATH

#
# Import CGI objects
#
. ./response resp
. ./request req

#
# Source in error code
#
. ./smuErr.sh

#
# Verify that you can use client ORB software
#
. ./smuORBverify.sh

#
# Functions for printing templates
#
doTopHalf()
{
  while read HTML
  do
    if [[ $HTML = "__TITLE__" ]]; then
      print "$1"
    else
      print "$HTML"
    fi
  done < ./smuTemplTop.tmpl
  return 0
}

doBottomHalf()
{
  cat ./smuTemplBottom.tmpl
  return 0
}

doConnectError()
{
  object=$1
  server=$2
  error="Failure retrieving object: $object<br>"
  error=${error}" from host: $server<br>"
  doError "$error"
  exit
}
```

```
doGreyTable()
{
  _greyMessage_=$1

  print "<table border=0 cellspacing=5 width=600>"
  print "<tr><td bgcolor=#330088 align=center>"
  print "<font face=tahoma,helvetica,arial color=white><b>"
  print "$_greyMessage_<b></font><tr><td bgcolor=#DDDDDD>"
  print "<font face=tahoma,helvetica,arial>"
}
#
# Begin MAIN program
#

#
# Determine object, server, argument list
#
if [[ $req_url_server = "" ]]; then
  error="Server undefined..."
  doError "$error"
  exit
else
  server=$req_url_server
fi

if [[ $req_url_object = "" ]]; then
  error="Object undefined...."
  doError "$error"
  exit
else
  object=$req_url_object
fi

arguments=$req_url_arguments

#
# Select case on object....
#
case $object in
  #
  # View Process Table
  #
  opViewProcessTable)
    #
    # acquire object from server
    #
    if ! ../connectionMgr.sh "$server" "$object" myOp "$arguments"
    then
      doConnectError $object $server
    fi

    #
    # Prepare for output
```

```
        #
        if ! resp_printHeader; then
          myOp_release
        fi

        if ! doTopHalf "Process Table"; then
          myOp_release
        fi

        doGreyTable "Processes For $server"

        #
        # print out process table
        #

        myOp_execute
        myOp_release

        #
        # finish table
        #
        print "</font></td></tr></table>"

        #
        # close page
        #
        doBottomHalf

        exit
    ;;
    #
    # View Disk Status
    #
    opViewDiskStats)
        #
        # acquire object from server
        #
        if ! ../connectionMgr.sh "$server" "$object" myOp "$arguments"
        then
          doConnectError $object $server
        fi

        #
        # Prepare for output
        #
        if ! resp_printHeader; then
          myOp_release
        fi

        if ! doTopHalf "Disk Statistics"; then
          myOp_release
        fi
```

```
    doGreyTable "Disk Statistics For $server"

    #
    # print out disk statistics
    #
    disk_data=$(myOp_execute)
    for each in $disk_data
    do
      if [[ $each = @(*%) ]]; then
        print "$each <br>"
      else
        print "$each"
      fi
    done
    myOp_release
    #
    # finish table
    #
    print "</font></td></tr></table>"

    #
    # close page
    #
    doBottomHalf

    exit
 ;;
#
# View Load Average
#
opViewLoadAvg)
    #
    # acquire object from server
    #
    if ! ../connectionMgr.sh "$server" "$object" myOp "$arguments"
    then
      doConnectError $object $server
    fi

    #
    # Prepare for output
    #
    if ! resp_printHeader; then
      myOp_release
    fi

    if ! doTopHalf "Load Average"; then
      myOp_release
    fi

    doGreyTable "Load Average For $server"

    #
```

```
        # print out load average
        #

        myOp_execute
        myOp_release

        #
        # close table
        #
        print "</font></td></tr></table>"

        doBottomHalf

        exit
    ;;
    #
    # Create Account
    #
    opAddAccount)
        #
        # acquire object from server
        #
        if ! ../connectionMgr.sh "$server" "$object" myOp "$arguments"
        then
            doConnectError $object $server
        fi

        #
        # Prepare for output
        #
        if ! resp_printHeader; then
            myOp_release
        fi

        if ! doTopHalf "Create Account"; then
            myOp_release
        fi

        doGreyTable "Creating Account on $server"

        #
        # print out Account Results
        #

        #
        # Translate space in gecos field to underscores, some
        #
        gecos=$(echo $req_url_gecos | tr \  \_ )

        acctString="$req_url_logID x $req_url_uid $req_url_gid "
        acctString=${acctString}"$gecos $req_url_hdir "
        acctString=${acctString}"$req_url_shell"
```

Chapter 13: Connecting from the Web   385

```
  print "$acctString" >> acclog
  if ! myOp_execute "$acctString"; then
    doError "Create Account Failed."
    exit
  fi
  myOp_release

  #
  # close table
  #
  print "</font></td></tr></table>"

  doBottomHalf

  exit
  ;;
#
# Delete an Account
#
opDelAccount)
  #
  # get ID from URL
  #
  arguments=$req_url_acct
  print "deleting account: $arguments" >> acclogdel
  if [[ $arguments = "" ]]; then
    doError "You must supply an account name."
    exit
  fi

  #
  # Check for a bad, bad idea
  #
  if  [[ $arguments = "root" ]]; then
    error="You <i>do not</i> want to delete this account"
    error=${error}" from a Web browser."
    doError "$error"
    exit
  fi
  #
  # acquire object from server
  #
  if ! ../connectionMgr.sh "$server" "$object" myOp "$arguments"
  then
    doConnectError $object $server
  fi

  #
  # Prepare for output
  #
  if ! resp_printHeader; then
    myOp_release
  fi
```

```
        if ! doTopHalf "Delete Account"; then
          myOp_release
        fi

        doGreyTable "Deleting Account on $server"

        #
        # print out Delete Account Results
        #

        if ! myOp_execute; then
          doError "myOp_execute: delete account failed..."
        fi
        myOp_release
        #
        # close table
        #
        print "</font></td></tr></table>"

        doBottomHalf

        exit
        ;;
esac
```

Security

This application may raise some questions of security. While some of SMU's operations are quite docile, such as disk statistics, the capability to create or delete an account may or may not be appropriate for a Web interface, depending on the environment in which you work. UNIX servers do a variety of work, and while browser-based account maintenance may be great for a research and development company, a secure banking network may not be the best place!

This application is designed to demonstrate the power of shell objects and how object-orientation can not only bridge the network rather painlessly, but also provide high-level objects to make quick work of complex operations. Creating a UNIX account involves touching a lot of different areas, and this CGI script demonstrates the process quite easily. The CGI script smuORB.cgi takes form information from a browser, creates a remote instance of opAddAccount, and passes the parameters off to the ORB. On the remote machine, opAddAccount is an encapsulation of finer grained objects such as user and account that actually pull off the account creation on your behalf. This configuration demonstrates the power of object-orientation. The user and account classes are reusable in many different types of scripts, including both distributed and local. The opAddAccount class, like the other operation classes, is a distributed facade, and allows for the attachment of multiple and concurrent distributed user interfaces. Ultimately, the HTML interface you've created may very well be the most portable and easy to use, although you could have created a fairly simple interface using the Java GUI libraries, or even in native code on Win32. After all, you can tailor any programming language or platform to speak KSOP, including Windows, without major difficulty.

The security implications of remote account creation are serious, and you should use this application as a model for any problem you need to solve in your domain.

Summary

In this chapter, you created a dynamic, Web-based front end to application objects you created in Chapter 10. Those application objects were geared to support multiple user interfaces, while the front end presented in this chapter is merely an option. The SMU application is the culmination of your efforts in developing functional object-oriented shell components and providing an efficient and object-oriented means of distributing these components across the network via the shell ORB and KSOP.

While shell objects may not be the best means for creating some applications, the techniques presented in this book shed new light in the area, and extend the capabilities of the Korn shell considerably. You can use the examples presented in this book to build and refine your existing applications, and improve the implementation and notion of object-oriented shell scripting.

Appendix A

GNU General Public License

Version 2, June 1991
Copyright © 1989, 1991 Free Software Foundation, Inc.
675 Mass Ave., Cambridge, MA 02139, USA

Everyone is permitted to copy and distribute verbatim copies of this license document, but changing it is not allowed.

Preamble

The licenses for most software are designed to take away your freedom to share and change it. By contrast, the GNU General Public License is intended to guarantee your freedom to share and change free software – to make sure the software is free for all its users. This General Public License applies to most of the Free Software Foundation's software and to any other program whose authors commit to using it. (Some other Free Software Foundation software is covered by the GNU Library General Public License instead.) You can apply it to your programs, too.

When we speak of *free software*, we are referring to freedom, not price. Our General Public Licenses are designed to make sure that you have the freedom to distribute copies of free software (and charge for this service if you wish), that you receive source code or can get it if you want it, that you can change the software or use pieces of it in new free programs; and that you know you can do these things.

To protect your rights, we need to make restrictions that forbid anyone to deny you these rights or to ask you to surrender the rights. These restrictions translate to certain responsibilities for you if you distribute copies of the software, or if you modify it.

For example, if you distribute copies of such a program, whether gratis or for a fee, you must give the recipients all the rights that you have. You must make sure that they, too, receive or can get the source code. And you must show them these terms so they know their rights.

We protect your rights with two steps: (1) copyright the software, and (2) offer you this license, which gives you legal permission to copy, distribute, and/or modify the software.

Also, for each author's protection and ours, we want to make certain that everyone understands that there is no warranty for this free software. If the software is modified by someone else and passed on, we want its recipients to know that what they have is not the original, so that any problems introduced by others will not reflect on the original authors' reputations.

Finally, any free program is threatened constantly by software patents. We wish to avoid the danger that redistributors of a free program will individually obtain patent licenses, in effect making the program proprietary. To prevent this, we have made it clear that any patent must be licensed for everyone's free use or not licensed at all.

The precise terms and conditions for copying, distribution and modification follow.

Terms and Conditions for Copying, Distribution, and Modification

0. This License applies to any program or other work that contains a notice placed by the copyright holder saying it may be distributed under the terms of this General Public License. The "Program," below, refers to any such program or work, and a "work based on the Program" means either the Program or any derivative work under copyright law: that is to say, a work containing the Program or a portion of it, either verbatim or with modifications and/or translated into another language. (Hereinafter, translation is included without limitation in the term "modification.") Each licensee is addressed as "you."

   Activities other than copying, distribution, and modification are not covered by this License; they are outside its scope. The act of running the Program is not restricted, and the output from the Program is covered only if its contents constitute a work based on the Program (independent of having been made by running the Program). Whether that is true depends on what the Program does.

1. You may copy and distribute verbatim copies of the Program's source code as you receive it, in any medium, provided that you conspicuously and appropriately publish on each copy an appropriate copyright notice and disclaimer of warranty; keep intact all the notices that refer to this License and to the absence of any warranty; and give any other recipients of the Program a copy of this License along with the Program.

   You may charge a fee for the physical act of transferring a copy, and you may at your option offer warranty protection in exchange for a fee.

2. You may modify your copy or copies of the Program or any portion of it, thus forming a work based on the Program, and copy and distribute such modifications or work under the terms of Section 1 above, provided that you also meet all of these conditions:

   a) You must cause the modified files to carry prominent notices stating that you changed the files and the date of any change.

   b) You must cause any work that you distribute or publish, that in whole or in part contains or is derived from the Program or any part thereof, to be licensed as a whole at no charge to all third parties under the terms of this License.

   c) If the modified program normally reads commands interactively when run, you must cause it, when started running for such interactive use in the most ordinary way, to print or display an announcement including an appropriate copyright notice and a notice that there is no warranty (or else, saying that you provide a warranty) and that users may redistribute the program under these conditions, and telling the user how to view a copy of this License. (Exception: If the Program itself is interactive but does not normally print such an announcement, your work based on the Program is not required to print an announcement.)

   These requirements apply to the modified work as a whole. If identifiable sections of that work are not derived from the Program, and can be reasonably considered independent and separate works in themselves, then this License, and its terms, do not apply to those sections when you distribute them as separate works. But when you distribute the same sections as part of a whole that is a work based on the Program, the distribution of the whole must be on the terms of this License, whose permissions for other licensees extend to the entire whole, and thus to each and every part regardless of who wrote it.

   Thus, it is not the intent of this section to claim rights or contest your rights to work written entirely by you; rather, the intent is to exercise the right to control the distribution of derivative or collective works based on the Program.

   In addition, mere aggregation of another work not based on the Program with the Program (or with a work based on the Program) on a volume of a storage or distribution medium does not bring the other work under the scope of this License.

3. You may copy and distribute the Program (or a work based on it, under Section 2) in object code or executable form under the terms of Sections 1 and 2 above provided that you also do one of the following:

a) Accompany it with the complete corresponding machine-readable source code, which must be distributed under the terms of Sections 1 and 2 above on a medium customarily used for software interchange; or,

b) Accompany it with a written offer, valid for at least three years, to give any third party, for a charge no more than your cost of physically performing source distribution, a complete, machine-readable copy of the corresponding source code, to be distributed under the terms of Sections 1 and 2 above on a medium customarily used for software interchange; or,

c) Accompany it with the information you received as to the offer to distribute corresponding source code. (This alternative is allowed only for noncommercial distribution and only if you received the program in object code or executable form with such an offer, in accord with Subsection b above.)

The source code for a work means the preferred form of the work for making modifications to it. For an executable work, complete source code means all the source code for all modules it contains, plus any associated interface definition files, plus the scripts used to control compilation and installation of the executable. However, as a special exception, the source code distributed need not include anything that is normally distributed (in either source or binary form) with the major components (compiler, kernel, and so forth) of the operating system on which the executable runs, unless that component itself accompanies the executable.

If distribution of executable or object code is made by offering access to copy from a designated place, then offering equivalent access to copy the source code from the same place counts as distribution of the source code, even though third parties are not compelled to copy the source along with the object code.

4. You may not copy, modify, sublicense, or distribute the Program except as expressly provided under this License. Any attempt otherwise to copy, modify, sublicense, or distribute the Program is void, and will automatically terminate your rights under this License.

However, parties who have received copies, or rights, from you under this License will not have their licenses terminated so long as such parties remain in full compliance.

5. You are not required to accept this License, since you have not signed it. However, nothing else grants you permission to modify or distribute the Program or its derivative works. These actions are prohibited by law if you do not accept this License. Therefore, by modifying or distributing the Program (or any work based on the Program), you indicate your acceptance of this License to do so, and all its terms and conditions for copying, distributing or modifying the Program or works based on it.

6. Each time you redistribute the Program (or any work based on the Program), the recipient automatically receives a license from the original licensor to copy, distribute, or modify the Program subject to these terms and conditions. You may not impose any further restrictions on the recipients' exercise of the rights granted herein. You are not responsible for enforcing compliance by third parties to this License.

7. If, as a consequence of a court judgment or allegation of patent infringement or for any other reason (not limited to patent issues), conditions are imposed on you (whether by court order, agreement or otherwise) that contradict the conditions of this License, they do not excuse you from the conditions of this License. If you cannot distribute so as to satisfy simultaneously your obligations under this License and any other pertinent obligations, then as a consequence you may not distribute the Program at all. For example, if a patent license would not permit royalty-free redistribution of the Program by all those who receive copies directly or indirectly through you, then the only way you could satisfy both it and this License would be to refrain entirely from distribution of the Program.

If any portion of this section is held invalid or unenforceable under any particular circumstance, the balance of the section is intended to apply and the section as a whole is intended to apply in other circumstances.

It is not the purpose of this section to induce you to infringe any patents or other property right claims or to contest validity of any such claims; this section has the sole purpose of protecting the integrity of the free software distribution system, which is implemented by public license practices. Many people have made generous contributions to the wide range of software distributed through that system in reliance on consistent application of that system; it is up to the author/donor to decide if he or she is willing to distribute software through any other system and a licensee cannot impose that choice.

This section is intended to make thoroughly clear what is believed to be a consequence of the rest of this License.

8. If the distribution and/or use of the Program is restricted in certain countries either by patents or by copyrighted interfaces, the original copyright holder who places the Program under this License may add an explicit geographical distribution limitation excluding those countries, so that distribution is permitted only in or among countries not thus excluded. In such case, this License incorporates the limitation as if written in the body of this License.

9. The Free Software Foundation may publish revised and/or new versions of the General Public License from time to time. Such new versions will be similar in spirit to the present version, but may differ in detail to address new problems or concerns.

    Each version is given a distinguishing version number. If the Program specifies a version number of this License which applies to it and "any later version," you have the option of following the terms and conditions either of that version or of any later version published by the Free Software Foundation. If the Program does not specify a version number of this License, you may choose any version ever published by the Free Software Foundation.

10. If you wish to incorporate parts of the Program into other free programs whose distribution conditions are different, write to the author to ask for permission. For software which is copyrighted by the Free Software Foundation, write to the Free Software Foundation; we sometimes make exceptions for this. Our decision will be guided by the two goals of preserving the free status of all derivatives of our free software and of promoting the sharing and reuse of software generally.

No Warranty

11. BECAUSE THE PROGRAM IS LICENSED FREE OF CHARGE, THERE IS NO WARRANTY FOR THE PROGRAM, TO THE EXTENT PERMITTED BY APPLICABLE LAW. EXCEPT WHEN OTHERWISE STATED IN WRITING, THE COPYRIGHT HOLDERS AND/OR OTHER PARTIES PROVIDE THE PROGRAM "AS IS" WITHOUT WARRANTY OF ANY KIND, EITHER EXPRESSED OR IMPLIED, INCLUDING, BUT NOT LIMITED TO, THE IMPLIED WARRANTIES OF MERCHANTABILITY AND FITNESS FOR A PARTICULAR PURPOSE. THE ENTIRE RISK AS TO THE QUALITY AND PERFORMANCE OF THE PROGRAM IS WITH YOU. SHOULD THE PROGRAM PROVE DEFECTIVE, YOU ASSUME THE COST OF ALL NECESSARY SERVICING, REPAIR, OR CORRECTION.

12. IN NO EVENT UNLESS REQUIRED BY APPLICABLE LAW OR AGREED TO IN WRITING WILL ANY COPYRIGHT HOLDER, OR ANY OTHER PARTY WHO MAY MODIFY AND/OR REDISTRIBUTE THE PROGRAM AS PERMITTED ABOVE, BE LIABLE TO YOU FOR DAMAGES, INCLUDING ANY GENERAL, SPECIAL, INCIDENTAL, OR CONSEQUENTIAL DAMAGES ARISING OUT OF THE USE OR INABILITY TO USE THE PROGRAM (INCLUDING BUT NOT LIMITED TO LOSS OF DATA OR DATA BEING RENDERED INACCURATE OR LOSSES SUSTAINED BY YOU OR THIRD PARTIES OR A FAILURE OF THE PROGRAM TO OPERATE WITH ANY OTHER PROGRAMS), EVEN IF SUCH HOLDER OR OTHER PARTY HAS BEEN ADVISED OF THE POSSIBILITY OF SUCH DAMAGES.

End of Terms and Conditions

How to Apply These Terms to Your New Programs

If you develop a new program, and you want it to be of the greatest possible use to the public, the best way to achieve this is to make it free software that everyone can redistribute and change under these terms.

To do so, attach the following notices to the program. It is safest to attach them to the start of each source file to most effectively convey the exclusion of warranty; and each file should have at least the "copyright" line and a pointer to where the full notice is found:

<One line to give the program's name and a brief idea of what it does.>
Copyright (c) 19yy (name of author)
This program is free software; you can redistribute it and/or modify it under the terms of the GNU General Public License as published by the Free Software Foundation; either Version 2 of the License, or (at your option) any later version.

This program is distributed in the hope that it will be useful, but WITHOUT ANY WARRANTY; without even the implied warranty of MERCHANTABILITY or FITNESS FOR A PARTICULAR PURPOSE. See the GNU General Public License for more details.

You should have received a copy of the GNU General Public License along with this program; if not, write to the Free Software Foundation, Inc., 675 Mass Ave., Cambridge, MA 02139, USA.

Also add information on how to contact you by electronic and paper mail.

If the program is interactive, make it output a short notice like this when it starts in an interactive mode:

```
Gnomovision version 69, Copyright (c) 19yy name of author
Gnomovision comes with ABSOLUTELY NO WARRANTY; for details type
 'show w'
This is free software, and you are welcome to redistribute it under
 certain conditions; type 'show c' for details.
```

The hypothetical commands `show w` and `show c` should show the appropriate parts of the General Public License. Of course, the commands you use may be called something other than `show w` and `show c`; they could even be mouse-clicks or menu items — whatever suits your program.

You should also get your employer (if you work as a programmer) or your school, if any, to sign a "copyright disclaimer" for the program, if necessary. Here is a sample; alter the names:

Yoyodyne, Inc., hereby disclaims all copyright interest in the program "Gnomovision" (which makes passes at compilers) written by James Hacker.

(signature of Ty Coon), 1 April 1989
Ty Coon, President of Vice

This General Public License does not permit incorporating your program into proprietary programs. If your program is a subroutine library, you may consider it more useful to permit linking proprietary applications with the library. If this is what you want to do, use the GNU Library General Public License instead of this License.

Appendix B
About the CD-ROM

THE CD-ROM CONTAINS all of the book's code, as well as Version 1.2.6 of the Apache Web server, and Version 5.2.12 of the public domain Korn shell (pdKsh). A standard ORB installation that can be applied to a server is also included on the CD-ROM.

Chapter Directories

If you browse the CD-ROM, you'll notice several chapter directories. These directories contain all of the code presented in a particular chapter of the book. You can use this code instead of manually typing in the listings. If you run into problems after completing an example, you can compare your results with the version listed here. All of the files are Java source files, Java binaries, Korn shell class files, or "compiled" Korn shell classes and Korn shell scripts.

The tools Directory

The `tools` directory contains the following subdirectories: `bin`, `classes`, and `ORBserv`. These subdirectories contain both compiled example classes and the final version of the `ORBserv.sh` application with its dependency repository and client scripts.

install.sh script

Also included in the `tools` directory is an `install.sh` script. If you run the `install.sh` script, you are prompted for a root path, with `/usr/local/uso` as the default.

The install script copies everything under the `tools` directory on the CD-ROM into the directory you specify. Once completed, this directory can become your default ORBserv location, and you can add its path to the necessary environments that will run the `ORBserv.sh` program.

ORBserv.sh program

In particular, anyone running the `ORBserv.sh` program needs the following in their path:

```
/usr/local/uso/ORBserv
/usr/local/uso/ORBserv/repository
/usr/local/jdk1.1.1/bin
```

Obviously, you want to substitute your location for these particular executables, but they all must be available to the user running `ORBserv.sh`. To set these paths, you can use the following commands:

```
$>PATH=$PATH:/usr/local/uso/ORBserv:/usr/local/usoORBserv/repositor
y:/usr/local/jdk1.1.1/bin
$>export PATH
```

You can also add the preceding to the user's profile in their home directory (see Chapter 2 for a discussion on the `.profile` file).

Also, any script or program that will be a client of the `ORBserv.sh` must have the client executables within its path. If you've run the `install.sh` script on the CD-ROM, these files are located in your `install` directory under `ORBserv/client` and contain the connection manager, proxy, and supporting scripts.

As many modifications are made to the `ORBserv.sh` and related tools throughout the book, it is strongly suggested that you use a "working" directory for these edits, and keep the final version in the main `/usr/local/uso/ORBserv` directory.

Apache 1.2.6

The Apache Web server is one of the most popular HTTP servers available. It's extendible, supports CGI, and is completely free. The version included on the CD-ROM is the default distribution, and must be compiled on your system. Under the `apache` directory on the CD-ROM, you'll find the compressed, TAR file. Unpack the file as follows:

```
$> uncompress apache_1_2_6.tar.Z
```

The preceding leaves a TAR file, with which you can do the following:

```
$> tar -xvf apache_1_2_6.tar
```

You should do the preceding from a directory such as `/usr/local` or wherever you want the installation to reside. Unpacking the TAR archive creates a new directory called `apache_1.2.6` — you don't need to create a special place for the archive. Once unpacked, consult the README file for the particular build options. This compilation is quite easy on Linux.

Also, if you're using a recent distribution of Linux, you probably already have Apache running on your server. You can check with the following:

```
$> ps -aux|grep httpd
```

If you receive several processes, the server is running. Even if the server is not running, you should consult your distribution's documentation to verify whether it was bundled.

The Public Domain Korn Shell

The public domain Korn shell is a freeware version of the popular Korn shell distributed with all commercial UNIX implementations. All of the code in this book was written under the pdKsh5.2.12, which was compiled both under Linux and Solaris 2.6. Although some of the newest features of the Korn shell aren't supported (such as compound variable assignments and advanced string parsing), this version is a great implementation and is the book's overall shell of choice.

The GNU zipped file resides under the pdksh directory on the CD-ROM. Open the file with the following:

```
gzip -d pdksh-5.2.12.tar.gz
```

Once unzipped, you can unpack the TAR files as follows:

```
tar -xvf pdksh-5.2.12.tar
```

This package also needs to be compiled for your system. The README file details the instructions, but for the most part, this book has had great success running the build scripts. The configure script checks your system, determining what pdKsh can use during compilation, and the subsequent make calls build the executable. The README file illustrates this process.

Once compiled, you should move your existing KSH executable out of the way as root:

```
cp /bin/ksh /bin/ksh.orig
```

Replace it with the pdKsh version, naming it /bin/ksh. Depending on how you chose to install it, your command should look like the following:

```
cp /usr/local/bin/ksh /bin/ksh
```

It then becomes the login shell for users, and your !#/bin/ksh causes your scripts to be run under pdKsh. All of the code in the book calls /bin/ksh as its "sh-bang" — you need to have pdKsh as your shell or change the "sh-bang" to reflect the location of pdKsh.

Please note: The use of the public domain Korn shell is subject to the terms of the GNU General Public License contained on the CD-ROM and Appendix A.

INDEX

& (ampersand), 132, 182
* (asterisk), 142
@ (at sign), 76, 223
\ (backlash), 3
: (colon), 207
{} (curly brackets), 3
$ (dollar sign), 223
. (dot), 44, 84, 205, 226
/ (forward slash), 142
() (parentheses), 25
% (percent sign), 29, 335, 337
| (pipe character), 24, 182, 338
+ (plus sign), 335
# (pound sign), 29
; (semicolon), 142
[] (square brackets), 45
_ (underscore), 52, 55, 64

A

accept function, 168
access control, 48, 57-60, 62. *See also* security
   encapsulation and, 4-6
   distributed clients and, 199
   Java and, 143, 144, 145, 155
   writing classes and, 48, 57-60, 62
access.conf, 326
account.cls, 90-92
add account operation, 264-266
_addHandler method, 118, 119
_addItem function, 64, 95-96
admin object, 113-114
admin_alert method, 119

_Age variable, 64
aggregation, 80-81, 148-149
AIX, 161
_alert method, 113
algorithms, 341
aliases, 45
_alrtRcpnt method, 123, 129, 130
ampersand (&), 132, 182
Apache Web server, 325-327, 332. *See also* Web servers
APIs (Application Programming Interfaces), 16, 113, 131-134
   Java and, 141-142
   networks and, 164-165
applets, 140. *See also* Java
application(s)
   breaking apart, 234
   goals, identifying, 239-244
   Java and, 140
   menus, 323-324
   objects, exploring, 237-238
   tracking, 243
architecture, 53-63, 237-240, 243-249
Args[] array, 151
ASCII (American Standard Code for Information Interchange), 43, 338
asterisk (*), 142
at sign (@), 76, 223
Atom object, 12-13
atomization, of objects, 50
awk utility, 23, 33, 41
AWT (Abstract Window Toolkit), 150, 248

B

backlash (/), 3
backups, 9
balance data member, 155
base classes, creating, 253-263,
　　317-319
Bash shell, 19, 25, 27-29
BASIC, 1
bdf statement, 84
bg_instances reference, 214, 217, 218
black-box methods, 4
blank lines (carriage-returns), 164
boolean data type, 172, 178
Bourne shell, 19

 tag, 275
browsers
　　cookies and, 342, 343
　　Java and, 141
　　object-oriented systems and, 244
　　response objects and, 342-345
　　TCP/IP and, 163
business processes, 288

C

C programming
　　API functionality and, 16
　　CGI and, 330
　　compilers, 232
　　Java and, 139, 140, 142-143, 152,
　　　　159
　　Korn shell and, 3
　　object-oriented systems and, 232,
　　　　236
　　polymorphism and, 10
　　references in, 89
　　wrappers, 133, 134
C++ programming
　　access rights and, 59
　　API functionality and, 16
　　benefits of OOP and, 1
　　compilers, 52, 56
　　destructors and, 62
　　distributed clients and, 192, 194
　　encapsulation and, 4-5
　　function names and, 4
　　inheritance and, 98
　　Java and, 139-141, 143, 145-146,
　　　　148-150, 152, 155
　　Korn shell and, 3
　　messaging and, 115
　　object-oriented systems and, 238
　　polymorphism and, 10
　　references and, 89
　　variables and, 55
　　wrappers, 133, 134
　　writing classes and, 52, 55-56, 59
callback.log, 316
callbacks, 292-303, 308, 312-322
carriage-returns (blank lines), 164
case loop, 77
case statements, 33-34, 352, 353, 378
casting, 167
cat command, 23, 24
cat statement, 22
cat utility, 22-24, 41
catch blocks, 159
CGI (Common Gateway Interface), 244,
　　250
　　environment, understanding,
　　　　329-332
　　error scripts, 363-365

examining, 324-327
examples, 346-355
HTTP headers and, 164
objects, creating, 332-345
security and, 386-387
TCP/IP and, 163
users, 329-330
using shell objects with, 323-356
variables, 330-332, 334, 352
Web connections and, 357-388
cgi.sh, 332-333
checkDisks interface, 94
_checkDisks method, 94
_checkDiskSpace method, 129, 257
child/parent classes, 96-99. *See also* inheritance
chkUser function, 35
class(es). *See also* classes (listed by name); inheritance
   architecture of, 53-63
   base, creating, 253-263, 317-319
   basic description of, 2-4
   changing, without breaking dependencies, 57
   design of, 52
   operation, 254-255, 263-277
   programming considerations for, 63-68
   writing, 47-78
classes (listed by name). *See also* classes
   Continuum class, 11-15
   controller class, 118-120
   Customer class, 155, 158
   DataInputStream class, 150, 172
   DataOutputStream class, 150
   Energy class, 15

   Fruit class, 6-7
   Galaxy class, 14
   InputStream class, 150, 166
   msgHandler class, 114, 117-119, 121, 130
   myServer.class class, 144
   newsys class, 121
   objlist class, 115-116
   opViewDiskSpace class, 270
   opViewDiskStats class, 272
   opViewProcessTable class, 274-277
   Orange class, 7
   OrbObject class, 13-14
   OutputStream class, 150
   Person class, 153, 155
   Planetary class, 13-14
   quark class, 12
   serverFactory class, 195
   ServerSocket class, 168
   servFactory class, 130
   sfile class, 81-82
   socket class, 186-189
   sunUserver class, 262-263
   system class, 118, 120-121, 150
   System.out class, 175
   Thread class, 157
   unixServer class, 80, 99-110, 149, 245, 254, 258
   UNIXSystem class, 8
CLASSPATH environment variable, 145
client(s)
   networks and, 164-165, 173-175, 185
   nondistributed, 279-282
   object responsibilities, 295-296
   proxy, 204-210
   -server model, 141

continued

client(s) *(continued)*
   sockets, 164-165, 173-174
   strings, formatting, 297
client1.java, 167-168
client2.class, 170
Client2.java, 170, 171
_clientCall function, 294, 295-296, 314, 317-318
clientCb_clientCall method, 315
clientCb.cls, 307, 318-319
.cls files
   account.cls, 90-92
   clientCb.cls, 307, 318-319
   controller.cls, 119-120
   disk.cls, 84-85, 123-126
   _execute.Objlist.cls, 95
   msgHandler.cls, 114, 117-119
   newsys.cls, 121
   object1.cls, 312-313
   object2.cls, 313-314
   objlist.cls, 95-96, 115-116, 225-226
   opAddAccount.cls, 265-266, 386
   opDelAccount.cls, 267-269
   operation.cls, 254-255
   opReboot.cls, 269-270
   opViewDiskSpace.cls, 271
   opViewDiskStats.cls, 272, 277
   opViewLoadAvg.cls, 272, 273-274
   opViewProcessTable.cls, 274-277
   person.cls, 54, 56-57, 65, 70-77
   request.cls, 333-334, 338-339
   response.cls, 344-345
   server1.cls, 316-317, 319-320
   servFactory.cls, 104, 105-106, 108-109, 130

sfile.cls, 81-82
shellobj.cls, 129
signal.cls, 123, 129-130
socket.cls, 186-189, 198, 202
sunServer.cls, 98-99
sunUserver.cls, 262-263
system.cls, 120-121
template.cls, 72
unixServer.cls, 101-104, 123, 126-131
users.cls, 86-88
uServer.cls, 254-262
co-ords value, 12, 14
COBOL processes, 194
colon (:), 207
colors, selecting, 352
COM model, 192-193, 288
command line(s)
   arguments, 26
   debugging and, 65
   eval keyword and, 69
   I/O (Input/Output) and, 150-152
   writing classes and, 59, 65, 69
commands (listed by name)
   cat command, 23, 24
   cp command, 19
   cut command, 33, 42
   env command, 27
   finger command, 33
   hostname command, 255
   if command, 61
   java command, 227
   javac command, 145
   kill command, 327
   killserver command, 204, 218

ls command, 19, 44, 45, 81, 92
mail command, 24-25
mkfifo command, 131, 187
mv command, 19
pipeclnt command, 187
print command, 133, 182, 216
ps command, 21, 274
read command, 133, 182
remsh command, 16, 99, 100, 161, 162, 164
rsh command, 16, 99, 164
sed command, 76
sendrecv command, 187
set command, 27, 65, 68
shift command, 26
sort command, 43
sync command, 262
tail command, 359
test command, 28, 30-31
time command, 41, 42
tr command, 298
unset command, 62
uptime command, 42
user command, 42
what command, 255
while command, 31-32
xargs command, 298
ypbind command, 240-241
ypmaps command, 241
ypwhich command, 240-241
comments, 142
communication, interprocess (IPC), 131-136, 139, 141, 159, 182, 197-201
communication, object. *See also* objects

basic description of, 111-138
critical and operational events example, 122-123
demonstrating, with classes, 119-121
event handling example, 123-131
object-to-object communication, 113-114
process boundaries and, 131-133
compilers, 52, 56, 232
components
building, 232-234
connecting, 357-359
distributed, 238-239
examining, 235
runtime, 232-235, 238-239
ComputeGravitationalPull function, 14
conf directory, 326
Connection Manager, 166, 196, 202, 205
basic description of, 210-212
creating multiple connections with, 211-212
creating persistent connections with, 210-211
modifying, 310-311
connectionMgr.sh, 205, 210-211, 227
constructors, 86, 97
overloaded, 56
Planetary class and, 13
Universe object and, 15
writing classes and, 54-56
containment, 148-149
Continuum class, 11-15
Continuum object, 14
Continuum structure, 10-15

controller class, 118–120
controller.cls, 119–120
cookies, 342, 343
coprocesses, 132–133
CORBA (Common ORB Architecture), 104, 176, 192–195, 246, 288
cp command, 19
cpsh.sh, 133
CPUs (central processing units), 42, 243, 246
Create Account menu option, 279
_createAccount function, 62, 295–296
_createDiskObjects method, 256, 257
createInstance function, 213–214, 216, 223
crontab, 241
curly brackets ({}), 3
custom.cgi, 354–355
Customer class, 155, 158
Customer1.java, 155, 156–157
Customer.java, 157–159
custom.html, 350–355
cut command, 33, 42

D

daemons, 327
data clashing, 63–64
data member(s)
    accessing, 48–49
    balance data member, 155
    distributed clients and, 199
    Java and, 143
    messaging and, 123, 126
    prefixing of, with an underscore character, 52
    properties and, 58–60
    strName data member, 143
    _this data member, 124, 126, 129, 334
    writing classes and, 48–49, 52, 58–60
data streams, 141
database(s), 235, 324
    polymorphism and, 8–9
    setting user names in, 58
    SQL lookups and, 57
    storing information for, 89
DataInputStream class, 150, 172
DataInputStream object, 175, 179
DataOutputStream class, 150
DBMSs (database management systems), 235
DCAC/MRM system, 192
DCOM model, 192–193
debugging, 20–21, 359. *See also* errors
    output, 66–68
    writing classes and, 65–68
default delimiters, 24
definition files, 277–278
Delete Account menu option, 280
delete account operation, 266–269, 280
_Delete function, 72
delete keyword, 62
_delete method, 49, 199
demo scripts, 228–230, 320–322
demo2.sh, 229–230
demo.sh, 228–229, 320–322
dependencies, 277
descriptors
    basic description of, 20–21
    redirecting, 20

STDERR (standard error) file
descriptor, 20, 65
STDIN (standard input) file
descriptor, 20–21, 23–25, 133,
140, 150–152, 165, 173–175,
178–179, 182, 187, 298, 335
STDOUT (standard output) file
descriptor, 20, 22, 25, 57, 60, 61,
92, 133, 140, 150–152, 165,
173–174, 175, 179, 182, 325
destructor(s)
functions, Planetary class and, 13
writing classes and, 62–63
devgate.connections, 211–212
directories
loading objects and, 293
path names and, 44
public, 44
disconnect messages, 187
disk(s)
objects, 84–85
space, tracking, 241–242
space, viewing, 270–271
statistics, viewing, 61, 272, 280, 283
disk_alert event, 129
diskalert.sh, 130–131
disk.cls, 84–85, 123–126
_diskStats variable, 61
Display object, 11
distributed clients, 191–230, 278–285
DNS (Domain Name Service), 175
doBottomHalf function, 377
doCallBack function, 298, 299, 303
doConnectError function, 377
doGreyTable function, 377
dollar sign ($), 223
DOS (Disk Operating System), 20

dot (.), 44, 84, 205, 226
doTopHalf function, 376–377
Draw function, 12, 15
_dumpState function, 59
dynamic binding, 9–10

E

e-mail, 162, 324
emp.cgi, 347–348
encapsulation, 96, 235, 238, 248
basic description of, 4–6
access rights and, 4–5
interface design and, 5–6
Java and, 145, 159
of networks, with components,
161–190
polymorphism and, 10
writing classes and, 58–59
END_OF_MENU, 22
END_OF_SCRIPT, 23
END_OF_TEXT, 22
Energy class, 15
env command, 27
environment variables
CLASSPATH environment variable,
145
$EVENTHANDLER environment
variable, 118, 119–120
MANPATH environment variable, 44,
45
error(s). *See also* debugging; exceptions
callback, 300
file descriptors and, 20–21
GPFs (General Protection Faults), 59
operation classes and, 267

continued

error(s) *(continued)*
  retrieving, 21
  scripts, 363-365
  standard, file descriptor for, 20, 65
  templates, 361-363
  variable clashing and, 64
  Web connections and, 358
  writing classes and, 55-56, 61, 64
  "X: Bad number" message, 55
errorlog.txt, 65
errors.txt, 20-21
err.tmpl, 362
/etc/passwd file, 60-61, 84-86, 89, 240-241
euid, 44
eval keyword, 52, 68-69
event(s)
  basic description of, 111-115, 122-131
  -driven programming, 111-112
  handling, 123-131
$EVENTHANDLER environment variable, 118, 119-120
events.sh, 115
example.sh, 93-94
example1.sh, 122-123, 134
example2.sh, 107-108
example3.sh, 135-136
exceptions, 160-161. *See also* errors
_execute method, 95, 175, 248-249, 257, 264-265, 267, 269-273, 280, 357
_execute.Objlist.cls, 95
exiting shell processes, 49
extends keyword, 155

F

-f option, 31, 359
features, providing, 240
_fields variable, 60
FIFO (First In First Out), 132, 134, 166, 173, 186-189, 194, 196-201, 217
file descriptors
  basic description of, 20-21
  redirecting, 20
  STDERR (standard error) file descriptor, 20, 65
  STDIN (standard input) file descriptor, 20-21, 23-25, 133, 140, 150-152, 165, 173-175, 178-179, 182, 187, 298, 335
  STDOUT (standard output) file descriptor, 20, 22, 25, 57, 60, 61, 92, 133, 140, 150-152, 165, 173-174, 175, 179, 182, 325
file extensions
  .bak, 28
  .cgi, 325
  .pid, 327
filestuff variable, 92
file.txt, 24
finger command, 33
flat files, 58, 89
fonts, selecting, 352
foo variable, 68
foobar variable, 68-69
for each loops, 23, 257-258
for loops, 32-33, 257-258
for statement, 33
forms, 328-329, 335, 338, 348-355. *See also* CGI (Common Gateway Interface)

gateway applications and, 350-355
main, in SMU applications, 369-375
questionnaires, 348-350
forward slash (/), 142
forwardMethodArgs function, 214, 216, 303
_fromStream method, 89
Fruit class, 6-7
FTP (File Transfer Protocol), 163-164, 327
functional classes, 81-96
functionality, 4, 16
  encapsulation and, 5
  inheritance and, 6-7
  object-oriented systems and, 236, 248
  polymorphism and, 10
  Web connections and, 378
  writing classes and, 50, 51
functions. *See also* functions (listed by name)
  basic description of, 34-35
  objects as collections of, 49
functions (listed by name). *See also* functions
  accept function, 168
  _addItem function, 64, 95-96
  chkUser function, 35
  _clientCall function, 294, 295-296, 314, 317-318
  ComputeGravitationalPull function, 14
  _createAccount function, 62, 295-296
  createInstance function, 213-214, 216, 223

_Delete function, 72
doBottomHalf function, 377
doCallBack function, 298, 299, 303
doConnectError function, 377
doGreyTable function, 377
doTopHalf function, 376-377
Draw function, 12, 15
_dumpState function, 59
forwardMethodArgs function, 214, 216, 303
getMessage function, 145
_getName function, 55, 57
_getUserFields function, 60-61
handleConnection function, 178-179
IncrememntCircularMotion function, 13
InsertUser function, 4
invoke function, 223-224
LaunchXwindow function, 7
main function, 144, 147-148
Move function, 12, 13, 14
_MyFunction function, 76
_parseURLenc function, 335, 336-341
_person function, 47
_printit function, 69, 170, 172
print_message function, 2
printMessage function, 145
RebootSystem function, 7
recursive functions, 14
_releaseObjects function, 217
restore function, 28
setMoney function, 147
_setName function, 58
Shutdown function, 7-8
squirtJuice function, 7

continued

functions (listed by name) *(continued)*
  _strName function, 58, 57, 59
  takeMoney function, 147
  _theirFunction function, 76
  virtual function, 297-298
  _yourFunction function, 76
function.sh, 69

G

Galaxy class, 14
garbage collection, 49, 140
gateway applications, 350-355
gecos field, 86
GET method, 55, 57, 332, 335-341, 346, 365
getargs.java, 151-152
_getClientMessage method, 315-316
_getDiskUsage method, 51, 52, 61, 101, 256-257, 271, 272
_getFields method, 61, 86, 88-89, 113, 290, 294, 295-296
get.html, 346
_getKbAvail method, 101, 104, 246
_getLastItem method, 95-96
_getLoad method, 51, 258
getMessage function, 145
_getMessage method, 312, 313-314, 315
_getName function, 55, 57
_getOwner method, 90
_getPercentUsed method, 104, 113
_getReference method, 90
_getState method, 123, 124, 126, 129, 246, 253
_getUserFields function, 60-61
_getUsers method, 51, 255

_getWindow method, 51, 262
GIDs (group IDs), 85
GODZILLA_HOME variable, 45
GPFs (General Protection Faults), 59. *See also* errors
grep utility, 23, 35
GUI (graphical user interface), 114, 123, 131, 386-387
  CGI and, 324
  Java and, 140, 150
  object-oriented systems and, 239, 248
  operation classes and, 267

H

handleConnection function, 178-179
handshaking routines, 164
has-a relationships, 51-52
headers, 163, 164, 247, 343
"Hello World!," 144-145, 325
Hello.class, 145
Hello.java, 144-145
hexadecimal codes, 337-338, 341
high_load event, 129
host.inf, 105-106, 254
hostname command, 255
hosts, rebooting, 248-249
HP-UX, 161, 195
HTML (HyperText Markup Language), 324, 325
  error templates, 361-363
  forms, 328-329, 335, 338, 348-350
  interfaces, creating, 359-360
  object-oriented systems and, 244, 250

operation classes and, 264, 274-277
request objects and, 335, 338
security and, 386-387
TCP/IP and, 163
Web connections and, 357-388
HTTP (HyperText Transfer Protocol)
    basic description of, 327-329
    daemons, 327
    headers, 163, 164, 247, 343
    object-oriented systems and, 250
    ports and, 176
    requests, 328, 332
    responses, 328, 342-345, 378
    TCP/IP and, 163
    variables, 332, 333
human.java, 146-148
Hungarian notation, 55

I

I/O (Input/Output), 150-152
identifiers, built-in, 25-27
IDL (Interface Definition Language), 194, 195
if command, 61
if-then evaluations, 29-31
IFS (Internal Field Separator) variable, 24, 207, 216, 217, 298, 303, 338
IIOP (Internet InterORB Protocol), 192, 238
inAr array, 206
IncrememntCircularMotion function, 13
index.html, 327, 328, 359-361
inetd.conf, 161-162
information.html, 327
inheritance, 80-81, 96-99

basic description of, 6-8, 50
Java and, 152-153, 155-157
writing classes and, 50, 51
initialization, 213
inout.java, 150-151
InputStream class, 150, 166
InputStream object, 166
InsertUser function, 4
install script, 53
installing tools, 53
instance(s)
    creating, 93-94, 213-214
    distributed clients and, 201
    processes, modifying, 307-310
    scripts, 379
instantiation, 84, 100, 101
    basic description of, 2
    Java and, 146-148
    Universe object and, 15-16
    writing classes and, 59, 63
interface(s), 239, 243-244, 250. *See also*
        interfaces (listed by name)
    changing the code behind, 288-289
    creating HTML, 359-360
    defining, 203
    design, encapsulation and, 5-6
    distributed clients and, 193-194, 203, 218-222, 225-226
    facilitating scalability with, 239
    Java and, 152-155, 159-160
    objects, 49-52, 376-387
    registering, with servers, 225-226
    requesting, 203
    reusable, 58
    unknown, 218-222

interfaces (listed by name). *See also* interfaces
  checkDisks interface, 94
  PersonInfo interface, 153-154
  Reboot interface, 7
  Runnable interface, 157, 158
  Shutdown() interface, 8
  takeMoney interface, 146-148
  unixServer interface, 50-51, 153, 195, 245, 248
Internet, 141, 236, 246. *See also* networks; World Wide Web
interprocess communication (IPC), 131-136, 139, 141, 159, 182, 197-201
invoke function, 223-224
IOException, 159-160
IP IP (Internet Protocol) addresses, 255
IPC (interprocess communication), 131-136, 139, 141, 159, 182, 197-201
IPX protocol, 163
is-a relationships, 51-52
_ItemList array, 64

J

Java, 16, 55, 386-387
  AWT (Abstract Window Toolkit), 150, 248
  binary executables, checking for, 364
  choosing, 140-141
  Database Connectivity (JDBC), 235
  Development Kit (JDK), 144-146, 160
  distributed clients and, 192, 194, 196, 204
  getting started with, 144-146
  input/output and, 150-152
  language features, 152-159
  networks and, 164-169, 173-175, 179, 184, 186-188
  object-oriented systems and, 142-149, 233, 235, 238, 245-246, 248
  operation classes and, 264
  packages, 159-160, 164
  syntax, 142-149
  using, from the shell, 139-160
  VM (Virtual Machine), 168
java command, 227
javac command, 145
java.net package, 164
JDBC (Java Database Connectivity), 235
JDK (Java Development Kit), 144-146, 160

K

keywords
  delete keyword, 62
  eval keyword, 52, 68-69
  extends keyword, 155
  private keyword, 143
  public keyword, 143
  super keyword, 155
kill command, 327
killserver command, 204, 218
Korn shell, 3, 193, 194, 250. *See also* KSOP (Korn Shell Object Protocol)
  basic description of, 19

building a model using, 10–16
callbacks and, 299
concepts, 20–29
CORBA objects and, 193
destructors and, 62
environment factors, 43–45
inheritance and, 96–99
object lists and, 94
parameter substitution and, 27–29
polymorphism and, 10
programming concepts, 41–43
programming examples, 35–41
as a user and programming
    environment, 19–46
.kshrc file, 45
KSOP (Korn Shell Object Protocol), 193,
    199–204, 206
    basic description of, 202–204
    callbacks and, 294–303
    .def files and, 319–320
    modifying, 296–297
    modifying the Connection Manager
        and, 310–311
    object release, 216–217
    one-way implementation and,
        290–292
    ORB and, 214–223
    proxy.sh and, 206–207
    strings, 318
    updating, 288

L

last-modification time, 81
LaunchXwindow function, 7
Linux, 35, 86, 100, 251

CGI and, 353–354
Java and, 140
_list array, 115
<List> variable, 32–33
load average operation, 272–274
localObject object, 310
log files, 242, 324
    debugging and, 65
    flushing, 63
    rotating, 63
    writing classes and, 61, 63, 65
login IDs, 280
loop(s)
    case loops, 77
    creating, 214–215
    distributed clients and, 207, 213,
        214–215
    for loops, 32–33, 257–258
    infinite, 134
    Java and, 151, 152
    named pipes and, 134
    networks and, 172, 178–179, 187
    parsing files through, 76
    request objects and, 336–337
    while loops, 23, 31–32, 167, 171–172
    writing classes and, 76, 77
ls command, 19, 44, 45, 81, 92

M

Macintosh, 141
mail command, 24–25
main function, 144, 147–148
MANPATH environment variable, 44, 45
memory
    allocation, 146

continued

414 Index

memory *(continued)*
  destructors and, 62–63
  exiting shell processes and, 49
  Java and, 140, 146, 149
  leaks, 146
  messaging and, 133
  object instances in, 149
  releasing, back to the operating system, 49
Message Queues, 133, 134
method(s). *See also* methods (listed by name)
  invocation of, 200, 203–204, 214, 216
  prefixing, with an underscore character, 52
methods (listed by name). *See also* method
  _addHandler method, 118, 119
  admin_alert method, 119
  _alert method, 113
  _alrtRcpnt method, 123, 129, 130
  _checkDisks method, 94
  _checkDiskSpace method, 129, 257
  clientCb_clientCall method, 315
  _createDiskObjects method, 256, 257
  _delete method, 49, 199
  _execute method, 95, 175, 248–249, 257, 264–265, 267, 269–273, 280, 357
  _fromStream method, 89
  GET method, 55, 57, 332, 335–341, 346, 365
  _getClientMessage method, 315–316
  _getDiskUsage method, 51, 52, 61, 101, 256–257, 271, 272
  _getFields method, 61, 86, 88–89, 113, 290, 294, 295–296
  _getKbAvail method, 101, 104, 246
  _getLastItem method, 95–96
  _getLoad method, 51, 258
  _getMessage method, 312, 313–314, 315
  _getOwner method, 90
  _getPercentUsed method, 104, 113
  _getReference method, 90
  _getState method, 123, 124, 126, 129, 246, 253
  _getUsers method, 51, 255
  _getWindow method, 51, 262
  opAddAccount_execute method, 290–292
  opDelAccount method, 264
  _opReboot() method, 269
  _parseGetPost method, 334–336
  POST method, 332, 335–341, 353, 365
  _printHeader method, 343
  readLine method, 172
  _reboot method, 98, 262
  _redirection method, 343
  _release method, 199, 217, 204, 208–211, 283, 303
  _removeItem method, 115
  _removeLastItem method, 95–96, 115
  run method, 159, 170, 175, 178
  _sendrecv method, 205, 227
  set method, 54, 55, 57, 58
  _setCookie method, 343–344
  _setHeader method, 344
  _setOwner method, 90
  shcc_delete method, 63

Index   415

_ShowDiskUsage method, 101, 129
_signUpSnazzyGuard method, 238
_strFields method, 294
_toStream method, 89
unixServer_reboot method, 242
uServer_getLoadAvg method, 272-273
middleware, 243-245
mkfifo command, 131, 187
Move function, 12, 13, 14
msgHandler class, 114, 117-119, 121, 130
msgHandler.cls, 114, 117-119
multithreading, 139, 141, 157-159
mv command, 19
MVS machines, 141, 161
myfile.txt, 22
_MyFunction function, 76
MyObject object, 4
MyPerson object, 63-64
myServer object, 192
myServer.class class, 144
myuser ID, 88
myvar variable, 28

N

_Name variable, 64
named pipes, 131-132, 134-136, 141, 245, 246. *See also* pipes
nested operations, 142-143
Netscape Enterprise Server, 327
Netscape Navigator browser, 342
networks
 distributed clients and, 191-230
 encapsulation of, with components, 161-190

interfaces and, 50
Java and, 141
object-oriented systems and, 50, 247-248
socket classes and, 186-189
understanding, 162-166
newline (\n) character, 23, 172
newname parameter, 143
newRef variable, 90
newsys class, 121
newsys.cls, 121
NIS, 4, 240-241
nLoad attribute, 51
Novell, 163
_nTotalDevs string, 255
_NUsers attribute, 51

O

object(s). *See also* objects (listed by name)
 basic description of, 49
 callbacks, 292-303, 308, 312-322
 definition files, 277-278
 design of, 52
 lists, 94-96
 releasing, 204
 requests, 333-341
 responses, 342-345
 two-way, 292
object communication. *See also* objects
 basic description of, 111-138
 critical and operational events example, 122-123
 demonstrating, with classes, 119-121
 event handling example, 123-131

continued

416 Index

object communication *(continued)*
   object-to-object communication, 113–114
   process boundaries and, 131–133
object instance(s)
   creating, 93–94, 213–214
   distributed clients and, 201
   processes, modifying, 307–310
   scripts, 379
Object Repository, 319–320
Object Request Broker (ORB), 16, 104–105
   callbacks and, 293, 294–297, 300
   creating, 213–225
   distributed clients and, 192–196, 199–201, 203–212, 217–218
   examples, 226–230
   Java and, 140
   modifying the Connection Manager and, 310–311
   modifying instance processes and, 307–308
   named pipes and, 132
   networks and, 166, 175, 185
   object-oriented systems and, 238, 241, 244–246, 247–249, 297, 300, 307–308, 310–311
   process, examining, 213–214
   registering interfaces with, 225–226
   repository, deploying objects in, 277–278
   Web connections and, 357, 359, 386
object1 object, 312–313, 314
object1.cls, 312–313
object2 object, 313–314
object2.cls, 313–314
ObjectID object, 69
ObjectId variable, 124
OBJECT_MAYBE_RELEASED message, 217
object-oriented systems
   building components for, 232–234
   designing, 231–252
   goals of, 231–239
   modifying, 287–293
   rethinking, 287–322
OBJECT_RELEASED message, 217
objects (listed by name). *See also* objects
   admin object, 113–114
   Atom object, 12–13
   Continuum object, 14
   DataInputStream object, 175, 179
   Display object, 11
   InputStream object, 166
   localObject object, 310
   MyObject object, 4
   MyPerson object, 63–64
   myServer object, 192
   object1 object, 312–313, 314
   object2 object, 313–314
   ObjectID object, 69
   opViewProcessTable object, 376
   OutputStream object, 170
   PrintStream object, 170, 175
   SnazzGuard object, 237–239
   sunServer object, 105, 202
   Universe object, 15–16
   unixServer object, 80, 192, 195, 202, 244
objlist class, 115–116
objlist instances, 108

objlist.cls, 95–96, 115–116, 225–226
ODBC (Open Database Connectivity), 235
opAddAccount.cls, 265–266, 386
opAddAccount_execute method, 290–292
opDelAccount method, 264
opDelAccount.cls, 267–269
opDemoDisk.sh, 283–285
opDemo.sh, 278–282
operation classes, 254–255, 263–277
operation.cls, 254–255
_opReboot() method, 269
opReboot.cls, 269–270
optimization, 42–43
opViewDiskSpace class, 270
opViewDiskSpace.cls, 271
opViewDiskStats class, 272
opViewDiskStats.cls, 272, 277
opViewLoadAvg.cls, 272, 273–274
opViewProcessTable class, 274–277
opViewProcessTable object, 376
opViewProcessTable.cls, 274–277
or operator, 32
Orange class, 7
ORB (Object Request Broker), 16, 104–105
  callbacks and, 293, 294–297, 300
  creating, 213–225
  distributed clients and, 192–196, 199–201, 203–212, 217–218
  examples, 226–230
  Java and, 140
  modifying the Connection Manager and, 310–311
  modifying instance processes and, 307–308
  named pipes and, 132
  networks and, 166, 175, 185
  object-oriented systems and, 238, 241, 244–246, 247–249, 297, 300, 307–308, 310–311
  process, examining, 213–214
  registering interfaces with, 225–226
  repository, deploying objects in, 277–278
  Web connections and, 357, 359, 386
OrbObject class, 13–14
ORBserv, 201, 202, 204, 277. *See also* ORBserv.sh
ORBserv.sh, 213–228, 246, 248, 277, 283, 293, 300, 303–307, 320–322, 358, 379. *See also* ORBserv
OutputStream class, 150
OutputStream object, 170
ownership, 55

P

-p option, 133, 182, 216
packages, 159–160
parameter(s), 86, 97, 245
  distributed clients and, 193, 199, 224
  Java and, 143
  messaging and, 118–119
  networks and, 166, 178
  passing, 35, 56
  substitution, 27–29
  writing classes and, 48, 55–56, 64, 65

parentheses, 25
_parseGetPost method, 334–336
_parseURLenc function, 335, 336–341
passwords, 58, 240, 243. *See also* security
PATH environment variable, 44–45, 53, 204, 226–227, 248, 278, 283, 369
path names, 44, 84
percent sign (%), 29, 335, 337
performance, evaluating, 42
Perl, 1, 139
   CGI and, 324, 329, 330
   interpreters, writing to, 22–23
   object-oriented systems and, 233, 250
Person class, 153, 155
_person function, 47
Person1.java, 153–155
person.cls, 54, 56–57, 65, 70–77
person.def, 225
PersonInfo interface, 153–154
PersonInfo.java, 153–154
person.java, 155–156
PIDs (process IDs), 186, 213, 327
pipe(s)
   basic description of, 24–25, 131
   distributed clients and, 194–195, 197, 200–202, 218
   messaging and, 131–132, 134–136
   named, 131–132, 134–136, 141, 245, 246
   networks and, 165–166, 173, 186
   object-oriented systems and, 234, 245–246
   optimization and, 43
   request objects and, 338

   synchronous, 206
pipe character (|), 24, 182, 338
pipeclnt command, 187
pipeclnt.class, 227
pipeclnt.java, 176–177
pipeserv.java, 180–181, 213
pipe.sh, 134, 136
Planetary class, 13–14
plus sign (+), 335
pointers, 140, 148, 149
polymorphism
   access functions and, 57
   basic description of, 8–19, 50–51
   dynamic binding and, 9–10
   system backups and, 9
   writing classes and, 50–51, 57
portability, 140–141
ports, 163, 175, 178, 247
POST method, 332, 335–341, 353, 365
post.html, 346–348
pound sign (#), 29
print command, 133, 182, 216
print statement, 197
_printHeader method, 343
_printit function, 69, 170, 172
print_message function, 2
printMessage function, 145
PrintStream object, 170, 175
private keyword, 143
process(es)
   boundaries, 131–133
   destructors and, 62–63
   IDs (PIDs), 186, 213, 327
   representing, 59
   tables, viewing, 274–277
   terminating, 186

processes.txt, 21
.profile file, 27, 43, 44
prog.java, 147–149
properties, 58–60
proxy servers, 58, 104–105, 195–210, 227–230. *See also* proxy.sh
proxy.sh, 199–210, 227–230, 293–303, 310–311. *See also* proxy servers
ps command, 21, 274
public keyword, 143

Q

quark class, 12
QUERY_STRING variable, 335
questionnaire.cgi, 349–350
questionnaires, 348–350
questions.html, 348–350

R

$RANDOM variable, 59
rcp, 164
read command, 133, 182
read statement, 197, 335–336
readability, 55
readLine method, 172
README files, 53, 204, 226, 325
read-only properties, 81
Reboot interface, 7
_reboot method, 98, 262
RebootSystem function, 7
rectangle objects, 55–56
recursive functions, 14
redirection

basic description of, 21–24
optimization and, 43
using pipes for, 24–25
_redirection method, 343
references, 80–81, 88–94, 148–149
regular expressions, 76
_release method, 199, 217, 204, 208–211, 283, 303
_releaseObjects function, 217
_removeItem method, 115
_removeLastItem method, 95–96, 115
remsh command, 16, 99, 100, 161, 162, 164
request brokers, 58
request objects, 333–341
request.cls, 333–334, 338–339
required services, 243–244
resolution
    Display object and, 11
    multiple levels of, 11, 12
response objects, 342–345
response.cls, 344–345
restore function, 28
result variable, 224
.rhosts file, 99–100
root users, 44
rsh command, 16, 99, 164
run method, 159, 170, 175, 178
Runnable interface, 157, 158
runtime integration, advantages of, 289
r-utilties, 99–104, 164, 195

S

scalability, 239
scale constant, 12

security. *See also* access control
    distributed clients and, 199
    Java and, 143, 144, 145
    object-oriented systems and, 243
    passwords, 58, 240, 243
    Web connections and, 386–387
    writing classes and, 48, 57–60, 62
sed command, 76
<selection> variable, 34
semaphores, 133
semicolon (;), 142
sendrecv command, 187
_sendrecv method, 205, 227
serialization, 126
server(s), 50, 240–245, 250. *See also* Web servers
    component, creating, 314–317
    configuring, 361, 365–369
    deleting, 365–367
    distributed clients and, 194–195, 203, 225–226
    facades, 245
    networks and, 171–179, 183–184, 186
    object responsibilities, 295
    objects, creating, 94–96
    processes, terminating, 186
    rebooting, 242–243, 269–270
    registering interfaces with, 225–226
    sockets, 164–165, 168
    strings, formatting, 297
    tracking disk space and, 241–242
server1.cls, 316–317, 319–320
server1.java, 168–169
server2.java, 170, 172–173
serverFactory class, 195
server.list, 366
ServerSocket class, 168
servFactory class, 130
servFactory.cls, 104, 105–106, 108–109, 130
set command, 27, 65, 68
set method, 54, 55, 57, 58
_setCookie method, 343–344
_setHeader method, 344
setMoney function, 147
_setName function, 58
_setOwner method, 90
sfile class, 81–82
sfile.cls, 81–82
.sh files
    cgi.sh, 332–333
    connectionMgr.sh, 205, 210–211, 227
    cpsh.sh, 133
    demo2.sh, 229–230
    demo.sh, 228–229, 320–322
    diskalert.sh, 130–131
    events.sh, 115
    example.sh, 93–94
    example1.sh, 122–123, 134
    example2.sh, 107–108
    example3.sh, 135–136
    function.sh, 69
    opDemoDisk.sh, 283–285
    opDemo.sh, 278–282
    ORBserv.sh, 213–228, 246, 248, 277, 283, 293, 300, 303–307, 320–322, 358, 379
    pipe.sh, 134, 136
    proxy.sh, 199–210, 227–230, 293–303, 310–311
    smuErr.sh, 363–365

smuORBverify.sh, 364
test1.sh, 182, 183-184
test2.sh, 184-185
shcc script, 3, 10, 53-65, 68-77, 332-333
    converter program, 73-76
    getting started with, 52-53
    inheritance and, 97
shcc_delete method, 63
shellobj.cls, 129
shift command, 26
_ShowDiskUsage method, 101, 129
Shutdown function, 7-8
Shutdown() interface, 8
signal.cls, 123, 129-130
_signUpSnazzyGuard method, 238
size arrays, 12
Slackware, 86
sleep statement, 197
SMU (System Management Utility), 240-244, 246, 248
    one-way implementation and, 290-292
    security and, 386-387
    Web connections and, 357-387
smu_action.cgi, 250
smuAddServer.cgi, 367-368
smuDelServer.cgi, 366-367
smuErr.sh, 363-365
smuMain.cgi, 370-376, 379
smuORB.cgi, 379-386
smuORBverify.sh, 364
smuTemplTop.tmpl, 362-363
SnazzGuard, 237-239, 288-293
SnazzGuard object, 237-239
socket(s)

API, 164-165
    distributed clients and, 215, 218, 227
    interface design and, 5-6
    Java and, 141, 142, 151, 158
    networks and, 164-182
    object-oriented systems and, 245, 246
    TCP/IP and, 163
    using, 166-173
socket class, 186-189
socket command, 173-182
socket.cls, 186-189, 198, 202
Solaris, 9, 43-45, 161, 262-263
    distributed clients and, 195
    pipes and, 24
    remote servers running on, 105
    sunServer.cls and, 98-99
sort command, 43
SQL (Structured Query Language), 22, 57
square brackets ([]), 45
squirtJuice function, 7
statistics, viewing, 61, 272, 280, 283
STDERR (standard error) file descriptor, 20, 65
STDIN (standard input) file descriptor, 20-21, 23-25, 133, 140, 150-152, 165, 173-175, 178-179, 182, 187, 298, 335
STDOUT (standard output) file descriptor, 20, 22, 25, 57, 60, 61, 92, 133, 140, 150-152, 165, 173-174, 175, 179, 182, 325
_strArguments string, 223
_strDevices[x] attribute, 51
_strFields method, 294

string(s)
    data type, 3, 145
    formatting, 297
    space-separated, 23
    testing, 29-30
    URL-encoded, 335-336, 341
strName data member, 143
_strName function, 58, 57, 59
_strName variable, 47
sunServer object, 105, 202
sunServer.cls, 98-99
sunUserver class, 262-263
sunUserver.cls, 262-263
super keyword, 155
symbols
    & (ampersand), 132, 182
    * (asterisk), 142
    @ (at sign), 76, 223
    \ (backlash), 3
    : (colon), 207
    { } (curly brackets), 3
    $ (dollar sign), 223
    . (dot), 44, 84, 205, 226
    / (forward slash), 142
    () (parentheses), 25
    % (percent sign), 29, 335, 337
    | (pipe character), 24, 182, 338
    + (plus sign), 335
    # (pound sign), 29
    ; (semicolon), 142
    [ ] (square brackets), 45
    _ (underscore), 52, 55, 64
sync command, 262
system backups, 9
system class, 118, 120-121, 150

System Management Utility (SMU), 240-244, 246, 248
    one-way implementation and, 290-292
    security and, 386-387
    Web connections and, 357-387
system.cls, 120-121
System.out class, 175

T

tab characters, 23
tail command, 359
takeMoney function, 147
takeMoney interface, 146-148
TCP (Transmission Control Protocol), 164, 185
TCP/IP (Transmission Control Protocol/Internet Protocol), 163-164, 246, 247
telnet, 111, 175
    sockets and, 164, 169
    TCP/IP and, 163
tempArray array, 217
template.cls, 72
templates, 72, 361-363
test command, 28, 30-31
test1.sh, 182, 183-184
test2.sh, 184-185
test.cgi, 330-332
testing
    CGI environments, 358-359
    consolidating, 42
    strings, 29-30
    variables, 27-28, 56

text.txt, 21
_theirFunction function, 76
_this data member, 124, 126, 129, 334
Thrd.java, 157-159
Thread class, 157
threads, 157-159
Thread.start() constructor, 157
time, last-modification, 81
time command, 41, 42
_toStream method, 89
tr command, 298
try blocks, 159, 178

U

UDP (User Datagram Protocol), 164
UIDs (user IDs), 35, 44, 85, 265
underscore (_), 52, 55, 64
UniqueInstanceIdentifier argument, 201
Universe object, 15-16
unixServer class, 80, 99-110, 149, 245, 254, 258
unixServer interface, 50-51, 153, 195, 245, 248
unixServer object, 80, 192, 195, 202, 244
unixServer.cls, 101-104, 123, 126-131
unixServer_reboot method, 242
UNIXSystem class, 8
"Unknown interface" message, 218-222
unset command, 62
uptime command, 42
URLs (Uniform Resource locators), 141, 162
    basic description of, 325

-encoded strings, 335-336, 341
HTTP and, 329
request objects and, 335-336, 338, 341
response objects and, 342, 343
user command, 42
user IDs (UIDs), 35, 44, 85, 265
user management, 240-241
user names, setting, 58
users.cls, 86-88
uServer.cls, 254-262
uServer_getLoadAvg method, 272-273
util variable, 352
util_info variable, 353

V

$var value, 23
<var> variable, 32, 34
variable(s). *See also* variables (listed by name)
    built-in, 25-27
    casting, 167
    CGI, 330-332, 334, 352
    data clashing and, 63-64
    HTTP, 332, 333
    names, 55
    scope, 63-64
    testing, 27-28, 56
    writing classes and, 55-56, 58, 63-64
variables (listed by name). *See also* variables
    _Age variable, 64
    CLASSPATH variable, 145

continued

variables (listed by name) *(continued)*
  _diskStats variable, 61
  _fields variable, 60
  filestuff variable, 92
  foo variable, 68
  foobar variable, 68–69
  GODZILLA_HOME variable, 45
  IFS (Internal Field Separator)
    variable, 24, 207, 216, 217, 298,
    303, 338
  <List> variable, 32–33
  MANPATH variable, 44, 45
  myvar variable, 28
  _Name variable, 64
  newRef variable, 90
  ObjectId variable, 124
  PATH variable, 44–45, 53, 204,
    226–227, 248, 278, 283, 369
  QUERY_STRING variable, 335
  $RANDOM variable, 59
  result variable, 224
  <selection> variable, 34
  _strName variable, 47
  util variable, 352
  util_info variable, 353
  <var> variable, 32, 34
VAX machines, 161, 194
vendor.java, 147
VI editor, 45
virtual function, 297–298
virtual ports, 163. *See also* ports
Visual C++ for Windows (Microsoft),
  114
VM (Java Virtual Machine), 168

W

Web browsers
  cookies and, 342, 343
  Java and, 141
  object-oriented systems and, 244
  response objects and, 342–345
  TCP/IP and, 163
Web servers. *See also* servers; World
  Wide Web
  Apache Web server, 325–327, 332
  CGI and, 325–327
  configuring, 325–327
  forms and, 328–329
what command, 255
while command, 31–32
while loops, 23, 31–32, 167, 171–172
while read loops, 23
while statements, 143
white space, 23
widgets, 131
Win32 code, 55, 238
Windows NT (Microsoft), 141, 195
words.txt, 21–22, 23
World Wide Web. *See also* Internet; Web
  servers
  -based applications, 242–244
  connecting from, 357–388
  system backups and, 9
wrappers, 133–134, 269
write statement, 197

X

X-Window system, 45, 136, 262
xargs command, 298

Y

Yellow Pages, 240
_yourFunction function, 76

ypbind command, 240–241
ypmaps command, 241
ypwhich command, 240–241

IDG BOOKS WORLDWIDE, INC. END-USER LICENSE AGREEMENT

This agreement does not apply to every program on the CD-ROM. Please consult Appendix B for details.

READ THIS. You should carefully read these terms and conditions before opening the software packet(s) included with this book ("Book"). This is a license agreement ("Agreement") between you and IDG Books Worldwide, Inc. ("IDGB"). By opening the accompanying software packet(s), you acknowledge that you have read and accept the following terms and conditions. If you do not agree and do not want to be bound by such terms and conditions, promptly return the Book and the unopened software packet(s) to the place you obtained them for a full refund.

1. **License Grant.** IDGB grants to you (either an individual or entity) a nonexclusive license to use one copy of the enclosed software program(s) (collectively, the "Software") solely for your own personal or business purposes on a single computer (whether a standard computer or a workstation component of a multiuser network). The Software is in use on a computer when it is loaded into temporary memory (RAM) or installed into permanent memory (hard disk, CD-ROM, or other storage device). IDGB reserves all rights not expressly granted herein.

2. **Ownership.** IDGB is the owner of all right, title, and interest, including copyright, in and to the compilation of the Software recorded on the disk(s) or CD-ROM ("Software Media"). Copyright to the individual programs recorded on the Software Media is owned by the author or other authorized copyright owner of each program. Ownership of the Software and all proprietary rights relating thereto remain with IDGB and its licensers.

3. **Restrictions On Use and Transfer.**

    (a) You may only (i) make one copy of the Software for backup or archival purposes, or (ii) transfer the Software to a single hard disk, provided that you keep the original for backup or archival purposes. You may not (i) rent or lease the Software, (ii) copy or reproduce the Software through a LAN or other network system or through any computer subscriber system or bulletin-board system, or (iii) modify, adapt, or create derivative works based on the Software.

(b) You may not reverse engineer, decompile, or disassemble the Software. You may transfer the Software and user documentation on a permanent basis, provided that the transferee agrees to accept the terms and conditions of this Agreement and you retain no copies. If the Software is an update or has been updated, any transfer must include the most recent update and all prior versions.

4. **Restrictions On Use of Individual Programs.** You must follow the individual requirements and restrictions detailed for each individual program in Appendix B, "About the CD-ROM," of this Book. These limitations are also contained in the individual license agreements recorded on the Software Media. These limitations may include a requirement that after using the program for a specified period of time, the user must pay a registration fee or discontinue use. By opening the Software packet(s), you will be agreeing to abide by the licenses and restrictions for these individual programs that are detailed in Appendix B, "About the CD-ROM," and on the Software Media. None of the material on this Software Media or listed in this Book may ever be redistributed, in original or modified form, for commercial purposes.

5. **Limited Warranty.**

   (a) IDGB warrants that the Software and Software Media are free from defects in materials and workmanship under normal use for a period of sixty (60) days from the date of purchase of this Book. If IDGB receives notification within the warranty period of defects in materials or workmanship, IDGB will replace the defective Software Media.

   (b) IDGB AND THE AUTHOR OF THE BOOK DISCLAIM ALL OTHER WARRANTIES, EXPRESS OR IMPLIED, INCLUDING WITHOUT LIMITATION IMPLIED WARRANTIES OF MERCHANTABILITY AND FITNESS FOR A PARTICULAR PURPOSE, WITH RESPECT TO THE SOFTWARE, THE PROGRAMS, THE SOURCE CODE CONTAINED THEREIN, AND/OR THE TECHNIQUES DESCRIBED IN THIS BOOK. IDGB DOES NOT WARRANT THAT THE FUNCTIONS CONTAINED IN THE SOFTWARE WILL MEET YOUR REQUIREMENTS OR THAT THE OPERATION OF THE SOFTWARE WILL BE ERROR FREE.

   (c) This limited warranty gives you specific legal rights, and you may have other rights that vary from jurisdiction to jurisdiction.

6. <u>Remedies.</u>

   (a) IDGB's entire liability and your exclusive remedy for defects in materials and workmanship shall be limited to replacement of the Software Media, which may be returned to IDGB with a copy of your receipt at the following address: Software Media Fulfillment Department, Attn.: *UNIX® Shell Objects*, IDG Books Worldwide, Inc., 7260 Shadeland Station, Ste. 100, Indianapolis, IN 46256, or call 1-800-762-2974. Please allow three to four weeks for delivery. This Limited Warranty is void if failure of the Software Media has resulted from accident, abuse, or misapplication. Any replacement Software Media will be warranted for the remainder of the original warranty period or thirty (30) days, whichever is longer.

   (b) In no event shall IDGB or the author be liable for any damages whatsoever (including without limitation damages for loss of business profits, business interruption, loss of business information, or any other pecuniary loss) arising from the use of or inability to use the Book or the Software, even if IDGB has been advised of the possibility of such damages.

   (c) Because some jurisdictions do not allow the exclusion or limitation of liability for consequential or incidental damages, the above limitation or exclusion may not apply to you.

7. <u>U.S. Government Restricted Rights.</u> Use, duplication, or disclosure of the Software by the U.S. Government is subject to restrictions stated in paragraph (c)(1)(ii) of the Rights in Technical Data and Computer Software clause of DFARS 252.227-7013, and in subparagraphs (a) through (d) of the Commercial Computer − Restricted Rights clause at FAR 52.227-19, and in similar clauses in the NASA FAR supplement, when applicable.

8. <u>General.</u> This Agreement constitutes the entire understanding of the parties and revokes and supersedes all prior agreements, oral or written, between them and may not be modified or amended except in a writing signed by both parties hereto that specifically refers to this Agreement. This Agreement shall take precedence over any other documents that may be in conflict herewith. If any one or more provisions contained in this Agreement are held by any court or tribunal to be invalid, illegal, or otherwise unenforceable, each and every other provision shall remain in full force and effect.